THE POLITICS OF DESIGN IN
FRENCH COLONIAL URBANISM

THE POLITICS OF DESIGN IN FRENCH COLONIAL URBANISM

GWENDOLYN WRIGHT

THE UNIVERSITY OF CHICAGO PRESS

Chicago and London

GWENDOLYN WRIGHT is professor of architecture and history and
director of The Temple Hoyne Buell Center for the Study of
American Architecture at Columbia University. She is the
author of *Moralism and the Model Home: Domestic Architecture
and Cultural Conflict in Chicago, 1873–1913*, also published
by the University of Chicago Press.

The University of Chicago Press, Chicago 60637
The University of Chicago Press, Ltd., London

Library of Congress Cataloging-in-Publication Data
Wright, Gwendolyn.
  The politics of design in French colonial urbanism / Gwendolyn Wright.
    p. cm.
  Includes bibliographical references and index.
  ISBN 0-226-90846-1 (cloth).—ISBN 0-226-90848-8 (paper)
1. Architecture, French—Morocco. 2. City planning—Morocco.
3. Architecture, French—Indochina. 4. City planning—Indochina.
5. Architecture, French—Madagascar. 6. City planning—Madagascar.
7. France—Colonies—Administration. I. Title.
NA1590.2.M44W75   1991
720'.1'03—dc20   90-45063

Contents

Acknowledgments

I FIRST BEGAN thinking about this project some twenty-five years ago as a student in France. Since then, I went on to become an American architectural historian, yet the questions, both theoretical and aesthetic, raised by the French colonial experience continued to be intriguing. Indeed I began to realize that I could think more clearly about the broader political implications of culture by briefly moving outside the familiar domain of American history.

The enterprise proved to be anything but brief, but it was even more engaging and valuable than I had originally anticipated. This book first began to take form as a collaboration between myself and Paul Rabinow. During an initial research trip to France, many friends helped us think about the issues we were raising, especially Jean-Louis Cohen, Daniel Defert, Michel Foucault, Annick Osmont, and Christian Topolov. I am grateful for their insights, their questions, and the encouragement they all gave.

As I began to explore my own particular interests in colonial architecture and urban design, a fellowship at the Stanford Humanities Center provided an ideal milieu; in this bucolic setting I could concentrate on the specifics of this research and the more general issues raised at every Friday lunch. I have since given several talks based on this material, learning a great deal from the audiences at Harvard, MIT, UCLA, Columbia, the University of Virginia, the State University of New York at Binghampton, and the New School for Social Research. Perhaps the most important forum for these ideas was the Washington Collegium for the Humanities, where Henry Millon, director of the Center for Advanced Study in the Visual Arts, invited me to give a lecture followed by a day-long seminar. During that lengthy and thoughtful discussion I heard questions, ideas, and comparisons which have helped me clarify many of these pages.

The *Cahiers de la recherche architecturale* published an early essay on Hébrard's work, which I co-authored with Paul Rabinow, and the *Journal of Modern History* allowed me to work out the basic argument of this book in a lengthy article. I would especially like to thank Bob Fishman and Carl Schorske for their thoughtful comments on that article.

I have benefited from lengthy conversations with several friends, most notably Charles Burroughs, Dolores Hayden, Tony King, Mina Marafat, and Peter Marris. Others have read parts or all of this manuscript and offered helpful advice. Without implicating any of them in the shortcomings which remain, let me thank Janet Abu-Lughod, Jean-Louis Cohen, Kenneth Jackson, Elizabeth Kendall, Philip Khoury, Tony Judt, Robin Middleton, David Van Zanten, and Marilyn Young. The range of their knowledge and the precision of their criticisms have been invaluable. The University of Chicago Press has continued to be a place of high intellectual ambition, careful attention to scholarly detail, and compassionate support. I especially wish to thank Karen Wilson, John McCudden, and Joan Sommers.

My children, David and Sophia, have been patient, or reasonably so, during the seemingly interminable years of my working on this book. Their own fascination with new places and the joy of words often gave me a fresh viewpoint. Both the book and I have benefited from my husband, Tom Bender, especially from the clarity of his historical logic and the richness of his appreciation for cities. He has given generously of his time and encouragement, and even more of his boundless intelligence and love.

Introduction

THE FRENCH ARCHITECT Joseph Marrast, like many of his compatriots, reveled in the elemental volumes and intricate detailing of Moroccan architecture when he designed Casablanca's courthouse in 1920 (fig. 1). Incised cedar woodwork, bands of delicate blue tiles, and colonnades of Roman arches set off the solid rectangular masses of the building. The architect also saw another reason, beyond sheer aesthetic delight, for using indigenous Moroccan motifs in the official buildings of the colonial government. By suggesting France's respect for Islamic culture, this formal homage might help quell the Moroccans' hostility toward European domination. "And thus, little by little," Marrast wrote, "we conquer the hearts of the natives and win their affection, as is our duty as colonizers."[1]

Such efforts to assuage nationalistic resistance represent only the most obviously political aspect of architecture and urban design in colonial cities. Perhaps even more important were the messages communicated back home, where design played a major role in promoting and justifying colonialism. In the eyes of most Westerners, colonial settings pointed up both sides of an inherent cultural dichotomy: the voluptuously ornamented temples and primitive housing conditions evoked a foreign way of life, fascinating yet far beneath their own, while the straight, tree-lined streets and new buildings in European districts exemplified the benefits of "civilization."

Literary, artistic, and ethnographic depictions of a distant "other" reality usually do seem worlds apart from Western life and values.[2] This cultural divide is far more complicated in the case of urban design and policy. The process of conceiving and implementing plans for colonial cities reveals European notions about how a good environment—including their own—should look and function. This projected ideal has been a dominant aspect of colonial urbanism

1

FIGURE 1. *Detail of the Palais de Justice, Casablanca, by Joseph Marrast, 1925. Photograph by Gwendolyn Wright.*

throughout history: for Greek settlers in Turkey in the seventh century B.C., Roman legionnaires in Gaul in the second century, Spanish conquistadors in Latin America in the sixteenth century, and for the governments of England, the Netherlands, or even Japan, as well as France, in more recent times.

The basic morphology and prevailing focus did change, of course, even in the history of a single national culture; there might be simple grids or grand boulevards; a fixed size or expansive boundaries; an emphasis on commerce, administration, health, or the arts; highly visible planning regulations or a less rigid "organic" environment. Beneath such formal variations, the new cities of the colonial realm usually shared a fundamental reference to the European countries that sponsored them, what the French called the *métropole*. However exotic certain districts might have seemed, the European sections of colonial cities not only evoked the capitals and provincial towns of home, they sometimes suggested future directions for Western cities.

The early twentieth century provides many such instances, especially in the French colonies. Colonial literature of all genres, from adventure tales to official reports, abounds with descriptions of model urban environments and the efficient techniques which engendered them. One novelist, for example, praised J. H. Collet de Cantelou, director of the architectural service of Madagascar in

2

the 1930s, because he "has asserted authority in directing new building, just as [the colonial administrators] are directing the economy: erecting rational, healthy, and elegant administrative districts and decorative prototypes for dwellings" (fig. 2).[3] In 1931, children's book author Jean de Brunhoff had Babar design and supervise the construction of Celesteville, City of the Elephants, with standardized shuttered huts arranged in neat rows below two grand monuments, the Palais du Travail and the Palais des Fêtes (fig. 3). Celesteville, too, was an appealing vision of social hierarchy, orderly growth, a thriving economy, and effective political authority, all accomplished without destroying what seemed to be an indigenous African urban fabric—as was too often the lamented result of urban reform in Europe.

A recurrent theme, echoed on both the right and the left, proclaimed the *outre-mer* as a terrain for working out solutions to some of the political, social, and aesthetic problems which plagued France. Urbanism, implying both policy and design, formed the core of such efforts. "In Morocco, people believe in urbanism," wrote one enthusiastic commentator in 1931, "while in France they do not. I cannot help comparing the results of this faith and skepticism."[4] "Use the Sudan to remake the City in France itself," implored Robert Delavignette, director of the Ecole Coloniale, in 1935.[5] Lyautey insisted that North Africa was for France "what the Far West is for America: an excellent testing ground for creating new energy, rejuvenation, and fecundity."[6] The tensions and weaknesses of Third Republic politics gave the premises of this experiment an additional weight: governmental factions and instability, conflicts between Paris and the provinces, the loss of Alsace-Lorraine to the Germans, a low self-image in general, especially in contrast to the illustrious national past. Social imperialism would not only pacify the colonies and make them more productive; it would also provide a way to revitalize metropolitan France, regenerating politics and culture with new leaders, fresh ideas, and proven methods (fig. 4).[7]

The colonies possessed as well an important pragmatic appeal. They offered opportunities for extracting wealth and labor, glorifying the preeminence of French civilization, and, through all these means, asserting the power of France to the world at large.[8] Yet ambitions alone did not generate capital investment or cultural pride. Recognizing this dilemma, colonial administrations embarked on an innovative approach to governance and self-promotion at the turn of the century. Aesthetic images formed a highly self-conscious element of this strategy. A proposal for an illustrated magazine on Morocco, sponsored by the colonial government, contended straightforwardly, "It is by images, widely distributed throughout the entire country [of France] that we will bring first tourists and then, following after them, capital to Morocco."[9]

FIGURE 2. *Drawing of the colonial administrative buildings at the Place Colbert, Antananarivo, by Jean-Henri Collet de Cantelou, 1931.* From L'Urbanisme aux colonies, 1931.

FIGURE 3. *The fictional African city of Celesteville from Jean de Brunhoff, Babar à Celesteville, 1931.* From Babar the King. *Copyright 1935 by Harrison Smith and Robert Haas, Inc. Copyright 1935 by Random House, Inc. Copyright renewed 1963 by Random House, Inc. Reprinted by permission of Random House, Inc.*

FIGURE 4.   *Mural of a French colonial urbanist and his "architectes indigènes," by Duclos de la Haille for the Colonial Museum at the 1931 Colonial Exposition in Paris. Courtesy of the Musée des Arts Africains et Océaniens, Paris.*

The images focused overwhelmingly on colonial "space"—groups of new monuments, streets of new housing, magnificent ruins from the past, as well as quaint scenes of "native" bazaars, rituals, and the natural beauty of the countryside. Books, magazine articles, posters, postcards, and exhibitions reiterated a narrative of colonial ambitions and accomplishments. The French found a compelling portrait of their own initiative, their benevolent spirit, and their sensitivity to those they ruled. They might be tempted as well by the delights of travel or life abroad, and the endless opportunities to develop and profit from the untouched natural resources. French citizens would also recognize the beneficent effects of professional experts and strong political leaders. And finally, in a more subtle but always present fashion, they saw how cities, whether at home or abroad, could look and function in the twentieth century, combining the benefits of modernity with a strong sense of place and local history.

When all is said and done, colonial cities did not provide a truly significant model or even a much-needed incitement for replanning cities at home. Only with the Vichy government plans and post–World War II reconstruction would France again enact and carry out major urban reforms.[10] Nor did these urban accomplishments weaken support for the nationalist movements which in time destroyed colonialism.

All the same, colonial cities deserve close scrutiny on a variety of planes. Certainly they provide insights into the beliefs and strategies which fueled twentieth-century colonialism and resistance to it. They reveal with startling clarity the aesthetic, cultural, and political dilemmas which preoccupied and often divided France during the first half of the century. Moreover, the writings and accomplishments of these professionals offer a vantage for analyzing two variations of modernism in architecture and urban design, often cast as polar opposites, contending forces that still vie with one another today: an avant-garde or universalist version, like Le Corbusier's Chandigarh, and a contextual, culturally relativist approach, such as Venturi and Scott Brown's experiment in "traditional Iraqi architectural forms" for Baghdad.[11] Here it is possible to see both approaches as the products of modern aesthetic philosophies and a modern political climate.

Colonial urbanism can be called modern in two senses. First, teams of professional advisers relied heavily on various social sciences to generate supposedly impartial, objective criteria and techniques. And it is here that the modern profession of urban design developed, with its battery of legal tools and artistic guidelines, in an effort to achieve a balance of historical continuity, profitable economic development, and public amenities.

Whether by international or indigenous architects, looking toward a romantic past or an equally idealized future, contemporary urban design still confronts the issues faced by colonial architects of the early twentieth century. Even our tendency to disregard the political implications of architecture and urban design has such antecedents. Colonial professionals claimed to be apolitical experts, involved in purely aesthetic or technical matters, yet they entered inevitably into the political realm.

By politics, I mean not so much European political parties, for these urban designers rightly claimed to be nonpartisan, in the sense that they could contentedly work for either socialist or conservative administrations. Nonetheless, a fundamental shift took place under their direction. Urban policies took on a new orientation, at once more technocratic and more cultural, which extended into many aspects of daily life. With the advice of architects and sociologists, art historians and geographers, colonial administrators sought to exert greater control over such matters as family life and working conditions, industrial growth and cultural memory.

Yet politics represents only one element of the picture we see here, one strand in the narrative. A multiplicity of meanings always coexist within any piece of architecture. The balance between them shifts continually. The designers' formal goals represent a significant facet, but these, too, are not absolute. The architects' concerns should never be dismissed as shallow, but neither should we single out these intentions as the quintessential meaning of a building. The same, of course, can be said of the programmatic and symbolic intentions which concerned the clients, in this case, colonial administrators.

If I emphasize what one learns about France itself and about Western concepts of urbanism, this is by no means to downplay the critical importance of analyzing these cities in their own right and acknowledging the toll that colonization took. Imperial policies, including aesthetic decisions, obviously affected how residents used and experienced their surroundings. The questions of how effective certain policies of control proved to be and, by contrast, how cities related to nationalist movements for independence remain to be answered, although I hope to address them in my conclusion. But my principal aim in this book is to consider the full meaning of urban design for the French in this colonial context. Such an understanding may help all of us who must now consider the future of cities, whether in Western Europe and North America or in other parts of the world.

Behind the research lies a concern to analyze the relations between culture and politics, specifically efforts to use architecture and urban design, ranging from ornamental details to municipal regulations, as part of a complex political agenda. The fact that culture and politics often affect one another, albeit in constantly changing ways, now seems self-evident. Yet among the historians and architects who acknowledge such a connection, only a few have sought to isolate the precise historical processes involved.[12]

The essential question that needs to be posed concerns direct influence, rather than passive "reflection," between these two domains. It can be asked in two ways. First, does a specific political intent generate particular urbanistic policies and stylistic preferences that advance the political goals? Conversely, can the evolution of certain styles, policies, or programs be seen as the product of a given political context, or are these indeed purely formal and professional matters, always in a hermetic realm of their own? In other words, can we learn anything new about either urban design or political processes by studying the two together? Is either one ever truly formative of the other, or is their relationship simply a matter of interesting background?

I wanted to focus on a setting that was both irrefutably political in nature and also innovative in terms of urban theory and practice. This would let me look at politics and culture simultaneously, as two complementary techniques or strategies for asserting power, two distinct approaches—each with its own internal imperative—woven together, each helping shape the other.

It is reassuring, with such ambitious goals, that the people I studied, the colonial administrators and urbanists, themselves perceived this connection. Political leaders like Hubert Lyautey came to view culture, and specifically urban design, as a key element in their efforts to curb resistance abroad and to win political and economic support at home. Architects Henri Prost and Ernest Hébrard recognized the need for strong, centralized governments to underwrite their plans; they worked out ideas about urban design in close collaboration with politicians like Lyautey of Morocco or Maurice Long of Indochina, administrators who considered themselves amateur urbanists. Both administrators and architects talked about culture and politics, linking the two themes. They explored the political potential or liabilities of European versus indigenous styles, the destruction or preservation of key symbolic monuments or established neighborhoods, the strengths and weaknesses of Haussmannesque boulevards or vernacular housing types. Aesthetic decisions, even for the architects, had decided political implications.

Political implications are by no means the full significance of this history, however. There is a new aesthetic to be explained, and a changing notion of culture which lay behind the forms. If culture was important to politics, this enlarged understanding derived in part from a new appreciation of aesthetic

8

diversity in the early 1900s, both vernacular and refined, traditional and con-temporary, indigenous and European, challenging a strict cultural hierarchy and the supposed universality of French art. Colonial civil servants also perceived culture in a more anthropological sense, as values, as ways of living which varied from one group to another, even within a single city. They observed the ways in which existing streets and buildings accommodated attitudes toward public life, or the separation of the sexes, or religious beliefs. These social conventions, acted out in public and private space, formed a complex ritual of order.

Administrators hoped that preserving traditional status-hierarchies would buttress their own superimposed colonial order. Architects, in turn, acknowledg-ing that resistance to new forms is often based on affection for familiar places, tried to evoke a sense of continuity with the local past in their designs. Both groups extolled traditions—often, in the words of Eric Hobsbawm, "invented traditions" which relied on pageantry or other symbolic expressions of a rigid social order, resuscitated and dramatized by the European authorities.[13] Such artificial revivals inevitably indicate a break in continuity: the forms could not have the meanings they once evoked. In essence, the apparent respect for other cultures involved European efforts to legitimate colonial power, thereby facili-tating the process of economic modernization, and parallel efforts to give mod-ernist aesthetics both sensuality and a sense of locale or place.

Let me pause for a moment to consider terminology. Modernization, a po-litical and economic concept, has a complex relation to two other, more cultural cognates of the term "modern." They are rarely discussed together and it is worth distinguishing between the terms.[14] Modernization concerns the infrastructure of cities, although it obviously in turn affects human experience. This term describes the shift from a local market to international capitalism, from produc-tion based on self-sufficiency and exchange to a system that responds only to distant consumer markets. Together with these systemic changes comes an array of highways and railroads, factories and plantations, banking and insurance firms, all geared to large-scale production and trade.

"Modernity" evokes the fast-paced experience of large cities, awhirl with recent fashions and exciting activities, constant changes in the environment, and a great diversity of people who come into some kind of contact with one another. This experience has probably characterized urban life throughout history, al-though the pace of change has unquestionably intensified since the nineteenth century.[15]

If "modernization" and "modernity" are quite broad-based, "modernism" represents a self-consciously limited definition, at least with art and architecture. A small coterie of early twentieth-century artists seized hold of the word to describe their work and its theoretical underpinnings. They proclaimed their affinity with the process of modernization, which they saw as an inevitable and progressive force; architects and other artists appropriated images of standardization, speed, and simple, unadorned volumes from machine technology. The modernist avant-garde carried these preferences to new limits, convinced that only their images represented a true expression of modernity. They condemned both historical styles and commercially oriented industrial design as sentimental compromise, pandering to an undeveloped bourgeois taste. This negative attitude toward their own culture combined with sheer visual exhilaration when they praised powerfully expressive forms of "primitive" art from the colonized world.

Most of the world has seen and experienced modernization since World War II primarily under the guise of an international architectural modernism that drew its essential forms from those espoused by this avant-garde: enormous highway projects, immense factories, vast residential superblocks, anonymous glass and concrete towers, many built after the destruction of earlier streets and buildings that were dismissed as outmoded and primitive. Today, amidst widespread critiques of stylistic modernism, branded as the embodiment of the ravaging and insensitive effects of modernization, it is important to clarify that relationship. In fact, many different formal vocabularies responded directly to the challenge of modern economic development in cities—not only the avant-garde modern movement or the monolithic International Style which succeeded it.

This book is concerned with the formal and political framework of several such variations in France and the French overseas empire. Some architects, confirmed modernists in certain ways, challenged the rigidity of the European avant-garde canon. They explored a complex multiplicity of images, drawing from the past and the present, juxtaposing the exotic and the rational, much as their counterparts in literature or painting tended to do. These designers felt it better to compromise purity of expression in order to temper the disruptions modernity was causing in the economy and society; they recognized the potentially disorienting quality of life in a fast-changing city. Architecture and site plans aimed for a synthesis of historic forms, indigenous to an area, with more abstract modernist imagery and real improvements—better roads for traffic and careful siting of industry, for example—that could fit anywhere.

We might now find these alternative aproaches to modernism rather appealing, both aesthetically and conceptually, when we look at the provincial regions where they thrived. The colonies present a more complicated situation. The proposals and policies of Morocco in the 1910s and 1920s, like those of Indochina and Madagascar, certainly represent a particular, "contextual" version of modern urban design. That approach varied from place to place, adapting to existing cultures and geography, to different architects and administrators, to the particular political climate within the colonial government and the private sector of European investors.

All the same, there is a fundamental commonality. The "contextual" aesthetic was applied to a consistent set of building types and programmatic imperatives that undermined the indigenous economy, the patterns of land use and social structure, and the cultural beliefs which once bound these together. As one scholar says of colonial port cities in the Far East, "If the results were far from uniform, that should have something to tell us about Asian regional differences, as the uniformity of design and ambition should tell us something about the nature of Western imperialism."[16]

The colonial setting derived in part from an imposed government's right to exercise power, an almost autocratic authority. Tempered by political opposition at home, certain local traditions they chose to honor, and the fiercely independent private sector of European *colons*—the term used for French businessmen, workers, and functionaries living in the colonies—this power was not absolute. Yet it far exceeded the authority of any official or urbanist in a democracy like France.

This book will consider the three French colonies—Indochina, Morocco, and Madagascar—that were the most discussed, most often photographed, and most admired showpieces of the French empire in the 1910s and 1920s. Presented in the order of the governments carrying out quite similar approaches to urban development, they were each indeed more advanced than France by several gauges. These three colonies had far-reaching legislation controlling building and requiring plans for future development (in the case of Morocco, five years before France's largely unenforced law of 1919). Moreover they implemented the legislation. Officials sponsored a high quality of public and private architecture, both in new construction and in the preservation of historic structures; the styles themselves, in each case, represented a conscious effort to blend modernistic forms with traditional motifs, responding to the local context rather than imposing a supposedly universal aesthetic. Colonial administrators proudly claimed that their public-health reforms lowered morbidity statistics for environmentally related diseases like malaria and tuberculosis. And they added a range of social reforms in education, local self-government, and public employment to the governmental apparatus.

As we shall see, each of these advances encompassed, quite intentionally, a fundamental inequality. The urban design reforms divided these cities as never before. The French did not acknowledge that contact with Europeans had introduced and certainly aggravated many public-health problems in colonial settings, problems from which they now wanted to protect themselves. The social reforms applied mainly to a small coterie of indigenous bourgeoisie who supported the French. But here, too, we should remember, one sees amplified a hierarchy that would have applied to French cities as well.

I certainly do not want to present these places as a vanguard; instead I intend to explore how the French responded to the challenge of urban design and planning, at home and abroad, and to ask how that response related to the power they held. The politicized climate of the colonies makes it clear that virtually any stylistic trend or policy reform can be used for political purposes. The possible implications of "traditional" or "modern" styles, of innovative or conservative policies, all come more sharply into focus. Here we discover not only an important aspect of the French justification of colonialism; we also discern how the leading professionals, intellectuals, and political leaders saw the problems of their own French cities—especially problems of cultural hierarchy, continuity with the past, social segregation, and economic development.

Within this shared perspective, one finds particular urbanistic issues, pressing concerns in France itself, which preoccupied the architects and administrators in different colonies. This book will first trace a common point of view about urbanism, then about urban design and the social sciences, situating the malaise in fin-de-siècle France. Succeeding chapters will then focus on the specific issues and aesthetic programs which seemed most critical in one of the three principal colonies. In Morocco this meant the need to boost development, commerce, and tourism; in Indochina, a balance of centralization with local control; and in Madagascar, efforts to achieve more rationalized work habits and more pervasive public health.

Indochina, Madagascar, and, above all, Morocco were much talked and written about throughout the French-speaking world (and even beyond) in the early twentieth century. They were seen as "laboratories"; again and again they were called *"champs d'expérience"* or experimental terrains.[17] As such they seemed unadulterated primitive lands where one could carry out controlled tests; yet each domain was also understood as a distinctive cultural setting. In a characteristic French manner, many colonialists wanted to combine these two aspects of experimentation: they were searching for universal rules, on the one hand, principles of urban design and urban policy that could be applied effectively in any context; and for the meaning of cultural particularities, on the other, for the specifics of artistic tradition, environment, and social life that defined each place, qualifying the kinds of change that would be feasible.

This book, too, seeks to relate the particular and the general, the cultural and the political. It offers a portrait of specific proposals in certain French colonial cities, analyzing the approaches taken in different countries. It is also an attempt to show how, in the larger setting of the French-speaking world of the early twentieth century, an overall shift occurred in the ways that urban cultural policies were bound up with political concerns. This relationship between history, power, and culture illuminates many of the problems that architecture then faced and faces still.

IMPASSE AND
AMBITION

ALTHOUGH *FIN-DE-SIÈCLE* despair resounded throughout all of Europe, the French intelligentsia confronted disturbing statistics as well as a forboding sense of moral decline. Their cities indeed lagged noticeably behind those of England, the United States, and, most distressingly, Germany. Many sectors of the urban economy appeared static and unproductive, although there was some promise in the new manufacturing of machine parts and automobiles on the outskirts of Paris.[1] Mortality rates for all ages surpassed those of other European countries.[2] Bitterness about the loss of Alsace-Lorraine mingled with the painful memories of violence during the Commune: street barricades, the destruction of public monuments, the loss of thousands of lives among the Communards and the army, not only in Paris, but in all large French cities.[3] Class antagonisms continued to build with increasing numbers of strikes, augmented by the growing political power of the Confédération générale du travail (CGT) and various left-wing parties.[4] As the housing available to urban working-class families declined in quantity and increased precipitously in cost, overcrowding became a glaring problem, especially in Paris, where the census of 1901 documented over half the city's population as living in "overpopulated" or "insufficient" dwellings.[5]

In a variety of disciplines the educated elite, most of whom resided in the capital city, sought to regain a positive sense of direction and control in metropolitan life. Jean Izoulet, for example, just a few years before he assumed the chair in social philosophy at the Collège de France, published *La Cité moderne et la métaphysique de la sociologie* (1894). This immensely popular book sounded an appeal for social unity through scientific research—research that would establish authoritative principles for urban hierarchy and segregation. "The great social problem," Izoulet declared, "is to equilibrate justly the Elite and the Crowd in the City."[6] He proposed to solve that problem through a combination of urban design and urban social policy—an approach which resonated in the empassioned books and speeches of numerous other French scholars.

Despite the exuberance of Parisian cabarets and the magnificence of the capital's boulevards, the mood among intellectuals seemed decidedly pessimistic. Some French scholars even expressed doubts about the benefits of new knowledge and technology when they reported the results of their studies. Emile Durkheim, in a celebrated passage documenting that France led all European countries in increase of suicides, took this melancholy tone:

> We must not be dazzled by the brilliant development of sciences, the arts and industry of which we are the witnesses; this development is altogether certainly taking place in the midst of a morbid effervescence, the grevous repercussions of which each one of us feels. It is then very possible and even probable that the rising tide of suicide originates in a pathological state just now accompanying the march of civilization without being its necessary condition.[7]

Whatever the terms of analysis, from statistics on urban growth to essays on mental health, France seemed caught in a disturbing decline, and her cities showed the worst effects of that precarious condition.

In France, as elsewhere, the theme of degeneracy which ran through novels, medical reports, political discourse, through treatises in the social sciences or in aesthetics, seemed especially grave in metropolitan areas. Doctors and reformers in the "social hygiene" movement called for controls over prostitution based on a progression of sanitary improvements, as much moral as physical: "cleanse the lowly places (the streets, sidewalks, brasseries, dance halls, wine shops, etc.) and you cleanse the rest . . . ; cleanse the large cities and you cleanse the entire country. Cleanse all the capitals and you cleanse the world."[8] Even architecture came under attack. Although the Ecole des Beaux-Arts enjoyed worldwide prestige, many French art critics condemned the majority of turn-of-the-century Parisian buildings as either "monstrous *palaces* . . . colossal edifices, surcharged with mediocre sculpture" or "prison houses along narrow, noisy, inhospitable streets."[9]

Aesthetic disarray and moral decay shared the same root, in that both seemed to reveal fundamental weaknesses, most notably a pervasive apathy, in French society itself. From university lecterns, church pulpits, and town council halls came repeated calls for "rejuvenation," "moral energy," and "moral education." New voluntary organizations vowed to break the debilitating lethargy afflicting both the state and the older, established social groups. Likewise, young

French architects, most notably the "Nouveau Paris" group around Frantz Jourdan, demanded innovations, certainly in style, but also in the choice of materials and the kinds of commercial or industrial commissions deemed appropriate for the new century.[10]

While the perception of a critical lack of direction permeated every stylistic creed, every field, and every ideology, from the Catholic extreme right to the socialist left, proposals to correct the situation could seldom generate enough support to be implemented. Civic authorities seemed impotent, unable or unwilling to act conclusively on any problem, whether aesthetic, social, or hygienic. Years later, after he had returned to France from Morocco, the architect and urban planner Henri Prost looked back on the frustration which had characterized this period:

> One had to have lived in Paris around 1900 to understand the motives [for the urban reforms which followed]. One had to have witnessed the disintegration of the grand STATE ADMINISTRATION which, from Sully to Colbert to Haussmann, had assured the harmony of our cities, in order to understand the anguish which afflicted young people before 1900.[11]

The sense of impasse cast its pall over every profession.

To list, even succinctly, the concrete and the theoretical problems disturbing educated Frenchmen, including young architects like Prost, goes beyond the more familiar parameters we associate today with urbanism. Nonetheless, most topics did suggest a way in which the city—as a physical setting, a symbolic reference, or a bureaucratic organization—could improve or harm human conditions. Issues as varied as the low national birthrate, poor industrial productivity, class antagonisms, inadequate housing stock, and a perceived decline in national prestige since the humiliation of the Franco-Prussian War, all these had urbanistic implications. So, too, did the problem of societal integration—given the name *solidarité* in 1895 by Léon Bourgeois (a senator and minister of education.) Professors and politicians alike invoked the term, although the need for orderly social cohesion had in fact preoccupied French intellectuals since the middle of the nineteenth century.[12]

By the end of that century the problem had two main cultural expressions: an obsession with the dangers of the crowd and a preoccupation with the creation of national identity. In these two subjects, and in other less pervasive themes as well, the theoretical influence of three very different thinkers—Gustave Le Bon, Emile Durkheim, and Frédéric Le Play—often overlapped: the first intensified fears that irresponsible mass movements would cause social breakdown; the second encouraged interest in collective symbols and social cohesion; the third, the most influential, promoted a strong reformist orientation, a belief that physical and social settings have a major impact on social life.[13]

None of these three key theorists took the city itself as a specific category for analysis (although Le Play helped organize the vast 1867 Exposition Universelle in Paris and his followers strongly advocated garden cities). However, each one did explore the need for *civisme* as a centripetal social force, drawing citizens into a collectivity which would encourage the subsuming of private interests into the larger public good. In diverse ways they linked this social cohesion to the transformation of the milieu—particularly the urban milieu—in physical, political, and social terms. The city could become a more positive setting for French cultural development.

The sense of crisis and the optimistic belief in reform through an improved milieu were, of course, especially evident in the texts on urban design. Such books appeared with considerable frequency during these years. Robert de Souza, for instance, discussing possible policies for the coastal resort of Nice, bewailed the general inattention to urban planning throughout France:

> In the field of civic improvement, our French towns have declined to a level of unbelievable stagnation. . . . The future of our towns is being choked off by chaotic outward growth. Not a trace of an overall plan! No attempt to complete or even to respect the fine work of our eighteenth-century predecessors! Our most recent tradition, Haussmann's, was shabby enough, but even that has not been continued. . . . French municipal enterprise had been completely outstripped by foreign countries, and especially by the United States, Sweden, Germany, and Austria. But we had no inkling of the depth and breadth of this new urban science, and of the extent to which it was being generally applied.[14]

Count de Souza did find some hope in the prize-winning examples of younger French architects who entered competitions held *outside* of France: Léon Jausse-ly's Barcelona plan of 1903, André Bérard's 1906 plan for Guayaquil, Ecuador; and Henri Prost's 1910 plan for Antwerp (fig. 5). He deplored the fact that no such opportunities existed in France itself.[15]

The major setting for transforming the concerns of architects and intellectuals into policies, for putting theories into practice, was to be not France or even Europe, but the cities of the French colonies. The reasons for this were imminently practical. The colonies had an immediate, pressing need for policies that could quell the possibility of social disorder and encourage economic development; they had to provide homes and workplaces for French settlers and for the indigenous populations drawn to the new colonial metropolises; most of

FIGURE 5. *Prize-winning plan for the redesign of Antwerp, Belgium, by Henri Prost, 1910. From* Urbanisme, 1965. *Courtesy of* Urbanisme.

all, their political system provided policy-makers with a degree of authority for carrying out their plans that simply did not exist in France. Writing in Morocco in 1914, Hubert Lyautey, the new head of the protectorate, expressed his belief that the regulations he had recently promulgated would bring stability and prosperity, relieving the "urban malaise," much as similar urban legislation was doing "in New York, Brussels, Frankfurt, and Lausanne"—all in distinct contrast to Paris, Lille, or Marseilles.[16]

Given this original impetus, theory and practice in the colonies often referred back to France, both its capital city and its provincial centers. An understanding of the state of French urban life and the appeals for urban reform, most of which had little effect in metropolitan France, provides an essential baseline for what happened in the colonies in the early twentieth century. The contrast between the *métropole* and the *outre-mer* explains the great sense of opportunity for those who ventured abroad: urbanists, architects, social scientists, and political administrators alike. It also suggests why these experiments generated so much interest in France at this time.

To comprehend this context one must recognize, as did these men who departed for the colonies, the sheer intransigence to change in France. The public monuments and even the infrastructure of French cities had been deemed the pinnacle of European urban glory for so many centuries, that many Frenchmen found it difficult to acknowledge that their cultural dominance could be displaced.[17] This was especially true of the rural and small-town politicians who dominated the Chamber of Deputies, which would have had to approve any national proposal to set aside funds for urban planning reform. The majority of French population growth, such as it was, took place in towns. (Paris, for example, doubled in population during the half-century from 1870 to 1920, increasing to just over four million persons.) Still, the country was by no means predominantly urban, and jockeying for funds to improve provincial public works continued to dominate legislative sessions.

One example may suffice. Not until 1902 was Jules Siegfried able to persuade his colleagues in the Chamber of Deputies to pass a much-amended version of the bill he had first presented in 1866, requiring all large towns to create and enforce public-health regulations, including powers to inspect and demolish unsanitary dwellings. Basically a variation of English statutes of a half-century earlier, it was the first French law in over fifty years to concern itself directly with insalubrious urban housing and the need for coordinated, overall planning in urban areas.[18] However, since the bill did not provide for enforcement, and all discretion was left with local authorities, the Siegfried law merely translated into the French language—but not into action—these English reform concepts.

As the public and private sectors turned, rather haltingly, toward urban reform, several distinct categories of issues emerged: the need for long-term urban and regional planning; a range of environmentally related health problems, including inadequate and unsanitary housing; and aesthetic conflicts about what, in fact, constituted civic beauty. Each topic combined aesthetic issues of architecture and urban design with the more social and political aspects of policy planning. Each one, moreover, eventually generated urban reforms in the French colonies, in many cases on a scale of innovation and success that far exceeded what France itself had done. This history has, of course, been analyzed elsewhere in great detail, but let me again outline the basic parameters of urban problems in France which preoccupied its population during the early decades of the twentieth century.[19]

The Need for Long-Range Planning

Founded in 1894, the Musée Social was one of several such "social museums" created in Western cities during these years. Its patrons sought to do for social and political economy what other museums did for the arts and sciences. They, too, brought together significant objects (in this case, data and books on social problems) so that specialists and the general public could better understand them. In terms of its theoretical positions and its intellectual impact on the future professions, the Musée Social dominated urbanism in fin-de-siècle France.[20]

Primarily engaged in efforts to improve labor-capital relations, the Musée took a new turn toward urban planning in 1907, with the establishment of a special Section d'Hygiène Urbaine et Rurale. The impetus for this new subgroup was the growing awareness of what other nations were accomplishing: German zoning on the peripheries of their cities, American settlement houses and civic centers, and the English decision to build a garden city at Letchworth. From its Parisian vantage, the Musée Social focused on the need for a master plan to coordinate the rebuilding of the former fortifications area on the outskirts of the city. The Section d'Hygiène put forth a detailed, long-range program for housing, new traffic arteries, parks, parkways, and stately public buildings all along this ring. Behind their proposal lay the larger goal of more effective planning legislation for the entire city, demanding action from an obstinate municipal council dominated by development interests.

The Musée Social did function as a lively meeting ground, bringing together innovative architects, social scientists, and political reformers, all of whom now looked upon urban planning as the best means for coordinating improvements in the capital city. Yet the group experienced only a series of rebuffs when it tried to implement any proposed reforms.

Like virtually every urbanistic reform group in the West during these years, the Musée Social stressed the urgent need for major transportation improvements, especially within cities. These concerns did not go entirely unheeded. Laws now stipulated that new streets had to be at least fifteen meters wide to facilitate increased traffic, and just before World War I Paris undertook a cautious program to widen certain existing streets. Several municipalities completed major boulevards, left unfinished after 1871, among them the Avenue de l'Opéra in Paris. Yet no one could put forward a vision of French streets that embodied both traditional elegance and modern efficiency—no one, that is, since Haussmann and Napoleon III. The council itself continued to mull over the unexecuted parts of Haussmann's plan, despite public outcry every time they attempted to implement some new or extended boulevard. A major commission report of 1913 decried any so-called improvements that would alter "the aesthetic of a city which must preserve and increase throughout the world its artistic prestige." [21]

Although the spacious thoroughfares could indeed accommodate the increasingly complex pressure of vehicles far better than the narrow streets they replaced, the municipalities seemed unable to make them work effectively. Complaints resounded about traffic congestion, the polluting smells of horse manure and gasoline fumes, the dangers faced by pedestrians with no protected intersections, and the lack of traffic regulations to control the speed or direction of vehicles. [22] Even sidewalks proved frustrating (fig. 6). *Flâneurs* skirted their way around a steeplechase of new fixtures: lampposts, kiosks, benches, public toilets, and numerous stands selling newspapers, flowers, food, or souvenirs. These installations were sometimes charmingly designed, and many of them brought in rental revenues for the city. But the picture as a whole stirred complaints that chaotic movement and crass commercialism had eroded the former elegance of the renowned French street.

Disdainful of the existing street system, Le Corbusier demanded a complete transformation in the pattern and the very premises of cities. His Contemporary City for Three Million People of 1922 was intended to demonstrate this agenda (fig. 7). The basic structure came from the transportation network: long expressways, connecting at right angles, pedestrian walkways in similar geometries, and a massive central terminal for cars, trains, and biplanes. Order also meant clear spatial differentiation. Tall office buildings and luxury apartment blocks appeared at regular intervals, each one standing free in an open lawn of greenery, while subordinate classes lived in modest garden-apartments, grouped in satellite towns.

Three years later, after the publication of two polemical texts on urbanism, Le Corbusier first suggested how he would use modern guidelines to transform Paris. This Plan Voisin was no modest reform proposal, cautious about disrupting familiar places or overspending a budget. Even if certain historic monuments would be retained, the surrounding context—repetitive series of identical skyscrapers set back from a grid of wide streets and limited-access expressways—disassociated those monuments from the city's history and from the new urban fabric.

The Municipal Council refused even to consider such a devastating plan. De Souza and many of his colleagues lambasted Le Corbusier's aversion to local history and his insistence on universal standards for urban design. [23] Preferring

FIGURE 6. *Typical street in Rheims, c. 1910. From M. N. Forestier*, La Reconstruction de Reims, *1925.*

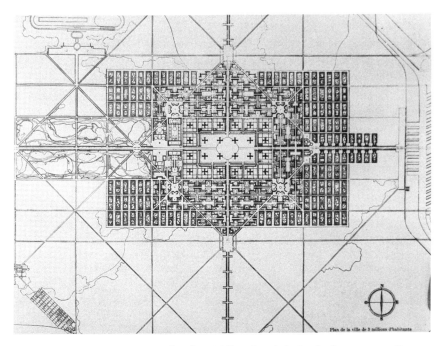

FIGURE 7. *Contemporary City for Three Million People by Le Corbusier, 1922. From his* Oeuvre Complète *1910–1929.*

23

regional styles in buildings and site plans, they still wanted modern traffic systems: "*Streets! Streets! Streets in every direction!,*" proclaimed an article on the 1919 Renaissance des Cités exhibition in Paris. "*Level streets! Direct streets,* if possible! *Solid streets! Large streets within the city! Give everyone the possibility of coming to the city and doing business!*"[24]

Twenty years before Le Corbusier's first major publication, the preeminent architect in the Musée Social proposed new ways to adapt cities to traffic. This, too, went largely unheeded. Eugène Hénard issued his eight-volume set of major modifications, *Etudes sur les transformations de Paris,* between 1903 and 1909. Only one proposal for automobile circulation was put into effect. Initiated in 1907 at the Place de l'Etoile, the symbolic gateway to the capital, the "simple and elegant" *carrefour à giration,* or roundabout, required that all vehicles proceed to the right as they entered a circular intersection, where the traffic flow would thereby remain continuous[25] (fig. 8). Five years later the first traffic regulations for the capital city required the *carrefour à giration* for all such *grandes places* throughout the city.

Jean-Claude-Nicolas Forestier, also associated with the Musée Social, discussed traffic problems at a local level and on a theoretical plane, without advocating a modernist grid. In a masterful urban comparison, Forestier's *Grandes villes et systèmes de parcs,* published in 1906, evoked the examples of English and American cities, praising in particular Frederick Law Olmsted's Boston plan.[26] To undertake such a scheme, Forestier stressed, a municipality had to override the political fragmentation which typically prevents large-scale development. And, he continued, even Parisians had to become more self-critical. Americans see Paris as a

> "finished City" . . . finished and perfect, an *objet d'art* . . . A "finished City" is one that, having attained its apogee, can only decline. . . . Paris has so often been given as an example, usually by foreigners who know only its beautiful districts, that we have ended up falling asleep, and only now do we realize that the population growth is continuing, that construction continues without cease.[27]

Forestier's concept of a centralized agency to oversee suburban development would play a role in the French garden-city developments. This did not take place until the 1920s. Even before World War I, his ideas received public endorsement outside of France—in Spain, Portugal, Latin America, and Morocco (fig. 9). In those places both professionals and administrators recognized the need for ample open space and traffic plans in all urban areas.

FIGURE 8. *Proposed* carrefour à giration *for Paris by Eugène Hénard. From Hénard,* Etudes sur les transformations de Paris. Fascicule 7, 1906.

In the hope that professional authority would strengthen their position, the leading architects and landscape architects in the Musée formed the Société Française des Urbanistes (SFU) in 1911 (first called the Société Française des Architectes-Urbanistes). All were internationally acclaimed urban designers. Forestier had undertaken a major plan for Havana and Lisbon, Jausseley for Barcelona, and Donat-Alfred Agache would soon oversee a master plan for Rio de Janeiro. Henri Prost was a founding member, and Ernest Hébrard served as the society's second president. These designers found virtually no opportunities to apply their talents in their own country.

The lack of commissions did not prevent deliberation about the premises French urbanists might use, should public authorities in time accept the need for their services. SFU architects debated whether the urban designer should be defined as a "sanitary engineer" or an "artist."[28] By and large, formal composition still remained at the center of French urbanistic philosophy, though the SFU designers believed it essential to balance aesthetic considerations with the scientific collection of social, hygienic, and economic data. "Urbanism is a science and an art," an early publication by the group intoned, and the urbanist must

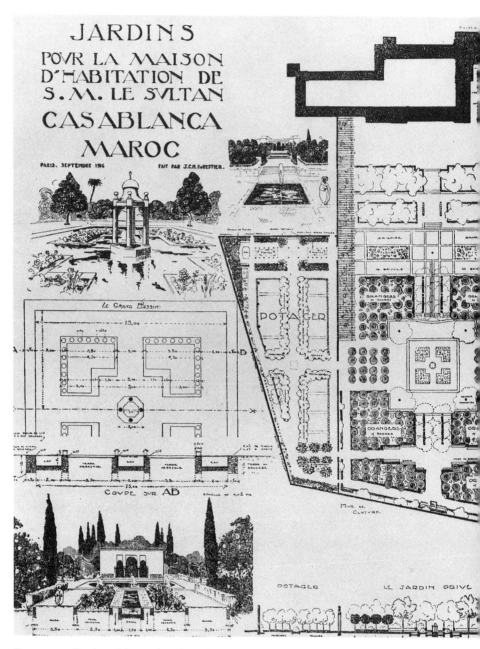

FIGURE 9. *Portion of the gardens for Sultan Moulay Youssef's new palace in Casablanca, designed in Paris by J. C. N. Forestier, 1916. From Forestier,* Jardins, *1920.*

"coordinate all the values in a conception that represents the whole; in other words, he must make a beautiful plan." [29]

Most professionals agreed on the need for state intervention and scientific data on urban development. [30] Georges Risler, a vice president of the Musée Social and honorary president of the SFU, outlined a program for collecting information about a city's "dominant economic and social character, . . . its hygienic condition, . . . its history and evolution," in order to generate a viable master plan for future development. [31] Urban legislation suggested by the SFU and the Musée Social stressed the need for long-term regional planning and improved sanitation, but always with reference to the historic tradition of urban beauty in each region of France.

The state, in turn, would need trained experts to direct its efforts, and several institutions now promised to produce them. The Musée Social sponsored a School of Public Art during the war years, offering public lectures virtually every day, in an effort to involve citizens in architectural issues. The Ecole des Hautes Etudes Urbaines and the Ecole Pratique d'Etudes Urbaines, founded just after the war, drew would-be professionals as their students. In 1919 these two schools combined to form the Institut d'Urbanisme of the University of Paris.

Behind the Institut's curriculum stood a belief in state legislation and subsidies for urban improvements, municipal control of each locale, and forceful architectural leadership. The teaching staff emphasized a combination of scientific analysis and artistic sensibility. [32] The historian Marcel Poëte explained to students that urbanism should be based first on the science of observation, dealing with specific places and needs; after that, the various particulars were to be classified into universal laws, applicable to all times and settings. [33]

Largely as a result of such efforts, stipulations for urban plans and municipal sanitation improvements pertained, at least in theory, in all post–World War I French building efforts. Modern water and sewer systems constituted one element of a major new law, passed in 1919, requiring official plans for all of the nation's large cities and for all cities and towns seeking reparations for war damages. The winning scheme for Paris emphasized a region linked by several modes of transportation, guided by the principle of " 'taylorization' which treated the city as a vast workshop where, for quite precise reasons, everything had its one proper place and should be only in that place." [34]

Unfortunately, planning for the future seemed antithetical to the mood of the times, when many Frenchmen felt a greater concern for rebuilding an idealized past which had deteriorated badly in recent generations. Despite a great deal of discussion and publicity, less than one-quarter of the towns which should have approved plans had begun to prepare them even twenty years later. Paris did not proceed with a plan until the 1930s, and other French municipalities seldom implemented any sort of master plan until after World War II, when the administrative mechanisms for municipal control over land had finally been installed.[35]

Industrial modernization also followed a pattern of metropolitan frustration and colonial experimentation. As early as 1904, Georges Benoit-Lévy, a lawyer active in the Musée Social, asserted the industrialist's prerogative. "Today's factories," he declared, "should create the centers of social life, as industrialists should create the new cities; it is their job to make such cities healthy and beautiful, and for this we should expect from them all our social improvements."[36] As France tried to gear up for renewed output after World War I, the heads of major industries had to acknowledge the low level of production in most sectors. This weakness was compounded by the difficulties of integrating new, relatively unskilled workers, after the war had so drastically reduced French manpower, and the reluctance of major joint-stock banks to invest in French industry.[37]

The principal pressure group for change was the Redressement Français, an organization founded in 1925.[38] Rallying to the slogan, "Enough politics. We want results!" this consortium of business and industrial leaders, headed by electrical mogul Ernest Mercier, promoted a neo-Saint-Simonian program of modern technocracy. They wanted an economy geared to mass production and a government run by apolitical experts.

In the eyes of the Redressement Français, better cities, and especially improved housing, would directly stimulate the entire economy while preventing social disruption. In terms of specific policy, the organization lobbied actively for passage of the Loi Loucheur, which subsidized 200,000 low-cost dwellings and 60,000 moderate-cost units in France over a five-year period beginning in 1928. The results were less than pleasing in both aesthetic and administrative terms. "Since the end of the war," warned the group's official magazine, "France has built very little and built badly. . . . In effect, the causes which have retarded urbanistic progress in France are quite grave, for they imply the profound alteration of our political mores and our public institutions."[39] Formal architectural issues, in this view, could scarcely be dismissed as incidental; the absence of an original new architecture in France represented nothing less than a "social impasse" for the nation.[40]

Leaders of the Redressement Français did not endorse any one aesthetic direction; rather they encouraged public discussion of the subject. A variety of aesthetic predilections posed no problems, for modern experts could supposedly choose correctly if they had adequate information. Towards this end, the Redressement Français brought together some quite disparate viewpoints about urban design. Le Corbusier participated in an urban study committee and then contributed two pamphlets, published as supplements to monthly *Bulletins* in 1928.[41] Other publications featured Henry Prost and Henri de la Casinière on the legal and urban design procedures recently evolved in Morocco, where historic preservation helped generate strict design guidelines in new building.

The group's pamphlets, newspaper articles, and even half-ownership in the journal *Le Monde colonial illustré* promoted a closer integration of metropolitan and colonial economies, with extensive, planned industrial development in both settings.[42] The Redressement Français advocated French capital investment in the colonies in a much larger and more centralized manner than even Jules Ferry could have envisioned.[43] At issue, in essence, was the need for a national economic policy to spur industrial development. It was not sufficient for a few individual companies to flourish if the country, indeed the whole of *la plus grande France*, did not prosper and become more efficient.

A fundamental point in the Redressement Français campaign involved supervising the location of future industrial expansion. After the destruction of World War I, leaders of this organization unsuccessfully advocated the relocation of factories to the peripheries of the northeastern cities, near major transportation lines, in order to stimulate national markets for goods. Likewise, they recommended sending workers to the colonies or to depopulated rural areas in France, as part of an effort to spread the nation's centers of industry. These proposals echoed those of the colonial proponent, Joseph Chailley-Bert, who envisioned the colonies as places where French workers and their children could find new opportunities, thereby complementing the needs of capital as it, too, invested abroad.[44]

The Redressement Français encouraged the state to promote a vigorous policy of *mise en valeur*, promoting both private investment and state-funded public works in the provinces and the colonies alike, as part of a vast modernization program. The major governmental spokesman for this approach was Albert Sarraut. A deputy and then senator from the Aude, Sarraut belonged to the Radical-Socialists, a party dominated by small-town businessmen and peasants. Sent off to the colonies in retribution for his outspoken critiques of governmental policy, he served as governor-general of Indochina (1911–14 and 1916–19), twice as minister of colonies (1920–24 and 1932–33), and as minister of the interior in the cabinet of Poincaré. Sarraut put forward an elaborate proposal for infrastructural improvements, scholarly and sanitary reforms, industrial development, and administrative decentralization—first for the colonies in 1921, then for the country as a whole five years later. Both instances followed the example of

Charles de Freycinet's regional public works in the provinces, initiated in 1878, an attempt to open up internal markets and to strengthen lines of contact between the center and periphery.

Sarraut's plans sought to tie metropolitan and colonial France more closely together, just as he hoped to strengthen national identity in the provinces. In either case, the development techniques would be much the same. "This policy creates banks and factories," Sarraut explained, "but also, all around them, it would build maternity clinics, schools, hospitals, and provincial administrative offices."[45] Legislators in the capital needed to provide such services. At home or abroad, only a "policy which thus realizes an alliance and an equilibrium . . . can justify the far-off 'domination.' "[46]

Environmental Health

Industrialists hoped to rationalize the French work force and depoliticize workers, accomplishing both goals through a concerted policy of zoning and limited social reforms. To assure high levels of productivity, the general health of the French working class also came under closer scrutiny. Five main subjects preoccupied health officials and forward-looking industrial reformers: inadequate health statistics; the surge of epidemics; the limited allocation of spaces for treatment; the relationship of physical and mental health to the low national birthrate; and the lack of acceptable, affordable housing, especially for urban workers and their families. Together with social policies to provide health services, the physical planning of cities emerged as an essential element in public health reform.

Intervention, when it did take place, usually emanated from private organizations of hygienists or social reformers. In 1901, for example, Dr. Albert Calmette, who had previously directed the Bacteriological Institute in Saigon, privately established France's first tuberculosis dispensary in Lille. The movement did not expand greatly until the Rockefeller Foundation provided funds during World War I, prompting Léon Bourgeois to lobby for passage of a bill in 1916 that set up governmental standards—but still little money—for antitubercular and antivenereal dispensaries (fig. 10).

The new dispensaries did imply a social-scientific model which viewed the city as a composite of distinct districts with different problems and needs.[47] Modern health problems were now seen, at least in part, as the results of broad-based demographic, industrial, and administrative conditions. The state required public action, as well as individual self-motivation, to improve epidemiological statistics.

FIGURE 10. *Office Public d'Hygiène Social, Paris, 1930. Photograph by Gwendolyn Wright.*

In time public-health records included not only morbidity rates but also indices of income levels and class, local economy, and even public morality—documented through the incidence of prostitution and venereal disease. As one medical reformer explained the complex vision of modern urban epidemiology:

31

Social hygiene is an economic science, having as its object human capital, its production or reproduction (eugenics and puericulture), its conservation (hygiene, medicine, and preventive health), its utilization
(physical and professional education), and its output (scientific organization of work). Social hygiene is a normative sociology.[48]

Yet this very scale of impact left many French citizens suspicious, wary that full-
fledged public health had socialistic implications. The implementation of reforms lagged far behind medical knowledge.

One disease, tuberculosis, did cause special concern when it showed no
signs of abating in the larger French cities. By 1920, 67,000 cases were still
reported—an incidence six times higher than in neighboring countries.[49] Continued documentation eventually led to urban renewal campaigns in those
working-class districts (called *îlots insalubres*) which recorded especially high
rates of the disease. The proposed remedy derived from the prevailing environmentalist interpretation of Robert Koch's research, which noted that the tuberculosis bacillum survived for long periods in dark, damp places. "We must destroy the house when it harbours the disease," declared one city official. "Any
palliative would be an illusion."[50]

This effort in fact shifted attention away from the working conditions which
caused most cases of tuberculosis, and from the kinds of treatment that were
necessary to alleviate the illness.[51] Other reforms—such as sanitoriums and especially shorter working hours—were dismissed as mere "palliatives." Even slum
clearance remained only the most acclaimed remedy rather than actual policy.
Nothing was done in Paris, for instance, until an outbreak of bubonic plague
occurred in 1921.[52]

In a similar vein, despite epidemics of cholera and typhoid and high inci-
dences of smallpox well into the twentieth century, controversy surrounded public efforts to control these diseases.[53] Many urban property-owners protested demands that they connect their houses with public sewers, such as the famous
tout à l'égout in Paris. (Compliance was so slow that, as late as 1925, almost
one-third of the houses in Paris had not yet made the required sewer connection.)[54] Slow to act in any case, public authorities demonstrated little ability to
carry out the reforms they had agreed to implement. Neither the legislators nor
the courts had been granted the powers to require that landlords conform to new
standards of environmental hygiene.

Public-health officials, physicians, and social scientists tended to scrutinize
the more sociological aspects of human biology, in particular France's disturb-
ingly low birthrate. National population growth, which had begun to level off

during the eighteenth century, first showed a disconcerting contrast with that of other European countries during the Second Empire. In the three decades between 1881 and 1911, the French population increased by only two million, while that of England rose by 10 million, and Germany's by 20 million; during one five-year period (1891–95), deaths exceeded births by 300.[55]

The role of "moral" diseases like syphilis caused much stir, for venereal disease unquestionably lowered the possibility of natality. Here, too, urban reform proposals came into play as the French sought a way to curb disease and protect public propriety on the streets—without following the lead of Anglo-Saxon moralists who hoped to abolish prostitution altogether. Regulations prohibiting prostitution had been passed in the fervor of the French Revolution. These laws granted special dispensation to certain houses, called *maisons de tolérance*, whose architecture and residents came under increasingly strict scrutiny during the course of the nineteenth century.[56] By the turn of the century, such artificially controlled environments seemed completely ineffective. Everyone acknowledged that the unregulated, impromptu *maisons de rendezvous* had become the scene of most liaisons. Accordingly, a government commission recommended that the police focus only on regular, mandatory health exams for all prostitutes, wherever they worked. When this effort, too, proved unable to stem the rising incidence of venereal disease, the state implemented new moral controls, and a "Sanitary Brigade" regularly inspected all settings known or suspected to be used for prostitution.[57]

As debate about controls over prostitution continued, the issue of the French birthrate was ever present. Voluntary low natality most often came under attack as the principal reason for depopulation, but so, too, did the very state of French cities—an opinion put forth by Lucien Merch, director of statistics for the French government, speaking before the Chamber of Deputies in 1913.[58] Again the colonies would represent a place to experiment fruitfully with solutions for the problems of the *métropole*. The Le Playians in particular insisted on the ways in which "civilization" weakened hereditary factors while it fostered irresponsibility in individual women and the culture as a whole. Hoping to reverse the moral and statistical trend, the National Alliance for the Increase of the French Population, founded in 1896 by Jacques Berthillon, was only one of many pronatalist groups which argued that the invigorating challenge of the colonies could provide the physical and cultural impetus to revitalize the French family.

French housing reform of the early twentieth century followed much the same pattern as that of public health; indeed, medical metaphors repeatedly evoked the dangers of "leprous" neighborhoods and "pestilent" tenements, linking the two problems.[59] The critical issue, once again, concerned the extent of state intervention that would prove acceptable to the electorate and sufficient to remedy the problems. As with public health, the initial action came from outside government. The Société Française des Habitations à Bon Marché, a private group (soon called HBM) founded in 1889, promoted inexpensive housing through tax exemptions and reduced-interest government loans. It remained only an advisory body, even after the passage of the HBM law in 1894, followed by the Ribot Law of 1908, facilitating home ownership with garden plots for working-class families. No funds were made available for either program until after the First World War.

Conditions had worsened considerably by then, given the extensive wartime losses sustained in the east and north of France, where some 600,000 dwellings had been destroyed or severely damaged.[60] This only compounded the prewar shortage of acceptable moderate-cost housing in all French urban areas. Paris, for instance, now estimated that 200,000 new units were needed to compensate for overcrowding and unacceptable housing conditions, as more people moved into the capital city.[61] But postwar inflation made private investment "impossible," according to the Le Playist journal *La Réforme sociale*.[62] The 1911 census had already identified close to two million persons in the Paris region who were inadequately housed—constituting almost half the area's total population—and the dearth of new housing made matters worse every year.[63] Suburban expansion was particularly alarming, as over a million new residents settled there during the 1920s; unable to afford Parisian rents, most of them lived in makeshift shanties they had built themselves, without adequate sanitation, water supplies, or paved streets.[64]

To most Parisians, the ugliness of the primitive settlements seemed as disturbing as the health dangers of the inadequate services. The existence of what one senator called a "miserable population . . . this rubbish [in a] sordid, sad quarter" made it difficult to take pride in their city (fig. 11).[65] The article then went on to explain:

> When one admired passionately the severe and grand lines of Paris's architectural beauty, the spectacle of incoherence, anarchy, and ugliness presented by the greater part of the Parisian suburbs cannot but afflict us. Yes, the Parisian suburbs are a great stain of ugliness on the beautiful face of France.[66]

If the *bidonvilles* of the colonial cities pointed out the inequalities—and the dangers—of that system, the outskirts of French cities posed a similar, highly visible critique of French republicanism at home.

FIGURE 11. *Housing in the Paris suburbs. Photograph by Henri Prost, c. 1925. Courtesy of the Académie d'Architecture, Paris.*

The HBM authorities, granted limited state funds in 1912, could only undertake the initial move of finding inexpensive land on which they hoped eventually to erect housing. They usually turned to the former fortifications areas, ringing the central core of many cities, or to the outlying suburbs. On the outskirts of Paris, under the direction of Henri Sellier, sixteen large *cité-jardin* projects, each comprising several thousand units, finally went up during the interwar decades (figs. 12, 13)[67] Likewise in Strasbourg, reclaimed from the Germans, officials made a marginal impact on the postwar housing crisis by erecting new HBM housing on the periphery (fig. 14). Yet the total number of new units did not approach the number torn down in the center of that city for the modern Grande Percée, which opened up the commercial district for modern buildings.[68] One could look upon the rehousing schemes of these cities largely as efforts to relocate workers to outlying districts, opening up new land in the center for commercial and residential development, while effecting greater overall class and ethnic segregation.[69]

In the face of diverse public-health issues, the colonies could, it seemed, provide techniques for revitalizing French cities, even as they accentuated the social and hygienic problems faced by all large cities. In the words of one commentator, after viewing a 1927 exhibit on colonial urbanism at the Grand Palais,

FIGURE 12. *The garden city of Plessis-Robinson outside Paris, by Maurice Payret-Dodail for the Office Public d'Habitations à Bon Marché du Département de la Seine, 1923–28. Courtesy of the Bibliothèque Forney, Paris.*

organized by the SFU and the Société d'Hygiène de France, "*Urbanism* is the *eugenics* of cities; and *urbanist* is a *specialized technician*."[70]

Aesthetic Debate

The appearance of the new housing projects stirred emotions, since the forms carried symbolic associations, and sometimes actual implications, about such issues as centralization versus local control. Only occasionally did the style of a new housing development follow the aesthetic of the avant-garde. The Parisian Société des Logements Hygiéniques et à Bon Marché commissioned several blocks of flats between 1903 and 1909, in which architect Henri Sauvage exposed the reinforced concrete frame, filled in with simple ceramic tiles or bricks, and maximized light and air through ample bay windows.[71] A generation later Tony Garnier oversaw 12,000 units of low-rise apartment buildings in the Etats-Unis district of Lyons (1924–35), together with ancillary schools, libraries, and community services. All of these structures brandished frankly modernist imagery such as unornamented walls and flat roofs.[72]

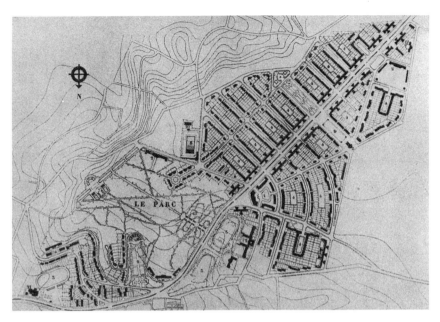

FIGURE 13. *Site plan of Plessis-Robinson. From Henri Sellier,* La Crise du logement et l'intervention publique, *1921.*

FIGURE 14. *Jardins Ungemach on the outskirts of Strasbourg by Paul de Rutté, 1923–29. Courtesy of the Bibliothèque Forney.*

One rarely saw modern lines or apartment blocks, especially outside major urban centers, certainly not until the 1930s. In 1916 the Société Française des HBM had stated its preference for regional styles, praising the "aesthetic diversity" France could thereby attain.[73] Many architecture critics, especially in the popular press, decried the use of universalist formulas. Yet they still considered themselves modernists. Léon Rosenthal and Léandre Vaillat were among the most vocal to call for a new architecture that would use contemporary materials and address modern urban problems, without sacrificing the multiplicity of the nation's regional traditions.[74]

Picturesque variations in massing, rooflines, and decorative detailing characterized most new housing that went up in the north and east of France after the war. Architects could still experiment with prefabrication and standardized elements, even as they utilized local construction techniques and the widespread desire for some diversity in appearance. Marcel Aubertin's Chemin Vert was typical. Situated on the outskirts of Rheims (1920–35) (fig. 15), it used twelve different types of blocks, balancing regional unity and visual contrast among the 600 individual units, resulting in what one observer called "a very special—and successful—effort . . . to give variety and cheerfulness of aspect."[75]

Much of the Art Deco movement should be seen in this light, as an effort to synthesize local forms with modern materials and consumer preferences. Energizing provincial traditions with the commercial excitement of modern life seemed a fitting reference to the culture all Frenchmen now shared. Unlike industry, the favored stylistic metaphor of the avant-garde, commerce carried a positive connotation of modernity for many people.[76]

In such a conception, traditional local norms would temper cosmopolitan innovations, just as more conservative public taste would supposedly restrain audacious architects. At least in theory, most French regionalist architects of the 1920s sought to combine local traditions with modernist concepts of universal standards, balancing charm with improvements, regional distinctions with general guidelines. France saw an outpouring of books in this vein just after the war. The most significant was the three-volume *Murs et toits pour les pays de chez nous* by Charles Latrosne, former president of the Société des Architectes Diplomés par le Gouvernement (SADG).[77] Letrosne explicitly emphasized the modernity of his designs and his intended clients. He also stressed the fundamental tenet of the regionalists: the need for buildings to adapt to their site, anthropomorphized as the "face" (*visage*) of the landscape.[78]

In his introduction to the 1922 French edition of Raymond Unwin's manual of garden-city design, Léon Jaussely reiterated this stand:

FIGURE 15. *Garden city of Chemin Vert on the outskirts of Rheims by Marcel Aubertin, 1920–35. From* The American City, *1923.*

> We do not think it would be particularly desirable to create from
> scratch—no matter how joyous, how seductive they might be—totally
> new cities, by which we mean true garden cities, completely self-
> sufficient and isolated from the older centers of our actual cities, with
> their histories and their traditions.[79]

Other members of the SFU articulated a similar agenda.

Debates about the meaning and effects of building style went beyond the professional boundaries of architecture and art criticism. Many political factions asked whether art and architecture could stir such emotions as national pride or class solidarity. Socialist Jean Juarès dismissed artistic propaganda as backward, declaring the "art forms can no longer, or almost not at all, play a role in that part of thought which translates into political and social action."[80] Despite such rebuffs, others on the left celebrated what Claude-Roger Marx in 1913 called *L'Art social*, referring to forms that would be generated by collective social life— not in the factory, in his modern definition of collective identity, but in the city itself.[81]

By the early twentieth century many French cities, especially those with strong leftist coalitions, decided to build new institutions to strengthen those collective bonds. Municipal subsidies and the national labor movement sponsored over one hundred and fifty Bourses de Travail in new or renovated buildings. An institution peculiar to France, these served initially as labor exchanges and then, increasingly, as trade union centers which collected information about workers' lives, lobbying for various improvements in housing and work condi-

FIGURE 16. *Hôtel de Ville, Lille, by Emile Dubuisson, 1926. Photograph by Gwendolyn Wright.*

tions.[82] Lille undertook an impressive new Hôtel de Ville, initiated in 1909 and inaugurated under a Socialist mayor in 1927 (fig. 16). Designed by Emile Dubuisson, the building used reinforced concrete to produce a modernized Flemish style that spoke of conspicuous local pride.[83]

The most visible representation of this ideal could be found in the *maison de tous* (also called the *maison de peuple* or *maison de la vie sociale*). This quintessentially public building provided citizens of all ages and backgrounds in a town or city with a myriad assortment of activities—public baths, gymnasia, library, social services, meeting rooms, child-care facilities, and collective gardens (fig. 17). Ideally, in such a structure, citizens would recognize the social and political ties which bound them together as a community. Many were proposed and a fair number built. Architect Achille Duchêne called the *maison de tous* "the office of human normalization," stressing the social and industrial research that could be conducted, even as citizens educated and reformed themselves. Like the good city plan as a whole, he wrote, the community building would generate "social order and cohesion."[84]

While socialists debated whether aesthetics could inspire political activism or mute its impact, French conservatives by and large agreed on the important role the arts could play in strengthening national pride and a sense of public

FIGURE 17.   *Maison de Tous at the Exposition des Arts Décoratifs, Paris, by Donat-Alfred Agache, 1925. From Pierre Selmersheim, L'Architecture à l'Exposition des Arts Décoratifs, 1925.*

duty. The historian Maurice Agulhon has described the "statuomania" rampant in the late nineteenth century, as national and local governments erected civic monuments laden with allegorical sculpture.[85] The church of the Sacré Coeur, the standardized Parisian *mairies*, the opulent train stations connecting Paris with the provinces, and the resplendent new Hôtel de Ville had all represented conscious efforts to let architecture encourage a sense of unity, even consensus, in the capital. Well into the twentieth century provincial cities continued to build ambitious municipal theaters, governmental buildings, train stations, and casinos in the resort spas, echoing the same desire for visible signs of their own civic well-being. Whether public or private, each expenditure sought to proclaim both the city's unique history and its place in contemporary fashion.

Professional identity for individual architects now involved two contradictory mandates: the need to provide public services and respect public taste, on the one hand, and the right to artistic freedom, on the other. Yet even the very definition of public taste and functional services raised difficult questions: where to draw the line between national standards and regional diversity? how to distinguish between cultural distinctions and economic inequalities? whether to accept or to elevate the prevailing public taste in the arts? whether to impose restrictions that would guarantee quality and harmony, or promote artistic creativity through lenient controls?

Professional commentators tended to assert a new kind of *demiurge*, a creative genius that talented men would inevitably embody. "The New Architecture," wrote art critic and gallery owner Léon Rosenthal, "demands unprecedented liberties—and responsibilities—for the architects charged with reconstruction. . . . France needs structures, fitting with the indications of climate and geography, that conform to our ideas, our usages, our needs."[86] Artists in other fields issued similar statements about the challenge of their time, often granting architects a privileged position to resolve the nation's problems. Raymond Escholier, winner of the prestigious Prix Femina in literature, predicted a new aesthetic for the capital that would respond to a wide range of social issues:

> The hope of renewing national traditions, while guarding their veneration; . . . research on the picturesque based on rationalist doctrines; fantasy spouting forth our necessities; a strong taste for the familiar and especially for logic and regularity; these are the dominant themes which inspire artistic life in the new Paris.[87]

But such earnest aspirations could not preclude considerable confusion and discord about how to undertake actual projects in French cities.

Nowhere was the confusion about appropriate styles, the tension between past grandeur and present disarray, more acute than in the capital city. The *maisons de rapport* along Haussmann's boulevards came under fire as early as the 1890s, when many Parisians came to see the facades as monotonous, "a tyranny of street architecture wrought by ordinances and old habits."[88] Now uniformity seemed boring to the public and unduly restricting to the artistic freedom of French architects. In response, largely under the instigation of Hénard and the architect Louis Bonnier, head of the municipal Department of Streets, the council passed a law in 1902 which encouraged more animated ornamentation, giving the architect complete freedom within a spatial envelope whose size was determined by the street width. After centuries of strict controls, buildings suddenly became taller, covered with lavish, deeply incised ornamentation.

The rococo surfaces in turn aroused critics, most of whom deemed both the new and renovated buildings garishly excessive (fig. 18). A storm of protest soon called for a return to architectural restraint, identifying this aesthetic with France

FIGURE 18. *Hôtel Lutecia, Paris, by Louis-Charles Boileau and Henri-Alexis Tauzin, 1910. Photograph by Melinda Maerher.*

itself, and branding the new trends in xenophobic terms. "Yes, they are ugly, all these 'palaces,'" deplored the legal historian Charles Lortsch,

> American in height, Germanic in ugliness, and Annamite in decoration. . . . Paris is the city of beauty, which is to say of order and harmony, the city of good taste, elegance, and refinement. We cannot allow Paris to be constructed absolutely by chance and whim, following the fantasies, perhaps fortunate but perhaps also monstrous, of architects and owners.[89]

Yet buildings unprecedented in height, bulk, and number continued to appear, not only in Paris, but in provincial cities as well.

Many observers saw in history a means for reestablishing sound aesthetic priorities. Criticizing the fussy ornamentation of apartment houses and the austerity of many business structures, they hoped that the grand monuments of France's past would furnish a countermodel: Parisian edifices of the seventeenth and eighteenth centuries represented stately, uniform architecture, while the smaller houses and shops of provincial towns showed how to provide variety and charm. Albert Guérard, in *L'Avenir de Paris* (1929), could dismiss all recent buildings, declaring, "To modernize is inevitably to make things ugly."[90] Somewhat earlier the legal scholar Charles Lortsch decried the decline of public responsibility among Parisian architects. "In order to have the pleasure of building a story higher here and there," he wrote, they "are in the process of destroying the work of three centuries."[91]

Architects seldom endorsed a historicist duplication of older forms. Guérard had contended that "To restore is to banalize," much as Lucien Magne, writing a generation earlier, had declared that archaeology is the "true obstacle to the progress of modern art."[92] The most vocal critics of the 1910s and 1920s—Robert de Souza, Emile Magne, Charles Magny, Léon Rosenthal, and Adolphe Dervaux, for example—all insisted that "pastiche" or "superfluous fetishism" would be a grave mistake.[93] They understood the dilemma of creating a historically sensitive modern architecture, but they were not sure how to achieve it.

Bitter conflict arose over the restoration of historic sites after the Armistice. Rheims Cathedral, for example, a controversial site, had been severely damaged by bombing during the war. Many architects believed that nothing should be done, other than installing an invisible reinforced concrete roof, so that the cathedral would stand "as a permanent witness to German barbarity."[94] Amateurs, on the other hand, clamored for idealized restorations.

A national preservation law had been enacted in 1913. The Bureau of Historic Monuments, headed by Paul Léon, now actively sought to classify buildings in order to bring them under governmental protection. Léon showed a particular interest in the building ensemble, and the law allowed the state the right to buy adjacent buildings (or to prevent inappropriate new structures) around a classified monument. During the 1920s the inventory included entire streets, then entire towns such as Collonques and Mont-Saint-Michel. (fig. 19).[95] When the bureau was brought under the auspices of the National Office of Tourism, tax relief and the right to charge entry for historic sites accentuated the economic benefits of preservation.[96]

French architects engaged in urban design had to choose between two paradigms. Although most endorsed some amalgam of the two, the polarity seemed absolute. One approach focused on preserving the particular charm of the towns in each province, even in the capital city itself. The other stressed the need for higher standards and modern improvements: wider streets, zoning, infrastructural services, and a regional analysis to promote industrial development through rational siting of future factories and workers' housing. Such improvements had no inherent local character; they would be applied without distinction in any setting.

FIGURE 19. *Mont Saint Michel after the removal of extraneous buildings under the auspices of the Historic Monuments Service, 1928. From Paul Léon,* La Vie des monuments français, *1951.*

The SFU strongly endorsed the first, more culturalist paradigm. At their exposition on "La Cité Moderne" held in Nancy shortly before World War I, Agache had formulated a clear set of priorities for the architect. His work, Agache stressed, should always put the public interest before any private interest. That public interest, he continued, in large part meant the responsibility to protect local styles and traditions, even as the architect helped improve public health and municipal development.[97] The culturalist credo was best formulated by the French and Belgian architects who organized "La Cité Reconstituée" at the Jeu de Paume in 1916, an exhibition which considered future rebuilding in the north and east of France, areas largely destroyed by German invasion. Speaking for the group, Agache again insisted:

It is not a matter of proposing omnibus plans which could be laid out here or there, regardless of the particular conditions of a setting. . . . The physiognomy of the rural agglomerations of our old France is diverse, and it is right that, even restored and resuscitated, they evoke, if not the souvenirs of a destroyed past, at least the charm of the territory which finds its exterior expression in the look and disposition of housing.[98]

In a catalogue introduction to the regional housing display at a related exhibition held at the Société des Architectes Diplomés par le Gouvernement a few months later, Léandre Vaillat anthropomorphized the distinction:

> It took the war for France to have a glimmering of the fact that, beside grand "Architecture" with a capital A, which sculptors once represented as a nobly draped woman, Vitruvius on her knee and a compass in her hand, there was a simpler "architecture" with a small a, which I envision as a good housewife, knowing well the recipes her mother has passed down to her.[99]

The appeal of regional styles rested, in part, on an appreciation of cultural diversity and a recognition of the limits of modern expertise (fig. 20).

What Le Corbusier would soon ridicule as "r-é-g-i-o-n-a-l-i-s-m-e" involved a desire to maintain not one but many cultural traditions in the face of modern uniformity.[100] The opposition to the "invasion" of prefabricated houses from other countries reverberated with strong nationalist opposition to the actual German invasions in the east of France, most bitterly to the loss of Alsace-Lorraine in 1871. Regionalist sentiment by no means opposed nationalistic emotions. Vaillat went on to praise Viollet-le-Duc and the Gothic revivalists of the mid-nineteenth century:

> What did they want if not the return to a national tradition, that is to say, to an architecture adapted to our soil, climate, landscape, to the inhabitants, and therefore abandoning an ultramontane architecture, imagined in Greece and Rome by Greek and Roman masters, consequently regional to Greece and Rome, but abstract in our country.[101]

Vaillat's ideal, in its essence, evoked an architecture of place, responding simultaneously to the city or town, the region, and the nation, while assiduously avoiding all abstract ideas that transcended these boundaries.

Such an aesthetic suggested distinct political overtones, for the regionalist movement had a resonant appeal throughout the French provinces. Since the late nineteenth century, a few political leaders had begun to acknowledge the weak sense of national unity, especially outside Paris. Regional dialects, unequal educational and economic opportunities, poor systems of communication, and primitive transportation services had created in France a situation several historians would later brand "internal colonialism."[102]

Two Parisian professors, Charles Gide and Jean Charles-Brun, led a new crusade for "patriotism and particularism" during the early twentieth century.[103] Themes of conciliation and growth distinguish this movement from sentimental nostalgia. As Charles-Brun explained, "stability and change, tradition and pro-

FIGURE 20. *Housing for employees of the Compagnie du Nord, Lille-Déliverance, by Gustav Umbdenstock, 1921. From* Arts et décoration, *1922.*

gress, these are terms that seem so obviously contradictory, but need not be, for regionalism brings them together."[104] Binding intellectual and peasant in a celebration of local cultural distinctions, their brand of regionalism stressed the need for economic decentralization. Yet the longstanding separatism of certain provinces remained and even intensified (notably in Brittany, the Auvergne, and Provence), spreading to other regions with the unequal industrial development following World War I. Demands for autonomy within the centralized French state continued to insist on both economic and cultural rights.

By and large, authorities bypassed economic, educational, and administrative concessions in favor of picturesque architecture. State-financed rebuilding usually followed this pattern. Industrialists, too, used a regionalist mode to present a benign portrait of their relations with workers. The railway towns of the Compagnie du Nord, built all across the northeast of France in the 1920s, featured the distinctly traditional aesthetic of each province (fig. 21). National geography texts issued by the government, such as *La France et ses colonies* (1930), praised the new villages, both publicly and privately funded (fig. 22), which had replaced "sad mining towns and crowded workers' quarters" in the regions devastated by wartime hostilities.[105]

The ideal of the small provincial town as a countermodel to the unhealthy, unwieldy city permeated many aspects of French life, fueling the legislature's refusal to tackle the planning problems of the large cities. Regionalist design

47

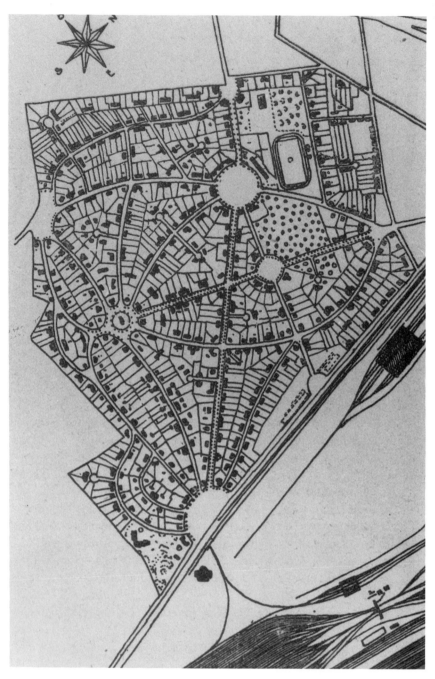

FIGURE 21. *Site plan of Lille-Déliverance by Gustav Umbdenstock, 1921. From Umbdenstock*, Recueil de compositions architecturales, *1922*.

FIGURE 22. *Housing for the Cité de la Société Mossant, Vallon et Argod, Bourg-de-Péage (Drôme), by Henri Prost, 1928. From* L'Illustration, *1938.*

allowed administrators and industrialists to imply their respect for the provinces which supplied workers for French farms and factories, just as their counterparts used indigenous styles in the colonies, suggesting greater tolerance and involvement than actually existed.

The other approach to rebuilding likewise sought to connect aesthetics and economic development, in this case through "scientific" principles. Exemplified by the American planner George B. Ford of New York, who oversaw relief efforts for the American Red Cross, the philosophy had already found favor among French politicians such as Edouard Herriot, *maire* of Lyons and soon to become president of the Republic. Speaking to a conference on urbanism he organized in 1914, Herriot had declared, "The administration of the smaller city should cease being empirical in order to become truly scientific."[106] Although he then went on to list a number of specific "scientific" concerns—health care, industrial development, modern education, improved housing—Herriot still acknowledged the important role of aesthetics and history in any urban plan. So, too, for that matter, did Ford, who had pointed out that rational planning could be destructive by "straightening out all the kinks in the streets, thereby losing all the personality and charm of the town."[107]

With these disclaimers, the scientific approach to urban design buttressed the definition of the urbanist as a rational expert, focusing primarily on zoning, infrastructure services, and a regional plan for development. Yet the "scientific" modernists did not, in fact, rely upon a truly neutral language. The preoccupation with large-scale programmatic reforms revealed an aesthetic predilection. Implicit in the scientific discourse of impartial rationality one finds a recurring pattern of neutral shapes arranged in a systematic pattern—a studied neutrality, to be sure, but a formal preference all the same. These architects assumed that standardized forms would guarantee both economy and health. This was a moralistic assertion, a symbolic association more than a truly scientific conclusion, and therefore all the more difficult to contest.

"Scientific" concerns resonated with the municipal council of Rheims, which had suffered the worst damage of the large French cities during the war. Inviting Ford to supervise postwar replanning efforts, they hoped to stimulate the local economy. That goal required not only a physical plan but also a strengthened central authority, including the government's right to regulate and even reorganize the use of private property. An expropriation law of 1918 allowed the city to take over a whole zone for public use in order to improve streets, sanitation, and the ventilation of rebuilt structures; ownership of land would be reallocated in a manner that replicated original land value, although here and elsewhere many citizens deplored the "fiasco" of biased expropriations tribunals.[108]

Armed with this legislation, Ford was able to impose wider, more regular streets in the center of Rheims, even in the historic areas surrounding the partially demolished cathedral and town hall (fig. 23). Over the next two decades, with significant modifications, "le plan Ford" gradually determined the course of postwar reconstruction in this, France's "martyr city" of World War I.[109]

It was not, however, the sharp distinctions between these two paradigms of urban design that hampered postwar building. Neither model prevailed in the actual course of reconstruction, largely because the financial provisions for remuneration encouraged the rebuilding of streets and structures just as they had been before the war. When the state undertook to indemnify losses, whether for factories, stores, or houses, repayments were higher and more prompt if new building took place in the same area—even if there were a more feasible alternative site. The policy led not only to fraud but also to the most expedient and least thoughtful kind of rebuilding.

By 1925, with no German payments and vast French outlays, the state was virtually bankrupt. French reconstruction—the nation's major effort before World War II to engage in urban planning—had provided no viable new model

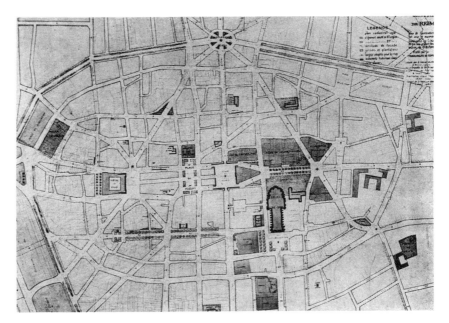

FIGURE 23. *Reconstruction plan for Rheims by George Ford, 1919. From the* Journal of the American Institute of Architects, *copyrighted 1920 by the American Institute of Architects, with the permission of the AIA under license number 90062. All rights reserved.*

for development. The issue of reconciling memory and modernization remained one of many urban dilemmas troubling French intellectuals. Health problems, industrial and financial sluggishness, class and regional conflicts, all seemed to call for a new vision of the city.

The ideal of a "municipal sociology in action," in the words of the architect and reformer Achille Duchêne, had elicited an outpouring of publications at the time of World War I.[110] New associations and long-established groups pleaded their cause, but neither could generate much action. The sense of impasse continued, until the frustrated critics of French cities began to look abroad.

2

COLONIAL
OPPORTUNITIES

WHEN GUSTAVE LE BON spoke about education at the 1889 Colonial Congress, he drew characteristic parallels between colonial and domestic reforms. While most Frenchmen agreed on the impossibility of "civilizing Negroes," Le Bon explained, they nonetheless felt the state should provide education for its charges. "We are in the same situation with respect to these colored peoples as we are with respect to our peasants," agreed one official who heard the speech. "We owe education to the former as to the latter." This obligation held even if, he added sarcastically, "some persons think that in sending our peasants to school, we are making them enemies of society."[1]

At times the language for describing colonies and capital city became virtually interchangeable. One critic, speaking of the Parisian suburbs, insisted:

> It is from the moral point of view, above all, that such *colonies* present
> the gravest dangers. The overcrowding, the habitation of entire families
> in the same room, have the most unfortunate results, and the old inhabitants of the country look with contempt (often exaggerated by hatred) on
> the immigrants, whom they frankly deem to be undesirable.[2]

In both settings leaders looked for reforms that would affect not only the poor or colonized populations, but the French working class and middle classes as well.

If the colonies seemed a potential liability, they could also provide benefits to France. Here the state could experiment with goals and tactics, deliberating about how best to progress into the twentieth century. Even Juarès's Socialist party had come to favor colonization, arguing that it would spread liberal principles of democratic equality and protect French workers from unfair competition elsewhere in Europe.[3] To French conservatives, benefits seemed beyond doubt and pervasively necessary. Charles Lemire asserted that by sending poor families from France to the colonies, the nation could address its own internal class tensions: "instead of making rebels, you will make *workers*."[4] Lyautey's concept of the leader's responsibility to know his staff and subjects should be applied, wrote one enthusiast, "not only for the barracks and the officer, but for the factory and the engineer, the office and the manager, the workshop and the foreman."[5]

Certainly economic benefits provided an important rationale for colonial expansion. This had been true during the nineteenth century, even in countries such as Morocco not yet officially colonized.[6] Indeed, as we shall see, European arguments about colonization as a nondisruptive force often involved protecting the "historic traditions" and "economic climate" they had helped create. By the early twentieth century, major benefactors became highly visible. These included the giant phosphate companies in Morocco, rubber and coal producers in Indochina, and real estate speculators everywhere who bought land cheaply— often confiscating it illegally.

All the same, economic self-interest can only be argued so far. In 1914 the vast French colonial empire was responsible for only 12 percent of French trade, exports being slightly greater than imports. Algeria and, far behind, Tunisia, Indochina, and the recently conquered Morocco headed the list. This balance of trade would not shift from a liability to an asset until the 1920s. Relatively little French capital was being invested in the colonies: less than 9 percent of the national total on the eve of World War I. That amount had quadrupled since the previous decade, but it was still scarcely larger than French investment in Turkey and behind that in Latin America.[7] These indications should by no means overshadow the enormous profits and exploitative tactics of major industrialists and land speculators in the colonies. They indicate the power the colonial pressure groups were able to assert in French politics, even when money invested in the *outre-mer* was scarcely helpful to the national economy as a whole. Other non-economic factors helped win support.

Policies for colonial cities in the 1910s and 1920s sought to address many problems which plagued France: overcrowding, poor sanitation, economic stagnation, class and ethnic antagonisms, fears about immorality and aesthetic squalor. Indeed, several metropolitan architectural critics recognized that the colonial example—Algeria for its mistakes, Morocco in particular for its achievements—could help the French planning efforts. Gaston Rambert explained the parallels in 1922, commenting on the master plans for French cities—as yet unimplemented—on display at Marseille's Colonial Exposition that year:

The principal ideas in these grand projects are definitely quite similar to those which presided over the creation of extension plans for the colonial cities. Everywhere the largest amount of space is reserved for public thoroughfares, gardens, parks, and playgrounds; everywhere one finds specialized zones based on climatic considerations and proximity to transportation; finally, the principal traffic system tends toward a spider's web pattern—the most favorable to the flow of traffic—while that of the secondary streets, especially in the better residential quarters, has been laid out to please the eye and make the drive more agreeable.[8]

In spirit and in actual programs, both the impressive examples of modern French urbanism for the *colons* and the efforts to exercise control over the larger dependent populations, provided a model for metropolitan cities.

If many French intellectuals were concerned about the state of cities at home, professional ambitions often drew them abroad. The colonies provided France with a cultural domain for expansion. During the first two centuries of imperialism this had involved the glorification of French culture: its language, institutions, and revered superiority as the epitome of civilization. In the early twentieth century a distinctive new approach to cultural politics would emerge, seeking a more supple approach to power. French colonial officials proclaimed their tolerance for difference, their appreciation for other cultures, their respect for tradition, and their ability to modernize in a sensitive manner.

Implementing these policies was a new generation of applied social scientists and self-declared "architect-urbanists." These young men found their first real opportunities abroad. Colonial professionals hoped to establish the significance of their work, to prove its applicability at home and its intellectual significance in general. If they emphasized the general or theoretical importance of their research and policies, in part perhaps to obscure its political intentions, they were also trying to win favor in the eyes of metropolitan colleagues.

It is the story of the would-be urban designers that deserves our attention first, for it is out of their youthful ambitions and frustrations that the aesthetic experiment in the colonies emerged. It is that experiment, arising in part from the theories formulated in Paris and Rome, which generated an important development in modern French architecture and urban planning.

The Profession of Urban Design

The recipient of the esteemed Prix de Rome in architecture, selected annually from the students of the Parisian Ecole des Beaux-Arts, spent four years in Rome with additional travel in Italy and Greece. At the state's expense, the country's artistic elite were to further their classical education, always following the strict "moral tutelage" of their mentors.[9] The Prix de Rome lionized the best young designers who worked within the classical tradition, thus reaffirming the styles long since deemed correct for the major monuments and institutional buildings of the French nation.

Sharing quarters in the Villa Medici, taking their meals communally and traveling in small groups, these young men enjoyed the privilege of time and the promise of elite professional careers once they returned to France. Yet the group that came together between 1900 and 1909 chafed at such facile privilege. They were certainly notable designers, including, first, Tony Garnier, then Henri Prost, Léon Jaussely, Jean Hulot, Paul Bigot, and Ernest Hébrard. While each was duly impressed with the glories of antiquity, they nonetheless questioned many of the stipulations that went with the prize. To do so implicitly challenged the authority of the French architectural establishment and the appropriate imagery for the French state.

The fundamental issue was their definition of the scope for architectural work. This group insisted that the twentieth century demanded new skills and priorities from the architect, and especially from the future leaders in that profession. They no longer considered formal training in composition and a thorough knowledge of historical monuments sufficient bases for good design. Even the most beautiful building, whether contemporary or archaeological, could not be studied in isolation from the larger urban context.[10]

It is sometimes difficult to grasp the insularity of this profession, so obviously based on a public world of clients and commissions. Yet it is exactly the desire to be removed from extraneous influences that characterized the profession of architecture in France at the turn of the last century. Of course, not every architect responded in this way. Groups or individuals who insisted on putting architecture squarely into the context of the social, technological, and political events of their time generated major aesthetic reformulations, as well as a more engaged role for the designer. This had been the case with Henri Labrouste and Eugène-Emmanuel Viollet-le-Duc at mid-century, as it was now with Tony Garnier and Henri Prost, or would be with Le Corbusier.[11] Such exceptions, and the response they elicited, only prove the point about the profession's prevailing conservatism.

Looking back over his career, Henri Prost wrote an unpublished paper entitled "Paris 1900," where he laid out the various influences that underlay the reforms this group had proposed as students, reforms they eventually carried out, in different ways, in their later professional work. "If sociologists, hygienists, and artists were concerned about the state of society," Prost declared, "the young students of the architecture section of the Ecole Nationale des Beaux-Arts also displayed a deep apprehension about the state of their art."[12] By this account, both formalistic debates and more purely social concerns provided the motivation for needed change.

In Rome, Prost wrote, he and his cohorts concurred on the need to shift emphasis, in their studies and their professional work, from isolated buildings to the city as a whole. Since the city was a complex intermixing of aesthetic, political, economic, and epidemiological parts, any building had to be designed with an awareness of all these elements. The paper then discussed their awareness of issues outside the aesthetic realm, including technical problems like traffic congestion and inadequate public transportation in a city like Paris which, as yet, had no traffic regulations whatsoever.

As fervent French nationalists, the Prix de Rome winners were all too aware that just such an urbanistic approach prevailed in other countries. "We learned," Prost recalled, "that in England and in Germany, planning for the extension of cities had long been a priority of governments and municipalities which, aided by sociologists and artists, had created an appropriate legislation for carrying out such projects."[13] These young Frenchmen did not see themselves as followers of Ebenezer Howard or Camillo Sitte, but they did want to study the ideas and projects of such urban reformers in order to apply the relevant principles in France. In their eyes, it was a matter of political necessity and artistic innovation.

Beginning with Garnier's Cité Industrielle and continuing through a ten-year cycle, these young architects undertook projects that changed the scale of their studies. They moved away from the accepted reconstruction of individual classical monuments to a larger complex of buildings and even entire antique or modern cities. Broadly speaking, four prevailing images dominated their work: the industrial city, the historic city, the republican city, and the imperial city.

Garnier's design for a Cité Industrielle was submitted in 1900, his first year in Rome (fig. 24). This elaborate *envoi* consisted of a site plan, accompanied by detailed architectural renderings of various buildings and districts and an impassioned statement. The scheme represented Garnier's effort to take into account many aspects of a real city, including governmental, cultural, residential, manufacturing, and even agricultural facilities; it linked certain of these functions and separated others through zoning. Even the uniform style of the buildings reflected resolutely modernist taste, with unornamented flat white walls in reinforced concrete.[14]

The Académie des Beaux-Arts in Paris reacted with violent outrage, charg-

FIGURE 24. *Tony Garnier's Cité Industrielle in 1917. From Garnier,* Une Cité industrielle, 1917. *Copyright renewed, 1982, St. Martin's Press.*

ing that Garnier had confused the "social tendencies that can impassion him and the forms of art with which he would be able to clothe them." [15] Refusing to accept the project, they demanded that he produce the kind of work expected of *pensionnaires* in Rome. Students at the Paris Ecole rioted to protest the opinion, but Garnier eventually complied, though he did so with a vengeance which reinforced his urbanistic focus, if not his modernistic aesthetic. In 1902 he submitted an entire set of restoration drawings of the Roman city of Tusculum.

Henri Prost observed Garnier's challenge at close hand. He also took on a historic city, and did so with less direct conflict. In his second year Prost reconstituted the essential lines of the Byzantine capital of Contantinople (renamed Istanbul since 1453), thereby extending the permissible geographical and cultural terrain as well as the accepted scale of Prix de Rome work. Prost's presentation drawings concentrated on the Church of the Hagia Sophia, built in 532 – 37, but he took care to show this edifice alongside the palace, baths, and fora Constantine had built on the shores of the Marmara (fig. 25). Other drawings focused on the church's dome as a major focal point in the city, showing a view toward the Hagia Sophia from several different vantage points. Once again, the social and emotional meaning of architecture was enlarged at an urban scale. Years later, in 1936, following his acclaimed career in Morocco, Prost was invited to do a master plan for this city, once more called Constantinople, under the Islamic nationalist leader Kemal Atatürk. [16] Prost's youthful exercises even-

FIGURE 25.   Envoi *of sixth-century Constantinople and the Hagia Sophia by Henri Prost, 1904. From* Urbanisme, *1965. Courtesy of Urbanisme.*

tually found application in a plan which balanced historic preservation, modernization, and Atatürk's authoritarian political goals.

The year after Prost's Constantinople *envoi*, Jean Hulot submitted a reconstruction of Selinus, the Greek maritime colony in Sicily, whose elegant orthogonal urban design plan by Hermocrates (408 B.C.) had been erected on earlier sixth-century B.C. foundations. Paul Bigot then reconstituted a vast section of fourth-century Rome, showing the tortuous winding streets, the cramped apartment *insulae*, and the grandiose public buildings surrounding the Circus Maximus.[17] For all these young architects, antique Rome embodied imperial power and the highest standard of urban civilization.[18] In terms of urban design and cultural policies, history had contemporary relevance at many levels.

Léon Jaussely put off his acceptance of the 1903 prize in order to take part in an international competition for Barcelona, a project sponsored by the Institute for Catalan Studies in that city.[19] Barcelona was the Catalan capital within a Spanish state; it epitomized demands for cultural autonomy, based on historical archaeology studies and broad class participation in government, which would later fuel the Spanish Republic.[20] Jaussely's winning plan focused on the role of public spaces, a coordinated street system, and industrial services in a republican capital city. Elaborating upon the scheme over the next four years (it would be partially carried out in 1917), he emphasized parks and open space, improved transportation facilities, and future outward expansion with anticipated economic growth. Jaussely respected and even highlighted the cultural

59

particularities of the city: the waterfront harbor, the Ramblas, Gaudí's Sagrada Familia, the Ciudadela Park (which he asked Forestier to relandscape). In developing these simultaneously as road networks and social gathering places, Jaussely sought to integrate cultural sensibility with economic progress through urban design.[21]

In Rome, continuing to work around some of these themes, Jaussely reconstructed a major section of Pompeii as his principal *envoi*. Capturing the color and complexity of this splendid retreat for Rome's major citizens during the last years of the republic, he portrayed the interwoven activities of public and private spaces. Minute details showed ordinary citizens going about their various domestic affairs in crowded streets, thriving in an animated urban setting.

The last in this succession was Ernest Hébrard's imperial city. Hébrard arrived in Rome in 1905, traveling to Istanbul with Prost his first year. His major Prix de Rome project consisted of a reconstruction of Diocletian's palace, built on the Yugoslavian coast in 305 A.D. The palace was sufficiently large and complex for Hébrard to consider it a model of an imperial city (fig. 26). (Indeed, Spalato functioned as a walled town for centuries after the fall of Rome.) Intended principally as a fortified stronghold for the retired emperor, the palace complex also showed a markedly political aesthetic sense. In an effort to represent the unity of an empire on the verge of collapse, Diocletian had freely intermingled Western and Eastern precedents—notably the prototypes for the Roman camp, or *cadastra*, and the Byzantine colony—just as Hébrard's later work in Indochina would do. A lavish two-volume publication on the reconstruction, with a text by the historian Jacques Zeiler, emphasized this intentional borrowing from the East, which "rejuvenates and soon leads to a new art" in the West.[22]

To be sure, the main goal in the planning of Diocletian's palace had not been an aesthetic formula so much as military strength and a well-organized grouping of administrative functions. The rigid, mathematically regular system of Spalato precluded further growth and development. This same static quality would not mark Hébrard's later work. Efficiency through design, particularly of administrative functions, like stylistic efforts to proclaim imperial harmony, would however continue to be central themes throughout his colonial career.

The work of these young architects continued to emphasize their commitment to urban design and their roles as urbanists, even if they sometimes produced rather truncated versions of cities. One project serves as a link between the early, more abstract analyses and the later, more concrete plans of this group in France and in the colonies. It underscores the desire for control of social, economic, and political problems through urban design, so evident in this group's endeavors.

FIGURE 26.　Envoi *of Diocletian's palace at Spalato by Ernest Hébrard, 1906. From Hébrard and Zeiler,* Le Palais de Diocletian, *1912.*

While in Rome, Hébrard had met Hendrik Christian Andersen, a wealthy young American sculptor devoted to the cause of world peace. He began to collaborate with Andersen on a grandiose scheme for a *Centre Mondial* (fig. 27), a vast world capital designed to further this goal. Their proposal was published in 1913 with simultaneous French and English editions, supplemented by a history of urbanism by the classicist Gabriel Leroux. Like Garnier, Hébrard conceived of a total plan for a modern city from his early student days. Unlike Garnier, he saw no need to challenge prevailing architectural styles or to make significant accommodations for modern industry and multiple dwellings.

This was not a model city in the sense that the garden city had been formulated: a diagrammatic prototype to be modified again and again, thereby taking into account all manner of urban distinctions. Hébrard imagined a single format for a true world capital, bringing together the leaders of all countries and all disciplines in a singular setting. "This World Center," declared the text, "was conceived as embodying and unifying all the world's scientific, artistic, and physical achievements, testing their values in relation to human progress, to the end that, after obtaining an international sanction of their excellence, they might be distributed throughout the world."[23] Hébrard and Andersen dreamed of centralizing, then disseminating the knowledge generated by their city's elite residents, rather than analyzing the strengths or weaknesses of the plan itself.

FIGURE 27. *Frontispiece of Hendrik Christian Andersen and Ernest Hébrard's* Creation of a World Centre, *1913*.

Hébrard believed he had isolated and consolidated essential rules of order. These principles included the new social and health priorities of professional urbanists:

> the amount of cubic space, hygienically proportionate to the needs of the people both in- and out-of-doors, free access to public baths, laundries, hospitals, churches, theaters, lecture halls, and markets, according to popular needs, all the various spaces necessary for human rest and relaxation, are considerations that in the last few years have been acknowledged by the world.[24]

It was his insistence on the idea of a world capital, linked to all parts of the globe by advanced communication technology, that represents the essential modernism of his scheme. In this sense, Hébrard actually went beyond the nineteenth-century industrial focus of Garnier's city. Moreover, with an envisioned population of 800,000 to one million, this metropolis anticipated truly urban proportions.

Hébrard's attention to the problems of a metropolis came through most clearly in his careful attention to transportation systems and technological services. Subways linked all parts of the city for rapid movement between work and residence, with automobile traffic anticipated in the outlying suburban grid. The engineer A. Beaurrienne provided detailed working drawings of centralized heating and water supplies with the plants on the outskirts of the city—thereby following the appeals of the French municipal socialists. Trees lined the broad main avenues, and small parks were interspersed regularly throughout the city. "It is now well known," Hébrard explained, "that more lives have been destroyed by lack of light, air, and cleanliness than by invading armies."[25] All in all, he took into account many of the contemporary ideas about public health, scientific zoning, and modern transportation that signaled the studious planner more than the aesthete.

Nonetheless, Beaux-Arts conceptions of style and composition dominated the proposal. Symmetrical axes and a long central vista commanded the site plan. Three consecutive cores of the city focused on an area for Olympic sports, a complex for the arts, and a communication center built around the monumental Tower of Progress. The buildings themselves bespeak a commitment to architectural tradition, specifically the neo-Baroque that had come to be called "Beaux-Arts" throughout the Western world (fig. 28). Hébrard made no efforts to modernize the plans or elevations, nor did he question the universal applicability of Renaissance and Baroque facades. Many of the particular buildings

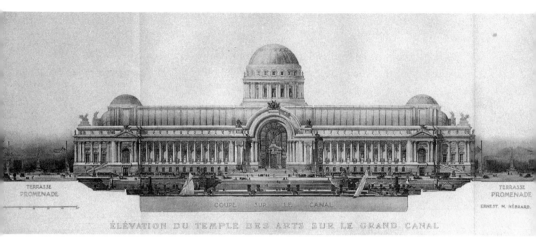

FIGURE 28. *Palace of Fine Arts in the World Center. From* Creation of a World
Centre.

made precise references to major seventeenth- and eighteenth-century monuments in Paris and Rome, including Le Vau's Institut de France, home of the
Académie des Beaux-Arts. Style provided the link to an orderly past, a fixed set
of aesthetic and social traditions in a world undergoing rapid technological
change.

The Tower of Progress, 320 meters high, stood as the single modern structure, the beacon from which innovations and accords would be broadcast. Hébrard realized that progressive research and debate could be carried out in aesthetically conservative buildings, the conclusions then instantly sent around the
globe. From their privileged citadel, the world's leaders would strive "to increase
the development of hygiene, make possible more elevated social conditions,
and, above all, uplift the oppressed and harmonize all human efforts."[26] Such a
portentous goal echoed the celebratory prose of colonialism, just as the administrative centers of power would also dominate their surroundings.

In one sense, Hébrard obviously wanted to conceive of the city as a unified
whole. He also insisted on a policy of carefully delineated zones, segregated by
socioeconomic class and by function. The monumental group of structures
along the main axis of the city, together with the six major residential districts,
were separated from the outlying areas by a wide canal. On the far side of the
canal Hébrard anticipated industrial development and nearby garden-suburbs for
workers' families—although he showed no interest in how this industrial section
would look.

While he spoke of the "need to plan for the entire population, not just the
elite," Hébrard meant by this a distinctly medieval view of social structure, with

each class provided for, but little chance to change one's status. He even praised medieval hierarchy as a specific influence on his view of society.[27] Thus Hébrard did specify that working-class areas, like the more prestigious neighborhoods, should be self-contained environments, politically and culturally autonomous, with their own museums, theaters, schools, and town halls. He acknowledged a universal need for "air, leisure, light, and the right to self-expression," mixing in one program physical and mental health, science, and culture.[28] For him, these benefits could only accrue to the public as a whole if segregation and separate local services kept that public divided.

Andersen contacted prominent world leaders and many of the hundreds of international peace organizations and municipal reform groups which flourished during the pre–World War I years. Feminist Charlotte Perkins Gilman, architect Otto Wagner, and black activist W. E. B. Du Bois were among scores of respondents who politely supported the project.[29] Andersen drew up detailed economic calculations for building the city, while Hébrard developed specific site plans for locating it adjacent to eight different metropolises, ranging from the New Jersey side of New York City to Tunis and New Delhi.[30] He never altered the city plan in any of these proposals, despite the great differences in topography, climate, and cultural tradition (fig. 29). As one critic bluntly wrote: "[In] the erroneous belief that a plan can be perfect . . . the love of grandeur sometimes develops into megalomania."[31]

The most auspicious prospect for the city's being realized came from Belgium, whose legislature offered a site on the outskirts of Brussels as a prospective center for world peace.[32] When the First International Congress of the Union of Belgian Cities and Communes convened in 1913, the group endorsed Hébrard's proposal; the government began to raise money under the instigation of Senator Lafontaine and the Brussels attorney Paul Otlet. But the outbreak of war intervened, and Belgium turned away from thoughts of peace. The idea resurfaced after the war, first with suggestions that the World Center be a commemorative monument, again on the outskirts of Brussels, and then that it be built as the seat for the League of Nations. Despite such expressions of continued interest, the expense of constructing an entire city relegated the hopeful project to the status of an impossible dream. The only individual to show much enthusiasm for the project during the 1920s would be the aspiring Fascist leader, Benito Mussolini.[33]

What remains prominent about Hébrard's city, linking it to earlier student work he and others carried out in Rome and to their later professional careers in France and the colonies, is the strong belief in the city itself as a force in progressive culture. The metropolis represented a vehicle for promoting peace and

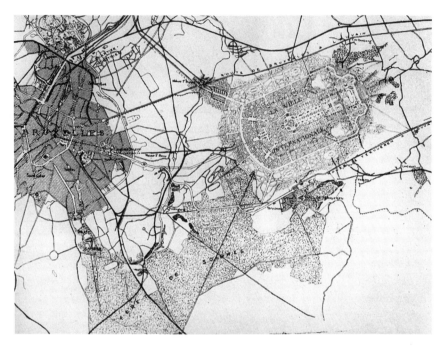

FIGURE 29.   *Hébrard's proposed siting of the World Center on the outskirts of Brussels. From Andersen and Hébrard,* World Conscience, *1913.*

prosperity, a visible sign of respect for the past and hope for the future. These sentiments took on different forms, but the fledgling urbanists all shared an emphatic commitment to a large metropolitan scale and a recognition of the complexity that scale entailed.

Urbanism and the Social Sciences

Careers in the social sciences, as in urban design, proved highly problematic in metropolitan France, where such disciplines remained on the fringe of academic acceptance until the years following World War II. Kept outside the lycées, and hence outside the license-agrégation sequence for teaching jobs, most social sciences tended to be loosely defined and intensely factional. Ethnography was sustained in a few small private institutions, such as the Institut Français d'Anthropologie (founded in 1911) and the Institut d'Ethnologie, first proposed in 1914 and established in 1924 with a specifically colonial focus. Future statisticians trained directly in ministerial offices, for there existed no sufficiently advanced courses in the universities.

To be sure, beginning in the 1890s, independent institutions appeared, such as René Worms's Institut International de Sociologie, Jeanne Weill's Collège

Libre des Sciences Sociales, and finally the Ecole des Hautes Etudes Sociales. These provided intellectual excitement, certainly, but not a university pedigree. Only in adjacent academic fields—history, geography, and the law—could one find an official setting for exploring issues of contemporary culture and society.[34]

In contrast, colonial administrations provided jobs for numerous French sociologists, anthropologists, and statisticians, as well as more specialized legal scholars, hygienists, and political economists. At Casablanca's Institut des Hautes Etudes Marocaines, Antananarivo's Académie Malgache (fig. 30), or the Ecole Française d'Extrême-Orient in Hanoi, scholars could study various languages and social groups, analyzing family patterns, legal traditions, and religious practices, for the governments believed that this information had direct political relevance. Moreover, beginning in 1896, these same colonial governments sponsored some of the few social-science teaching positions in Paris, such as a chair in Muslim sociology at the Collège de France and courses in the principles of colonization at the innovative Collège Libre des Sciences Sociales.[35] René Worms himself headed a session on sociology and ethnography at the 1906 Colonial Congress. The Parisian Institut Franco-Musulman—a scholarly center for practicing Muslims, together with a mosque and *hammam* designed by Maurice Mantout and completed in 1926—received substantial funding from the French colonial government. (fig. 31).[36]

In addition, the Ecole Coloniale prepared skilled technocrats for colonial service in both the public and the private commercial sectors. Opening in Paris in 1889, the school first took in Indochinese students preparing for administrative positions through studies in the capital, as well as French students destined to be the supervisors of such staffs. Four years later, the Ministry of Education added a commercial section to improve the technical skills of those who would oversee colonial businesses. The enterprise had now become so successful that a new building was needed, and a competition took place in 1894. Maurice Yvon's winning entry, completed in 1898 and still standing on the Avenue de l'Observatoire, provided more than larger quarters for the Ecole Coloniale (fig. 32). The facade combined Oriental and Moorish motifs in an effort to have the style itself play a part in promoting colonial careers. In architecture as in the classrooms, a move to integrate aesthetics and administrative policy in the colonies was underway.[37]

By the mid-1920s, incoming colonial administrators were required to undertake specialized studies, rather than to rely solely on experience in the field for their promotions. Lyons and Strasbourg established branches of another official study center, the Ecole de Préparation Coloniale, replacing earlier informal classes with closer study of languages, culture, and ethnography. All the

FIGURE 30. *The Académie Malgache, housed in the former Tramovola or Maison d'Argent, built in Antananarivo by Louis Gros in 1854. From* La Revue de Madagascar, *1933.*

FIGURE 31. *The Institut Franco-Musulman, Paris, by Maurice Mantout, 1926.*
Photograph by Melinda Maerher.

FIGURE 32. *The Ecole Coloniale, Paris, by Maurice Yvon, 1898. Photograph by*
Melinda Maerher.

same, teaching continued to stress general themes and principles. The French, in contrast to their English counterparts, contended that cultural variations within their empire did not permit detailed study of specific instances.[38]

As the most prestigious forum for such experts, the Académie des Sciences d'Outre-Mer stressed a "moral crusade" and intellectual cachet. Founded in 1922, the academy expressly rejected "the inexplicable intrusion of politics" and the "economic exploitation" of mercantile interests in the elaboration of colonial policy. Its members advocated programs based on serious scientific research and idealistic intellectual principles, seemingly unmindful of the fact that such programs could easily mask political and economic interests.[39] Members of the academy, chosen from the elite of geography, history, ethnology, economics, the physical and natural sciences, and colonial politics, included Lyautey, Sarraut, and Gabriel Hanotaux, the anthropologist Lucien Lévy-Bruhl, and the physician Albert Calmette. Their aim, elaborated in the group's initial meeting, called for:

> Exacting knowledge of our colonial domain; a scientific inventory that will guide us; the study of the races and peoples who inhabit our colonies, including their history, their folklore, and all manner of their customs and traditions; generating further research and the best regulations, all on a scientific basis, which will preside over the government and administration of our colonies.[40]

These goals involved an exciting new mission for all the social sciences, in which the most thorough research would lead to actual social policy.

Colonial social science should be considered in the broad nineteenth-century sense of the word "sociology," with its numerous and quite diverse advocates. One group pursued their subjects with scholarly fervor, focusing in particular on the critical study of texts written in oriental languages. This fascination with the Orient usually kindled a "kind of voyeurism, an emotional ethnography of the other" that refined and strengthened the Western sense of power.[41] Such Orientalists dominated institutions of higher learning in France.

Colonial administrations and institutes offered opportunities for applied social scientists as well. While some were academically trained, many can only be labeled enthusiasts or amateurs, overly eager to gather information and assert its potential usefulness. The "vast ethnographic literature" on North Africa, in the opinion of the respected Jacques Berque, provided "no significant contribution to general sociological theory."[42] Nor, it must be said, could these specialists adequately explain the nationalist movements for independence, either in the 1920s or the 1950s, for the unspoken purpose of their discipline was to defend and justify European colonization. These failures require close analysis. We must try to dissect the multiple contexts—intellectual, political, and aesthetic—in which these individuals existed.

Geography, nor surprisingly, emerged as the academic discipline most strongly oriented toward the colonies. Here scholars could study the interrelations between a group and its environment, a French concept known as *genre de vie*; here cities as well as the rural countryside still seemed fixed, harmonious settings. The discipline did not seek idealism. The most original figure in the French field, Paul Vidal de la Blache, asserted that modern geography, while essentially descriptive, relied on "the scientific study of places."[43] However, like the urban historian Marcel Poëte, Vidal presented his ideas in a language more poetic than scientific, evoking the narrative of local history and a romanticized cohesiveness in other cultures. Vidal thereby hoped to establish the state of ecological equilibrium that he believed existed between a group's natural or built environment and their essential way of life.[44]

This is not to say that Vidal and his generation eschewed practical matters of colonial expansion. The concentration on transportation systems is only the most obvious instance of a scholarly concern which directly related to imperial goals and techniques. Vidal repeatedly called for a trans-Saharan railroad to link the various parts of French North Africa.[45] As early as 1905 Augustin Bernard, another French geographer specializing in this area, argued for the French to establish their permanent colonial capital for Morocco on the coast at Rabat.[46] These advisors cannot be understood as willing agents of colonialism. But they were nonetheless dependent upon colonial authorities for the opportunity to carry out their work, and often for material support as well. It therefore seemed prudent to suggest possible benefits from scholarly research.

By the late 1920s a new generation of French geographers sought to codify Vidal's concepts. They shifted even more resolutely toward larger regions, the complex development of urban areas, and applied research in general. Pierre Lavedan, for example, analyzed comparative urban morphology and street patterns. His *Géographie des villes* (1936) emphasized the control of nature and the urban system (through legislation and master plans) as the basic distinctions between a city and a town.[47] Georges Hardy, long an administrator in Morocco and by now the director of the Parisian Ecole Coloniale, discussed more openly how such studies could aid colonial governments:

> Whether it is a matter of European settlements or the simple indigenous
> environment [*encadrement*], the occupation of a populated country or
> taking possession of a deserted land, colonization would essentially seem
> to rely upon the transformation of a region that has been retarded or ne-

glected in the development of human potential. It therefore requires, above all, a perfect knowledge of the regions to be transformed.[48]

Even at the time, prominent professional geographers criticized Hardy's disdain for intangibles and his overly pragmatic focus on material topics.[49]

Jean Brunhes gained professional respect for this studies of artifacts and his topical comparisons between diverse settings. Brunhes, too, celebrated the benefits of applied geography in governmental or industrial decision-making. Discussing the issue of colonial land tenure, for example, he affirmed the claims of Governor-General Martial Merlin of French East Africa:

> The conquering state does not possess property since it can at any time take possession of it. On the other hand, the natives cannot possess it, since they have no such idea. . . . When we arrive in these new countries, the ground belongs to no one; it is in an indeterminate state, which must be determined. Now this state can be determined only by exploitation and by creating value. The land must be given only to those who exploit it and make it useful.[50]

In particular, Brunhes praised roads and zoning, claiming they signified the growing strength of "world commerce, world circulation"—and hence modern improvements.[51] Nonetheless, he warned readers, this fast-paced life with little contact between different groups or classes could create a "sick agglomeration," peopled by individuals with no sense of place or common commitment, and therefore prone to social anarchy.[52]

Even the rather abstract quality of French social life and social criticism in this period played a role in the fascination with the colonies. In 1911 Alfred de Tarde coauthored an influential analysis of contemporary attitudes among *Les Jeunes gens d'aujourd'hui*.[53] The son of one of France's most distinguished sociologists and later the author of an enthusiastic book entitled *Le Maroc, école d'energie* (1915), de Tarde embodies the links between the worlds of French social science and colonial administration. The book concluded that, since 1890, a desire for action had become the preeminent theme for educated French youth: experience and results seemed far more meaningful than intellectual constructs.

In much the same tone, Joseph Chailley-Bert's *La France et la plus grande France* (1902), ostensibly calling for scientific research in the colonies, had pointed out that the overseas terrain could provide both theoretical challenges and personal excitement for Frenchmen. He characterized the colonies as "experiments, in whatever sense, whether laboratory or greenhouse, enterprises on a small scale." Here one could take part in a mission "instituted uniquely with the goal of extricating, with no thought of cost, some truth, applicable or not, profitable or not."[54]

The sense of mission extended beyond the intellectual world. For many Frenchmen of the turn of the century, the colonies seemed a way of inducing new spirit and vigor in all aspects of their national life. As Chailley-Bert wrote in 1903, introducing the French public to the impassioned speeches of Theodore Roosevelt, "new blood is infused by youth into the elderly, by the young colonies into the old *métropole*."[55] Lyautey himself eloquently asserted that the colonies provided "the most glorious school of energy, in which our race is being tempered and recast, as if in a crucible."[56] And Edouard Herriot, socialist *maire* of Lyons, extolled Lyautey's work in Morocco as "a sort of laboratory, an admirable experimental terrain . . . where thought and action come together, as in the best of French thought."[57]

Amateur observers or professional social scientists who looked to the colonies dealt by necessity with existing patterns in circumscribed places, each one distinct in terms of geography, history, ethnography, and cultural life. By the early twentieth century they also sought to relate these particularities to a more general vision of the problems and potentials of the modern city, specifically the contemporary French city. It is, in part, the effort to strike a balance between these two dimensions—the specific or local and the general or universal—that characterized the important role, both theoretical and practical, of the colonies for so many French intellectuals.[58]

Associationism and the Colonial City

By the turn of the century, French concepts of colonial power fell into two camps, one still asserting universalist principles and the other promoting respect for cultural differences. In books and public assemblies—notably the National Colonial Congress of 1889–90 and the International Congress of Colonial Sociology in 1900—delegates debated the merits and often the very definitions of these two approaches to colonization, which they called assimilation and association.[59] To most observers, the underlying premises of assimilation were twofold: the cultural predominance of the European country, in its language, its laws, and even its prevailing architectural styles—the famous *mission civilisatrice*; and the military prowess of the European country, demonstrated through destruction of indigenous cities and towns, embodied in a continuing, visible military presence. In contrast, most advocates of association insisted on respect for and preservation of distinctive local cultures, even cultural differences among indigenous people, including tribal councils and historic monuments; and the realization that this respect, when combined with social services like schools and hospitals, might counter resistance far more effectively than military strength.

All the same, throughout the controversies of the nineteenth and twentieth centuries, the two policies and their advocates were often closer together, in principles and practices, than most commentators acknowledged. Both approaches were fundamentally variations on the colonial exercise of power over a subject people. Gustave Le Bon's pseudo-scientific theories about the inheritance of mental characteristics condemned educational efforts in the colonies, while Paul Doumer's reforms in Indochina, as we shall see, represented an effort to "protect" the majority of indigenous children from contact with Western ideas. With different rationales, each restricted the colonized population's access to Western education.

Only rarely would a commentator rise above the conflict to make a more general point about the inherent power of the social analyst. Durkheim was such a critic, who pointedly warned the *colon* against "unlimited confidence that too often promotes the virtue of principles one does not challenge with other approaches, thus not risking becoming unsettled by experimentation."[60] In *La Sociologie des colonies*, René Maunier exposed an underside to the preservation strategies so integral to associationist colonial policy:

> The tendency sometimes desired by the rulers, sometimes not, to preserve and confirm the natives in their own traditions, to fix and fossilize them therein, has sometimes gone so far as to arrest the natural evolution of the native traditions, which are in fact plastic, growing things.[61]

A respected legal scholar and a member of the Académie des Sciences d'Outre-Mer, Maunier dared be so critical because, as he stated openly in the introduction to his text, he was *not* himself a sociologist.

The impassioned deliberation about assimilation and association reverberated with all the tensions indigenous to France itself during these years. Caught up in the similarities, most commentators ignored the fundamental difference between *métropole* and *outre-mer*. Only the least parliamentary colonial reformers, those like Lyautey who deplored the political effects of democracy in France, could construct a coherent policy that they might in principle apply in either setting. As Prost explained to the Redressement Français, his work in Morocco was destined to "assure the permanence of ideas and the will of municipalities, indispensable for the execution of plans for cities, by protecting these realizations from *too frequent electoral variations*."[62]

The new associationist policy found a forum in the Musée Social and the Groupe Colonial du Sénat, both presided over by Jules Siegfried, whose son André was a disciple of Vidal de la Blache.[63] Reformulations in the social sciences, domestic urban reform, and colonial administration reform thus engaged a common group of intellectuals. Officially endorsed by the minister of colonies, Etienne Clementel, in 1905, the position was finally given official sanction in a resolution of the Chamber of Deputies in 1917. France pledged "its determination to pursue ever more effectively towards the colonial peoples the generous policy of association which will continue to assure their progressive incorporation in the national unity."[64]

Two books had already made the principles of association accessible to a larger French public, echoing the familiar chords of cultural politics and design at home and abroad. In *Dix années de politique coloniale* (1902) Joseph Chailley-Bert argued that a "native policy [*politique indigène*]," as he called it, should recognize "the differences of race, of genius, of aspirations and of needs between the native inhabitants of a possession and their European masters," culminating in different institutions for different settings.[65] A few years later Jules Harmond, in *Dominations et colonisation* (1910), reiterated that the word "association" (which he had first proposed in 1887) meant "scrupulous respect for the manners, customs, and religion of the natives."[66] In neither instance did the ultimate goal revolve around cultural benevolence; the authors were searching for a policy that would make European economic and political power work more effectively, reducing the need for force.

The nineteenth-century policy of assimilation was officially rejected, partly for moral reasons, but as much on the pragmatic grounds that it had proved to be politically and economically inefficient. This was precisely when colonial opportunities for French urbanists and social scientists opened up. These two groups helped rationalize new approaches to colonial administration and commerce, mitigating dramatic modernization with a conjoint policy of protecting cultural traditions. All this implied a particular cultural interpretation of association: in its implementation, this colonial policy tended to have a strong basis in architecture and urban-planning reforms.

Most Frenchmen associated the new policy with two contemporary administrators who articulated quite vividly what they were doing in the colonies. Both Joseph-Simon Gallieni and Hubert Lyautey believed in the political efficacy of cultural policies in general and urban policies in particular. In Indochina from 1892 to 1897 (where Lyautey, as a young lieutenant, first met General Gallieni in 1894), then in Madagascar from 1897 to 1902, finally in Morocco (where

Lyautey served as head of the protectorate from 1912 to 1925, Gallieni having retired), these men elaborated and carried out a new strategy for French colonization.

The approach was not entirely original with them. Gallieni and Lyautey admired the English system of colonization, especially the general principle of "indirect rule," using the local elite and their existing institutions of power, rather than imposing European authority in the destructive way which had characterized French colonial exploits of the eighteenth and nineteenth centuries. Jean-Marie de Lanessan, a Radical-Socialist legislator "exiled" to Indochina as governor-general during their tour of duty, provided an important link, for he too strongly advocated integrating the indigenous mandarin elite into the French administration.[67]

The innovations begun under Gallieni and championed by Lyautey derived from basic notions about social and cultural life. In essence, those in command had to acknowledge the diversity of peoples over whom they wielded power. This is the basis of how people live together in any city, especially those with large and complex populations. Of course, Gallieni and Lyautey were fundamentally concerned with the exercise of power, even if they did sincerely appreciate the characteristically urban cultural diversity which they made one of their techniques.

Gallieni and Lyautey articulated their principles and strategies in various discussions with staffs and admirers. Many of these statements were subsequently published and widely circulated in France. The initial statement, formulated in 1898, was Gallieni's famous "Instructions" to his staff in Madagascar. Outlining three tactics for colonial policy, the "Instructions" gave a political rationale and administrative precision to the associationist policy.[68] Gallieni called for simultaneous military and political action; flexibility and accommodation to cultural differences; and the establishment of permanent posts, notably market towns, showing the local population that the French intended to stay and develop the region. This came to be known as the *tâche d'huile* ("oil stain") approach to pacification.

Following his mentor's example, Lyautey elevated these tactics to three basic premises of social and cultural action. The first and most abstract precept was that power should be exercised, Lyautey wrote, "not as a matter of destroying [people], but of transforming them."[69] This stance toward power, specifically military power, had emerged early in Lyautey's career, when he decided that the modern army would have to be based on a dramatic shift: replacing military force with social benefits. The attitude was epitomized in his often-repeated statement: "Un chantier vaut un bataillon."[70]

Lyautey wanted such a transformation to pervade the army itself, not only in its dealings with the people it colonized but in relations between French officers and conscripts. His 1891 article, "Du Rôle social de l'officier," published in *La Revue des deux mondes*, caused a furor by insisting that, in an era of universal conscription, the military officer had a responsibility to know and understand his men, helping them learn to respect all leaders through the bonds forged in military ranks.[71] The author could not remain anonymous after he contended that most officers knew their horses better than they knew the soldiers in their unit. In a very real sense, Lyautey's view of colonial administration grew out of his conviction that the army offered a means for civilizing Frenchmen themselves, instilling in them a sense of respect for authority through mutual understanding between superior and inferior.

The second aspect of Lyautey's colonial policy involved respect for the cultural forms of other peoples. A French colonial administration should not seek to destroy the indigenous legal system, aristocratic lineages, or the patterns of family life and religion; rather the administration would work with local elites, preserving traditional cultural forms. Lyautey's earliest images about adapting to existing conditions, penned in Indochina and Madagascar, referred to the fecundity of the local soil; after 1900 he turned toward architectural metaphors of restoring an old house. As Lyautey told the scholars at the Congrés des Hautes Etudes Marocaines in 1921:

> We have found here the crumbling vestiges of an admirable civilization, of a great past. You are restoring the foundation, renewing construction work, and on the foundation which you rebuild in good cement you are undeniably aiding us to build the marvellous future that we wish to make spring from this past.[72]

The ultimate goal, however it was expressed, always concerned a benevolent French presence, made stronger in both political and economic terms.

In many ways this policy was clearly a cover for exploitation. The local leaders were puppet figures placed in power by the French. In Morocco, for example, Moulay-Hafid was forced to abdicate as sultan and was replaced by his brother Moulay-Youssef, "who immediately demonstrated," wrote one colonial officer, "a strong sense of politics and showed his confidence in France."[73] Lyautey then explained that the protectorate "required reviving around the [new] sultan the ancient traditions and old ceremonies of the court."[74] We should not be surprised to see the protectorate erect a sumptuous "Arabicized" palace for Moulay Youssef in 1917 (see fig. 43).[75] Lyautey himself could occasionally describe the political intentions of his policies quite accurately. In 1920 he wrote

of the sultan, "All administrative measures are taken in his name. He signs the
dahirs [decrees]. . . . But in practice he has no real power. . . . His advice is
requested only for the sake of form."[76]

Nonetheless a change did take place. To grasp the importance of these new
principles of colonial reform, one could look back to the history of French involvement in Algeria and Indochina in the mid-nineteenth century. When the
French captured Algiers in 1830, the destruction of the existing city—its streets,
its monuments, and its population—seemed to be the primary goal. As the
official record noted two years later, "Since then we have continued, and today
we are still at work seizing the mosques to make them into hospitals, stores, and
a church; several have even been closed down without having a new use. As for
the demolition of properties, it is something that does not seem to be near an
end."[77] Wide new streets and formal *places* were soon cut through the medina;
barracks and a spacious Place d'Armes on the city's northern periphery indicated
the strong military presence which formed the backbone of French urbanism
there (fig. 33).

The French seized control of Saigon in 1859, when Napoleon III and his
prefect, Baron Haussmann, were at the height of their imperial glory. Having
burned the city, the French troops proceeded as if they had a *tabula rasa*. In an
effort to encourage real-estate speculation, an engineer's gridiron dominated the
plan of the proposed new city, embellished with a few wide streets to evoke
Haussmann's grand boulevards. The government then erected a number of
French cultural emblems—cafés, a racetrack, a lavish opera house, a post office,
as well as two successive palaces for the new government—before installing a
sanitary water system (fig. 34). Ordinary living conditions in Saigon remained
quite spartan. As one early resident put it, "Nothing was wanting—except necessities."[78] Xenophobic architectural pretense best represented the power of colonial domination.

These examples contrast with Lyautey and Gallieni's third principle, the
view that cities should be the cornerstone of an associationist policy. Already
markets and cultural centers, often royal or religious capitals with great symbolic
significance, existing cities had to be protected. When Gallieni and Lyautey
undertook pacification campaigns in the countryside, they used such towns as
the centers of their strategy (hence the *tâche d'huile* appelation), always radiating
out from a secure base where good relations had been established. The day after
taking a town or village, Gallieni told his troops, they should rebuild what had
been destroyed, then erect a new market and a school.[79] In this strategy, too,
Lyautey accentuated the most lyrical and opportunistic aspects of Gallieni's "Instructions":

As pacification takes hold, the countryside is cultivated, the markets re-open, commerce is renewed. The role of the soldier passes to the second stage: that of the administrator begins. He must, on the one hand, study and satisfy the social needs of the subjected populations and, on the other, favor the colonial expansion which will increase the natural riches of the area and open the markets to European commerce.[80]

Colonial cities were artifacts of other cultures to be respected and manipulated by the French. Here administrators could demonstrate the benefits of colonial social services.

This attitude toward cities developed over the time the two men spent to-gether in Indochina and Madagascar, where Lyautey laid out a plan for two provincial capitals, Ankazobé and Fianarantsoa, in the first year of French oc-cupation (see figs. 168, 169). During his tenure in Morocco, Lyautey perfected his idea of "dual cities" or geographical "association." This meant the strict pres-ervation of monuments, streets, and all kinds of ordinary cultural forms in the existing cities, with some attention to the differences between various religious and ethnic groups within the indigenous population. Alongside the "traditional" cities he envisioned expansive extensions for the French, called literally *villes nouvelles* or new cities, where all the benefits of modern urbanism would be applied and appraised. Here the architecture displayed the imagery of European modernism in its clean lines, standardization, and ample open space. As Lyau-tey explained the dual-city approach, one should

> Touch the indigenous cities as little as possible. Instead, improve their
> surroundings where, on the vast terrain that is still free, the European
> city rises, following a plan which realized the most modern conceptions
> of large boulevards, water and electrical supplies, squares and gardens,
> buses and tramways, and also foreseeing future extensions.[81]

By conserving one culture while introducing planned modernization to the other, Lyautey's urbanism represented the culmination of his belief in the cen-trality of culture—not one culture, but cultural diversity—for his vision of power.

As the most visible locus for reforms and the prime repositories of cultural traditions, cities were the key to Lyautey's larger vision. Many times he pointed out that two aspects of his long career had given him the greatest pride: his so-called "native policy," or "tribal policy," which emphasized respect for indige-nous traditions and the integration of indigenous people, by their respective tribes, into colonial administration; and his city-planning accomplishments.

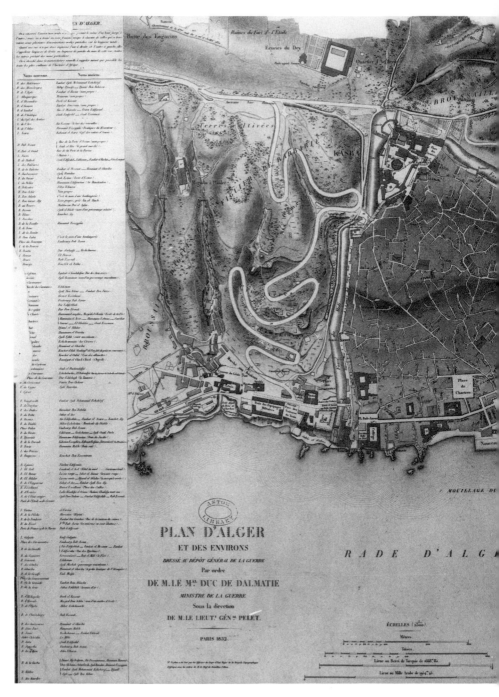

FIGURE 33. *Plan of Algiers in 1832, showing numerous French places and military*

barracks occupying buildings formerly used as mosques. Library of Congress.

FIGURE 34. *Central Post Office, Saigon, by Alfred Foulhoux, 1876. Postcard.*

"One never sees too grand a vision when it is a matter of building for centuries to come," he wrote in 1926, "When I look back over my colonial career, if you will permit me, one of my greatest satisfactions is to have brought the urban condition [*urbs condita,* harking back to the Romans] into being in so many parts of the globe."[82]

Lyautey's eloquence won him a place in the Académie Française in 1920. "I find other joys opening roads, inventing a city, creating schools," he wrote his mentor, Eugène de Vögué, from Madagascar in 1897, in a letter that was later published, "and especially seeing houses spring from the earth, rice fields dug into the soil, markets swarming with people, there where six months ago I saw only darkened pieces of rubble, uncultivated land, and a deserted horizon."[83] On closer inspection, such lyricism cannot disguise the policies of military pacification, rigid social stereotypes, and cultural domination; rather it explains how these ideas, in the colonies as in France, could seem so compelling. His colonial urbanism represented, Lyautey acknowledged, "a pacifist arsenal destined to give these people a way of life they know nothing about."[84]

Elsewhere Lyautey elaborated on the colonial administrator's duties as a preservationist. Addressing the Ecole des Hautes-Etudes Marocaines, he extolled its mission: "In Morocco, it is our honor to say, 'we *conserve*'; I would even say 'we save.' "[85] Once again, other writings reveal the complex rationales underlying such ambitions. "Do not offend any traditions, do not change any customs," Lyautey wrote in his journal while in Indochina. "Say that in all societies there is a governing class, born to govern, without whom one can do nothing, and a class to be governed. Put the governing class in our interests."[86]

Lyautey's career and his writings give an initial focus to the themes I want to cover here. He is something of a literary convenience, a man vividly articulate about the issues, engaged in each of the colonies I will discuss. Yet Lyautey was not single-handedly the engineer of the new policies. Nor was he the only spokesman, if perhaps the most rhapsodic, for the principles of modern urbanism which represented such an important aspect of twentieth-century colonialism and which bind together my narrative.

His vision was shared and implemented by his staff and his many admirers. As Lyautey wrote of Prost, celebrating the architect's election to the Académie Française in 1932:

> The art and science of urbanism, so flourishing during France's classical age, seemed to have suffered a total eclipse since the end of the Second Empire. . . . Prost's election seems to me the triumph of ideas I have held dear for forty years, ideas to which new countries as well as old will have to refer when they consider the present order and the future development of human settlements.[87]

For Lyautey, as for the professionals he brought to the colonies, the role of the city was critical. It provided an expression of diversity in apparent social harmony; a tool for economic and artistic development; and a strategy for creating and maintaining order. This attitude affected the kinds of cities built in the French empire and the policies carried out there.

The colonial experiments in turn demonstrated a complex modern role for architecture and urban design in any setting; it was in these terms that colonial urbanism was so often discussed in France. That role encompassed several progressive attitudes about cultural tolerance: an awareness of different social groups, a commitment to historic preservation, an aesthetic of complex variety. All the same, at least in this extreme context, aesthetic appeal cannot mask the unrelenting quest for political control and economic modernization.

At the end of his Madagascar campaign, Lyautey mused, "To build, this is the goal, and the unique goal, of every colonial war."[88] Indeed, many sorts of construction took place in the cities of the French colonies. Not the least of these involved the structuring of a modern role for the architect-urbanist and social scientist, supposedly above politics, responsive only to science and cultural ideals, but, in reality, caught in an intricate web of power. In each colony administrators and professionals faced somewhat different circumstances as they built, evolving particular urban and architectural solutions. Two constraints remained. To a surprising extent, their concerns and the proposals they formulated referred back to the problems of the modern French city. In a less surprising manner, the urban plans—whether an architectural design for a city hall or a public-health policy for an entire city—represented efforts to consolidate power. This applied to the dominant authority of colonialism and to the more subtle control of professional expertise.

3

MOROCCO:
MODERNIZATION AND
PRESERVATION

ON A VISIT to Morocco in 1930, the Parisian art critic Léandre Vaillat was enraptured with what he saw (fig. 35). Admiring the beautifully preserved medinas, or old Arab towns (fig. 36), and the stunning new French cities built alongside them, he realized that important social considerations underlay the aesthetic effects. Morocco, Vaillat wrote, is "a laboratory of Western life and a conservatory of oriental life."[1]

For those who fell under its spell, colonial Morocco represented at once a modernist vision of formal order—smooth white planes of building facades aligned along broad straight boulevards—and an exotic dream of voluptuousness. The combination did not by any means seem a random feat or purely architectural phenomenon. Calculated strategies buttressed the urbanistic achievements there: Resident-General Hubert Lyautey had carried out a well-articulated agenda. A deputy investigating conditions in the colonies, Maurice Long, soon to be the governor-general who established Indochina's first urbanism service, praised the political effectiveness of his cohort's cultural policies. "The work General Lyautey has accomplished in Morocco since the war," Long declared in 1916, "will remain an unperishable title of glory for France."[2]

From their different perspectives, Long and Vaillat reached far toward, but did not fully grasp, the significance of Lyautey's Moroccan achievement, at once aesthetic and political. What Lyautey and his associates sought can also be summarized under two other somewhat disparate headings: modernism and preservation. Their goal, in sum, was to protect certain aspects of cultural traditions while sponsoring other aspects of modernization and development, all in the interest of stabilizing colonial domination.

The protectorate government aimed to introduce and appraise the latest concepts of contemporary city planning in the *villes nouvelles*, enabling these

FIGURE 35. Ville nouvelle *and medina, Casablanca, c. 1926. The Place de France is still small, and the Boulevard du IVᶜ Zouaves, not yet widened or straightened. From* La Construction moderne, *1930.*

European centers to flourish economically. Simultaneously they tried to shield traditional Moroccan artistic and social life from the destructive impact of that modernization. In public Lyautey stressed architectural intrusions like skyscrapers. He was equally concerned about current political ideas, most notably Arab nationalism from Egypt, Zionism from the Middle East, and the French concepts of *liberté* and *égalité*.[3] "The problem we envisage," he explained succinctly in a memorandum of 1913, less than a year after the protectorate was established, "is to let modern civilization, with all its progress and economic exploitation, penetrate [into Morocco], while preserving what exists here that is of the greatest interest."[4]

Lyautey adroitly linked the concepts of aesthetic response, economic development, and political goals in his use of the word "interest." Likewise, the references to modern civilization and preservation were not used lightly or without deliberation. Both terms point out the serious attention given to cultural forms and the important role of specialists, especially in the fine arts and ethnography, under the French protectorate.

Modernity was understood in two senses, as an urbane existence which derived from diverse commercial activities and cultural institutions, and as a panoply of urban problems largely caused by industrial conditions. The colonial

FIGURE 36. *The medina in Casablanca, c. 1920. Postcard.*

administration proposed strategies to accommodate some of the difficulties and the opportunities modern life entailed for all cities. If the cosmopolitan center could not exist without an industrial district, for example, strict zoning could keep these spheres of activity quite separate. The tiny village of Kenitra expanded as a specialized industrial port, briefly renamed Port Lyautey (fig. 37). In Casablanca, Prost designated the industrial zone as the area around the enlarged port, together with a wide, rocky strip of adjacent land known as Roches Noires (fig. 38). He had duly noted that this area could not sustain the lush vegetation envisioned for the elite residential and commercial districts; equally important, the prevailing winds would blow factory smoke and smells toward the east, away from the well-to-do neighborhoods. Many factories of the 1920s exemplified the unadorned, well-balanced aesthetic of the European modern movement. Prost himself undertook the design of a handsome hydroelectric plant in the country-side at Saïd Machou (1920–25), near the recently discovered phosphate sites (fig. 39).[5]

Alfred de Tarde, a lieutenant in Lyautey's army and later editor of *France-Maroc*, lauded the opportunities this colony offered: "It is a matter of coming to the city of tomorrow. . . . To organize a new country is essentially to invent— to invent the future."[6] Lyautey himself spoke glowingly of spaciousness and ser-

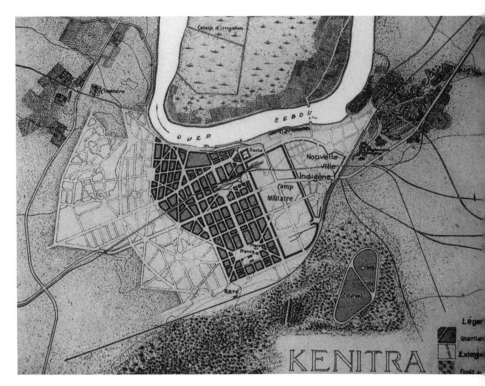

FIGURE 37. *Site plan of the industrial town of Kenitra, later Port Lyautey, by Henri Prost's Architecture and Urbanism Department, 1916. From Léandre Vaillat,* Le Visage français, *1931.*

vices to describe the urban enclave where the French would live: "the European city takes form on the vast open spaces, following a plan which achieves the epitome of modern conditions, with broad boulevards, water and electrical supplies, squares and gardens, buses and tramways, and also foreseeing future extensions."[7] For the French, Morocco offered a chance to create *de novo* a vision of the contemporary metropolis as a clean, efficient, and elegant setting. Lyautey could even claim, rather facetiously, "to have been one of the precursors of Le Corbusier."[8]

The concept of the traditional received at least as much attention, although here the French referred to a supposedly timeless continuity, in contrast to a sudden recent transformation. Most accounts ignored the effect of nineteenth-century European economic penetration on Moroccan life. The French claimed that they had stabilized the Sharifian administrative structure and tax system, without altering any long-standing patterns. "I want to see to it," insisted

Lyautey, "that ranks and hierarchies are preserved and respected, that people and things stay in their established places, that the natural leaders command, and that others obey."[9] The protectorate professed to leave intact all prerogatives of the *makhzan* (the Moroccan state administration under the sultan), including the right to levy taxes called "traditional," namely the *terbib*, which fell more heavily on Moroccans than on foreign residents.[10]

French historians contended that Moroccan culture had not changed significantly since its height in the late twelfth century, when Yacoub el-Mansour had laid out the first plan for Rabat as a magnificent royal capital.[11] Prost spoke of the need to "maintain in its setting a civilization intact for centuries."[12] This emphasis on continuity had its advantages, in that it implied no need to provide modern amenities for the Moroccans. Perhaps more importantly, it suggested that this somewhat backward nation—"a retarded brother whom we should love," in the words of Socialist Lucien Deslinières—could not responsibly be given control over its own destiny.[13]

The truth of the matter, of course, involved careful manipulation of individuals and symbols. Many Moroccan taxes in fact dated from the late nineteenth century, levied in response to increased European economic exchange and military threats.[14] Moreover, the various protectorate taxes went to pay for municipal improvements and services that primarily benefited the European districts of cities. The few exceptions concerned French efforts to buttress the authority of those Moroccans who accepted the colonial presence. As Lieutenant-Colonel Huot told an audience at the Parisian Musée Social, "The prestige of the Sultan is one of the constant preoccupations of the Resident-General. He is continually engaged in enhancing it."[15]

A clear political agenda overwhelmed any true respect for history or tradition, tainting the otherwise positive preservation efforts. The protectorate system was indeed a "fiction," where "colonization imposed on the country not only its authority, but a whole set of descriptive symbols. These replaced and repressed an ancient system, affecting towns and villages, pastoral and agricultural lands: a whole cycle of politics and piety."[16] One goal was indeed cultural, for Lyautey and his staff sincerely wanted to build modern cities and preserve the beauty of the medinas. The other imperatives were more conspicuously exploitative. Four such categories can easily be listed: first, the desire to consolidate and stabilize political power under the figurehead of the sultan; second, the need to centralize and rationalize government bureaucracies, without ousting the existing *makhzan*; third, the need to stimulate the economy by a strategy which joined centralized commercial enterprises, decentralized regional industry, and promotion

CASABLANCA

FIGURE 38. *Zoning plan for Casablanca by Prost's Architecture and Urbanism Department, 1917. The Roches Noires district is immediately southeast of the port and upper-class French residential districts are anticipated to the west. From* L'Architecture d'aujourd'hui, *1930.*

of tourism; and finally, the key point for the other three, the imperative of quelling potential revolt by a combination of modern "improvements" and respect for "traditional" ways of life. Urbanism played a key role in each of these scenarios.

"A Definitive Presence"

Although commercial ties had been developing throughout the nineteenth century, intensifying after 1900, the French did not penetrate into Morocco until 1907, when the army unit commanded by Colonel Lyautey approached from western Algeria. Military posts were established on the sandy plateaus adjoining the Algerian border and at the small port town of Casablanca, following orders that these settlements should give "indigenous people the impression, not of a provisional stronghold, but of a definitive presence."[17] Recalling his experiences

Figure 39. *Hydroelectric plant at Saïd Machou by Henri Prost, 1920–25. From* Vaillat, Le Visage français.

with Gallieni, Lyautey specified that the posts be sited alongside existing market cities to assure the future *colons* of commercial activity, drawing both sides more closely into the world market. "Economic considerations," he explained, "go along with military considerations."[18]

It took five years for the European powers to decide how to divide up Morocco. In the presence of Sultan Moulay Hafid, the Treaty of Fez, concluded in March 1912, gave most of the country to France. Yet architecture had come into Lyautey's strategy as early as 1907. The French had recently invaded Casablanca, claiming that the Treaty of Algeciras, signed the year before, gave them the responsibility of preserving order in Moroccan ports. Soon afterwards they proceeded east, where Lyautey met Maurice Tranchant de Lunel, a young artist touring Morocco. Aghast at the prefabricated French barracks being erected in Rabat's medina, Lyautey immediately commissioned Tranchant de Lunel to "reclothe" the colonel's own four-room residence in Rabat as well as the adjacent barracks, all "in the Arab style, making them tolerable"—or so he assumed—to the Moroccans in the surrounding medinas (fig. 40).[19]

FIGURE 40.   *"Arab" barracks in Rabat, refurbished for Lyautey by Maurice Tranchant de Lunel, 1907, and later converted into a hotel. Postcard.*

In 1912, with the establishment of the French protectorate, Poincaré named Lyautey both resident-general and head of the army. With virtually complete authority over the country, Lyautey could carry out the cultural policies he wished. Above all this meant a vision of urban design. Lyautey harshly criticized earlier French colonial town-planning, notably that of Algeria, where every action had been under the jurisdiction of the Ministry of War in Paris rather than local officials familiar with the culture. This, he lamented, had led to the demolition of major Algerian monuments and the destruction of established towns, replaced by monotonous gridiron city plans for the *colons* drawn up by military engineers, lined with heavy-handed pastiches of nineteenth-century French architecture.[20]

The resident-general's first acts included major decisions regarding the urban future of the country. Vaillat compared these moves to the founding of seventeenth-century cities like Neufbrisach, where "Vauban modeled the French presence along the frontier" of the emerging nation-state.[21] Within a few months, heeding in part the recommendations of Augustin Bernard, Lyautey decided to transfer the capital from inland Fez to Rabat, on the Atlantic coast (fig. 41). Its lineage as an imperial capital, like that of Fez, would give symbolic historical continuity to the new government. Rabat also offered better opportunities to build an impressive modern setting for political control. This decision

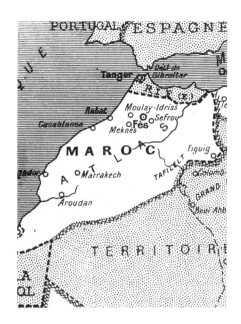

FIGURE 41.
Map of French Morocco,
showing network of colonial and royal
cities. From Jean de la Roche, La Féde-
ration française, 1945.

FIGURE 42. Avenue Dar-el-Maghzen, Rabat, c. 1930. From Vaillat, Le Visage
français.

represented, in part, a military maneuver, given the continued resistance to the French presence in Fez, but it quickly took on new meaning as part of a strategy for a more centralized locus of power. Closely tied to France by sea, the diplomatic capital would eventually be the nucleus for seven national roads, linking it to all parts of the colony. Moreover, many French administrators and scholars felt ill at ease in the inland cities, describing Fez as a "sad and gloomy town with its labyrinth of narrow and dark streets"; they preferred a more contemporary setting where they could help evolve "modern Islam." [22]

If Casablanca could be likened, in Lyautey's eyes, to New York, then Rabat was his Washington, D.C. [23] Here he intended to build an imposing cultural and administrative capital, combining symbolic references to a glorified national past with an equally strong commitment to the latest advances in design and technology. The results proved to be compelling (fig. 42). Vaillat considered Rabat "one of the most beautiful modern cities in the world. . . . The urbanism and the architecture make a Frenchman from France, strolling these streets, become jealous." [24] Writing in the *Encyclopedia of Islam* in 1936, Evariste Lévi-Provençal simply declared, "French Rabat at the present day is a masterpiece, famed throughout the world, of successful town planning and architecture." [25]

Lyautey then ordered a new harbor dug at Casablanca, ninety kilometers southwest of Rabat, together with massive jetties and extensive docklands, eventually creating one of the largest ports on the African continent. Casablanca was still not much more than a scruffy village, its expansion due to recent European migration, not to long-standing royal patronage. The city could easily be transformed into the financial and industrial metropolis for the colony; this in turn would allow Rabat to develop in a more peaceful and controlled manner. [26]

To be sure, Lyautey was concerned about the future development of all four traditional royal capitals: the *makhzan* or imperial cities of Fez, Marrakesh, and Meknes, as well as Rabat. He wanted European settlement there to proceed in an orderly manner through *villes nouvelles*, all following the same principles, without disrupting the medinas and palaces in any of these cities. The *makhzan* cities were ancient urban centers with long-established prestige as markets and courts—for over a thousand years in the case of Fez. As royal capitals they were also spiritual centers, since the sultan, considered a descendant of the Prophet and Commander of the Faithful, was the object of great veneration. To disrupt this would go against Gallieni's principle of colonial "posts" drawing the two cultures together while keeping each distinct.

French social scientists in the colony were astute enough to know that the sultan had experienced difficulty collecting taxes and assuring peace, especially in the arid Berber lands to the west of the Atlas Mountains. Ethnographers stressed the difference between what is called *bled-el-makhzan* (the major cities and coastal areas of Morocco, strongly Islamic and accepting the sultan's reign) and the *bled-es-siba* (the nomadic regions to the south, marginally Islamicized and prone to revolt against the sultan's rule).[27] This situation, they realized, in part explained the previous lack of a true capital, as the sultan had meandered, with a retinue of some forty thousand attendants, between the four imperial cities in different regions of the country.

The French wanted the sultan ensconced primarily in one spot, just alongside their own administrative headquarters at Rabat, to demonstrate his acceptance of their newly centralized political presence. Stifling Moulay Youssef's ceremonial movement would also deprive the ruler of much of his predecessors' power. The elaborate ritual of movement reinforced the sultan's *baraka*, or charismatic power, noted Walter Harris among others in 1921, citing a Moroccan saying that "The king's throne is in his saddle."[28]

It was thus strategic for the French to honor many of the sultan's claims over the extensive royal gardens which surrounded the mid-nineteenth-century palace in Rabat, a palace the French expanded and "restored." Within a few years, Casablanca, which had not been a royal capital, would also require a royal presence to legitimate its commercial purposes. The sultan commissioned an extensive palace on the outskirts of the city from the French architects Louis-Paul and Félix-Joseph Pertuzio (fig. 43). Born in French Algeria, the Frerès Pertuzio had joined Prost's architectural bureau in 1913. It was perhaps at his suggestion that they asked J.C.N. Forestier to design the palace gardens, hoping to achieve a balance of French formal order, Arabic motifs, and respect for local horticultural tradition (see fig. 9).

Thus a centralized urban and social order was established from the start, based first upon two poles situated on the coast, both looking toward Europe— one the administrative and cultural capital, the other a commercial and industrial center—rather than upon the traditional Moroccan system of several regional royal capitals. Simultaneously the protectorate created a dual urban-regional system in Morocco, favoring the development of the major coastal cities tied to the French economy and the extraction of wealth from the inland regions. Although Prost did later carry out *villes nouvelles* in Fez, Meknes, and Marrakesh, to attract *colons*, the European population there always remained substantially lower than in the two coastal cities.[29] To reassure these tiny minority populations, Prost sited military camps close to the European residential and commercial districts, unlike the pattern used in Casablanca and Rabat (fig. 44).

With French authority over Morocco recognized by Europe and the sultan, Lyautey turned his attention to the cities he hoped would draw large numbers

FIGURE 43. *New palace for Sultan Moulay Youssef, Casablanca, by Louis-Paul and Félix-Joseph Pertuzzi, 1916–19. Postcard.*

of *colons*. Georges Risler, whom he knew from the Musée Social, suggested the protectorate should undertake exemplary metropolises, true *villes nouvelles* that would dazzle and teach France.[30] The resident-general immediately commissioned Forestier to document the existing Arab gardens and suggest plans for parks and open space in the future metropolises. Forestier astutely advised setting aside all the coastline as public domain, purchasing land for parks and parkways, and preserving the sultan's gardens in Rabat as public parks (fig. 45).[31] Casablanca's spacious Public Garden (later the Parc Lyautey, alongside the administrative square, now the Parc de la Ligue Arabe) and Rabat's Jardin d'Essai resulted from his suggestion that the protectorate take over the sultan's domainal lands for public open space (fig. 46).

The rapidly rising cost of land precluded Forestier's other recommendation from being implemented, much to the detriment of later urban growth. The protectorate would in time pay dearly for the open spaces around Rabat's Municipal Park, the Triangle Park near the Andalusian Wall, and the cleared area around the Tour Hassan.[32] Most domainal lands—which the French contended were under their jurisdiction since they belonged to the state—were considered too valuable to be left undeveloped. The state auctioned off even the coastal land for future European settlement. The development of the Océan Quartier

FIGURE 44.   *Plan for the* ville nouvelle *in Fez by Henri Prost's Architecture and Urbanism Department, 1915. From* L'Architecture d'aujourd'hui, *1930.*

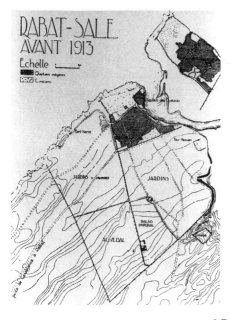

FIGURE 45.   *Pre-1913 plan of Rabat, drawn up by Prost's Architecture and Urbanism Department, 1914. Courtesy of the Académie d'Architecture, Paris.*

FIGURE 46. *Public Garden, Casablanca, on former domainal lands of the sultan c. 1920. Postcard.*

in Rabat (fig. 47) or Roches Noires and Anfa in Casablanca effectively hemmed in the medinas, precipitating increased overcrowding and preventing orderly growth in the Arab cities.[33]

Forestier also told Lyautey about the new "urban technicians" who wished to combine formal urban design with social and economic planning. When asked to suggest the name of a professional urbanist for Morocco, he thought back to the Musée Social and the fledgling Institut d'Urbanisme; Forestier nominated his young colleague Henri Prost.[34]

Prost was then traveling, surveying urban legislation in England, Italy, and Germany for the Musée Social. He returned to Paris and accepted his new post in 1913, somewhat hesitant about the continued violence in Fez, yet enthusiastic about the chance to explore his professional predilections. Invited for a twelve-month stint, Prost remained in Morocco for ten years, until 1923, drawing up master plans for nine cities: Casablanca, Rabat, Fez, Marrakesh, Meknes, Sefrou, Ouezzane, Taza, and Agadir. The Architecture and Urbanism Department, established on his arrival, became the first such governmental agency in the French world. The success of his efforts is captured in the description of Edith Wharton, who visited Rabat in 1918. She first remarked on the

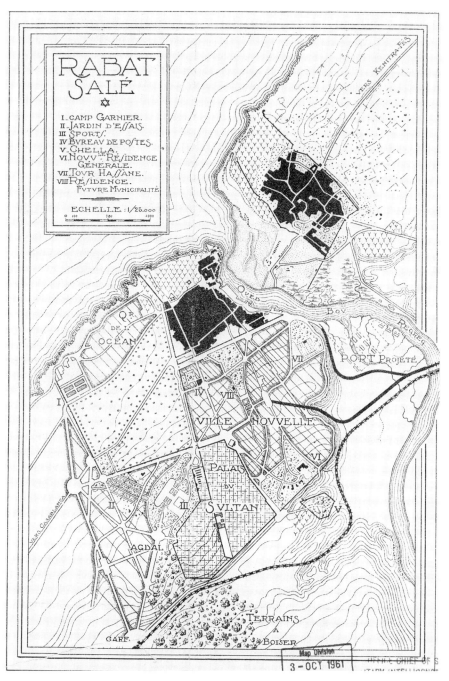

FIGURE 47.   *Map of Rabat in 1918, showing initial development of newly acquired French land. Library of Congress.*

L'HIVER à CASABLANCA

Edition Flandrin
Reproduction interdite

FIGURE 48. *Postcard ridiculing conditions in Casablanca during the winter months,* *1914. Drawing by Robert Birké, copyright C. Editions Flandrin.*

quaint beauty of the old walled medina and then exclaimed, "Set in this legendary frame was the unexpected spectacle of an intensely modern community, leading a life of European activity and usefulness."[35]

Prost disembarked in Casablanca in March 1914, carried through the water from the boat to the shore on the shoulders of a Moroccan dock worker, for the port was not yet deep enough to accommodate large vessels.[36] The state of the city did not improve once he reached land (fig. 48). "At first glance, it was unbelievable chaos," he later recalled. "*Nothing kept foreigners from building wherever they wanted. . . .* It was impossible to grasp the actual density of buildings; impossible to decipher the path of any street." Casablanca, Prost resigned himself, "will always bear the mark of its chaotic origins."[37]

Those chaotic origins derived largely from political instability in Morocco. During the years before the French formally set up their protectorate, speculators and adventurers did not bide their time. They avidly bought up land, especially in Casablanca, often using illegal methods, hoping these holdings would then be protected and increase in value when colonization became official. European governments encouraged this frenzied buying to augment their national presence in the disputed territory. In Prost's words, "Casablanca was composed almost entirely of plots laid out haphazardly. . . . Frantic speculation took place, everybody picturing his own plot as the center of the future city."[38] The characterization of Casablanca as a Wild West town or, in Lyautey's terms, the

Moroccan equivalent of New York City, implied energetic development but also anarchic growth, determined solely by the fluctuations for the market, with no direction over how land was used or streets were laid out.[39]

Standardization was not unheard of in the early years of colonial construction in Casablanca. Two notable European modernists undertook commissions there, even before Prost began his work in earnest. Between 1912 and 1916 Auguste and Gustave Perret designed and supervised several reinforced-concrete structures, including the Hotel Excelsior, the Paris-Maroc Department Store (later the Galleries Lafayettes), warehouses (fig. 49), and apartment buildings. Yet the city was, as a whole, quite disorderly. No coherent street system had been imposed; crude wooden and tin shacks stood randomly alongside five-story buildings, some precariously constructed out of rubble and others in brick (fig. 50). However welcome the work of the Frères Perret, the whole was not the image Lyautey wanted to project for Morocco's commercial capital.[40]

Lyautey remained more absorbed with the possibilities of Rabat and the other royal capital than with this uncouth metropolis. His early memories of visual disorder and ugly buildings in Casablanca would always linger, giving him a certain distaste for that bustling city.[41] A typhus epidemic in the winter of 1913–14, as Prost was setting sail, impelled Lyautey to take some action. He sent a military officer, Colonel Targe, to undertake an "energetic clean-up" by burning down a group of hovels in the market beside the medina walls at the gate of Bab el-Kebir, declaring them to be health hazards. Lyautey then gave Prost his first assignment: a plan for Casablanca's *ville nouvelle*, to be completed within three months.[42]

The new director of urbanism realized that he could destroy the small medina and Arab cemetery for access to the future port. Fear of political reaction prevented this solution. In Tunis, he explained, "grave incidents followed a similar move, with repercussions throughout the Islamic world."[43] Despite pressure from the military and the *colons*, he moved to the periphery of the city all but one of the barracks being built on the land Targe had cleared. In their place he envisioned a grand monumental axis, the Boulevard du IVᵉ Zouaves (today's Boulevard Mohammed el-Hansali) (fig. 51). This would proceed grandly from the port to a major commercial square in the transformed Place de France. (In popular usage, the site continued to be called the Place de l'Horloge, after the town clock erected by the French on the nearby medina wall in 1908; today it is the Place Mohammed V [fig. 52]). Lyautey immediately likened the street to the Cannebière of Marseille, and indeed, at this point, Prost had not yet made any effort to have his plans respond to their locale.[44]

FIGURE 49. *Warehouses made of thin concrete arches, Casablanca, by Auguste and Gustave Perret, 1915. From Bernard Champignuelle*, Perret, *1959.*

The scheme for the whole of the *ville nouvelle*, as it evolved over the next year, offered not so much an imitation of existing French cities as a vision of how they might look and function, just as the process behind the design suggested how planning might eventually be implemented at home (see fig. 38). Prost organized the city in a fan pattern around the Place de France and its two economic poles: the port, which tied Casablanca to Europe, and the railway station, which tied it to the interior of the country. From these nodes he defined zones for particular functions within the *ville nouvelle*: administration and commerce in the center; elite residential and recreation areas (racetrack and beaches) to the west; industry and European working-class residential district to the east; military and health-care services along the southern periphery. Trained to stress the Beaux-Arts principles of articulation and separation of function in a building plan, Prost could now apply these principles at the scale of a city.

In his master plans for cities, Prost did not insist on the absolute axial symmetry which dominated most recent Beaux-Arts plans. Instead he modified each design to accommodate zoning and topography. Casablanca's circulation pattern

FIGURE 50. *Typical streetscape in Casablanca, c. 1914. Postcard.*

of broad radial and peripheral boulevards facilitated movement between the districts. It also anticipated a rate of growth that seemed wildly unrealistic in 1913, when Casablanca had only 59,000 people and Prost foresaw 150,000. Prost's

FIGURE 51. *Initial sketch of the Boulevard du IVe Zouaves, Casablanca, by Henri Prost, 1914, showing the street prolonged by the demolition of earlier walls. From France-Maroc, 1917.*

FIGURE 52. *The Place de France, Casablanca, 1913. From* Le Monde colonial
illustré, 1929.

prediction was reached by 1930 and soon surpassed, such that by 1968 the city
registered a resident population of 1.5 million.[45]

French commercial and residential growth, still paramount, now came
under much tighter control. The all-important *dahir* of April 16, 1914, required
each Moroccan municipality to establish a master plan and local administrative
services to ensure its enforcement. Mandatory height limits based on the width
of streets prohibited any building over four stories, including the ground floor;
minimum dimensions for rooms and courtyards guaranteed sunlight and fresh
air; sanitary and construction codes promoted health and safety. These specifications clearly derived from the suggestions of European public-health advocates. In addition, Prost imposed aesthetic controls to create the visual unity and
the special sense of place he desired. These regulations, called *police des constructions*, did not directly legislate style, but they did set rigorous guidelines for
scale, materials, services, or alignment in various districts. Specific regulations
required that street facades and even the landscaping of public gardens be in a
style which would harmonize with the architectural character of the surroundings.[46]

Prost was not seeking to restrain artistic creativity so much as he was seeking
a way to guide and civilize it, looking back to the Haussmannian tradition of

FIGURE 53.   *Arcade along the Boulevard de la Gare, Casablanca. Photograph by Henri Prost, c. 1920. Courtesy of the Académie d'Architecture, Paris.*

Paris. Although arcades were required amenities along certain streets, for instance, different architects could interpret the forms in quite distinct ways, using graceful arches, heavy square columns, or geometric patterns to enliven the entrances from the street (fig. 53). Prost endorsed "great architectural liberty" for individual buildings, yet he insisted that all designs be carried out within the restraining context of the larger street, district, and cityscape.[47]

In essence Prost hoped to generate a thriving, orderly metropolis, especially for French Casablanca. Anticipating the growth of the industrial port, he projected a plan for future development there. This included the expectation that the French would, in time, be able to utilize part of the adjacent cemetery to enlarge and straighten the Boulevard du IVe Zouaves. The urbane world of commerce and entertainment was equally important to the kind of city he envisioned. Prost set aside space for theaters, department stores, a market, even an eventual *maison de tous* where the working class could gather. He thereby hoped to draw Moroccans and Europeans into a public life of leisure, consumerism, and civic pride. Prost even thought about the housing problem. He specifically hoped that he could alleviate the diminishing French birthrate through verdant

FIGURE 54. *An unnamed Moroccan medina. Photograph by Henri Prost, c. 1920.*
Courtesy of the Académie d'Architecture, Paris.

garden cities and workers' housing estates, using standardized construction to facilitate the availability of single-family dwellings. Depopulation, he contended, "is intimately tied to the problem of housing."[48]

Many French observers insisted that Paris would do well to learn from his efforts. The modern city, viewed in this way, was a universal phenomenon. Albert Laprade specifically contrasted the use of zoning in Morocco with the state of cities in France, "where factories, housing, and commercial buildings are mixed together in the most atrocious disorder, a lamentable situation for industrial development, and lamentable, too, for the tranquility and health of the residents."[49] Vaillat credited Lyautey and Prost with understanding what the author called the three perceptual and social values of any piece of architecture: "social responsibility, expressed in the facade; a program, affirmed in the interior plan; and urban design [*emplacement*], which translates the relations of the building itself into the larger fabric of the city."[50]

As they pursued this course of study, French architects and writers began to look around for clues and inspiration. Respect for the grand monuments of Islam had been in evidence since Napoleon's Egyptian campaigns of the early nineteenth century. Now the vernacular culture of ordinary houses received just as much attention (fig. 54). Prost himself developed such an appreciation, and newcomers to his design team followed in his footsteps. As one later recalled:

> The significance of my boss's first act—sending me, before doing anything else, to breathe the air of the medinas—drove home the point that it would be through us that a new style would be elaborated, executing his plan day by day, aided, even carried away, by his profound sympathy for this people and their culture.[51]

The official publication, *La Renaissance du Maroc* (1923), captured the Western cultural bias that pervades such sentiments. Comparing themselves to the early masters of the European Renaissance in the fourteenth and fifteenth centuries, artists like Prost admired the vitality of the vernacular culture around them. They, too, sought universal principles of beauty and order to elevate their surroundings. The colonial architecture of Morocco even conveyed a belief in its own ability to represent civic morality, quite similar to what Jacob Burckhardt had described in his history of Renaissance Florence.[52]

The result is a style which François Béguin has aptly named "Arabisances" (fig. 55). The effect was at once functional and romantic, contemporary and responsive to local history. The functionalism, codified in part in Prost's design guidelines, encouraged orderly new construction and sanitary technologies— without foreclosing any of the regional adaptations to climate, such as terraces, courtyards, and screened balconies or loggias.[53] The romanticism expressed a lyric fascination with Moroccan design arts. European architects freely adapted the white wall of stucco (*naqsh hadida*) and details like the interlaced wooden screen (*mashribiya*); porcelain or tile mosaics on columns or at the cornice line (*zellij*); a prayer niche (*mirhab*) indicating the direction of Mecca; pointed or horseshoe (outrepassé) arches; and vaulted corbelling (*muquarna*). Both private and, even more so, public buildings in Morocco made abundant use of these elements, a use encouraged by fashion and regulations.

French architects had become far more sophisticated since the generation which had worked under Célestin-Auguste-Charles Jonnart, governor-general of Algeria between 1903 and 1911 and Lyautey's former commander (fig. 56). Lyautey now branded this "a period of romantic bad taste when people believed they could create Arabic art by covering the facades with excessive exterior ornament. That is heresy."[54] In Lyautey's Morocco, few Western architects fes-

FIGURE 55. *Central Post Office, Casablanca, by Adrien Laforgue, 1920. From Henri Descamps*, L'Architecture moderne au Maroc, *1930.*

tooned an entire facade with Moorish-inspired details. They now understood something of the basic typologies of this other tradition: the stark simplicity of volume and contour; the relation of blank facade to carefully placed concentrations of ornament; the inward focus on the family that explained modest domestic facades; the interconnections between architecture, landscape, and urban design that generated the typical street pattern of Islamic neighborhoods (*humā*).[55] Again, the parallels with contemporary artistic and intellectual movements in France help explain the attraction.

Vivid descriptions of Moroccan architecture came from the French writers who visited Morocco during this era, notably Vaillat, Pierre Loti, and Jean and Jérôme Tharaud. Jean Gallotti captured the setting with typical rhapsodic appreciation:

> The materials, baked or sun-dried brick, gain force only from their massing, and brightness only from the [white] limestone and the reflections of the sun. . . . The unity of surfaces seems dedicated to the glory of the

FIGURE 56. *Courtyard of the archbishop's residence, Algiers, 1907. From Pierre Dumas*, L'Algérie, *1931.*

sun, the walls and terraces spreading out without any order, each one shading the others, creating a magical instrument, a grand organ of sunlight, for the play of light and shadow. Tell yourself that the gift of humble proportions and narrow spaces has now been bestowed upon you. You have rediscovered this pleasure, forever lost to us: the intimacy of the street.[56]

Gallotti stayed in Morocco to become an inspector for the Bureau of Fine Arts and Historic Monuments, which oversaw historic preservation in the medinas. He soon joined forces with one of the most visually responsive of the French architects working in Morocco, Albert Laprade, to publish a two-volume study, *Le Jardin et la maison arabes au Maroc* (1924), in which Gallotti's text was interspersed with delicate drawings by Laprade (fig. 57). The basic organization of the book corresponded closely to prevailing Beaux-Arts techniques of visual analysis, beginning with the plan as the generating form, then continuing with construction, decorative elements, and finally variations among house types. Decorative elements that the authors considered most typical of Moroccan architecture—the pointed arch, the stalactite *muqarnas*, stone frames around doors and windows, tilework, flat undecorated whitewashed wall surfaces, and so on—were thus canonized. With this guidance, French architects were eager to show their adaptation to the surrounding culture.[57]

FIGURE 57. *Sketch of a doorway in Salé by Albert Laprade. From Jean Gallotti,* Le Jardin et la maison arabes au Maroc, 1926.

The dangers of romanticism in a purely visual analysis intruded all too easily. Laprade's enthusiasm, while certainly genuine, could not generate a real understanding of the complex history of Moroccan architecture, especially in its relations with Europe. "Up until 1909," he asserted, "custom (*cïada*) had not changed [since the fifteenth century]. Mason, sculptor, carpenter, ironworker, each enjoyed himself on his own without breaking the harmony among them, so much had traditions remained stable in these countries situated outside the grand currents of Europe."[58] Historical and stylistic evolution could only be perceived in terms of Western trends, which made the Islamic countries seem to exist outside of time.

Further compromising any sense of cultural development was the fact that most Europeans in Morocco considered Islamic architecture a more or less universal set of elements from Spain to the Middle East. Architects freely incorporated motifs indigenous to Moorish Spain, Syria, or Egypt. Nor was there even a consistent recognition of the various local traditions within Morocco. French designers tended to glorify the richly ornamented houses and mosques of Fez as the culmination of a national style.[59] Despite good intentions and even a certain amount of historical knowledge, the result was inevitably an architecture of pastiche.[60]

But no matter, for the purpose of "Arabisances" was to cheer and inspire Europeans. As Laprade wrote:

Above all it is their popular culture that comes across in the ensemble of
these buildings. . . . In these countries architecture (like music and
dance) is for us an antidote to the sadness and the emptiness that our
triumphant materialism gives us in excess.[61]

Gallotti had been even more explicit about purpose and audience:

I offer here neither a study with scientific pretensions nor a purely literary
work. One will find here, continually juxtaposed, descriptive passages
and technical indications. I have written the one to give an idea of the
particular charm of these Arab houses and gardens, and the other with
the intention of facilitating the task of those Europeans who wish to build
in the indigenous style.[62]

Both authors presented the French with an intriguingly complex image of colonial Morocco: exotic and experimental, traditional and modern.

Was collaboration possible between the French architect who designed a
structure and the Moroccan building craftsman who would apply the essential
ornament? Prost confronted this problem by referring to history:

Our situation is analogous to that of the Normans when they occupied
Sicily [in the twelfth century]. We are the architects, and Morocco fur-
nishes us with artisans. The Frenchman establishes the structure of the
edifice, considering its function, and the indigenous decorative art will
truly be his collaborator.[63]

The statement dismissed the human craftsmen and anthropomorphized the art
itself. Artisans were not acknowledged as skilled designers; they were merely
conduits of a remarkable tradition from which the French could draw at will.
As Bernard Huet has pointed out, this represents the antithesis of traditional
Islamic architecture where the person who conceives and he who builds (if indeed they are different persons) operate within the same conceptual framework
about the design process—though the knowledge of one may vastly surpass that
of the other.[64]

Prost soon faced the problem of remunerating the Moroccan craftsmen at a
level commensurate with their skills. "If we pay them enough to keep them at
handicrafts," he mused, "the work will become too costly—or too organized by
official training."[65] While he wanted to "use indigenous arts for the decoration
of cities," Prost was caught between the contradiction of cost and culture. Forced
to choose, his solution was to endorse only minimal wages for the craftsmen he
so admired.[66]

In other ways, too, allusions to power intruded into design decisions. The basic proportions, even the evident symmetry of French buildings and streets-capes in Morocco, betray what Brian Brace Taylor has called "an indelible imprint of a European aesthetic sensibility."[67] Axes and symmetrical ordering are regularly used in Arab-Islamic composition, but one can only perceive axiality in a fragmentary manner, space after space. The view that encompasses the overall ordering of volumes is always blocked; the perception of symmetry can occur only in the mind's eye of the viewer. This concept in part determines the labyrinthine pattern of streets and building complexes.[68] French architects and their clients insisted upon visible control over such elusive patterns, making manifest their authority.

A complex semiology of architectural messages—a certain respect for and knowledge of the other, but still a clear dominance by the West—was, of course, especially evident in public buildings. Under Prost's direction, a Special Architecture Bureau was created in 1916 to oversee governmental structures. Lyautey and his staff again looked to France as well as the colonies in insisting on the need for strict urban-design controls, especially in major public settings. Evoking the ordered beauty of Nancy's eighteenth-century Place Stanislas, close to the village where he had grown up, Lyautey regretted that "such mediocre new districts had been created since that time, when it would have been so simple to impose a more enlightened planning ordinance that respected sites which should have been made inviolable."[69]

The Grand'Place in Casablanca (soon renamed the Place Lyautey and now the Place des Nations Unies) exemplifies Lyautey's policy of association. (fig. 58). Prost made the Grand'Place a key element in his master plan of 1914, envisioning it as an architectural expression of French authority and munificence in Morocco. His earliest guidelines specified the use of indigenous Moroccan ornament in a restrained but impressive manner; they also stipulated that different French architects design the various buildings in order to generate a pleasing sense of vitality.

A European spatial hierarchy commands the composition. Albert Laprade's Hôtel de la Subdivision (1919) employed regular arched windows and balconies to adorn the cubic white facade. Nearby, magnificent blue mosaics adorn the porch and cornice of Adrien Laforgue's central post office (1920) (see fig. 55). Joseph Marrast's courthouse (Palais de Justice, 1921–25) featured elaborately carved cedar brackets for the colonnaded galleries which connect the various pavilions (fig. 59). His city hall (Hôtel de Ville, 1922–25) featured magnificent interior patios, graced with fountains and tilework (fig. 60). In each instance the details are distinctly Islamic, while the symmetrical, centrally focused organi-

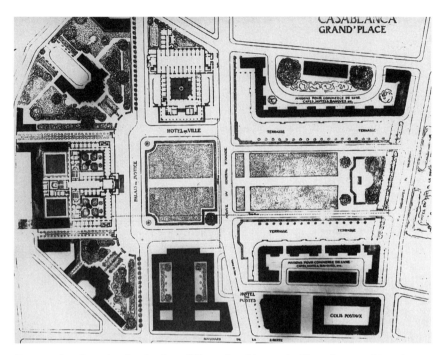

FIGURE 58.   *Site plan for the Grand'Place, Casablanca, by Henri Prost and Joseph Marrast, 1914–1917. From Descamps*, L'Architecture moderne.

zation of the building and, even more so, the axial site plan of the whole assert French control of the setting and its institutions.

The integration and hierarchy of spatial imagery was intentional from the start. Prost had envisioned a series of open interior courtyards for the city hall, embellished with fountains, pools, and lush tropical landscaping, derived in large part from the Islamic patio house, a scheme Marrast carried out with extraordinary skill. Yet one could never mistake this building for an Islamic *mahakma* (the pasha's administrative offices for a municipality), given the distinctively Western proportions, the formal main entrance at the center, disengaged siting, and the conspicuous campanile tower to the side (fig. 61). There can be no doubt that this building belongs to the tradition of European city halls rather than Islamic municipal institutions.

We can even document the self-conscious effort to assert the protectorate's cultural ideal. The initial work for the Grand'Place was carried out on a tight budget, aggravated by expenditures for World War I and the ongoing war in the Rif. Prost therefore resorted to what he called an "architecture of surface," instructing staff architects to design only the principal facades; construction would have to be completed gradually, awaiting additional funds in the future.[70]

FIGURE 59.   *Gallery in the Palais de Justice, Casablanca, by Joseph Marrast,*
1925. Photograph by Gwendolyn Wright.

The most important public commission was Rabat itself (fig. 62). Here Prost
oversaw a centralized administrative district, encompassing Lyautey's own residence alongside offices for the various French state bureaucracies. The street
connections and vistas into this district received careful attention. The straight
line of the Avenue Dar-el-Maghzen (named for the sultan's palace, now the
Avenue Abderrahmen Areggai) extended the principal street of the medina, the
rue El Gza, creating a sense of continuity with the *ville nouvelle*. Nearest the
Andalusian wall, the street consisted mainly of small-scale apartment buildings

FIGURE 60. *Patio in the Hôtel de Ville, Casablanca, by Joseph Marrast, 1922–25. Photograph by Gwendolyn Wright.*

with porticoes; it then widened majestically to provide a proper setting for imposing public buildings such as the Banque du Maroc, the post office, and the train station (see fig. 42). At the junction with the palace grounds, the boulevard was again transformed into the gently curving Avenue des Tourarga (today the Rue du Chellah), ending in the office of the resident-general himself.

The decision to place the residence symmetrically with the sultan's palace, while also emphasizing its connection to the medina, symbolized the bonds of colonialism. Prost chose the site over an earlier location because of these strategic associations, and because the plateau offered "a superb panorama of Rabat, Salé, and the estuary of Bou-Regreg."[71] He preserved three such picturesque views of the medina, making manifest both control and aesthetic appreciation. A pleasing vista, like axiality, was not simply a matter of European aesthetics; it represented European power.

Historic monuments likewise served a conspicuous political function. As early as 1915 Lyautey initiated a survey of the country's artistic resources, on the occasion of the first Franco-Moroccan trade exposition in Casablanca. That same year the archaeologist Marcel Dieulafoy began to supervise the excavation of Rabat's Roman and Merinid monuments, as part of an effort to date ancient ruins exactly. On the south side of the Residence district, Lyautey's home overlooked the ramparts of the Chella, a fourteenth-century Merinid fortress, now in ruins, built on the remains of the Roman town of Sala (fig. 63).[72] Land was cleared around the walls, and no construction was allowed near the historic site. The same approach applied to the monumental late-twelfth-century minaret of an unfinished Almohad mosque called the Tour Hassan, even though both sites were in the fast-growing European city (fig. 64). The fashionable Hotel de la Tour Hassan was erected in the neo-Moorish style at a discrete distance.

Historic preservation had a deeply political aspect, providing the French with additional justifications for their domination. Their most significant historical precedents recalled Roman colonization. The impressive remains at nearby Volubilis, just beyond the Roman *limes* south of the Chella, were carefully preserved.[72] If the Islamic sense of history and architecture found the concept of setting off monuments entirely foreign, this strategy gave the French proof of the conviction that only they could fully appreciate the Moroccan past and its beauty. The archaeologists and historians of the Institut des Hautes Etudes Marocaines made the point explicitly. Emile Pauty, writing in *Hesperis*, the official journal of the institute, chided the Muslims, "for whom the passage of time is nothing, [who] let their monuments fall into ruin with as much indifference as they once showed ardor in building them."[74]

In the French Administrative Quarter (now called the Ministries) the imagery of modern life again found a counterbalance with certain Moroccan design elements. While Lyautey wanted this to be "a factory of work," he also envisioned a setting that was "smiling and welcome."[75] Here Prost carried out his

FIGURE 61. *Elevation of major facade treatments on the Grand'Place,*

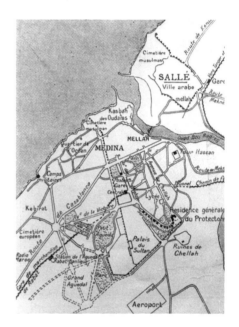

FIGURE 62. *Site plan of Rabat showing major streets and monuments built and restored under the French, 1930. From* La Construction moderne, *1931.*

most accomplished evocation of the modern urban fabric. Combining aesthetics with sociology, his design tried to soften both the appearance and the actual day-to-day process of modern political administration, at least for the colonial functionaries—who constituted almost half of Rabat's 14,000 Europeans in 1926.[76] Rather than one massive complex, separate pavilions housed each branch of the administration. A 500-meter-long curved colonnade with vine-covered pergolas linked the pavilions, and each structure harbored a lush courtyard where gardens, pergolas, and fountains offered contemplative respite (fig. 65). The decision to make each pavilion a separate commission reinforced the effect of diversity within a strong overall plan.

Casablanca, by Joseph Marrast, 1915. From Descamps, L'Architecture moderne.

FIGURE 63. *View of the ruins of the Chella, a fourteenth-century Merinid fortress, from the patio of Lyautey's Résidence de France. From Vaillat,* Le Visage français.

The setting won enthusiastic compliments from French visitors. Architect Henri Descamps wrote that "one is especially struck by the unity, the beauty of simple lines, the logic of the plan, the indefinable charm which liberates the ensemble. . . . Already architects and artists from all over the world have come here."[77] Duly impressed, Vaillat also recognized a clear shift over time in terms of design concepts. The earliest buildings—the simple tile-roofed prisms of Laforgue's Bureau of Mines (1918) (fig. 66) and Laprade's remarkable Résidence Générale (1918) (fig. 67), with its marble colonnades and mosaic courtyards

FIGURE 64. *The Tour Hassan, a late twelfth-century minaret in Rabat, after the French cleared away surrounding buildings, c. 1925. Postcard.*

carrying the play of geometric ornament down to the most minute details—showed an "ingenious concern for social and artisanal conservation."[78] In contrast, within a few years, Laforgue's cubist Forestry Division (1922) and, even more, Antoine Marchisio's offices for the Bureau of Health (1929) (fig. 68) turned toward a mix of luxury and industrial materials in a contemporary stripped-classical mode, one less specifically related to the buildings' context. With this stage of stylistic development, Vaillat felt, "the science of reinforced concrete renders construction easy, almost banal," especially in comparison with the earlier buildings.[79] Thus the architectural interpretation of French colonial policies underwent a subtle but marked transformation, as both administrative and design preferences changed, especially after Lyautey's departure in 1925.

From the start of colonization, one can clearly see political issues underlying architectural choices in the protectorate's educational program. The first stage involved "saving" the Islamic tradition while introducing a small number of the elite to Western culture. Several long-established *medersas* (Quranic schools attached to major urban mosques) were rehabilitated, made more pleasing to the Western eye, in order to better reflect the desired image of unchanging Islamic culture (fig. 69). A restricted set of schools was then established for those Moroccans who would ultimately take part in the colonial system. The Ecole de Fils de Notables began in 1914 in Fez—the first government-sponsored school in a country where religious institutions had always overseen education.

120

FIGURE 65.   *Aerial view of the Résidence de France and the colonial Administrative Quarter, Rabat. From* L'Art vivant, *1930.*

A Collège Musulman at Fez (1914) and another at Rabat (1916) provided the next stage of training for this group.[80] The restrained lines of Fernand Baud's college in Rabat (fig. 70), with its graceful horseshoe-arched entrances and arcaded courtyards, exemplified the claim that the French preserved the best of Moroccan culture while preparing its leaders for positions of authority in a cosmopolitan world.

FIGURE 66. *Service des Mines in the Administrative Quarter, Rabat, by Adrien Laforgue*, 1918. *From Vaillat*, Le Visage français.

FIGURE 67. *Résidence de France, Rabat, by Albert Laprade*, 1918. *From* L'Art vivant, *1930.*

FIGURE 68. *Main offices of the Service de Santé in the Administrative Quarter, Rabat, by Antoine Marchisio, 1929. From* La Construction moderne, *1930.*

This was not in any way to be an educational system designed to change Moroccan society. As Georges Hardy, then director of public education, explained, "[Do] not dream of the emancipation of the Moroccan citizen, nor the enfranchisement of the slave, nor the freedom of women: when you know the Moroccan milieu, you will realize that these commonplace ideas, transplanted here, become dangers."[81] Separation supposedly meant "*la droit à la différence*," necessary lest the Moroccans become "alien" from their own culture—and then, in Lyautey's words, "bitter, malcontent, potential recruits for opposition movements, recrimination, even revolution."[82]

The response on the part of the Moroccans surprised the protectorate officials, as local leaders set up some twenty "free schools" in the medinas of the major cities, seeking to modernize and strengthen traditional Islamic education as an alternative to the French system.[83] Here was content and self-determination—rather than simply architectural substitutes for these qualities, such as the schools built by the French relied upon.

Colonial officials tried unsuccessfully to stifle these schools, then turned to another tactic. Lyautey and Hardy decided to centralize the education they offered to the local elite. This new initiative involved more technical schools and the Institut des Hautes Etudes Marocaines, established in 1921 under Hardy, which would bring together a small number of Moroccan and French specialists to chart the country's past and its future. Even the architecture of these schools

FIGURE 69. *Courtyard of the twelfth-century Medersa Bouanyia, Marrakesh, rehabilitated under the aegis of the Ecole des Hautes Etudes Marocaines, c. 1925. From Charles Terrasse*, Medersas du Maroc, *1928.*

Collège musulman.

Photo Résidence g¹ʳ

FIGURE 70. *Collège Musulman de Rabat by Fernand Baud, 1916. From Vaillat,* Le Visage français.

represented a shift in policy. The buildings were less pseudo-historical than earlier ones had been, their Islamic ornament more abstract (fig. 71). The institute contained laboratories and offices, while the technical schools used large modern facilities to instruct students in business, metallurgy, and other Western skills. The building program could thereby indicate changes in administrative policy.

Architecture in the private sector, less constrained by official ideology, was also more visually daring, though still quite responsive to the Moroccan setting. More than a hundred European-trained architects practiced in Morocco during the 1920s, and more than three hundred developers underwrote buildings; yet a common approach prevailed in the commercial centers and villa districts.[84] This remarkable uniformity was the result of a thriving speculative market for both commercial and residential buildings. With very active practices, architects and developers preferred to rely upon successful formulas.

Casablanca's Boulevard de la Gare (today's Boulevard Mohammed V) evolved in an typically orderly, yet exuberant, manner during the early 1920s. Over a thousand meters long and twenty meters wide, including ample sidewalks shaded by *allées* of palm trees, this street joined the port with the railway station. Prost achieved a strong visual unity with continuous street-level arcades, uniform building heights and set-backs, and repeated but varied patterns of neo-Moorish ornament along the bright white facades (fig. 72). His own headquar-

1 2 5

FIGURE 71. *Ecole des Hautes Etudes Marocaines, Rabat, 1921–23. From Georges Hardy*, Les Colonies françaises: Le Maroc, *1930.*

ters for the Compagnie Algérienne de Crédit (1924–30) (fig. 73), done in collaboration with the modernist Antoine Marchisio, exemplifies the aesthetic that Prost sought and that business clients readily accepted. In such instances, private development interests abided by Prost's strict urban-design guidelines, rather than hold up construction. They in turn recouped some of the most valuable commercial property in the city.[85]

The aesthetic strategy of inclusion, with its emphasis on cultural interplay within a strong and emphasized overall order, can be found in the French residential districts, too (fig. 74). Many villas were privately commissioned, but the majority of houses for Europeans were speculative ventures, much as the apartment buildings in the city centers were. The land became available when the municipality bought it outright (or later when it could be expropriated for the "public purpose" of European settlement). This land was then sold at auction to private developers, with the profits from the sale used to pay for the site improvements (roads, drains, water, and electricity) which gave the *villes nouvelles* their impressive modern appearance.

FIGURE 72.   *View of the Boulevard de la Gare, Casablanca, c. 1930. Postcard.*

127

FIGURE 73. *Compagnie Algérienne de Crédit, Casablanca, by Prost and Marchisio, 1924–30. Courtesy of the Académie d'Architecture, Paris.*

FIGURE 74. *Apartment block in Rabat by Cadet & Brion, 1925. From* La Construction moderne, *1930.*

Since Prost's *police des constructions* did not apply in the villa districts, the fundamental preoccupations of the French architects and wealthy *colons* show most conspicuously. By and large, residences still followed common alignments for walls and setbacks, reinforcing the sense of uniformity with almost universal use of white or pastel stucco. The geometry of volumes varied greatly, as did the landscaping, yet the predominant effect remained one of visual cohesion. Moroccan decorative ornament seemed less a preoccupation than in the downtown public areas, though it was often present. Most architects and builders sought a combination of economical simplicity, abstractions of Islamic motifs, and fashionable allusions to European Art Deco and modernist movements.

By the mid-1920s, the authors of an official report for Hardy's Office of Public Instruction proudly described the aesthetic that prevailed, again comparing Morocco favorably with contemporary trends at home. In Morocco, French architects could experiment freely with

> a new architecture born in Europe, which accords better with Morocco than with the sky of Paris or Germany. And what architecture! A return of sorts to antiquity (and to modesty) by the starkness of plans and the disposition of volumes. No vain bourgeois ornament (much expense on the cheap). . . , the calm of facades in contrast with the excitement of the streets. . . , the taste of the harmonious whole once again given the place of honor in a well-ordered composition of blank walls and bays.[86]

Laprade insisted that this simplicity could "stir the imagination of French architects." And Henri Descamps, editor of *La Construction moderne*, called this "a logical architecture which is neither *Arabic* nor of the *Parisian suburbs*, but quite simply French architecture well adapted to the sky and climate of Morocco."[87]

Indeed, the interlocking cubist planes of houses by Balois, Marchisio, or even Prost himself follow much the same lines (fig. 75). In surveying the work of the colony's architects and developers, *L'Afrique du Nord illustrée* proclaimed "the spirit of France abroad, with the nuances of individualism tempered by a willingness to submit to rules and a hierarchy."[88] Vaillat evoked the famous passage in Descartes' *Discours de la méthode* which praised the uniform beauty of a city overseen by a single architect, and then explained:

> These houses avoid looking ridiculous because they copy each other. . . . The unity of style, adhesion to the shared constraints of climate and materials, the patient adjustment of each case to an ideal solu-

FIGURE 75. *Villas in the* ville nouvelle *of Rabat, c. 1930. From L'Art vivant, 1930.*

tion, the scarcely modified repetition of a type attains an effect as pleasing to the eye as to the mind. [89]

The esteemed French urbanist Gaston Bardet would look back fondly upon this setting a generation later, when he praised Prost's balance of dissymmetry and harmony in the Moroccan *villes nouvelles*. [90]

The use of architectural symbols to reinforce national culture extended to the medina as well. Lyautey established the Bureau of Fine-Arts in 1912, during the first months of the protectorate, appointing Tranchant de Lunel as the first director. A somewhat flamboyant aesthete, Tranchant de Lunel had become a great favorite of Lyautey, who granted him unprecedented powers, greater than anywhere else in the French-speaking world, to regulate new construction and restore existing buildings in the Moroccan medinas and *mellahs*. "Because tradition is the solid base on which all Moroccan art rests," Tranchant explained to a Casablanca audience in 1916, the bureau staff must be "servants of art, the faithful guardians of Tradition." The formula was simple enough: " 'Intervene everywhere, but change nothing.' "[91]

Self-righteous aestheticism could not generate an understanding of Moroccan art or the complex architectural problems raised by new building in a historic area. In terms of conservation and design, the staff was enthusiastic but scarcely scholarly in its early years. Prost called for the director's demotion, complaining to Lyautey that he and others found Tranchant de Lunel "lightweight, terribly lightweight," nothing more than an amateur artist who cared only about "cute, amusing details."[92]

Under new leadership after 1914, the Bureau of Fine-Arts quickly initiated some clear-cut procedures that preservationists in France would have welcomed. Perhaps the most important principles concerned the preference for protecting entire districts rather than individual buildings. Administrative measures to protect a single monument could not prevent its being surrounded by new buildings as land values increased: such surroundings would undermine all sense of historic character, even if the structure itself remained untouched. Pursuing this point, Lyautey and his legal consultant, Guillaume de Tarde, advised the staff that "the beauty and historic interest of Moroccan architecture resides not only in the important monuments, but also—even especially—in the ensemble of constructions."[93]

Tranchant de Lunel was decidedly more romantic than his colleagues. He wanted to return Morocco to the integral, exotic world he believed had once existed there. The principal purpose of the Bureau of Fine-Arts, he wrote Lyautey, should be "the exacting reproduction of parts of early Moroccan monuments now fallen into disrepair."[94] The definition of such monuments liberally extended to include canals and water systems as well as palaces and *medersas*—most of which the French considered to be on a par with those of Granada, and indeed the best had been erected by Andalusian Moors in the twelfth century. Yet the temptations to fantasize about this earlier period proved too alluring. One sees the result in Tranchant de Lunel's 1915 design for the garden and "Moorish café" of the Casbah des Oudaïas, the twelfth-century fortress in Rabat overlooking the sea (figs. 76, 77). While visually appealing, the results were far more scenographic than archaeological.

In time Tranchant de Lunel became completely caught up in the commercialization of Moroccan art, past and present, again in the guise of protecting it. Transferred to the new Bureau of Native Arts in 1917, he decided to send Moroccan handicrafts to all French trade expositions. Tranchant himself designed the Moroccan section of the North African Pavilion for the Arts Déco show of 1925 (fig. 78). To supply these European markets he set up official schools in the traditional crafts: rug-weaving, bookbinding, metalwork, and woodwork.[95] In *L'Art de reconnaître les styles coloniaux de la France*, Emile Bayard praised these efforts to "develop art in the colonies without denaturing it," expressing the hope that French crafts workers, whether in decorative arts or the building trades, could also be encouraged to "respond to new conditions without abandoning old techniques."[96]

Crafts were becoming moribund, not because of a lack of skill or motivation, but because of the impact of the world market on the production and sale

RABAT — Café Maure

FIGURE 76. The "Moorish café" in the Casbah des Oudaïas, Rabat, by Maurice Tranchant de Lunel, 1922. Postcard.

FIGURE 77. Gardens in the Casbah des Oudaïas, Rabat, by Maurice Tranchant de Lunel. Postcard.

of goods. Since the nineteenth century, in Morocco as in Europe, objects once made by hand had become less profitable and fashionable. Tranchant de Lunel's workshops faced a crisis when the initial overproduction of goods flooded the European department stores, lowering prices and standards, and soon saturating the mode for exotic handicrafts.[97] As a result, production techniques came under even more rigorous control by French experts, and the market shifted toward state museums and local tourist shops.

By 1920, in any case, Lyautey had reorganized the office into the Bureau of Antiquities, Fine Arts, and Historic Monuments, placing Jules Borély at its head. (In its first new incarnation, it was called the Bureau of Historic Monuments and Imperial Palaces, suggesting the continuing preoccupation with maintaining the status of the sultan's royal property. Headquarters for the bureau later moved to the Mamounia Hotel in Marrakesh, designed by Prost and Marchsio in 1926.) The initial impetus for the change came when Lyautey discovered the wires of a towering telegraph pole across from the beautiful Bab er-Ronad gate in Rabat, and then a huge electrical installation going up alongside the medina wall.[98] While in theory the bureau should have protected these sites, Lyautey realized that the personnel was more involved with the pleasures of historically inspired design than the pressures of surveillance. If he decried strict formalism—the staff should act "less as functionaries than as artists and men of taste"—Lyautey still demanded "watchdogs," always on the lookout for the intrusion of inappropriate modernization.[99]

With the *dahir* or Sultan's decree of April 1, 1925, Borély was able to require a one-month design review of any proposed new structure or renovation in a medina, and the right to refuse a building permit for any change deemed inappropriate. Following de Tarde and Prost's approach in the *villes nouvelles* for the French, Borély set up design guidelines for the medina: a maximum height of four stories; courtyards covering at least one-fifth of the surface enclosed; and facades "conceived in a style that relates to the importance of streets and public places, in harmony with the architectural character of the surroundings."[100] That character was given explicit formal qualities: tile roofs, untinted whitewash finish on the walls, exacting proportions for doorways and windows. Borély specified that his staff should respect the local characteristics of each city and region, rather than mix regional traditions arbitrarily. The Rabat headquarters of the Fine-Arts Bureau assembled a sizeable library of books on Moroccan art and architecture, together with 25,000 photographs of historical monuments and vernacular architecture throughout the country, to provide the basis for careful choice.[101]

FIGURE 78. *North African pavilion at the Exposition des Arts Décoratifs, Paris, with the Moroccan section to the right by Maurice Tranchant de Lunel, 1925. From* Le

The goal of these controls went beyond the desire to preserve "intact" the artistic and social life of the medinas. Whether under Tranchant de Lunel, Emile Pauty, or Borély, the Bureau of Fine-Arts oriented itself toward charming streetscapes that would appeal to French residents and tourists (fig. 79). Sablayrolles spoke of the "picturesque aspect of the medina," and Prost stressed the need "to conserve the physiognomy, so characteristic of their marvelous panoramic aspects, which give superb views from the principal vantage points of our Modern Cities." [102] Lyautey articulated the conscious effort to promote a tourist industry by maintaining the visual charm of Morocco's cities and countryside. "Since the recent, intense development of large-scale tourism," he explained to a gathering in Paris, "the presentation of a country's beauty has taken on an economic importance of the first order. To attract a large tourist population is to gain everything for both the public and the private budgets." [103]

Monde colonial illustré, 1925.

Appraising Colonial Architecture

Today we can appreciate the visual appeal of Morocco's colonial architecture, yet we also recognize the need to expand upon a purely formal appreciation. At issue are two points: a definition of what in fact is modern, essentially an aesthetic and cultural issue; and a hard look at what abuses were suffered because this cultural "renaissance" took place under a colonial regime, and whether those problems are specific to colonialism, obviously a political question.

To take up the aesthetic aspect first, it is essential to frame the issue broadly to include both France and Morocco. Between the two world wars Morocco provided a foil to architecture and urbanism in France. One textbook on urban design compared Casablanca, Paris, and Marseille on the same terms, without suggesting that the North African example was in any way distinct. Another cited

FIGURE 79.   *Chemins de Fer de Paris poster promoting tourism in Morocco with a modernist representation of tradition in Fez. Courtesy of the Bibliothèque Forney.*

Morocco as the great success of modern urbanism, "disproving critics who suggested that the field was not yet sufficiently developed."[104]

Discussions about architecture and urbanism in Morocco were often translated into proposals for reform at home. Lyautey clearly envisioned applying the Moroccan formula to France: "Conserve the traditional fabric of Paris," he advised readers of *L'Architecture d'aujourd'hui*, "but outside of Paris be as daring as possible."[105] The regionalists of the 1910s and 1920s were especially attuned to the similarities, as they too sought to combine modern materials with local aesthetic traditions. Georges Hardy stressed the lines of influence from the colony to the *métropole* when he wrote, "How many architects and decorators, they too searching for renovation, have discovered in Hispano-Moorish art, or even Berber and Sudanese, a prefiguation of their formulas!"[106] The goal involved artistic inspiration for the French, rather than the fixed tenets of a new stylistic fashion. As Laprade stressed, Lyautey had "waged war against formalism, against preconceived ideas, against the 'canon' that anyone tried to patent, whether it came from the Ecole de Guerre, the Ecole Polytechnique, or even the Ecole des Beaux-Arts."[107]

All architects did not concur with these positive judgments. The fight between avant-garde modernists and those architects attached to a local vernacular proved to be just as bitter in the colony as at home. At least in his polemical writings, Le Corbusier insisted at just this moment on an absolute commitment to universal modernism, with no sentimentality about specific places and their pasts. He declared unequivocally that the time had come for tearing down "false . . . sad, and ugly" relics from the past and instead building truly modern cities, based on universal "human standards of spirituality and a physiology of sensations." While visiting Fez in 1931 he deplored what he saw: "Prost's urbanism is all confusion. The medina is too compressed. . . . France has won over people with its bugle and drum, which represent the most formal order, incisive firmness, a clearly articulated formula." Le Corbusier was fascinated by the opportunities to fulfill "the destiny of the West, to act, to compose, to create modern life" in North Africa, but he did not find enough contemporary vision, at least not in Morocco.[108]

The Parisian architectural community of the 1920s exploded in a barrage of verbal crossfire about what was correct for cities, a fight that has yet to conclude. The architectural community of North Africa soon joined the fray. As early as 1924, Jules Borély began a "war against this . . . pseudo-Moroccan style . . . of trumped-up little Alhambras."[109] A convinced modernist as far as contemporary work, Borély also valued the history of Moroccan architecture, serving as director of the Bureau of Antiquities, Fine Arts, and Historic Monuments. (Antoine

Marchisio, too, became an advisor to the bureau in 1927). Protection of the historic, pre-colonial fabric in Moroccan cities could coexist with a staunchly modernist orientation in new architecture. But this group disdained any design that tried to bridge the two cultural worlds, the two aesthetic domains.

North Africa seemed an ideal setting for European modernism. *Chantiers nord-africains*, an architectural journal published in Algiers, adopted a strict Corbusian line beginning in 1927. Repeated illustrations of Le Corbusier's buildings and city plans accompanied articles by members of the Société des Architectes Modernes: Frantz Jourdan, Adolphe Dervaux, Henri Sauvage, and André Lurçat. One representative piece called for forms that offered a "symbol, an emblem of the age we live in"; another wondered whether it would be necessary to demolish Casablanca as "an anachronistic city." Prost's Urbanism Department came under attack for its attachment to old-fashioned local traditions and the "fallacious utopia of [the] garden city," instead of "frankly cubist" forms.[110]

Morocco was not entirely seen as a desert, however. Here the editors could also find "the exaltation of the most modern formulas of urbanism."[111] By 1927 Lyautey, Prost, and Laprade had all returned to France, and a new team of official architects—led by Marchisio, Laforgue, and Borély—now controlled architectural commissions and standards for the medinas and the *villes nouvelles*. They turned away from Moroccan ornament and urban-design traditions, except for the most abstract references. Laforgue's monumental and severe courthouse in Rabat (1930) won praise from the *Chantiers nord-africains* (fig. 80), as did Marchisio's train station in Rabat (1935), a low and streamlined structure with industrial windows and underground tracks, its only local motif a delicate decorative frieze. Laforgue and Borély collaborated on a music pavilion in Rabat (1930) which used Moroccan-inspired patterns only to provide a subdued backdrop to sparse classicism. A 1930 project by Marchisio, now chief architect for the Résidence, to erect thirty-two identical skyscrapers near the port in Casablanca (fig. 81), each rising twenty-two stories high, resembled Le Corbusier's "skyscrapers in the park" in a very self-conscious manner. Echoing critic Henri Descamps' criticism that "the street . . . is the great mistake of contemporary urbanism," Marchisio envisioned pedestrian walkways and gardens high above the wide thoroughfares for speeding cars.[112]

In theory, these modernist symbols of universal beauty would serve the indigenous people of Morocco, bringing them into modern society. There was really no need, in this outlook, to consider the particular conditions of North Africans, no reason to deliberate about their architecture or social problems, no cause to solicit their opinions. In *Chantiers nord-africains* modernism meant a

Figure 80.   *Palais de Justice, Rabat, by Adrien Laforgue, 1930. From* Cahiers nord-africains, *1930.*

celebration of the new unornamented aesthetic as inherently progressive. Architectural modernists in North Africa associated equality with a standardized formula for architecture. They did not admit that colonialism inevitably prevented equality, no matter what kind of architecture was built. Their diatribes against the earlier Arabisance style had much validity: it did tend toward a sentimental portrayal of Moroccan history and culture. Yet the new architecture of North Africa took no heed of that history or culture, nor of the realities of colonial conditions which affected the area.

The remedy is not simply to embrace another aesthetic paradigm, but rather to probe them all more thoroughly. Many of us can now appreciate the visual delight which infuses many designs of Prost's era, and the awareness of cultural particularities behind that interpretation of modern urban design. The need for symbolic content, for history—as memory, as ornament, as a basis for building the future—is no longer necessarily at odds with modernism, as that word comes into yet another historical usage. We must give Prost his due, acknowledging that he was thinking primarily in terms of formal ideals. In that sense, he even seems rather progressive, calling attention to general principles that have become important to the future of our cities today: designing streets before buildings; allowing public spaces to generate the plan and give it order; turning away from monumentalism; basing urban design on local traditions and vernacular motifs rather than on universal standards or a dominant grand tradition; and symbolizing the cultural connections between and distinctions among the different groups in a city through architectural design.[113]

At the same time, we must acknowledge, as these architects did not, the limits of aesthetic success. Architectural forms in and of themselves, no matter

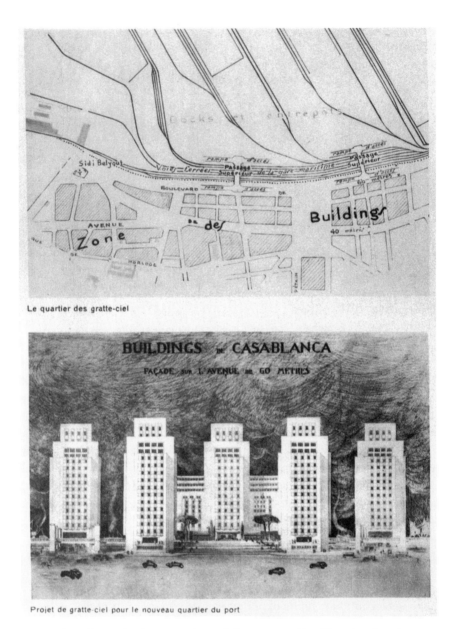

Le quartier des gratte-ciel

Projet de gratte-ciel pour le nouveau quartier du port

FIGURE 81. *Project for thirty-two identical skyscrapers in Casablanca's enlarged port area by Antoine Marchisio, 1930. From Vaillat,* Le Visage français.

how culturally sensitive, cannot substitute for social and political justice. If the tension between good intentions, even visually pleasing results, and the political repercussions of urban policies exists in any setting, it is especially keen under colonialism.

This leads us into the second, more directly political aspect of our analysis. The fact of colonial power is inescapable: it was authoritarian, discriminatory, and debilitating. No account of the benefits can evade or counterbalance this stark truth. Given this reality, there were fundamentally distinct ways to exercise such power. The different policies affected the people and the cities of each colony, and such policies have had their effects on the aftermath of colonialism, too.[114] Relativism is a mirage of sorts, of course, and one can easily misread events and their meanings by comparing obvious mistakes with mixed successes. Let me bracket this problem for the moment by keeping with the theme of modernism and conservation, now asking what political compromises were attempted under the colonial regime. What efforts were made to control and improve conditions for the French and the Moroccan populations? What policies were directed toward metropolitan France as well as colonial Morocco?

In the field of jurisprudence, Lyautey initiated urban laws controlling construction, preservation, and future development. What he accomplished was both earlier and more inclusive than comparable legislation in France, although he hoped to see the procedures duplicated there. As the French civil servants in Morocco proudly pointed out, their first urban legislation of 1914, requiring master plans for all cities, preceded by almost five years the passage of similar (though not nearly so far-reaching) legislation with respect to French cities, and by two years the famous New York City Zoning Resolution. The protectorate's administrators insisted on the right of public authorities to envision a master plan for cities, taking into account all dimensions: surface, underground, air rights, and change over time.

In her history of Rabat, Janet L. Abu-Lughod explains how "the French devised an elaborate system of laws and regulations that gave a patina of legitimacy and equity to the process" of colonial urban planning.[115] The Moroccan laws under the protectorate, called *dahirs*, were issued jointly by Lyautey and Youssef, yet they derived solely from the French legal staff. In his general report of 1914 Lyautey spoke proudly of this collaboration: "In fact, the sultan now possesses a true right to examine [what we are doing] and we even solicit his opinion in many instances."[116]

The most general and innovative legislation governing cities came from Guillaume de Tarde, who had joined the entourage in 1913, arriving with Prost, serving first as auditor for the State Council, then quickly appointed secretary-general of the protectorate. Let me briefly outline the Cartesian logic of his landmark piece of planning legislation, the *dahir* of April 16, 1914. The first section dealt with street alignments and easements. It established a procedure whereby land could be expropriated for these "public purposes." But as the text duly pointed out, alignments made sense only within a larger plan for a district and a city. Therefore the second part of the *dahir* enabled the creation of a legally binding plan for each city in the French zone to be drawn up or approved by Prost's service. The next logical step proceeded to the houses bordering the streets, creating regulations to control the quality of new construction or renovation in terms of hygiene, traffic, public safety, and beauty. In French and Moroccan districts alike, the authorities had aesthetic police power, and made extensive use of it. They could "require a wide setback to create more open space, . . fix the proportion of land coverage . . . and establish the architectural style to which the facades of buildings must conform." [117]

These far-reaching powers encompassed both general principles of urban design and exacting specifications to ensure compliance. In the *villes nouvelles*, for example, rooflines had to be at least partially slanted, Western bathrooms were required, and the height of gates or walls allowed houses to be seen from the street. In the medinas flat roofs were required, no posters or European signs were permitted, and visual overviews of adjacent courtyards or terraces were prohibited, thereby protecting the privacy of the women in the households. In other words, cultural adaptation harmonized with strategies to keep populations separate.

Not all urban land came under this jurisdiction. Every municipality divided streets into "urban streets" and "private streets"—the latter narrow dirt paths for the most part, often in residential districts, where the owners had not yet agreed to abide by the government's proposals for the enlargement and alignment of thoroughfares. A *dahir* of November 10, 1917, created the system for generating new "urban streets," largely derived from the *grands travaux* of Haussmann. Syndicates of adjacent property-owners, under the supervision of a planner, would temporarily pool their land, deed to the city those easements needed for streets or utilities, and then reapportion and redistribute the residual lands among themselves according to an elaborate formula. This process allowed for the gradual implementation of Prost's plan, notably in the center of the cities, even when the state did not have the funds to buy all the land in question. Through the special "benefits tax," the government rather than the landowners would recapture the surplus value created by any improvements. [118]

Administrative power was unchecked by law; neither Europeans nor Arabs had recourse to the courts if they did not agree with the general principles or the specific interpretations of the planner or inspector. [119] Lyautey's vision of the city was, in many ways, positive and complex, but it was a vision commanded into effect. He sought to preserve the beauty of the Moroccan medinas and to insure the beauty of the French settlements. Indeed, his personal revulsion against "some hideous constructions already half-finished" in Rabat, just after he returned there in 1912, had fueled the decision to enact the urbanism laws as soon as possible.[120] Lyautey, like Prost, believed that the only means for protecting beauty and quality was an authoritarian hand.

Authoritarianism was not meant only for the Moroccans. The protectorate also wanted to control the French *colons*, the speculative developers, provincial bourgeoisie, and urban proletariat, none of whom inspired much confidence or respect in Lyautey. One letter bluntly decried those *colons* with their "theories about inferior races destined to be exploited without mercy. They possess neither intelligence nor humanity."[121] Safeguards over the Moroccans' culture and well-being showed a paternalistic superiority, to be sure, but also a recognition of the racism that prevailed in the French community.

Lyautey deplored even more the prevailing aesthetic taste among the *colons*, and the ease with which they sacrificed beauty to economic gain. Official ire fell on the developers who would sacrifice the integrity of the larger setting for their private gain. "It is a matter above all," declared Prost, "of orienting the merchants and builders toward the true sense of the future city."[122] The legal scholar Louis Sablayrolles also criticized the social injustice of speculators making money on the increased value of land.[123]

As a consequence of these sentiments, regulations over architecture, construction, hygiene, and land use applied throughout the city, in French and Moroccan districts alike. Lyautey did not trust the *colons* to have the foresight to develop their own *villes nouvelles* in a manner that would epitomize modern standards of health, efficiency, and beauty.

Did these criticisms entail a criticism of Western capitalism? Lyautey was an old-fashioned conservative, disdainful of popular taste, democratic compromise, and conspicuous economic self-interest. For all these reasons he looked down on the upwardly mobile Europeans who came to the colonies, seeking their fortune. He admired those who knew their place—a category which included major financial and commercial investors whom he sought to attract to Morocco. Lyautey's close friends, the international banking team of the Lazard Frères, found a warm welcome. Prominent French industrialists like the Compagnie du Sebou and representatives of other major banks, most notably the Banque de Paris et des Pays-Bas, found no limits on their activities in Morocco—to the point of major financial scandals by the early 1920s.[124]

Vaillat endorsed the need for strict regulation and expert authority. He found these ideals exemplified not so much in Lyautey's "political mimetics" as in

Prost's dictatorial control over the colonial environment.[125] But he was wrong to pose the two approaches as oppositional. If anything, the resident-general proved quite astute about the techniques for legitimating the control that Prost needed to carry out his plans. Lyautey even sought to justify the system in terms of Quranic law, where "the general interest is higher than individual interest. The construction and enlargement of streets being an unquestionable public good, anyone owning land or a building where a public road is planned must sell."[126]

At first glance, this might seem to us more like a variation of the familiar power of eminent domain. Yet, as Abu-Lughod astutely demonstrates, the right of ownership was determined only by French title, and appeals could be heard only in the French courts. One telling example she cites is the expropriation and demolition of Moroccan shops, houses, and the *qaysariya* (cloth market) for the projected Boulevard du IVe Zouaves in Casablanca, when Lyautey insisted that the thoroughfare be immediately completed in the opening months of 1922, in time for President Millerand's first state visit (fig. 82). The buildings were cleared and within three months the boulevard—decked with curbs, sidewalks, and an esplanade planted with an *allée* of palms—was ready.[127] Clearly, if French interests were at stake, the expropriation system could ruthlessly deny Moroccan claims to title and just indemnities in the *villes nouvelles*.

In 1925 Lyautey was called back to France after he failed to subdue the rebellion in the Rif led by Abd-el-Krim. Foreign ownership of land now increased dramatically, soon far exceeding that of the Moroccans in both acreage and value. The property system was modified "in a very modern spirit," according to Sablayrolles: a syndicate could be set up simply because "the execution of work would procure a notable increase in value for the buildings in question."[128] In 1927, new *dahirs* decreed that French settlement itself was one of the principal "public purposes" which justified expropriating land from Moroccans.[129]

Although the disparity in ownership was not so great in the first decade of colonization, the techniques do date from this epoch. The system for colonial acquisition of land, drawn up in 1913 by Lyautey, de Tarde, and de Tarde's associate, Henri de la Casinière, formed the legal structure which allowed Europeans to buy land cheaply and to profit from it quickly. This did not come as a surprise to the professional urbanists. Now working in France, Prost straightforwardly told one audience that careful zoning was designed to prevent declines in property values.[130]

Lyautey's entourage of urban designers and legal advisors described their goals and methods quite clearly. Neither formal strategies nor long-range goals applied only to colonial settings, however. At many levels, we can also recognize Prost's implicit references to French cities, specifically to their commercial cen-

FIGURE 82. *Boulevard du IVe Zouaves, Casablanca, c. 1925. From Vaillat*, Le Visage français.

ters and the fortifications zone surrounding Paris. This was an area he had studied with the Musée Social, where he would later, in 1934, propose the basis for
a regional plan encompassing parks and parkways, preservation of natural and
historic sites, and subsidized housing.

In his Moroccan version of the *"fortif"* zone, separation between the medina
and the *ville nouvelle* culminated in a district of *non edificandi* where all construction was prohibited. The method and scale varied from one city to another.
Fez, Marrakesh, and Meknes exemplified Prost's vision, with greenbelts ranging
from two to three kilometers abutting the walls of the medina, reinforced by
geological barriers like the ravines of Meknes or the steep hills of Fez. In Rabat
and Casablanca, European construction before Prost's arrival precluded this
strategy, and he resigned himself to thoroughfares, roughly 250 meters wide,
augmented by large public parks. The open zones of *non edificandi* had clear
aesthetic and social purposes, marking the distinctions between the two parts of
a city, setting off two scales of construction, two cultures, and two periods of
history—at least in the eyes of the French. The term *cordon sanitaire* suggests
the health precautions inherent in this familiar colonial policy of separation. In

FIGURE 83. *Bab el'Alu gate ("Gate of the Winds") in the twelfth-century Almohad wall of Rabat, enlarged with traffic viaducts. From Henri Terrasse*, L'Art hispano-mauresque, *v. 2, 1930.*

an off-guard moment Prost once acknowledged that the no-man's-land existed as well "for military reasons," allowing the rapid mobilization of French troops in the event of violence.[131] Prost had absorbed all the implications of Haussmann's boulevards.

The ramparts and monumental gates of the medinas often remained, rendered more decorative than functional. A notable case is the Bab er Rouah in Rabat, a gate with delicate floral relief in the late-twelfth-century wall; the three domed chambers adjoining the original gate became a small museum. Three arched entries were then cut through here and at Rabat's Bab el'Alu gate, facilitating traffic along the Avenue de la Victoire, the broad, paved coastal road. Incoming vehicles from Casablanca now had a dramatic view of the city, comparable to the visual impact of the Arc de Triomphe straddling the Champs-Elysées. (fig. 83). Elsewhere, too, the French administration maintained historic walls, as much for aesthetic continuity as for the perceived protection of those *outside* the medina. In Fez, for instance, soon after his arrival, Lyautey ordered the Bab Boujeloud gate cut into the reinforced medina wall, in order to frame a splendid view of the minaret and medersa.[132]

Lyautey and his entourage claimed that their approach to urban design would distinguish between two cultures without resorting to discrimination. By

FIGURE 84. *Street in the Jewish* mellah *of Fez. From Vaillat,* Le Visage français.

and large their view of cultural difference and separation derived from a pater-
nalist conception, rather than ideas of contamination. In fact, the system drew
upon certain urban precedents in the area, for separation of foreigners had ancient roots in North Africa, reaching back to Greek and Egyptian towns, to
medieval Muslim *funduq* (hotel-warehouses) for Christians, and the still extant
mellahs for Jews. (Distinct from the medina, the *mellah* had straight, parallel
streets ending in gates that had, until recently, been closed at night) (fig. 84).
The French even asserted proudly that their urban policies gave the Moroccan
Jews, for thousands of years restricted to the *mellahs*, much greater residential
and economic mobility.[133] Nor was the housing of Islamic Moroccans of a uniform quality within the traditional medinas. The population typically split into
two divisions: one wealthier and more urban, the other poorer residents with
rural roots.[134]

The French extended existing geographical and social divisions to an elaborate interplay of spatial and architectural distinctions, all the while paying
homage to the indigenous cultures they had isolated. Officials went to great
length to insist that this system did not constitute racial segregation—a colonial
policy for which they harshly criticized the British. Even years later Prost would
argue that "it was never in the Resident-General's mind to prevent natives from
living in the European new towns if they would adapt to our customs. It was not
a matter of *segregation*."[135] The customs to which Prost referred included both

FIGURE 85. *House for the vizier El-Mokri in the French district of Anfa in Casablanca, by Maurius Boyer, 1929. From Cahiers nord-africains, 1929. Courtesy of the Bibliothèque Nationale, Paris.*

formal and social codes in the *villes nouvelles*; in addition, the cost of land and minimum size of dwellings in the villa districts made these inaccessible to all but the elite of Moroccan society. Among this group, several tens of thousands of Jews and Muslims chose to live in the European districts by the late 1920s, usually in villas that combined elements of the traditional *menzeh* (a pavilion with central courtyard) and the modern Western dwelling (fig. 85).[136]

Constraints pertained as well to Europeans. Lyautey's notes show his specific efforts to prevent them from living in the medinas through short-term leases for foreigners, the prohibition of all industry, and the curtailment of automobiles. Despite these efforts—or, more precisely, because of the setting they helped pre-serve—many artists and writers would continue to reside in Rabat's *casbah* and other similar enclaves, fascinated by their beauty and exoticism. They were soon joined by numerous European workers, *petit-blancs* who found themselves un-able to afford rents in the *villes nouvelles*.[137]

In any case, Lyautey never legally imposed restrictions by race or nationality in either part of his dual city. He did not actually establish a policy of apart-heid.[138] This was a more subtle cultural system which generated, but did not enact, economic and racial imbalances. That system has become the prevailing mode in modern cities, where liberal opinion shuns overt inequities and official segregation laws. Cultural and aesthetic differences became the focus of benign protection, often well-meaning and even positive in certain respects. One must acknowledge the potentially insidious implications of such efforts. The very concept of preserving cultural communities is so positive that it is difficult to recognize the prevailing pattern of injustices which often overlap with cultural preferences.

In all these ways Prost's first colonial master plan represented a modernist evocation of the efficient, well-organized metropolis. He envisioned urban design that would facilitate growth, commerce, and industry while providing pleasant residential and recreational areas—some in urban high-rises but most in the villas of the peripheral "garden cities"—as respites from the bustling workplaces. Solely through architectural specifications, each enclave would be implicitly segregated by race, ethnicity, and even by class among the Europeans.[139] As in other modern capitals, poverty was by and large hidden away, though manual workers were always accessible. Years later, preparing a course on urban design for the Institut d'Urbanisme in Paris, Prost identified the issues he had concentrated on in Morocco, calling his list the basis for planning a modern city anywhere: "Housing, traffic, work, health, and aesthetics."[140] He stressed the need to put sociological and technical considerations on a par with those of aesthetics, often using aesthetics to accomplish social goals, or using economic and cultural preferences to assure the formal pattern he wanted.

Prost succumbed to the tendency of many modern urbanists who believe that they have solved complex problems simply by identifying them, then sheltering a small group of prominent people from the difficulties. A case in point is his belief that he would be able to control land speculation and visual disorder, even in Casablanca. Instead, as soon as the general lines of the master plan became known, even for a single district, those with money bought up land along the newly designated boulevards. Small investors formed consortiums to buy land in the less expensive suburbs. Many speculators then held back from building, hoping to recoup higher profits in the future with open land on which to build, creating what André Adam calls "a no-man's-land of speculation" in the midst of highly developed areas.[141] This economic climate intensified the housing crisis for both European and Moroccan workers as new residents poured into Casablanca, causing rents to soar. As Brian Brace Taylor sums up the planners' relation to rampant speculation and unregulated growth:

[They] were at least *naive* in believing that technical expertise and aesthetic good taste could be sufficiently effective antidotes. Their naiveté is to be suspected when they returned to Europe to apply the same tactics such as "freezing" building heights in Paris suburbs, and creating entire new towns, segregated from existing centers.[142]

We should take care not to perpetuate that naivieté by restricting our analysis to purely formal considerations.

Aesthetic strategies, in and of themselves, could not rationalize and contain private development practices. Formal analyses of the commercial streets of Casablanca bear this out. In detail and overall pattern, they ultimately fall short of the public control to which Prost aspired. After World War I, for example, many buildings in the center city had only a provisional roofline at the fourth story, anticipating the amendments in 1923 that would allow for much taller buildings. Along certain principal thoroughfares such as the Boulevard de la Gare, the foundations were intentionally suitable for a minimum of six stories. Design anticipated future changes based on increases in the value of land and the loosening of architectural controls.

Efforts to assure visual harmony proved most effective on state-owned land set aside for public buildings, most notably the Administrative Quarter in Rabat and Casablanca's Place Lyautey. But here, too, the toll for the Moroccans must be taken into account. For example, the dimensions of the Place de France were substantially increased in 1927 through the destruction of the existing medina walls, adjacent *suqs* (markets), and a large portion of the *mellah* (fig. 86).[143] Rather than containing laissez-faire economic policies, Prost's guidelines and master plan served primarily to assure the financial gains of major landowners in the commercial center, while further undermining the Moroccans' access to land that had once been theirs.

Technically and legally, Lyautey did establish the infrastructure for a modern state in Morocco. Most improvements primarily benefited French residents, and if certain changes did serve Moroccans, too, the costs were high at every level. Using the benefits tax, the government established the first public garbage collection throughout the larger cities (fig. 87). Engineers restored the existing urban sewer network in several medinas and added to them considerably—primarily in the *villes nouvelles*.[144] (The "traditional" Moroccan practice of an open, recessed rain gutter in the middle of the street was retained in all non-European districts.) The public works service spent most of its effort and tax money constructing a half-million meters of paved city streets and five thousand kilometers of interurban routes during the first decade of the protectorate. This constituted nothing short of a revolution in transportation for a country where nineteenth-century visitors had remarked on the complete absence of roads or wheeled vehicles.[145] Obviously the network of streets and highways was intended

FIGURE 86. *Enlarged Place de France, Casablanca, 1928. Compare with figures 35 and 52. From* Le Monde colonial illustré, *1929.*

LA FRANCE AU MAROC — Enlèvement des cadavres dans les rues de Casablanca

FIGURE 87. *Postcard showing "La France au Maroc," represented by the collection of cadavers from the streets as a public health benefit, c. 1913.*

to facilitate the movement of raw materials, commercial goods, workers, and, if necessary, troops. It was a system based, in other words, on economic growth and stability to benefit European investors.

Pressure on the Medinas

While all French commentators eagerly awaited French migration to Morocco, both permanent and temporary, none of them anticipated the exponential expansion of the indigenous Arab population in the cities. The number of European residents did increase substantially—in Casablanca, for example, from 1,000 in 1907 to 20,000 in 1917 and 35,000 in 1926—but land had been set aside in the *villes nouvelles* to meet most of their housing needs, an amount more than twenty times that of the medina.[146] The Moroccan population during that same time went from 24,000 to 39,000 and then to 72,000 in 1926—almost tripling in just under twenty years—with virtually no space allocated for this influx.[147] The de facto enclosure of tribal farming and herding lands for French agricultural and mining interests intensified the shift toward the cities, as did pressure on merchants in small inland towns who now had to compete with stores selling Western goods. Urban wage-labor became imperative for many once self-sufficient families.

Given the expectation that much of the construction work, industrial labor, and domestic labor for Europeans would fall to the colonized populations, it is surprising that the French administrators did not adequately plan for this shift. In part the insensitivity derived from a legitimate esteem for the traditions of indigenous housing. The geographer Augustin Bernard wrote that "social transformation cannot be rushed by imposing new housing before people are ready. Houses are a natural, evolutionary, spontaneous expression of a way of life."[148] This seeming appreciation of difference did not protect that way of life; it only justified the colonial reticence in providing sufficient new housing for the thousands of Moroccans moving into the cities. When Prost began to realize what was happening, he still failed to comprehend the true complexities. Instead he placed the blame on the automobile and the appeal it held for "natives":

> From the farthest mountains and deserts, from the most inaccessible villages, the native leaves his indigenous home with all his family, amused by these means of transportation we have just given him, attracted by the great cities, especially in North Africa.[149]

His analysis failed to grasp what kinds of pressures forced people to move, or indeed, what benefits were available to which groups. Like many urban planners in complex situations, Prost had identified a problem without recognizing that his professional actions had helped create it.

Plans for the *villes nouvelles* had in every case encircled the medinas with European development, and Lyautey's principle of separation by and large held firm. As a consequence, overcrowding in the medinas became a major problem. Bourgeois houses were subdivided into one-room apartments; soon courtyards and rooftops were rented out and built upon, intensifying the congestion. Even in Salé, which had retained a slower provincial charm across the river from the *ville nouvelle* of Rabat, all available open space had been given over to housing by the 1920s, including cemeteries and courtyards.[150] The regulations of the Fine-Arts Bureau under Borély, while in part an acknowledgment of this problem, could do little to stop necessary but illegal building by the Moroccans.

Bidonvilles—illegal encampments of self-built shanties in tin, scrap wood, and other industrial refuse—appeared as early as 1907, when European pressure on space and the availability of discarded European supplies began to change the appearance of towns like Casablanca.[151] In 1912 the industrial town of Port Lyautey, created virtually *de novo* by military engineers alongside the tiny coastal *casbah* of Kenitra, seems to have had the first officially recorded bidonville in Morocco, where Arab workers constructing European houses and workplaces put together impromptu shelters for their own families.[152] Even before the 1914 plan for Casablanca had been approved, the bidonville of Derb Rhallet extended some two kilometers to the south of the city, in an area Prost had designated for future European settlement. In 1920 construction workers putting in an electrical plant at the quarries of Carrières Centrales on the outskirts of Casablanca built makeshift shacks with leftover construction materials (fig. 88). *Karyân*, the Moroccan word for "bidonville," refers to those quarries, although the rural term *doar* is used in Rabat.[153] Rabat's first notice of clandestine bidonvilles came in 1921 when the city tore down housing on land set aside for European residences (the Orantines and Océan districts) and then allowed two official bidonvilles to proceed at Douar Doum (on the pasha's land) and Douar Debbagh (on the oceanfront route to Casablanca.[154]

Families in an underdeveloped economy usually make do, not only for income but even for the bare minimum of shelter, with only marginal assistance from the developed world's economy. That help includes industrial refuse, but little in the way of public policy or financial assistance. At this level, the housing problem had a basis in class as much as race. The same pressures affected the poorer members of the European working class in Morocco, especially Portuguese and Spanish laborers, many of whom found themselves living in bidonvilles alongside the Moroccans in the early 1920s.[155]

Fifteen years later, at the 1931 International Congress on Colonial Urbanism, Prost would declare the bidonvilles to be the gravest problem facing colonial planners. Having left Morocco eight years earlier to undertake a regional plan for the Var, he still saw resonances between the urban problems of France and those of the colonies. How, he wondered, could one build new cities for these "brave but poor" newcomers, "without increasing their costs of living and their salaries to a point where this abundant but inexperienced labor force would become unusable"?[156]

The only solution, he had long ago realized, was to go outside the housing market. Prost had come up with several possible tactics in his efforts "to rehouse this labor force in good conditions of moral and physical hygiene by creating new native districts."[157] In 1916 he first encouraged industrialists to subsidize "garden-suburbs" for their workers. While the Société des Chaux et Ciments and the Compagnie des Phosphates did begin such settlements, the program had little effect (fig. 89). The protectorate did not initiate its own public housing until the late 1930s, when Marchisio built the massive complex of Aïn Chok

FIGURE 88. *A bidonville outside Casablanca, c. 1930. Postcard.*

FIGURE 89. *Housing for the Compagnie des Phosphates, Kouribga, by Edmund Brion,*
1926–30. From L'Architecture d'aujourd'hui, *1945.*

outside Casablanca (fig. 90), its severe cubist forms giving the most abstract
references to traditional Moroccan housing prototypes.

Prost's other approach did not serve a sizable Moroccan population, but it
received considerable attention from visitors to Morocco. In 1916 a consortium
of French, Jewish, and Arab benefactors first put forward the idea of controlled
rents in a government-sponsored project to be built on land owned by the habous
(*ḥubus* in Arabic, an Islamic religious foundation). The evolution of this scheme
shows the intricacy of colonial cultural politics and is therefore worth explaining
in some detail. When a wealthy Moroccan Jew offered to give the Casablanca
habous a large tract of land to help alleviate the housing crisis, its director asked
the sultan to serve as an intermediary, for the habous could not accept a gift

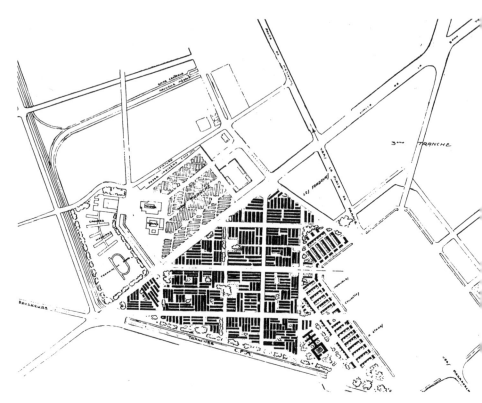

FIGURE 90. *The "model city" of Aïn Chok, outside Casablanca, by Antoine Marchisio for the Office Chérifien de l'Habitat, 1938. From* L'Architecture française, *1946.*

directly from a Jew. Moulay Youssef agreed; he had his own interests to serve, for he wanted a new palace in Casablanca.

One-quarter of the land was then deeded to the protectorate, plus another parcel sold at a reduced price, together adding up to nine hectares. The targeted group was not Moroccan workers, however, but Arab functionaries and bourgeois merchants, especially newcomers from Fez.[158] The sultan then set aside three-quarters of the gift of land for his palace, gardens, and housing for his retinue—much of this built with French support.

Prost and his staff liked the idea so much that they soon claimed land from the habous in Rabat and Meknes, creating similar districts, again for bourgeois Arabs and Jews. These areas, too, are still called habous districts, or *Derb el-Hubus* in Arabic. In each case the French architects in Prost's service took on the task of designing the streets, houses, and public buildings. They sought an aesthetic that would harmonize with the old medinas, even though the land was not continuous. In certain ways, the habous districts also followed modern design concerns, providing electricity, central heating, and water for individual dwellings. By and large, hygiene was superior to what existed in the older medinas, especially as they had become more overcrowded. Cars were allowed only on the wider commercial thoroughfares, in order to preserve the historic feeling of the side streets, although public transit did connect this area to the old medina and the central business district.

Site plan and architecture referred to traditional principles of Moroccan design and the established mores of Moroccan urban life, at least as far as they were understood by the French architects (fig. 91, 92). All the same, most Moroccan families did prefer a setting familiar to them. For instance, the seclusion of women in courtyards and the shielding of family life from the street largely determined the arrangement of houses in existing Islamic towns and cities. "From one house it is impossible to look into another," explained Albert Laprade, the chief designer of the Casablanca habous district in 1918. (When he was called to Rabat to design Lyautey's residence, Cadet and Brion took over for the final stages.) "On a given street the doorways of houses never face one another. Everything has been put together in an effort to respect the taste for mystery with which each Muslim envelopes his private life."[159]

Each habous district was conceived as a synthetic quarter (humā) which could meet all the traditional needs of the inhabitants. Casablanca's contained a funduq, a hamman, suqs, a qaysariya, public bread-ovens, both Quranic and Western schools, and three mosques. The suqs provided premises for over 150 commercial establishments, as well as open space for acrobats, magicians, storytellers, and snake-charmers. To a remarkable degree, especially for a twentieth-century effort to recapture the past, these districts did sustain the social and commercial life destined to take place in a true ethnic neighborhood.

The designers' prime concern, all the same, had been aesthetic: the romantic evocation of another typology for streets, shops, and houses, self-consciously distilled and artfully rendered by Western architects. Rabat's habous district was built in 1923, following the designs of Pierre Michaud in collaboration with Cadet and Brion. They evoked the local vernacular with archways over an irregular maze of narrow streets, the plain white facades contrasting with doorways brightly painted and studded with large handmade nails (fig. 93). Laprade had filled his sketchbooks with measured drawing and quick croquis of the "poor dwellings of Rabat and Salé" in preparation for the project in Casablanca. "Every house was designed with love," he wrote. "We taxed our ingenuity to create the maximum impression of serendipity, so dear to the Muslim."[160]

Laprade's oversimplified generalization about Islamic aesthetics suggests a darker side to the apparent cultural sensitivity, quite similar to the academic

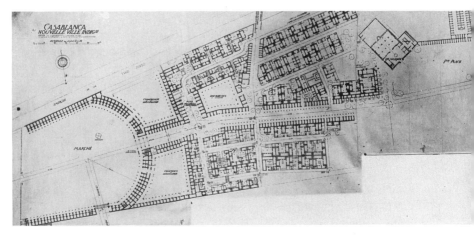

FIGURE 91. *Plan of the "new medina" or habous district in Casablanca, by Albert Laprade, 1918.* From L'Architecture d'aujourd'hui, 1936.

FIGURE 92. *View of the habous district, Casablanca, by Albert Laprade with Cadet & Brion, 1918–30.* From Vaillat, Le Visage français.

prejudices and policies Edward Said has labeled "Orientalism."[161] As a design, this district was a Western stage-setting for Moroccan life, a Disneyland world. It evoked the supposed harmonies of a traditional way of life that, in the Westerner's eyes, had not changed over time.

If the architects fell prey to the desire for stopping time and history that is always implicit in a preservation campaign, the rationale goes deeper than their own tendency to romanticize. Colonialism could not provide for innovation or progress in the Moroccan districts; this prospect the French had reserved for themselves. Aesthetic predilections again had a definite political aspect. Design decisions froze development for the Moroccans, both politically and economically, at an archaic level of the picturesque, in sharp contrast to the visible advances and opportunities available to Europeans. In part for these very reasons, conscious and unconscious, the habous districts, especially that of Casablanca, won abundant praise from European visitors. Vaillat called them "not a copy, nor a pastiche more or less adroit, but a meditation on the part of European artists savoring the theme of oriental life." [162]

The essence of the French efforts to win over both the Moroccans and their own countrymen at home relied on a concept of the city. In a very modern sense, that concept accepted the simultaneity of multiple urbanistic images, coexisting in apparent harmony, offering different experiences, embellishing distinct settings, providing the milieu for unique cultures to grow and coexist. Commen-

FIGURE 93.   *View of the habous district, Rabat, by Cadet & Brion with Pierre Michaud, 1923. From Vaillat,* Le Visage français.

tators described urban civility and respect as the cornerstones of the associationist policy. Sablayrolles's treatise on protectorate legislation made just such a point:

> "Urbanity," as the name implies, is an urbane quality; it consists in the discipline of words and gestures, a sort of politeness which one acquires in a city and which facilitates everyday relations between the people who mill around and group together at each moment of the day. If we transpose this quality into the material realm we have "Urbanism," which obliges that things—as urbanity obliges persons—make reciprocal concessions: houses, buildings, monuments, streets, open spaces, [all are made to be civil]. [163]

It is undeniable to us today, as it was to most Moroccans at the time, that the urbane arena of these cities included less gracious realities. Within these spaces one culture overwhelmingly dominated the others. The French urbanists explored an aesthetic of pluralism, providing an important alternative to the Corbusian ideal of a universal standard for beauty and human development. Yet seldom are all cultures equal in such artificially constructed settings, striving to tout their pluralistic diversity. The multiplicity of urban spaces in colonial Morocco revealed and perpetuated a pervasive domination by one group, not an equal coexistence.

The protectorate of Morocco, especially under Lyautey, undertook a conscious effort to instill a new approach in urbanism and in colonization. As Sablayrolles described the relationship:

> It seems that France . . . is sending the best of her pioneers to these exotic shores, to carry out experiments there. These experiments make tangible the success of the French enterprises in Morocco. [164]

The Moroccan cities proved to be more complex environments than the early colonial urbanists had anticipated. Their efforts to harmonize modernization and tradition, while commendable and visually impressive, could not cover over inherent problems.

The challenge came from two quite different sources. At an aesthetic level, other European architects attacked the design philosophy of the 1910s and 1920s for its sentimentality, lavishness, and tendency toward exaggerated historicism. At a political level, the Moroccans themselves refused to accept the premise of the protectorate's colonial urbanism: the assertion that the dual system of design protected everyone's best interests. While we can now debate the aesthetic merits of the towns and buildings constructed during this epoch, the political issue is irrefutable.

4

INDOCHINA:
THE FOLLY
OF GRANDEUR

A SMUG SELF-ASSURANCE prevailed among those late-nineteenth-century Frenchmen who, looking around at Saigon or Hanoi, could feel they had successfully replicated the urbane beauty of cities in their homeland (fig. 94). The traveler Gaston Bonnefont, visiting Saigon in the 1880s, found "well laid-out streets, planted with trees and aligned with pretty houses, handsome public buildings, commodious docks, a powerful arsenal, a governmental palace that would not be out of place across from the Louvre." Equally French, he noted with amusement, was "a large hospital that is always full, and a large cathedral that is always empty."[1] Alfred de Pouvourville, a novelist and respected commentator on southeast Asia, glowingly described Hanoi only a few years later, soon after the French had taken full control of the city in 1888. He especially praised the European district growing up south of the Petit Lac, "now featuring broad, well-cut boulevards, and the execution of recent projects by the municipality which makes this, without doubt, the most beautiful city of the Far East"[2] (fig. 95).[2] Such magnificence in urban design seemed, indeed, to embody France's cultural superiority and a strong connection to the prestige of Paris itself.

But others considered architectural display only an embarrassing pomposity. The *anciens* who had lived in Saigon from its early, quite primitive days as a French possession often viewed with hostility the indulgent extravagance which soon dominated there.[3] De Pouvourville, charmed by the overall impression of Hanoi, nonetheless disdained the cathedral (1888), built on the ruins of the demolished Bao Thein pagoda, with its alternating bands of dull black and white stone (fig. 96), as "a masterpiece of grandeur and ugliness."[4] Lyautey, describing Saigon to his sister in 1894, ridiculed "all this cardboard decoration."[5]

161

FIGURE 94. *Quai de Commerce, Saigon, c. 1870. Courtesy of the Fonds
Documentaire, Asie de Sud-est et le Monde Indonesien (ASEMI).*

By the early 1900s this critical view had become the dominant perspective. The urban architecture of Indochina represented extravagance and the loss of a sense of proportion rather than a proud symbol of French elegance. One member of the French Academy, writing in 1910, lambasted the Hanoi Opera House as "a pretentious caricature" of the Paris Opéra (fig. 97). Had it been completed as originally planned in 1886, the building would have seated at one time the entire European population of the city. "It is, moreover, a troubling symbol . . . where all our faults come together: love of pleasure, of artifice, of the artificial, unreflective enthusiasm, and a careless lack of foresight."[6] The taste for extravagance which characterized both Hanoi and Saigon now came to seem vainglorious, and their late-nineteenth-century architecture earned the derogatory appellation *"la folie des grandeurs."*[7]

Compared with the bombastic self-aggrandizement so evident in the first phases of French city-building in Indochina, the moralistic self-criticism of the early-twentieth century points out fundamental shifts in colonial urban policies and prevailing tastes. We see, as well, the legacies of each country's distinct history, both before and under colonial domination. While Morocco embodied

FIGURE 95. *Grands Magasins Réunis on the Rue Paul Bert (formerly the Street of the Inlayers) in the French Quarter of Hanoi, just south of the Petit Lac (Hoan Kiem Ho), c. 1910. Courtesy of the Musée de l'Homme, Paris.*

the associationist policies of Lyautey from the very start of the protectorate, Indochina had suffered for decades from the myriad problems of an assimilationist policy. The French slowly assembled this colony over a thirty-year period (see fig. 148). Three provinces of Cochinchina (Nam Bo) nearest Saigon came first, in 1862, then the other provinces in the south of what had been the ancient Empire of Vietnam, followed in 1885 by Tonkin (Bac Bo, the northern part of Vietnam), Annam (Trung Bo) in the center, then the separate kingdoms of Cambodia and Laos—each quite distinct in terms of population, culture, and history.[8] The French brought all these territories together under the Indochinese Federation of 1893, while maintaining different military and political conditions of rule in each of the five "states."

The vulnerability and the very artificiality of French authority in Indochina encouraged a ruthless colonial policy—and strong resistance. From the start of

FIGURE 96. *Hanoi Cathedral, 1888. Postcard.*

the French presence, demonstrations and acts of violence by highly educated nationalist groups in the cities, together with marauding anti-French "pirates" along the borders, continually challenged colonial control. The government also had to contend with volatile Frenchmen who demanded a different kind of autonomy. Commercial interests based in Saigon (most notably the Banque de l'Indochine, established in 1875, and gradually other less potent allies, too) resisted all efforts on the part of the central political authority to direct policy, especially in Cochinchina, where they managed to control affairs virtually on their own terms for almost thirty years.

FIGURE 97. *Hanoi Opera House and Municipal Theatre, 1900. From Eugène Teston and Maurice Percheron*, L'Indochine moderne, 1931.

Nor was support at home unfailing. From the initial intervention in 1858, many French citizens has questioned the wisdom of maintaining this expensive and often explosive colony. The shift from military to civilian government in 1879, with the creation of the Third Republic, did not bring a clear sense of purpose or even geographical limits to this distant national endeavor. Jules Ferry, who had come to be known as "Ferry le Tonkinois," lost his seat in Parliament for defending the invasion of Tonkin in 1885. In response to this ambivalence at home, the military officers stationed in Indochina often adopted a policy of *le fait accompli*, acting without authorization from Paris and then demanding official endorsement for the accomplished fact. They recognized correctly that national pride would usually back their conquests in the end.[9]

An administrative quagmire seemed to hamper all efforts to govern the colony in an intelligent manner throughout the history of French domination. If Indochina's problems proved even more exasperating than those of Third-Republic France, the two situations were quite similar in their cultural, economic, and political stalemates. The cultural and linguistic diversity of the regions united in the Indochinese Federation seemed to confound most French functionaries—when they paid these traditions any mind at all. The French banks and the Chamber of Commerce in Saigon believed they should have the upper hand in determining governmental policy, or at least the right to prevent Paris and the colonial government from interfering in the *colons'* ability to exploit the colony as they wished. Even as French economic investments flourished after 1922, internal political tension continued to block most efforts at social or political reform, such that the lot of Vietnamese peasants and workers worsened precipitously under French domination.

There was little opportunity for a coordinated, long-term policy. During the forty years between 1886 and 1926 Paris appointed no fewer than fifty-two different governments for Indochina, including both regular and interim governors.[10] In Indochina even more than in metropolitan France, the instability and weakness of political authority encouraged grandiose and vain acts of assertiveness. Civic architecture tried to convey the impression of authority and continuity where they by no means existed.

In 1901 Eugène Jung, the vice-resident of Tonkin, complained about the underlying chaos in the colony. "Everywhere there is disarray," declared a character in his novel, *La Vie européene au Tonkin*, "an incoherence of orders, the lack of any guiding idea that can direct administrators and regularize the movement of the city."[11] Twenty years later, as the first director of urbanism for Indochina, Ernest Hébrard also deplored the physical manifestation of this deepseated disorder, together with the means most often used to correct it: the monotonous and inefficient street grids laid out by surveyors or military engineers, relieved only by monumental but poorly sited public buildings and statues.[12] To grasp fully the innovations and constraints of twentieth-century urbanism in Indochina after the arrival of Hébrard in 1921, we need to see in more detail what these cities had been like before the French arrived.

From Citadels to Cultural Capitals

Although Vietnam and especially Cambodia possessed majestic religious and imperial complexes from centuries ago, these were not predominantly urban civilizations. Most of the population lived a rural existence, as it does today. Regional differences were considerable, with the well-established settlements and local social services concentrated in the northern Red River delta of Tonkin. Traditional Vietnamese settlements were, in fact, collections of small and relatively closed communities, often with a specialized trade. Each village was its own small republic, with shrines to the village dieties and much of the land owned and worked communally.

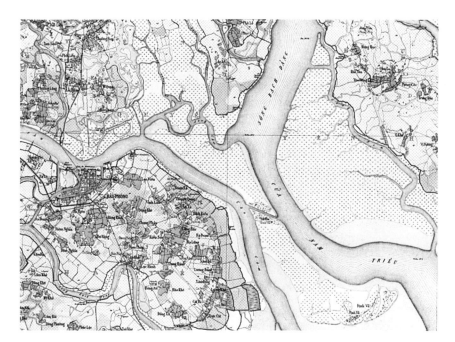

FIGURE 98. *Map of the citadel town* (thành-pho) *of Haiphong with surrounding* thi-trân, *1910. Library of Congress.*

Two basic types and morphologies of villages had first emerged in the seventeenth century: the *thi-trân* or market village had only narrow paths crossing a principal street, with bamboo palings at each end of the main axial thoroughfare and an open area all around, providing some security from marauders and wild beasts (figs. 98, 99). Much less vulnerable was the *thành-pho* or citadel, its streets wider and often arranged in a grid, protected all along its regular periphery by walls and moats, whose orientation and proportions were decided by royal geomancers (fig. 100). As Vu Quoc Thuc explains, "between these two and a 'city' [in the French sense of the word] there is a difference in nature and not just a difference in degree."[13] Without idealizing their collective life—we can say that the village, like the family, did provide a fundamental bond within Vietnamese society.

The French invaded Cochinchina in 1859, soon capturing Saigon's citadel and withstanding a major Annamite offensive at the nearby fortified camp of Ki-hoa the following year. In the process, their army destroyed large parts of the forty Vietnamese villages along the Saigon River and the two creeks (*arroyos*) which made up the civilian area surrounding the vast citadel. This fortress was a somewhat smaller modification of a huge Vauban-inspired citadel built for the

FIGURE 99.   Thi-trân *format of a gated street in Hanoi, c. 1880. From Henri Russier,*
L'Indochine française, *1931.*

future emperor, Gia Long, in 1790, the work of the French engineers Olivier
de Puymanel and T. Brun.[14] The citadel, renamed Fort Neuf, was soon repaired
and expanded, its new prefabricated barracks serving as public buildings and
residences for the nascent French colony (fig. 101).

For several years only crude wooden cottages appeared outside the citadel,
providing cafés, homes, or business offices for Europeans (fig. 102). This gave
Saigon more the appearance of "a temporary camp . . . in the Wild West,"
commented one visitor, than of a fledgling French capital.[15] Nonetheless a military engineer, Colonel Coffyn, envisioned a plan in 1861, rather crude in form
but majestic in scale, for a future metropolis of 2,500 hectares and half a million
people (fig. 103). At the time, European residents numbered fewer than 600,
and the indigenous populations of Vietnamese and Chinese had not yet reached
50,000.[16] From this projection, with its awkwardness and its grandiose vision of
the future, would emerge the spirit, if not the actual physical form, of the future
French metropolis.

Admiral Bonnard, head of the military government, used Coffyn's sketch as
the basis for early platting of lots, anticipating a major port along the Saigon
River (with access to the broad Mekong Delta) that he hoped would rival Hong
Kong and Singapore, as well as a commercial and governmental complex near
the citadel area (fig. 104). Bonnard did substitute a simple grid plan for Coffyn's
more irregular street system, with one radial *rond-point* at the Quai de Com-

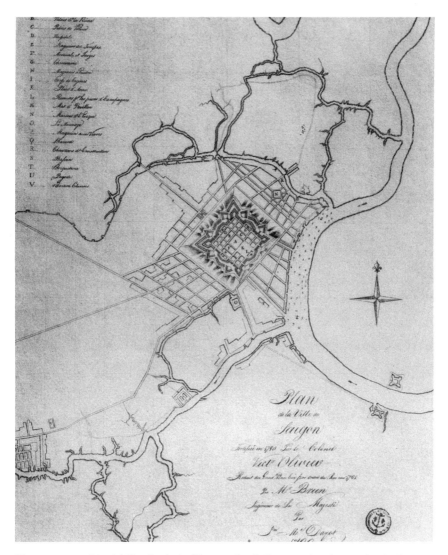

FIGURE 100. *Citadel* (thành-pho) *of Saigon, by de Puymanel and Brun for the future Emperor Gia Long, 1790. From Paul Boudet and André Masson*, Iconographie historique de l'Indochine française, *1931.*

merce. From this *place*, the oldest street in French Saigon, the Rue Catinet (Dong Khoi today) would extend into the future commercial center.

During the early years the admiral and his successors purposely kept down land prices and promoted development far from the rebuilt Vietnamese villages and the adjacent Chinese town of Cholon, hoping an influx of French *colons*

FIGURE 101.   *French colonial barracks in Saigon, 1865. Courtesy of ASEMI.*

FIGURE 102.   *First café in Saigon, 1865. From Boudet and Masson,* Iconographie.

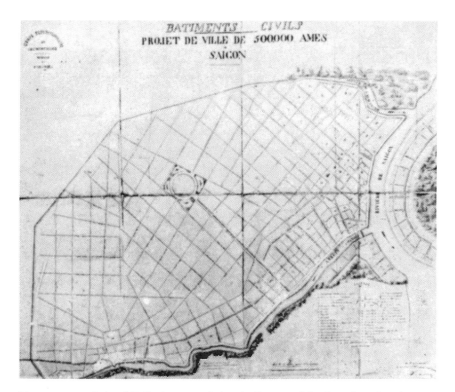

FIGURE 103. *Colonel Coffyn's proposed plan for Saigon, 1861. From Jean Bouchot,* Documents pour servir à l'histoire de Saigon, *1927.*

would assure continued support for the somewhat unpopular colony. An *arrêté* (decree) of 1864 interpreted the Vietnamese legal code to mean that most lands belonged to the emperor; acting on Tu Duc's behalf, the colonial government then asserted its right to sell or cede to Europeans both abandoned municipal land and rural property worked by tenant peasants.[17] Faced with a peasant rebellion to the north, the emperor had to accede to French demands. Court mandarins who had left their bureaucratic posts to protest the French takeover had destroyed many records, and the resulting confusion made it easy to disregard any assertions of previous title, even in lawsuits. Despite such efforts, few French settlers or investors were enticed to Cochinchina. Only after 1874 would the French begin to offer free concessions to Europeans, with the sole stipulation that they build a house and begin cultivation of adjacent land within three years.

By 1865 commerce at last began to develop, and security regulations forbade hunting tigers within the city. The precarious colony of Cochinchina now seemed sufficiently stable to merit serious urban design. New streets soon ran through the citadel, and parade grounds replaced the moats that once contained

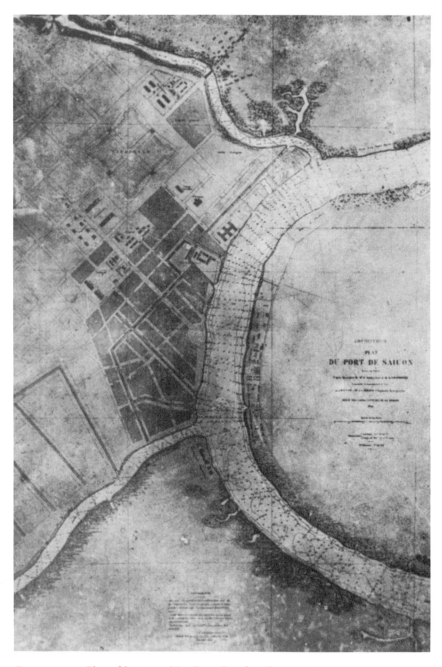

FIGURE 104. *Plan of Saigon, 1863. From Bouchot,* Documents.

172

FIGURE 105. *Plan of Saigon, 1878. The name of the Rue Impériale has been changed to the Boulevard Norodom. The palace of the governor-general stands in a large park at one end of that boulevard and the Botanical Garden at the other, facing the river. New York Public Library.*

the fort; the docks along the river banks were strengthened with new English equipment. Several hotels and restaurants, a central prison, and a state printing office proclaimed French priorities. Instead of simple numbers, the twenty main streets of Saigon received the names of illustrious French citizens, emblazoned on blue plaques.[18] At a rudimentary level, the enterprise paralleled the contemporary work of Haussmann, for the new streets evoked the state's military protection, its love of glory, and its modern commercial ambitions. Yet the configuration of Saigon's broad Rue Impériale, which overlay the former moats around the citadel, aligned rather awkwardly with the new streets (fig. 105). (Later the name was changed to Boulevard Norodom, honoring the Cambodian emperor who ceded his nation to France; it is now called Le Duan.) While the colony responded to the prevailing fashions in urban design from Paris, the military engineers could not replicate the elegant composition and majestic proportions of a European capital in this provincial setting.

173

As in Paris, landscape architecture was not neglected. A military engineer and veterinarian by the name of Alphonse Germain began work on a thirty-acre botanical garden facing the Arroyo de l'Avananche. A few years later, under the direction of a professional agronomist, J.-B. Louis Pierre, the site included elegant *allées*, an orchid garden, a zoo, and a music pavilion, across the *arroyo* from more functional experiments in industrial crops like sugar cane and jute (fig. 106). Replicating the exoticism of the eighteenth-century Jardin des Plantes, as well as Alphonse Alphand's more recent parks in Paris, Pierre could emulate Continental fashion while he probed the remunerative aspects of the colonial natural world. Almost a century later, the Botanical Garden, still a popular area for promenades, won praise as "a fortuitous juxtaposition of oriental picturesqueness and French method."[19] This orientalism had come indirectly, through the popularity of the so-called English-Chinese garden in Europe.

The first Beaux-Arts trained architect to work in Saigon, Georges Lhermite, arrived from Hong Kong on a lucrative retainer in 1866, invited to design two monumental buildings, the Cathedral of Notre-Dame and the palace of the governor-general. These would supplant the primitive structures built only a few years before. Coffyn had designed the first small wooden church to replace the

FIGURE 106. *Botanical Garden, Saigon. Nadal photograph from* Saigon-Cholon, *n.d.*

FIGURE 107. *Prefabricated admiral-general's palace, Saigon, 1862. From Boudet and Masson*, Iconographie.

converted pagoda that had originally served French Catholics in the city, as it had done for the sizeable number of Vietnamese converted by French missionaries before colonization; the original admiral-general's "palace" (fig. 107) had been a demountable wooden structure, three stories high, shipped over from Singapore.[20]

Squabbling and irresolution immediately came to the fore, a pattern that would continue through future generations of architects and governmental clients. Within a few days of his arrival, Lhermite submitted a design for an opulent baroque palace dominated by a majestic sweep of stairs, vaguely reminiscent of Versailles, set in a large formal garden. He found his proposal blocked by Paulin Vial, the first director of the Bureau of Governmental Buildings, who had been promised the commission. The fracas delayed construction, and Lhermite had already left the colony by the time the palace was finally completed in 1873, its effigies of Napoleon III now quite inappropriate (fig. 108).

The cathedral was postponed for almost another decade, awaiting a larger subvention, during which time mass was held in the vast *salle des fêtes* of Lhermite's palace for the governor. In the meanwhile, the government dropped Lhermite's design, although they retained the site he had proposed, a large oval *place* cut into the Boulevard Norodom. An international competition in 1875 awarded the commission to the Parisian architect Jules Bourard. When Notre-Dame was finally completed five years later, the French architectural press showed considerable interest in his work, vaguely Romanesque in its red-brick

FIGURE 108.   *The governor-general's palace, Saigon, by Georges Lhermite, 1873. From Albert de Pouvourville,* Histoire populaire des colonies française: L'Indochine, *1932.*

facade and granite base, with Gothic vaulting inside (fig. 109). No one acknowledged that the hot, humid climate of Saigon required better ventilation than this structure, more suited to northern France, could offer. Two spires were added in 1894, but not until 1942 would the French finally concede the need to pierce additional openings in the lateral chapels, following more or less the traditional Vietnamese practice for ventilating pagodas. [21]

Alfred Foulhoux became director of the Bureau of Governmental Buildings in 1875, replacing Vial, who was transferred to Hanoi. Among Foulhoux's many commissions, the Palace of Justice (1885), Customs House (1887), and the Palace of the Governor of Cochinchina (1890) still stand out (fig. 110). This last building (today the War Museum, often called the Palace of Gia-Long after the street it now faces, formerly the Rue Lagrandière) embodied the architectural sentiments of the period. For his sources Foulhoux looked to Claude Perrault's colonnade for the Louvre, a masterpiece of stately French classicism, designed in 1670 for Louis XIV. Appropriately enough, both palaces signaled a desire for absolute political power coupled with schemes for commercial expansion. Yet the Saigon palace had no planned relationship with the streets and buildings around it, only a small landscape garden.

FIGURE 109.   *Notre-Dame Cathedral, Saigon, by Jules Bourard, 1880. Courtesy of ASEMI.*

FIGURE 110. *Palace of the governor of Cochinchina, Saigon, by Alfred Foulhoux,
1890. From Pierre Gourou, L'Indochine, 1929.*

The long, arduous history of Saigon's Hôtel de Ville, like the more turbulent and mannerist idiom of its design (fig. 111), epitomizes the highly charged antagonisms of the epoch. The municipal council had first voted to build a city hall in 1871, hoping to replace the Chinese mansion they had been using for the past five years. The first stone had barely been laid, following the plans of the architect Pierre Codry, when the scheme was declared too costly. Not until 1898 would the new city hall, this one by Fernand Gardès, finally go into construction, and other delays obstructed completion for another ten years.[22]

The opulent baroque design resembled the overdecorated official elegance of the recent Hôtel de Ville in Paris, itself a caricature replica of the city hall burned down by Communards in 1871. Conflicts with the Parisian artist Antoine-Justin Ruffier, who designed the murals and sculptural ornament, aggravated the *colons'* frustration over the high costs. When finally completed, the building immediately came under attack in the local press as "grotesque," "a complete failure," and outright "bad taste."[23] (Even a later art-historical study of Saigon's major public monuments "scarcely dared interpret" Ruffier's writhing figures or Gardès's facade, "invaded by geometric and vegetal ornament").[24]

If the *colons* of Cochinchina expected glory in their monuments, they also wanted symbolic allegory they could comprehend. They abhorred Gardès's city hall but appreciated Foulhoux's governmental palace. Its elegant restraint and

FIGURE 111. *Hôtel de Ville, Saigon, by Fernand Gardès, 1908. Nadal photograph from* Saigon-Cholon.

figurative busts of the Republic inserted into Corinthian capitals and pediment seemed to evoke the "French order" which Perrault, among others, had once sought. Not incidentally, these references to a democratic republic, immediately recognizable to French residents, did not yet carry any political associations for Vietnamese inhabitants of the city, for French history classes in their schools omitted all mention, even iconographic, of the French Revolution.[25]

Ornate or restrained, nineteenth-century public buildings were architectural expressions of the assimilationist policy toward colonial cultures, asserting the universality of French concepts of formal beauty, just as the political system asserted the universal benefits of French economic growth and sovereignty. Sumptuousness that evoked French glory won support, while experiment with illegible symbolism did not. The worst architectural sin, however, was any intrusion of Indochinese architectural motifs. For the *colons* such designs seemed to be as an admission of their own nation's inadequacies, even a transgression against the sanctity of French culture. The result of such a merging of cultures, in architectural as in racial terms, was branded with the epithet *"métis."*[26]

Public works in Indochina showed the same grandiose vision, all too often exploitative, which characterized this colony. Governor-General Jean-Marie de Lanessan initiated a vast public works program in 1893, having secured a large state loan with overblown promises of future colonial prosperity. He focused on the outlying regions, only recently brought under French domination. Whereas de Lanessan's *Principes de colonisation* (1897) outlined a nascent associationist policy, this suggestion of cultural respect did not soften the imperative of French domination. Under de Lanessan the architect Eugène-Victor Fabré transformed Phnom Penh with a peripheral canal system, new streets, and French military installations. His alterations segregated the French population while adhering to the strict grid plan of the original Khmer palace complex.[27]

Even more important to de Lanessan's strategy were the fortified towns to the north, near China, where Gallieni and Lyautey were charged with protecting French settlers against peasant rebels and Chinese "pirates." Here Gallieni developed his *tâche d'huile* strategy: he solidified support in walled towns, both new and established settlements, providing Vietnamese peasants and persecuted Catholics with public services and security, before he moved farther into the countryside (fig. 112). In effect, Gallieni's *politique des races* exploited long-standing ethnic and religious tensions within Vietnamese society; likewise, his base of operations recognized the familiar morphology of the *thành-pho*.

While he professed no specific aesthetic ideals in this mission, Gallieni understood the importance of siting principal towns and even buildings strategically. That strategy involved symbolic domination of a traditional culture, as well as military considerations. Lyautey described their new base of operations at Long-Son, writing to his sister in 1895:

> Sensations of America: a town is born, on the naked soil, its avenues traced on a vast scale. The first work dates from only four months ago, at the beginning of the good season, the only time of year when any work is feasible, and some fifty houses are already half-finished, following the rectangular street pattern, that of an American grid. In the middle stands the future residence of Colonel Gallieni, almost a palace, conceived to affirm French power here.[28]

There was, as yet, little sense of drawing from an indigenous aesthetic in these settlements, only that of imposing nationalistic images of domination. An ambivalent fascination with America would haunt Lyautey throughout his colonial career; he delighted in the spirit of action but increasingly criticized the lack of an overall plan and the monotony of the grid.

FIGURE 112. A *Gallieni donjon at Ta Sung in northern Tonkin, near the Chinese border, 1895. From J. S. Gallieni*, Gallieni au Tonkin, *1941. Courtesy of Editions Berger-Levrault.*

By the 1890s, having reached a low point in imperial prestige, Indochina was widely considered the greatest failure in the French empire. Rebellion still continued, almost four decades after the initial French invasion of Saigon. Even worse, there was virtually no utilization of the country's vast resources which had, after all, been the principal motive for French colonial expansion in the region. One fervent critic was Paul Doumer, a deputy from Auxerre, finance minister in the cabinet of Léon Bourgeois, a regular at the Musée Social, who would later take part in the Renaissance des Cités activities and would serve briefly as president of France. A rising leader of the Radical party, Doumer championed the party's call for *solidarité,* which stressed the sharing of technical expertise throughout France. To punish Doumer for his criticisms and limit his political future, the deputy's rivals had him appointed governor-general of Indochina in 1897. This proved to be an unsuccessful tactic. The Radicals could seldom attain either reform or modernization at home, but they provided the established way to build a political base in France during these years. In the colonies Doumer could freely indulge his political ambitions, without challenging the party structure in France.

Most writers on Vietnamese history credit Doumer with turning the economic situation around, making Vietnam France's "richest colony" in the exploitation of natural resources. "This is the age of iron and bridges," trumpeted Doumer, and Paris responded with a 200-million franc loan, most of which he spent on roads, bridges, and, especially, railroads.[29] The urgent vision of a modern transportation system concentrated on technical feats, not human costs or even actual needs. The colonial Ministry of Public Works had the power to requisition labor, which soon became an ill-disguised deportation system. Of the 80,000 Vietnamese and Chinese employed in building the Yunnan-Fou line, less than 300 miles long, more than 25,000 died in the course of construction, surpassing the earlier tolls under de Lanessan.[30] Complaints about high costs, graft, and the callous treatment of Vietnamese and Chinese coolies soon filled even the Saigon newspapers; when the Parisian press picked up the stories, the French public was again scandalized by this distant colony.

Nor could the new technology produce the resources Doumer imagined. The Vietnamese railways built by the French cost more than twice the original estimates, and they were among the most expensive in the world to run, chiefly because their freight services were among the smallest. Interest on the loans perennially drained the colony's budget, and the railroads were never paid for themselves. As a later critic put it, "Doumer's vast program was based on the idea that railways, merely by their passage through a country, would create wealth. No one foresaw that there was little to transport."[31]

Doumer's mania for transportation services, a mainstay of economic modernization and architectural modernism, eventually produced two major rail lines: one went from Haiphong to Hanoi and then up the Red River Valley into the Chinese town of Yunnan Fou, which the French mistakenly considered an important market depot; the other, the 1,000-mile-long Trans-Indochinese (finally completed in 1936), connected Hanoi and Saigon, paralleling the existing and cheaper water routes, as well as the Mandarin Road, the colony's longest highway.

Although these routes consisted mostly of empty countryside, a battery of train stations had to be built. Even in small villages, the *gare* assumed majestic proportions and formal Beaux-Arts facades, as if to assert the monumental importance of the railway system for the colony (fig. 113). One did not find the picturesque Gothic-revival shelters that appeared in European or American towns during this era; nor would a traveler see architectural testaments to industrial modernism. If Doumer's language suggested a modernist imagery, enthralled with machinery and the materials from which it is wrought, the stations themselves never showed this aesthetic. Each one could have fit unobtrusively

FIGURE 113. *Train station at the village of Dong-Dang, Tonkin, c. 1900. Postcard, courtesy of the Bibliothèque Forney.*

into a large provincial French city. In the heat of Saigon or the chill of Haiphong and Hanoi, these stone behemoths offered little comfort or uplift to those awaiting trains. While the stops along the way never developed into sizeable markets, it was not until the late 1920s that the large urban stations of Doumer's era would handle enough passengers or freight to justify their scale; by then their center-city locations and exposed tracks would seem problematic (fig. 114).

The railroads, like the highway system of *routes coloniales* begun in 1918, served "a political and touristic rather than an economic interest," argued Paul Bernard in 1937.[32] Even more than the French investors, Vietnamese peasants found both transportation networks totally unsuited to their needs, and often highly dangerous. This dynamic infrastructure demonstrated Western power but did so in a way that was at best narrowly partisan exhibitionism, and all too often mindless display. A remarkable example is the costly 1902 bridge named for Doumer; more than a mile long—the largest such structure in Asia—its cast-iron supports reached down some one hundred feet into the turbulent Red River near Hanoi (fig. 115). When Eugène Brieux drove close enough to discover that the bridge had only one lane, he exclaimed, "If one didn't believe in the future of Hanoi, it would be useless; if one did believe, it was inadequate."[33]

Surprisingly, public works in the cities received much less attention, for here municipal governments preferred to invest in visible pleasures rather than unseen services. Saigon had an elegant racetrack, a philharmonic society, and the

FIGURE 114. *Central train station of Hanoi, 1896–1900. From Teston and Percheron,* L'Indochine moderne.

FIGURE 115. *The Pont Doumer over the Red River at Hanoi, by Daydé & Pille of Creil, 1898–1902. From Georges Maspero,* Un Empire colonial français, *1930.*

best theater in the Far East—a majestic hall seating 800 people, designed in 1895 by a resident architect, Joseph-Victor Guichard (fig. 116); here French classics performed by visiting Parisian troupes alternated with plays the colonial officials had written themselves. It was a curious commitment of resources, literally a superficial urbanism, since the municipal council which commissioned these structures declined to remedy the city's defective water supply.[34] The glory of France did not radiate in such mundane matters, neither in Paris nor in Saigon.

Following a fire in 1888, the French expanded their efforts to transform Hanoi. The resident-general ordered the demolition of all straw houses along the Rue Paul Bert. Brick and tile structures now appeared, facing new sidewalks and a wide paved street. Military engineers then demolished the gates of about one hundred traditional *thi-trâns* north of the lake, as well as many houses and pagodas. Five years later they tore down the ramparts and walls surrounding the citadel to free more land. Some European settlement took place there, but mostly on adjacent marshland to the south, drained by the developers, usually at their own expense. This land belonged to fifteen or twenty Europeans who had bought it very inexpensively at the time of the first French concession.[35] The layout of new streets and residential districts took place under the supervision of Paulin Vial, who later lamented that he "had not counted on the [inept] municipal administration, [nor] on the fever for destruction and change which brutally stopped construction barely begun in order to replace it with a bizarre barrage of new experiments."[36]

All the same, Hanoi soon had lovely villa sections, famous for the flowering trees adorning the sidewalks, an impressive theater, and fashionable shops and cafés along the Rue Paul Bert. But here, too, the municipal council would not release funds to improve the city's sewer system until the 1930s, even though public-health specialists criticized the inadequacies of the primitive installation, most of which predated the French concession of 1884.[37] The "City of Perfume" took on less pleasant connotations with the addition of a number of scattered industrial sites between the river and the Petit Lac (fig. 117).[38] Nonetheless, by the early twentieth century, 7 percent of Hanoi's budget was being spent on public buildings and still only 2 percent on sanitation.[39]

Neither Hanoi nor Saigon had any sort of overall plan until the mid-1920s, nor even an official agency to regulate aesthetic, social, and public-health matters in a coordinated manner. In part because of the lack, transportation services were notoriously bad. A proposal for a tramway system in Saigon was first presented to the council in 1879 but was not realized for a decade. The Compagnie Française des Tramways went bankrupt, and a later incarnation, also a private

FIGURE 116.   *Saigon Theatre by Joseph-Victor Guichard, 1895. From Gourou,* L'Indochine.

venture, did little to extend lines into the outlying Vietnamese villages whose population needed them.

Most French *colons* preferred the *pousse-pousse* or rickshaw, finding it quicker and more in keeping with the imagery of power they enjoyed. Unknown in Cochinchina before the French, the rickshaw had long served well-to-do Chinese and seemed appropriately exotic to the French. By 1903 some five hundred Vietnamese men were pulling rickshaws through the largely unpaved streets of Saigon, when they confronted a new form of private transportation: the colony's first automobile. Traffic in the city soon became anarchic, leading the municipal council to impose speed limits of 12 kilometers an hour and stoplights along the busy Rue Catinet as early as 1909.[40] The preponderance of narrow streets usually slowed traffic in any case. Only by chance did the former canals and citadel moats form the principal infrastructure of Saigon's streets, resulting in a few spacious boulevards with asphalt paving. The siting of major nineteenth-century monuments on islands at the axes of these boulevards usually blocked the flow of traffic, especially when automobile registration soared after World War I. With no peripheral ring roads, most cars had to move through the center of the city, adding to the congestion.

The lack of a centralized public authority to oversee urban planning in any of the major Indochinese cities did not, by any means, imply a diminished staff of bureaucrats for the colony. In 1896, with only 4,000 Europeans in Cochin-

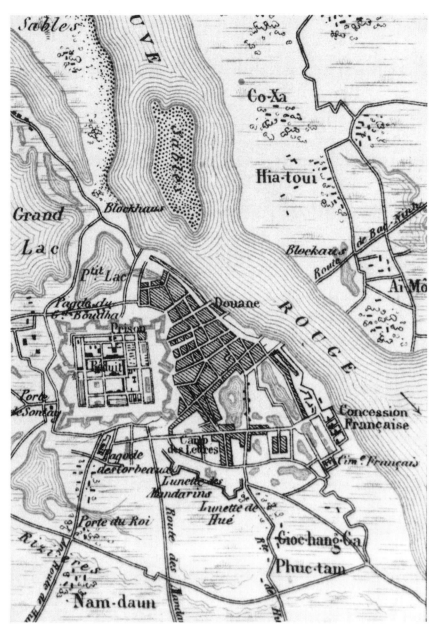

FIGURE 117. *Map of Hanoi, 1885, with the citadel* (thành-pho) *to the left. The French concession is along the river, although settlement had already extended into the marshy area between the citadel and the river. A number of* thi-trân *in the "native city" as the French put it, would soon have their gates removed to produce a more unified city. From Claude Bourrin,* Le Vieux Tonkin, *1935.*

china, over 1,700 of this number held governmental posts.[41] Most applicants were accepted, so the quality of personnel was notoriously low among this "vast administrative proletariat," this "host of incommpetent newcomers."[42] Doumer, like other liberal governors who followed him, vowed to reduce the number of French officials. But he also wanted to move the capital of the Indochinese Federation to Hanoi, a more temperate site, far from the interventions of Cochinchina's French commercial interests. In this new setting the state bureaucracy again multiplied, as it would under Doumer's successors. The number of governmental functionaries for the entire colony increased from 2,800 in 1897 to twice that by 1911, despite Doumer's hostility toward the expense and the petty self-interest which he felt characterized the bureaucratic mentality.[43]

The burgeoning number of French functionaries had many implications for the Indochinese people. Those who could find positions as interpreters or clerks in the inflated administrative system received wages far below those of Frenchmen in the most menial positions. More significantly, the entire indigenous population had to underwrite the bureaucracy through higher taxes, direct and indirect, while most French *colons* paid only a tiny fraction of their income in taxes (an average of three-tenths of 1 percent as late as 1930).[44]

The Architecture of Association

In 1900 Doumer centralized the colonial government in a new capital at Hanoi, commissioning a grandiose governmental palace with adjoining formal gardens, completed in 1902 (fig. 118). Doumer intended to strengthen the government's hand against Saigon's commercial elite, but primarily his aim was to take stronger control of the last vestiges of traditional Vietnamese political culture—without destroying the outward semblance of respect for these traditions.

One of the first such gestures is a representative example. In 1897, at the celebration of the young puppet emperor's coming of age (the lawful emperor had fled in 1885), the governor-general chose to emasculate the last embodiment of Vietnamese political sovereignty, the Secret Council or Comât. Doumer reorganized it, so that every Vietnamese member had a French counterpart and the institution as a whole came under the control of the French resident-general of Annam.[45] With the larger entourage, the Comât headquarters in Hué eventually had to be enlarged in 1913. To underline the supposed continuity with the earlier imperial version of the council, the architecture suggested nothing of France (fig. 119). Instead, the proportions and ornament imitated those of the original building. A 1919 photographic guidebook to French Indochina praised the refurbished building as "a clever adaptation of local architecture for modern construction."[46]

FIGURE 118. *Paul Doumer's new palace of the governor-general at the entrance to the Botanical Garden, Hanoi, 1902. Postcard, courtesy of the Bibliothèque Forney.*

FIGURE 119. *The new Comât in Hué, 1913. From* L'Indochine française, *1919.*

The shift in architectural style related directly to a new cultural and political policy for the colony, just as the new building stood as evidence of the inflated state bureaucracy. In the early twentieth century French public opinion had again been stirred up against Indochina, fueled by the passionate books of Jean Ajalbert.[47] Official reports submitted to the Chamber of Deputies between 1909 and 1912 condemned the economic and social policies of the colony so vehemently that a new direction became imperative. In April 1909, the Chamber first called for a new political course to be adopted in all French colonies, singling out Indochina as a particularly egregious example of what had gone wrong. The policy of association thus gained initial legal sanction, requiring a visible attention to the needs and traditions of colonized peoples.

Albert Sarraut, who commissioned the new Comât building, introduced the policy of association to Indochina. A Radical-Socialist deputy and later senator from the Aude, he served two terms as governor-general (1911–14, 1917–19). Sarraut's justly famous oratorical skill in defense of associationist policies gave hope to many Indochinese people, while infuriating conservative French residents. The rhetoric in fact produced little of fundamental substance, even if it did extend from the realm of words to that of architecture.

To provide office space for the fast-growing legion of functionaries, and to collect the many taxes that fueled the colonial budget, a new panoply of governmental buildings had to be erected: stamp and tax offices, customs houses, and treasuries proliferated in cities and provincial towns (fig. 120).[48] Under Sarraut the colony began to adopt indigenous motifs for these public buildings. The architecture replicated the basic theme of the governor-general's speeches: the contention that colonialism respected and served the Vietnamese, giving them greater representation in the running of their own country than they had previously enjoyed. So smooth was his eloquence that Sarraut could even admit some of the deficiencies of French colonialism: "Less generous perhaps than other nations in the verbal liberalism of the constitutions granted, we compensate for the parsimony of our colonial franchise with sincere feeling."[49]

The governor-general took special pride in the educational advances instituted under his leadership, an opinion echoed by later historians sympathetic to France's *mission civilisatrice*. After disbanding the last vestiges of the earlier mandarin system, Sarraut then increased the number of lycées. There were now six for the entire country, three of which reserved all their places for the children of the few thousand French families. The three lycées open to the children of the twenty-five million Indochinese "natives" had fewer places than the all-French schools—less than one thousand in all. The only truly progressive aspects to Sarraut's educational policy involved the integrated student body and

FIGURE 120.   *Provincial treasury in Indochina, c. 1925. From Teston and Percheron,*
L'Indochine moderne.

curriculum in these three select lycées of the major cities and the gradual opening of all levels of schools to girls—a reform only recently initiated in France
(fig. 121).[50]

Both "native schools" and the more cosmopolitan Franco-Vietnamese lycées infuriated the majority of *colons,* an anger reminiscent of more recent antagonisms over racial integration and curriculum reform in American education. They seemed less troubled by the fact that academic quality did not meet
metropolitan standards; until 1930, any student wishing to pursue studies in
France had first to repeat all classes taken abroad. Nor did the situation improve
at the lower levels, even though the primary schools only admitted about 10
percent of the two million Indochinese children who wished to attend.[51]

While most of the new schools built under Sarraut suggested some version
of "local color" in their ornament, the enormous lycée named for him, completed soon after his departure in 1919, truly exemplified the colonial government's educational policies (fig. 122). Technical specialization seemed to dictate
a rather spartan appearance, reminiscent of a cloister or a military barracks, self-
enclosed on its interior quadrangles.[52] If scant architectural ornament enlivened
the facade, neither did the building evoke a modernist version of streamlined
surfaces and industrial materials. Its architecture described only the dull routine
of training young people for future lives as bureaucrats; the site, directly on axis

FIGURE 121. *Ecole des Jeunes Filles Annamites, Saigon, c. 1919. From Gourou,* L'Indochine.

FIGURE 122. *Lycée Sarraut, Hanoi, 1919. Doumer's palace is to the left. From* Le Monde colonial illustré, *1925.*

with the 1902 palace of the governor-general in Hanoi, suggested the close ties and clear hierarchy between governmental goals and educational priorities.

Not until 1917 did Sarraut dare reopen the University of Hanoi, created in 1907 but closed down only a year later in retaliation for the students' involvement in the violent nationalist demonstrations of 1908. To placate the hostile *colons*, he made no apologies for the university's mission: the training of more qualified Vietnamese candidates for poorly paid jobs at the lower administrative levels in commerce and government. Despite the sumptuous Beaux-Arts building, few Vietnamese students considered any of the ten professional degrees worthwhile, for the diplomas were not honored in France and offered little chance for real mobility at home. At all levels, then, colonial education promised far more than it delivered.

The much-touted educational reforms under Sarraut must be seen in contrast with precolonial education in Vietnam, when free general and higher education had been widely available, and at least 25 percent of the population had been literate to some degree (in romanized *quoc-ngu* if not in Chinese).[53] The mandarin system's respect for scholars had created obligations for all persons of learning to teach others. But the French, by and large, had little interest in maintaining traditions of oriental scholarship, except for a few highly visible Vietnamese scholars who shared their knowledge with French orientalists.

Nor did the French want to spread the ideas of the Enlightenment or the inquisitive tenets of modern science. The French Chambers of Commerce endorsed only vocational training, approving funds for six new technical schools by 1924. Most *colons* considered it dangerous to permit their subjects even technical education beyond the most basic level, lest the Vietnamese become ambitious. Occasional reforms cannot excuse the more general effect of colonization on education in Vietnam: at no point during the 1920s and 1930s were even 10 percent of school-age children actually attending school, and fewer than 10 percent of the indigenous population were now literate.[54]

By the twentieth century, with the advent of associationist policies, the French colonial government could ill afford to suggest disdain for the nation it now dominated. To demonstrate their respect for the cultural traditions of Indochina, the government gave new prominence to an institute of scholarly research, the Ecole Française d'Extrême-Orient. Founded by Doumer in 1899 at Saigon, it was soon moved to Hanoi, where the initial headquarters consisted of a renovated building near the governmental palace, one of the few structures still extant which dated from the first French concession. Doumer obviously took as his model the prestigious French Schools at Rome, Athens, and Cairo, where renowned specialists studied the great classical civilizations of the Western

past. His enabling decree spoke of an institution that would "work at the archaeological and philological exploration of Indochina, assure the conservation of
historic monuments, and contribute to the erudite study of neighboring countries."[55] Despite its name, the Ecole did not involve teaching but "research in a
purely scientific vein" and, significantly, "public service, such that the members
are integrated into the governmental system of the colony."[56]

In 1905 Henri Parmentier and his staff architects organized a specialized
archaeological service at the Ecole, but the government did not pass any historic
preservation legislation until 1913. This consisted of a vague statement of respect
for the great monuments of the colony's past, somewhat strengthened in 1924
with Hébrard's support. The excavations undertaken by the French specialists at
the Ecole concentrated on two sites: Annam's monumental brick and stone
sculptures, eerie vestiges of the lost Cham civilization of the fifteenth century
(fig. 123); and the extraordinary remains of Khmer civilization in Cambodia,
especially the twelfth-century ruins of Angkor Wat (an area they forced Siam to
return to Cambodia for this purpose) (fig. 124). The French architects Charles
and Gabriel Blanche and the sculptor Eugène Auberlet supervised the cleaning
and recording of over eight hundred temple sites at Angkor during the 1920s.
Their restoration techniques proved to be somewhat controversial, notably the
use of reinforced concrete to hold up fragments of stone ceilings, walls, or lin-
tels—an approach taken by George Ford in the reconstruction of Rheims Cathedral. Yet these gigantic ruins, evoking the majesty of a once powerful and
highly artistic culture, did elicit the admiration, even the awe, of European
scholars and amateur archaeologists.[57]

In the opinion of a Vietnamese scholar who later joined the staff of the
School, Angkor's magnificence was "more to the taste" of the French, who rel-
ished the abundant ornament and believed that the monumental stonework revealed thoughts of eternity, suggesting the timelessness of true human nobility.[58]
Although the intervention of the school did help conserve several Buddhist pagodas in Hanoi, as well as the palace and imperial tombs at Hué, many other
important monuments were demolished without protest as French commercial
and residential districts were developed. Aware of the development issues that
preservation raised in cities, the Ecole successfully protected the picturesque lake
between the European and "native" districts of Hanoi and restored the Temple
of the Single Pillar on an island at its center (destroyed by bombing in 1954)
(fig. 125). This act enhanced adjacent property values to the south by distancing
the poorer Vietnamese and providing a romantic oriental vista for European
homes.

FIGURE 123.   *Fifteenth-century Cham sculptural monuments. From Gourou,*
L'Indochine.

A prominent aspect of the Ecole's public service involved tourism to historic
sites in the colony. While the scholars disdained amateurs, especially those like
André Malraux caught pilfering sculpture from the distant ruins, they recognized the need to stir the imagination of the French public with images of exotic
Indochina and its glorious past. Gigantic replicas of various temple ruins were
erected in plaster for the major colonial expositions, most spectacularly that of
Angkor Wat itself at Paris in 1931 (fig. 126), celebrating the completion of

FIGURE 124. *French tourists visit the twelfth-century Khmer temples at Angkor Wat.*
From L'Illustration, *1922.*

twenty years of restoration work. All the same, scholars insisted upon limits to promotional activities. The Ecole petitioned Governor-General Long not to allow a luxury tourist hotel at Angkor Wat, built in 1928, to be sited conveniently close to the ruins, thereby detracting from their grandeur (fig. 127). It was with mixed feelings that the school heard Governor-General Pierre Pasquier praise tourism as "probably the only practical application that archaeology might have, up through the present day, in Indochina." [59]

The school's mission embodied a statement about the relations between culture and power. The French self-consciously placed themselves in a line of great foreign powers which had long ago controlled the culture and politics of Indochina. Studying the aesthetic domination of India and China in the past, these scholars could help Governor-General Pasquier speak about contemporary politics. "Let us not maladroitly cut the spiritual ties which join Indochina to the great Powers of her Past," he implored at the inauguration of the school's most important museum in 1932; "these ties are tangled up with those of our own day, attaching her to France, a new incarnation of those Powers in the present." Present-day Vietnamese culture would be more difficult for the French

FIGURE 125. *Temple of the Single Pillar, Hanoi. From Martin Hurlimann*, Burma, Ceylon, Indochina: Landscapes, Architecture, Inhabitants, *1930*.

to admire, given the claims to superiority which buttressed colonialism. In their appreciation of the colony's august past, the French could also issue a warning: "Only the Western nations," Pasquier continued, "which have pushed their progress to its limit can recognize how foolish it is to break too brusquely with a past one gives up . . . under the pretext of modernization."[60]

If the Ecole provided moral and political lessons for Indochina, it also

FIGURE 126. *Reconstruction of a temple at Angkor Wat for the 1931 Colonial Exposition, Paris, by Gabriel Blanche. Postcard.*

FIGURE 127. *Hotel des Ruines, Angkor Wat, 1928. From Teston and Percheron,* L'Indochine moderne.

198

served to reprimand. The French could assert that they appreciated the glories of earlier civilizations in the colony, whereas the descendants of those civilizations left their own legacy in ruins. This attitude denied the legitimacy of allowing ancient palaces or pagodas to decay if they no longer retained sacred meaning. All historic architecture was aestheticized, then classified according to Western criteria. Archaeologists and government functionaries lauded the Ecole's formal classification system and its exacting reconstruction effort as the only legitimate way to honor the great art of the past.

In celebrating the splendid accomplishments of earlier eras, the French assured themselves, if not their subjects, of their respect for a bygone way of life, and of their inherent superiority in the present day. The parallel implication of cultural decline became explicit when Martial Merlin, an earlier and avowedly repressive governor-general, spoke of the French mission to "reawaken" a civilization that had been "for centuries now . . . mentally retarded, more or less asleep."[61] The glories and accomplishments of the Orient lay in the distant past, disallowing any suggestion of eventual independence based on respect for present-day southeast Asians.

The Ecole's research fell primarily into the realms of linguistic studies, architectural and archaeological research, and historic preservation. This research then provided the basis for scholarly references in public speeches and indigenous styles in the official buildings of the twentieth century. Public architecture, like Sarraut's speeches, implied that French functionaries appreciated traditional Indochinese cultures, that functionaries appreciated traditional Indochinese cultures, that colonialism would preserve and even advance these other cultures in an equitable manner. These principles can perhaps best be seen in Sarraut's Comât headquarters and the provincial Chambers of Representatives, set up throughout Tonkin and Annam at the end of his second term. Only the colonial government took pride in the *maisons communes* (fig. 128) which housed these bodies, confident that the gestures of respect in local architectural idioms and dignified titles would win the gratitude of the people, or at least assuage suspicious Parisians who demanded signs of greater cultural tolerance and political participation. Powerless as institutions of government, for they possessed only the right to offer advice, the provincial chambers seldom attracted individuals who were respected by their communities. Vietnamese nationalists considered them "reactionary delegations of natives under the influence of the French."[62]

Although we could dismiss the new trends in colonial architecture, first visible under Sarraut's direction, as dishonest and shallow reforms, they do indicate a profoundly different stance toward French cultural hegemony—in

FIGURE 128. *French-built* maisons communes *in various Vietnamese provinces. From Teston and Percheron,* L'Indochine moderne.

France as in the colonies. The breakdown of the nineteenth-century Beaux-Arts ideal of universal beauty signaled a new climate of opinion, in both political and aesthetic terms. By World War I it no longer seemed appropriate, even in the *métropole,* to insist on a single, unified image for beauty or for French political authority. Starting with Art Nouveau and the Fauves, an appreciation of varied aesthetics stirred artistic sensibilities, as it had during the heyday of the picturesque and Gothick in the early nineteenth century. Now even more exotic styles captivated imaginations. What represented sheer visual delight for artists like Picasso or Matisse, for architects like Henri Sauvage or Donat-Albert Agache, invigorating their sense of aesthetic possibilities after decades of academic rigor under the tutelage of the Beaux-Arts establishment, had other implications for clients.

In France as in Indochina, the efforts to incorporate vernacular motifs into public architecture often signaled a rather superficial acknowledgement, even an outright manipulation, of political demands and cultural distinctions. The ideal of a universal aesthetic representing the highest ideals of beauty had come under attack, in part because it related so conspicuously to the reality of a central government making all decisions, without the participation of other groups, or even much consideration of their actual needs and preferences. Activists in the French provinces demanded economic assistance and greater political autonomy. They received only a formal deference to their pleas in the newly fashionable regionalist architecture. Even more insistent were the Vietnamese nationalists, whose hostility to a centralized colonial government and sufferings at its expense fueled repeated attempts at uprisings against the French.

Nationalist sentiments intensified after World War I, in which 140,000 Vietnamese had served, many of them forcibly "recruited."[63] Liberal promises that the *français de couleur* would win greater freedoms, having helped France maintain her own independence, went largely unmet. The government provided only architectural concessions to the demands for political and economic self-determination.

"A Worthy Ensemble"

Questions of aesthetic sensibility, administrative authority, and industrial expansion underlay Governor-General Maurice Long's decision in 1920 to request funds for a new technical council in Indochina, headed by a professional urbanist. He had long admired Lyautey's accomplishments in Morocco, and indeed Long's intimate knowledge of the Moroccan situation, as well as his long parliamentary experience in the Republican-Socialist party, had favored his selection for the post of governor-general.[64] An astute politician, Long recognized the shift taking place in official urban policy, in France as in the colonies, toward a more exacting and self-conscious use of local cultural prototypes. That very year, Albert Sarraut, recently appointed minister of colonies, suggested through telegrams that all overseas administrators study the efforts of the Renaissance des Cités and the Société Française des Urbanistes to reorient French postwar rebuilding along regionalist lines. Brochures of their expositions could be ordered from the ministry.[65] Long recognized the implications of this recommendation when he made his proposal.

Ironically, Sarraut was involved in the request in another way, one not immediately disclosed to him by the new governor-general. Long detested the immense lycée that had just been completed alongside the governor-general's palace in Hanoi, named in honor of his predecessor, finding the lycée's size and austerity "an alas! irreparable mistake."[66] Accordingly the new governor intended to give Doumer's 1902 palace to the Colonial Council; he had bought up a sizeable property west of the former citadel where he planned to install a new governmental complex, bringing together the various scattered services of the colonial regime in a manner reminiscent of Prost's Administrative Quarter in Rabat. Long recognized the need for "a qualified and proven Urbanist" who could take on more than individual buildings, creating an urban design at once grand and efficient. This result, he felt, would be an "ensemble worthy of a great country."[67]

It was with the recommendation of Prost (as well as Louis Bonnier) that Ernest Hébrard was offered the position—more than a year after Long's initial request.[68] Prost's friend from the Villa Medici and the Société Française des Urbanistes had spent the war years in Greece, serving as director of the archaeological service of the French army stationed in Thessalonika. He had been able to apply several years of research when a fire and earthquake in 1919 destroyed much of the center of that city, such that extensive rebuilding was necessary.

Hébrard's plan reconstructed a sizeable historic district much as it had been in late antiquity; he also imposed building codes and guidelines for aesthetic unity in the commercial area, extended the port, and isolated the maritime industries from the reconstructed historic center (fig. 129). Admiring the results, the Greek government called Hébrard to Athens, where he issued controls to protect the entire historic district around the Acropolis, preventing new buildings that would block views of the Parthenon. When a Greek plebiscite returned Constantine to the throne (the king whom the Allied forces had forced to abdicate), the French army withdrew in protest. Although Hébrard remained as the king's advisor, his career as a French urbanist in Greece was in jeopardy. Hébrard accepted the offer to come to Indochina, arriving in the fall of 1921.[69]

Hébrard appealed to Maurice Long because of his familiarity with French civic grandeur, evident in all Beaux-Arts-trained architects, especially one who had designed an ideal city based on a majestic complex of administrative buildings. But grandeur alone could not suffice. In line with associationist values, the colonial government now had to suggest a greater Vietnamese involvement than had hitherto been the case under the French. Long had responded administra-

FIGURE 129.   *Reconstruction plan for Thessalonika, Greece, by Ernest Hébrard, 1919.*
From L'Architecture, *1923.*

tively with what he termed lateral ranks (*cadres lateraux*), where educated Annamites held offices parallel to French positions in terms of their titles and responsibilities, though the prefix *indigène* indicated their much lower salaries and
status. This compromise understandably did not satisfy the ambitions of talented
Vietnamese, while it further aggravated the bureaucratic overload by duplicating
many positions. The number of state employees multiplied again, with the
French staff alone doubling between 1919 and 1925—when some 50 percent of
the adult French men in Indochina held governmental positions.[70]

Hébrard responded to Long's call for an aesthetic in the associationist spirit
as thoughtfully as he could. He traveled extensively, photographing the high art
of Angkor and the Buddhist pagodas, as well as simple rural habitations and
narrow streetscapes in the eighteenth-century districts of Hanoi (fig. 130). These
studies resulted in several brief articles about the cultural traditions of Indochina, and others on India, Siam, Burma, and the Phillipines, as part of the
1931 Colonial Exposition.[71] Hébrard presented not so much a sophisticated
reading of formal ideals, stylistic rules, or historical variations as a lesson about
adapting local environmental controls to French architectural purposes.

In Hébrard's eyes, "indigenous construction always harmonizes with the en-

FIGURE 130. *The Rue des Caisses (Hang Thung) an eighteenth-century market street in Hanoi, paved by the French. Photographed c. 1925. Courtesy of ASEMI.*

vironment; . . . it becomes part of the landscape."[72] Beneath the surface of that simple observation lay a theory of culture and cultural evolution. In much the same spirit, the geographer Paul Vidal de la Blache or the anthropologist Bronislaw Malinowski, also writing during the 1920s, sought to show that one could find practical reason beneath the seemingly strange superstitions and erratic forms of primitive tribes. For Vidal or Malinowski, other cultures remained stable precisely because they had a relatively high degree of technical mastery over their environments, which in turn sustained a coherent social organization.

Hébrard sought to discern the principles of orientation, site planning, ventilation systems, and the choice of materials which prevailed in the seemingly exotic architectural styles of the Far East. One could comprehend the way traditional cultures functioned, he suggested, by analyzing how their buildings adapted to the specific problems of the climate with verandas, overhanging eaves, stilts, or thin walls.[73] Hébrard had come a long way from the universal aesthetic of his World Center, applied without change in prospective sites around the world, but he still assumed that other architectural systems evolved more or less unself-consciously in response to physical needs, without the intellectual sophistication of his own tradition.

Hébrard did not challenge the Beaux-Arts tradition with these suggestions; rather he called for French architects to live up to its true ideals. One could grasp different principles of construction and layout, he believed, without imitating the historical forms they had taken. In this view, other cultures necessarily and properly followed their own unchanging rules, while the independent spirit of creativity associated with the modern West could combine continuity with innovation, avoiding the cultural inertia he associated with the Orient.

In good Beaux-Arts fashion, Hébrard denigrated direct imitation by French architects in Indochina, whether it was based on the indigenous styles of the colony or the academic monuments of his own homeland. He chastized those who might blithely adorn a train station with Naga (Siamese) serpents, for this "would show a profound scorn for the traditions of the country, while shocking the religious sentiments of the natives."[74] One could not simply paste dragons on new buildings, thinking such superficial veneer represented a style appropriate to Indochina. Likewise, he criticized those who continued to replicate European neoclassical, baroque, or even modern iron and glass architecture in the colonies; only servile designers mindlessly attempted to reproduce the kinds of buildings they had known in France, without taking into account their actual surroundings. The *colons* who encouraged them, clamoring for French pseudo-majesty, deluded themselves if they believed that certain styles would always embody beauty and elegance. It was even doubtful, Hébrard suggested wryly, that "Gothic architecture is the only style acceptable to God."[75]

At issue, then, was Hébrard's notion of architectural creativity and responsibility—which he defined solely in aesthetic terms. Hébrard hoped to redefine the priorities of his profession. If he could do this in difficult circumstances, surely colleagues at home would follow his lead. Here, in a setting where the climate posed major difficulties, where stylistic references carried such dramatic meanings, where modern urban problems like traffic planning and historic preservation has to impress a conscientious architect, Hébrard wanted to teach fellow practitioners in France how to innovate. The critical move, as he explained, involved taking all these constraints into account as one designed. He did not venture to consider the real constraints posed by colonialism: European hegemony, fundamental inequalities, and economic exploitation.

In conference proceedings published after the 1931 Colonial Exposition, Hébrard expressed the hope that, at the next exposition, visitors would see not another copy of the "immortal but incommodious Angkor-Wat," but rather a well-planned, functional building that represented a true, and truly innovative,

"Vietnamese style."[76] In his reasoning, this new direction could come only from the French, for the best of their architectural theory, most notably the work of Viollet-le-Duc, taught how to discern the *caractère* of a culture and its architecture, and then build upon that essence. Strangely enough, he never even considered the possibility that the Vietnamese themselves could develop their own version of a "Vietnamese style." Hébrard's principal goals involved French architectural theory, rather than local Vietnamese culture. While the buildings he hoped to see would be appropriate to their exotic setting, the fundamental principles of design would apply in any context.

If Hébrard's buildings used local motifs, these resulted primarily from climatic and other functional considerations. Political symbolism was inherent, of course, in his ideas about separation, hierarchy, and the timeless quality of oriental culture. His was an inquisitive personal search for modern forms and principles of architecture, based in part on local systems of environmental controls and the styles he felt they had generated. Local traditions might inspire the Westerner, but they had little inherent significance for Hébrard, and he certainly sensed no conflict to be resolved. In essence, like a present-day postmodernist, Hébrard wanted to use history and a certain cultural sensibility in order to infuse a fresh vitality into French architecture.

The terms of reference always looked back to Europe. Admiring the "very picturesque" streets of Hanoi, each one named for its original artisanal specialization, Hébrard mused upon "what the cities of antiquity and the Middle Ages" must have been like. This view of European history was illusory. Nor did it show any effort to comprehend how each *phô* (the main market street) had once provided administrative services, security, and identity to the residents, before the French tore down the protective walls. Indeed, Hébrard dismissed the indigenous architecture of Cochinchina as "poor in ancient monuments, imposing no particular context, [such that] it was more or less reasonable for the first colonial architects to have looked modestly to the *métropole* for their architectural examples."[77]

Hébrard's own generation, on the other hand, lived in a larger and more complex colony, incorporating regions like Cambodia and Annam with grand traditions of monumental architecture. He envisioned a political environment, of course, when he called for architecture that responded to the entire Indochinese Federation—an artificial colonial unit, rather than a unified whole. Moreover, as Hébrard realized full well, the academic styles of France and even the single-minded focus on each building as an isolated phenomenon were no longer adequate references for a modern architect. Given this complex framework, Indochina might be a place to forge a new basis for French urban design, at home and abroad:

> Let us hope that French urbanism has found an experimental terrain in Indochina that will be fertile in producing results. It is especially in countries still young that this modern science, which consists above all in predicting future developments and putting current circumstances in order, will facilitate the construction of healthy, convenient cities which are pleasant to live in. [78]

Only with a myopic focus on the European colonial presence could one see Indochina as a "young country."

Hébrard's architecture in Indochina—for example, the new Ministry of Finance (1927), the Institut Pasteur (1930), and the Museum of the École Française d'Extrême-Orient (1931), all in the capital city—attempted to carry out this dictum. Site plans reveal his efforts to relate new structures to the larger urban design of a district, in formal and functional terms (fig. 131). Each building was carefully set in landscaped surroundings, near others of similar purpose, and easily accessible via an improved system of streets and avenues. The scale was, by and large, smaller than that of earlier French public institutions. Connected pavilions would avoid the ventilation problems which plagued the massive structures of the nineteenth century, while arcades and overhanging porch roofs provided protection from the sun. Hébrard never made a mistake like that of Foulhoux, when he mounted an enormous glass dome over his Saigon Post Office (1876) and created an insufferably hot greenhouse climate within a public building.

One finds a curious mixture of religious, civic, and residential decorative motifs here, even if none can be classified as exact allusions to existing structures or typologies in the Far East. Oblivious to centuries-old cultural rivalries in this part of the world, Hébrard freely mixed elements from different regions or entirely different countries, in order to generate his ideal of an innovative, adaptive aesthetic. As a result his buildings usually resemble a pastiche of exotic details superimposed on a Beaux-Arts plan, rather than the more radical change in direction that he advocated.

The Hanoi museum of the École Française d'Extrême-Orient is especially instructive in this regard (fig. 132). One sees Hébrard's enthusiastic observations of architecture in the Far East—all the Far East, which the school, in theory at least, took as its purview. The museum, begun in 1926 and inaugurated five years later, was named for Louis Finot, an early director of the École. Its design

FIGURE 131. *Proposed plan for Hanoi by Ernest Hébrard, 1923–25. The outlying suburbs and new industrial areas are across the river; three grand commercial boulevards traverse the former citadel area, radiating from the new administrative center. From* L'Architecture, *1928.*

constituted a hodgepodge of architectural motifs: the polychrome facade evoked Japanese Shinto temples; steep tiled porch roofs recalled Hindu temples in India; while the two-tiered roof of the central core alluded to Siamese, Cambodian, and Laotian temple structures. Hébrard was appealing precisely to the French archaeologists and historians, to their knowledge of a diverse range of oriental stylistic traditions, much as Beaux-Arts architecture referred to an educated observer's knowledge of classical and neoclassical monuments in Europe.

For the architect and, it appears, for his friends on the staff of the École, French influence pervaded the composition, embodied in Hébrard's integration of all these separate architectural references. As an early account in the *Bulletin* of the École put it, "these coordinated elements cannot, all the same, fail to make us recognize the French inspiration of the whole."[79] If the very idea of a

museum as an institution represented a strange intrusion in Vietnamese life—
isolating objects out of their daily existence, venerating but also emasculating
cultural practices—Hébrard's aesthetic made even the design of the museum a
statement of cultural dominance.

Long created an official Urbanism Department in 1923, more than a year
after Hébrard's arrival. Through this office Hébrard drew up plans for the principal cities of Indochina, even as far away as Pnom-Penh. The principles underlying his proposals for the major centers of Hanoi, Saigon, and Haiphong followed more or less the same lines. Apart from the preservation of important
monuments, Hébrard paid little attention to the existing indigenous cities. He
assumed that most Vietnamese would be shifted to peripheral workers' towns,
leaving the core open for new development among the beautiful historic artifacts.

Hébrard wanted rational zoning plans that would override the individualis-
tic economic interests which had, heretofore, determined the patterns of growth
in these cities. Each plan now provided five use-categories: an administrative

FIGURE 132. *Louis Finot Museum of the Ecole Française d'Extrême-Orient, Hanoi, by
Ernest Hébrard , 1926–31. From the* Bulletin de l'EFEO, *1936. Courtesy of the Ecole
Française d'Extrême-Orient, Paris.*

center, residential districts, recreational space (parks and cultural centers), commercial districts, and industrial sectors. Hébrard usually presumed extensive future expansion, charting specialized districts that anticipated growth over the next twenty-five years.

In promoting zoning, Hébrard referred directly to American ordinances of the decade, arguing that such controls would prevent installations which lowered property values and created unpleasant vistas. He pointed out the repercussions of a large distillery in Hanoi, sited so that the southwest winds carried its pollution into the most fashionable residential neighborhoods. Not until 1928 was legislation finally approved, demarcating zoning and design guidelines for future extensions of the colony's cities. Such restrictions seemed unwarranted controls to French real-estate interests and industrialists. Hébrard complained:

> The representatives of the powerful corporations who oversee the installation of new factories do not preoccupy themselves thinking much about the damages they might cause, and when we try to curtail their fantasies, they accuse us of wanting to halt the economic development of the Colony![80]

Like Prost and Lyautey, he scorned the speculative mentality, without questioning the rights of Western governments to dominate.

Hébrard by no means ignored economic development. He simply wanted to control it, civilizing the effect it had in urban settings. In the major cities of Indochina and at new industrial installations—Nam Dinh in particular, as well as Ben Tuy outside the Laotian city of Vinh, or Danang, the port for Hué—he envisioned vast arenas for productivity. The colony enjoyed exceptional prosperity during the 1920s, when French capital invested there as never before: close to three billion francs between 1924 and 1930, almost 60 percent of the total since French arrival. In 1922 Long obtained a state "loan" to encourage commercial and industrial development—of which the Indochinese people contributed 95 percent through increased taxes.[81] Such public and private investment encouraged modernization—new factories, stores, banks, and offices, what Albert Sarraut, as minister of colonies, called the *mise en valeur* of the colonies, purportedly bringing improvements to the *colon* and the colonized alike.[82]

Benefits did not accrue equally. It was European commerce that thrived, and construction thrived with it. New financial societies were formed; the Banque de l'Indochine opened more commodious offices (fig. 133). Attractive new hotels and department stores appeared along Hanoi's Rue Paul Bert and Saigon's Rue Catinet. All these developments took place in the "European commercial districts" of Hébrard's zoning maps. The imbalance extended throughout Viet-

FIGURE 133. *New headquarters of the Banque de l'Indochine, Saigon, by Georges Trouve, 1930. Courtesy of ASEMI.*

namese society, in urban and rural areas alike, though a small proportion of wealthy urban Vietnamese families also profited. Even Alexandre Varenne's agricultural credit banks, established in 1927, did not promote the Socialist governor-general's laudable aims (fig. 134). The Saigon-based Vietnamese bourgeoisie who administered the banks used them to augment their own rural landholdings, thereby dispossessing even more peasants. Not until 1927 did a Vietnamese-owned bank, the Société Annamite de Crédit, appear on the streets of Saigon, and this institution was dominated by prosperous rural landowners.[83]

"The preeminent economic objectives of the French [in Indochina] was to develop a modern export sector," contends David Marr, an economy focused primarily on rice and mining, and somewhat later on rubber production as well. "To provide the physical labor," Marr recounts, "somewhere between 100,000 and 200,000 Vietnamese were deceived or dragooned into the 'red earth' rubber-growing region of Cochinchina during the boom years of the 1920s."[84] From a quite different perspective, writing in 1949, Charles Micaud deplored the backwardness of those Vietnamese who were reluctant to abandon their ancestral farms for this isolated, "bad water" country supposedly inhabited by evil spirits.[85]

In the "native area" of the southern rubber plantations, workers were housed in camps or rural villages, each one holding between 300 and 500 coolies, separated according to ethnicity. Accommodations usually consisted of long brick or wood buildings, called *trai*, arranged in rows (fig. 135). Dozens of workers slept

FIGURE 134. *Agricultural Syndicate in Cantho, built under the Socialist governor-general Alexandre Varenne, 1927. From Teston and Percheron,* L'Indochine moderne.

side by side in each structure, beneath a straw or corrugated-iron roof.[86] The conditions were sufficiently bad that the plantations occasionally elicited criticism from officials and in the French public; more importantly, they would play an important role in the rise of Vietnamese communism during the 1930s and 1940s.

The French touted the extraordinary increase in rice production in the Mekong Delta, enhanced through immense colonial landholdings, extensive drainage, and a state-funded system of large rectilinear canals, providing both irrigation and transportation. Indeed, Indochina exported 700,000 tons of rice in 1900, and 2 million by 1937. While generating sizable profits for French and Chinese firms, the increases pertained primarily to export and actually depleted the supply of this basic food in Vietnam, causing widespread malnutrition.[87] Before the French, the emperors had banned the sale of this precious commodity outside the country in order to assure enough rice for their own people. One's perspective on colonial development depends on whether the observer is concerned with the disruption of the traditional agrarian economy or the failure to transform Indochina completely into a modern industrial nation.

FIGURE 135. Trai *or workers' housing at the rubber plantation of Suzannah in the "red earth" areas of Cochinchina. From Teston and Percheron,* L'Indochine moderne.

Raw materials were processed and shipped back to France in the cities of Vietnam, primarily Saigon and Haiphong. The environment of the major metropolises vividly evoked the inequities of the colony's economic growth. In the heart of Saigon's business district stood the European temples of commerce, many of them institutions unknown there before colonial conquest: banks, shipping offices, insurance companies, trading companies, and the business houses of the large French corporations. First constructed in wood or brick, the early buildings were quickly replaced with more permanent and impressive stone edifices (fig. 136). Beginning in the 1920s municipal ordinances drawn up by Hébrard regulated the somewhat uneven and episodic alignment down the principal commercial streets, although only the unstable soil imposed a de facto height limit.

At some distance from the economic center stood the main industrial district, by 1920 a concentrated mass of corrugated-iron or reinforced-concrete structures: rice-husking plants, sugar refineries, textile mills, cement works, hydraulic plants, distilleries, warehouses, and loading docks (fig. 137). The construction itself, like the work that went on there, relied on capital-intensive tech-

FIGURE 136. *Chamber of Commerce and Agriculture on the rue Jules Ferry, Saigon,* 1928. *Courtesy of the Musée de l'Homme, Paris.*

nology and materials which had never been known in traditional Indochina. Nearby stood a profusion of bars, brasseries, and houses of prostitution.

To these examples of colonial architecture must be added something seemingly traditional: the densely built housing in the "native sections" where the industrial laborers and their families lived. By the 1920s the majority of urban wage-earners in factories had become a permanent population, no longer able to spend part of their time farming, usually living below the poverty level, even when they worked steadily. They resided in makeshift housing on the outskirts of the manufacturing cities such as Saigon-Cholon, Haiphong, Hanoi, Ben Thuy, and Tourane, renting a room or a flimsy, dilapidated hut without any sanitary facilities. By doing nothing to improve the quality or availability of this housing, even as the population increased dramatically, the colonial government could spend more funds on public works to serve the French economy.

Preoccupied with the administrative center, Hébrard gave some thought to the large urban industrial zones. He sited vast processing areas alongside the enlarged ports and warehouse districts, charted extensive canal systems, and

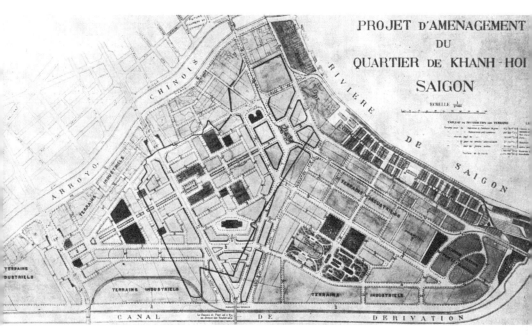

FIGURE 137. *Detail of Hébrard's plan for the industrial district of Saigon, in the marshy triangle south of the* arroyo *and west of the Saigon River, 1925. From* L'Architecture, *1928.*

zoned out residences—at least for the French. Criticizing the train stations of Doumer's era, finally coming into service for the transport of goods, Hébrard wanted installations near the ship-loading areas in order to minimize the expensive, inefficient movement of industrial products through the city centers. The goal, in sum, was to order two forms of chaos—"native" life and industrial growth—a disorder in fact caused, in large part, by the insensitive planning of colonial governments.

Concentrating and expanding industrial and commercial zones for the major Vietnamese cities, Hébrard defined their very character. Shipping and processing totally dominated Haiphong, especially after Hébrard's partially realized plan of 1924 (fig. 138). The major expansion here occurred in industry along the busy harbor and through the addition of a new "native" hospital and prison district near the slaughterhouse. One major part of Hébrard's proposal, endorsed by metropolitan financial interests, was not implemented. Hébrard had recommended the construction of new shipping facilities outside the delta, in order to avoid the constant dredging operations necessary to maintain open shipping lanes. Powerful colonial interests already entrenched in Haiphong successfully derailed the change, diverting the funds to more improvements for the existing

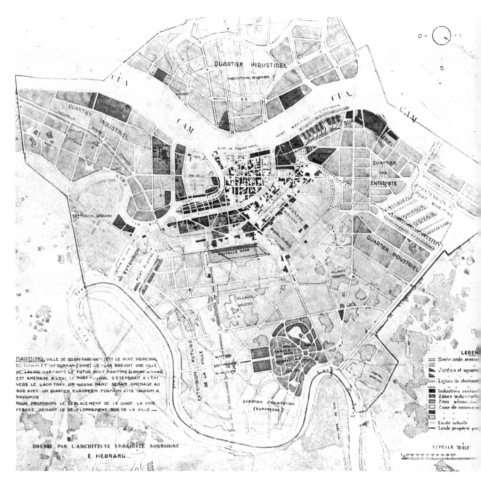

FIGURE 138. *Partially realized plan for the redevelopment of Haiphong by Ernest Hébrard, 1924, with larger industrial districts to the east, north, and west of the commercial core. From* L'Architecture, *1928.*

facilities. They were able to maintain their installations as the principal entrepot for Tonkin, even if the location was highly inefficient.[88]

Jean Chesneaux calls Haiphong the very essence of a colonial implantation, "a city detached from its land, from its natural context, with no roots in local reality."[89] Of 120,000 residents by 1930, only 3,000 were Europeans; another 8,000 were Chinese merchants and coolies; most of the population were Vietnamese, including women and children, who earned their meager livings in one way or another through the bustling industrial port. The working-class Vietnamese found their lives and livelihoods determined by the colonial system and its focus on a European market. The expanded maritime wharfs and quais serviced the large ships bound for France, alongside the industrial processing areas (see fig. 139). As T. G. McGee writes, "thus the smoking chimney stacks of the Western industrial cities were replaced by the long, corrugated-iron *godowns* (warehouses) of the [southeast Asian] port city."[90] Only a much smaller-scale indigenous economy remained, based around small jetties scattered along the riverfront (fig. 140).

Likewise, by treating Saigon and Cholon as one metropolitan region in his 1923 plan, Hébrard clarified the character and planning priorities of these cities (fig. 141). Production and consumerism would be geared even more primarily to European markets. Industry, long a mainstay of Cholon, now attained unprecedented proportions with Hébrard's enlarged industrial area. Commercial vitality, associated with Saigon since the early days of French occupation, was now dominated by larger enterprises grouped in a concentrated business district.

Hébrard's definition of this extensive industrial-commercial region did, in fact, take hold only a few years later, when the two cities merged in 1931. Their combined population, tripling over the past forty years, had reached 400,000— almost as large as Coffyn's wildly visionary plan of 1861. Only 10,000 of this number were Europeans, even in Hébrard's accounts, yet both cities oriented their economy toward Europe.[91] As in other industrial centers, the escalation in population consisted largely of Vietnamese peasants forced off their land by voracious French plantation and mine owners. Neither Hébrard's official reports, his articles, nor his plans and drawings ever addressed the housing problems of this group, the overwhelming majority of the urban population. His only concession to the difficult life of Vietnamese laborers was the passing suggestion that the French government should provide more parks for their recreation—a reform popular among urban designers in Europe and the United States.[92]

As a traditional Beaux-Arts-trained architect, Hébrard could never see his true mission in Indochina as the development of industry or the provision of mass housing. He envisioned his role as that of a master-urbanist, giving artistic form and efficient overview to the morphology of entire cities. With this self-image, he came into direct conflict with the Ministry of Public Works, within which his Urbanism Department was lodged. The engineers in this division— mostly graduates of the École des Ponts et Chausées, the École des Mines, or the École Militaire Supérieure—gravitated toward certain priorities, still much like those of Doumer: roads, bridges, railroads, and canals to transport material from the countryside to the ports; irrigation systems and dikes to increase the production of rice, the colony's principal export product; and large camps for Chinese and Vietnamese laborers in the mines, plantations, and agricultural estates. In all these services they obviously found themselves allied with the

FIGURE 139. *Standardized warehouses in Haiphong's main harbor district, c. 1925.*
National Archives.

FIGURE 140. *View of the local port of Haiphong, c. 1925. From Gourou,* L'Indochine.

VILLE DE SAIGON - CHOLON

FIGURE 141. *Plan for a unified Saigon-Cholon, by Ernest Hébrard, 1925. From*
L'Architecture, *1928.*

commercial interests of the local *colons*, and with the major French corporate
powers in Paris, Lyons, and Marseilles, who had begun to invest their capital in
the colony during the 1920s.

Hébrard not only distanced himself from these economic concerns, he publicly criticized speculative interests as a basis for policy in Indochina. He disdained even the aesthetic associated with public works, repeatedly disparaging
the nineteenth-century urban plans done by military engineers as dull, inefficient, lacking any civic grandeur. The more recent buildings by public-works
engineers he likened to "hideous hangars covered with industrial siding . . .
which have destroyed the countryside."[93]

The sense of conflict was not, in fact, misguided. The public-works engineers and the *colons* together envisioned extensive environmental changes in the
countryside—drastically altering its appearance, its political economy, and its
social life. They made only minimal changes in the cities of Indochina. This
did not result, as in Lyautey's case, from an argument about preserving traditional Vietnamese culture. The *colons* wanted public subsidies for their industrial and agricultural enterprises, without constraints on how the modernized
environment might look and function; the engineers, too, preferred an unham-
pered rural landscape which they could transform at will through their technical
skills.

A. A. Pouyanne, head of Public Works after 1925, was an educated man,
close to the inner circle of the École Française d'Extreme-Orient, but he found

no place for artistic or cultural concerns in his professional work. He met regularly with representatives of the most powerful private enterprises in the city, soliciting their advice. Pouyanne issued several reports, describing in vivid detail the alterations being undertaken in the Vietnamese countryside. The reports outlined three categories of public works that could benefit the colony: projects with direct benefits to the French, such as hydraulic irrigation systems; projects with indirect benefits, such as highways; and projects with social benefits to the government, a minor category which included urban design, relegated to a few dismissive paragraphs.[94] To Pouyanne, Hébrard's vision of the cities seemed frivolous: he did not provide immediate economic gain for colonial commercial interests. In 1931 the Comité de l'Indochine, made up of the most important investors in the colony, voiced their appreciation to Pouyanne: the colonial administration had followed their recommendations for infrastructural projects almost to the letter.[95]

The effort to separate himself from the public-works office resounded even in Hébrard's own urbanism proposals. His transportation network for Saigon, Hébrard explained, was not a mere map of technologies, but rather a professional system based on statistical research, aerial photographs, and a careful appraisal of comparable services in other great cities of the world.[96] Professional antagonisms between engineer and architect, common in Europe since the nineteenth century, suggested two quite different approaches to urban design: one based directly on technical feats as irrefutable signs of progress; the other self-consciously derived from an abstract process of scientific analysis and rational composition. It was this process of representation that underlay the aesthetic of the modern movement. Hébrard therefore regarded himself as a modernist. The conflict is remarkable for the supreme confidence of both sides; today it has become obvious that neither of these approaches, in and of itself, is a means for producing just, humane, and efficient cities.

An artist and professional urbanist, Hébrard considered himself above politics, uninfluenced by factional disputes and petty departmental intrigues. "We have proposed new goals [for the major colonial cities]," he declared straightforwardly; "it is the administration's job to find the means to realize them."[97] This distancing did not imply a subservience to government; in fact, Hébrard resented any governmental interference in his professional right to create plans and assume they would be implemented. He considered the Urbanism Department an independent professional agency with absolute power to plan cities; all urbanistic legislation should come from professional experts like himself, rather than from elected legislatures. In France, he feared, "the man of Art" could all too easily be limited by "the absolute technical incompetence of [local democratic] assemblies," notably the municipal councils which had a voice in determining the specific criteria for any implementation of the 1919 urban plans.[98]

In the colonies Hébrard was continually thwarted by actual political conflicts at many different levels: professional antagonisms with the engineers, lack of funds from new governors, ambiguous relations with the indigenous cultures of this colonial possession, poverty and revolt aggravated by that foreign domination, hostility from the major corporate and financial interests in Saigon. Although these forces largely determined the future of urban design and urban life in Indochina, he never tried to comprehend how they worked.

As a case in point, through all of Hébrard's writing about urbanism in colonial Indochina there inevitably lurks the question of racial segregation. He sought to sidestep the significance of racial policies by occasionally acknowledging his concerns about the poverty and poor health of Vietnamese villages and urban enclaves, problems from which the elite had to be protected, without showing any particular sense of France's responsibility for the situation. Hébrard thus tried to placate French liberals who condemned racial prejudice and at the same to avoid antagonizing the *colons* who certainly harbored such sentiments. On the one hand, he acknowledged that "for multiple reasons, the native districts should not be integrated with European districts"; on the other, he stressed that racial segregation laws had no place in good colonial urbanism, where the "new districts built in a European manner, and in principal destined for Europeans, are also peopled with a crowd of natives who can install themselves there freely, with the sole reservation that they abide by the codes imposed on everyone."[99]

Contact between the races was an inevitable aspect of colonial life, Hébrard contended, deploring the petty racism of the French *colons*. That contact had to be organized, sanitized, and rationalized by professional urbanists. If the mixing of the races constituted "an irrestible aspect of modernism,"[100] domination did not abate.

> [E]very European district needs a native district in order to survive; it will provide indispensable domestic servants, small businesses, and labor [*travaux d'exploitation*]. . . . [These districts] correspond, in essence, to the business districts and working-class residential neighborhoods of our own modern cities which are, in truth, separated from the bourgeois neighborhoods without a definite line being drawn on a map.[101]

This, in essence, is what happened in Indochina. In 1922 the city of Saigon established a zone reserved for the construction of "European-style houses"—permanent, detached, of minimum size and maximum occupancy, following strict sanitary standards.[102] According to an official municipal report that year, the ordinance was designed "above all to isolate from this part of the city the poor Asiatic element whose proximity constitutes a real danger because of the ignorance of the most elementary rules of hygiene."[103] Class, as much as race alone, determined segregation. It is ironic, if quite telling, that this same municipal council did nothing to regulate the corrupt Compagnie des Eaux et d'Électricité, a water and electricity monopoly which set exorbitant prices and provided substandard service, threatening the health of the European and Vietnamese populations alike.[104]

We learn a great deal about Western racial attitudes by looking at the more extreme segregation techniques of colonial cities.[105] Race became the overwhelmingly characteristic criterion for social stratification, even for the indigenous bourgeoisie who chose to live in the French neighborhoods, where this mixing was permitted (unlike in Dutch or English colonies). The exceptions reveal layered dimensions of racial prejudice, if not strict apartheid, though we should not forget the blatant racism of many French *colons*. Racial segregation based on medical or pseudo-functional grounds could easily lead to racial segregation on other grounds as well, as Philip D. Curtin has pointed out in his study of African colonial urbanism.[106] In Europe or the United States today, as in colonial Indochina, segregation policies purportedly based on class lines or health standards, demanding certain standards without making such standards of living widely available, will usually become a de facto form of racial segregation.

Some wealthy Vietnamese and Chinese families did live in the European residential districts of Saigon or Hanoi—just as they took a minor role in the governmental bureaucracy or local Chambers of Commerce and built their modern pharmacies (not traditional apothecary stores, at their own insistence) or luxury boutiques in the European commercial districts (fig. 142).[107] This new social class, soon to become a critical factor in Vietnam's history, was the product of colonial policies: land allocations, political favoritism, restricted educational opportunities, and the urban zoning plans Hébrard had drawn up and implemented. The Vietnamese bourgeoisie usually obtained their wealth and status through the French; if colonialism created them, most of this class respected its values and were given free access to the reserved elite neighborhoods of the colonial city. This applied to high-ranking clerks and translators as well as to professionals—journalists, doctors, lawyers, and especially teachers. It was certainly the case with officials who collaborated with the French; such officials received sizeable rural landholdings for their endorsements of the colonial re-

FIGURE 142. *Vietnamese and French commercial establishments on the same street, Saigon, c. 1930. National Archives.*

gime, endorsements that extended to such specific policies as the demolition of pagodas, the suspension of land titles, and the like.

Preference for the city among these highly educated families marks another dramatic break in Vietnamese history, for precolonial mandarins had identified with the court and the countryside, not the marketplace. While the lot of the vast majority of Vietnamese people worsened under colonialism, given its economic and educational priorities, this minority group flourished in the colonial cities of the 1920s, assuaging the consciences of liberal Frenchmen.

To direct the growth of an increasingly complex and modernized urban society, the colonial government instituted a new set of reforms, providing Hébrard with several commissions in the process. Under Governor-General Merlin new medical research facilities constituted the focus of such benefits, for health dangers in the cities, notably malaria and tuberculosis, remained a prime concern. Hébrard designed a new headquarters for the Institut Pasteur in Hanoi (1925–30) (fig. 143), while other architects in the service undertook additional hospitals and scattered dispensaries.[108] In each instance, the new buildings provided a picturesque composition of small pavilions with ample porches and balconies, thereby maximizing ventilation inside.

More important were the educational reforms, renewed under Long, disrupted by Merlin (who was deeply suspicious about giving the Vietnamese access

FIGURE 143. *Institut Pasteur, Hanoi, by Ernest Hébrard, 1930. From Laurent-Joseph Gaide,* L'Assistance médicale et la protection de la santé publique, 1931.

FIGURE 144. *Lycée Petrus Ky, Saigon, by Ernest Hébrard, 1925–28. From Teston and Percheron,* L'Indochine moderne.

to critical thinking and the ambitions education represented), then taken up again under the Socialist Alexandre Varenne. An important result of this effort was Hébrard's Lycée Petrus Ky in Saigon (1925–28), considered such a model of French colonial beneficence that a model of the school was put on display at the Colonial Exposition of 1931 (fig. 144).[109]

The lycée housed and taught 600 young Vietnamese students, providing a few classes in Chinese and Confucian ethics, but primarily technical training and French instruction that would prepare them for professional schools in the future. The setting, like the curriculum, sought to suggest the correct relations between French and Vietnamese culture, between health and learning, ambition and decorum. A series of elegant courtyards led out to soccer fields and a gymnasium—physical education that was unheard of in the mandarin system. Arcaded walkways connected classrooms, library, meeting rooms, dormitories, and a science laboratory—again a radical departure from mandarin practice. The orderly setting derived from Hébrard's Beaux-Arts plan, in perfect symmetrical balance and based on functional circulation paths. The subtle references to indigenous architecture consisted primarily of environmental controls, rather than decorative motifs.

One realizes the significance of the aesthetic choice by comparing this lycée with another school Hébrard designed during this same period, the Collège de Saigon (1926–28) (fig. 145). The more visible local motifs—tiered and upturned roofs covered in tiles, polychrome bands of colors along the walls—together with a rather spartan site and a more practical curriculum, made it another setting altogether.[110] The graduates would seek no higher education; they would remain more or less within the constraints of traditional Vietnamese culture, while they served French commerce and administration in useful ways. In contrast, the Lycée Petrus Ky prepared a future intelligentsia who would attend local professional schools under the aegis of the colonial government, or possibly complete their studies in Paris.

Those who went to Paris would live at the Maison des Etudiants de l'Indochine at the Cité Universitaire (fig. 146), a building designed by Martin and Vien in 1928. Here one sees the far-reaching reorientation of the colonial experience at home and abroad. This residence, too, represented a French perception of Indochinese aesthetics, evoking an exotic distant world for the Parisians, articulating a complex cultural milieu of power and history for the Maison's residents and their French neighbors.

Vietnamese students represented only a small proportion of the country's young people. Even those with access to education saw a limited horizon, mainly directed toward facilitating the French colonial presence. Merlin, for example, opened an École des Beaux-Arts as an extension of the University of Hanoi in 1926. This did not indicate a lessening in his hostility to education so much as an extension of his efforts to generate more income for the colony. In an extraordinary passage, meant to compliment the governor-general, the ama-

FIGURE 145. *Collège de Saigon by Ernest Hébrard, 1926–28. From* Urbanisme, *1932. Courtesy of* Urbanisme.

teur colonial historian, J. B. Alberti, explained the primary rationale behind the new school:

> In the fifteenth, eighteenth, and nineteenth centuries, the Annamites created architectural and decorative works of an original character, but since the end of the nineteenth century a considerable decline in the Indochinese arts has become apparent. Given that the vogue for Far Eastern works of art is steadily increasing in France and in all of Europe, Mr. Merlin judged it appropriate to select from the elite of indigenous artisans those able to create works in keeping with the genius of their race. He thought that France should make the Annamites understand how important it was for them not to abandon their traditional art while, at the same time, allowing themselves to be led in new directions. [111]

In other words, the École des Beaux-Arts would produce "authentic" oriental works of art for a European luxury market, with its directors deciding which materials and detailing an artist should use on the objects to be sold in European boutiques and department stores.

A minor division of the school trained a class of some thirty Vietnamese as *architectes-indigènes*, which is to say, low-paid draftsmen. Hébrard expressed no regrets about their lack of opportunity as architects. He associated Vietnamese designers with an artistic taste he deplored, that of "the abominable commercial terra cotta turned out in the Gay May factory of Cholon: minuscule elephants,

FIGURE 146.   *Maison des Etudiants de l'Indochine at the Cité Universitaire, Paris, by Martin & Vien, 1928. Photograph by Gwendolyn Wright.*

turquoise-blue hand railings in the shape of turnips, and an entire arsenal of architectural ornament of a quite dubious taste."[112] Of course, he also faulted the French architects who concocted designs using such opulent orientalism.

Hébrard assumed no possibility of development within Vietnamese culture. Again and again he reiterated the fantasy of French professional autonomy and disciplinary innovation, triumphant in the colonies. If the young Vietnamese in the architecture program should concentrate on drafting skills in their drawing classes, the French practitioners in Indochina should strive to find a balance between art and science, between preservation and innovation, in their commissions. Then the colonial architect would be graced with a "certain authority."[113]

Hébrard's major preoccupation was not individual buildings or even pedagogy but urban design. To him this meant the grouping of major governmental buildings and public open spaces in an impressive and efficient manner. His first duties when Long invited him to Indochina included two such settings: the new governmental district in Hanoi and a renewed plan for a summer capital at Dalat, high in the Lang-Bian mountain range.

For the governor-general and his architect, the proposed governmental center of 1923–25 exemplified a grand modern vision of colonial urbanism (see fig. 131). Hébrard's site plan recalled Versailles—and his own World Center. Taking Long's site west of the Petit Lac, in an area still relatively unencumbered yet close to the burgeoning French residential district, Hébrard sketched a magnificent Beaux-Arts plan. A strong central axis emerged from the new governor's palace, with ministries grouped in an enlarged park. At the edge of the expanded Botanical Garden, a baroque trident would reach out into the city. The scheme set aside space for later expansion in the governmental complex, while it concentrated future commercial development along three major boulevards that would replace the military installations in the former citadel district. Like the single existing avenue to the southeast, which led to the prestigious Rue Paul Bert, the new avenues would terminate at historical colonial settings: the picturesque Gate Jean Dupuis at the entrance to the "native city," and the grand Chateau d'Eau dating from the concession. These were not simply exciting vistas. The ideals of French colonialism literally radiated outward in this scheme.

Martial Merlin, appointed governor-general after Long's sudden death in 1924, enthusiastically endorsed the plan. Yet Hébrard was compelled to proceed in a piecemeal fashion due to budgetary constraints and the continuous internecine rivalries within the French population. Slowly, a few new streets were laid out as he envisioned, and the park was extended, but the new radial avenues did not materialize. The large circular *place* at the entrance to the park would

FIGURE 147. *Ministry of Finance, Hanoi, by Ernest Hébrard, 1925–27. From the* Eveil économique de l'Indochine, 1927.

eventually be named in Hébrard's honor but was completed only after his death in 1932. In 1925 construction commenced on the first administrative building, Hébrard's Ministry of Finance, with its pagoda-like roofs, where the emperor's elephant stables once stood (fig. 147). Ground was broken for three other ministries (agriculture, education, and justice), but work did not proceed.[114] Nor was Hébrard successful in implementing many related urbanistic projects for the capital city, such as removing the large factory near the Petit Lac or modernizing the river front.

Since the colony's economy, at least for the French population, reached its zenith in the mid-1920s, we must ask why so much of Hébrard's grand scheme was curtailed. One answer might indeed be aesthetic, for it surely displeased many *colons* and bureaucrats to see Indochinese architectural motifs on the ministries they would use; hitherto this practice had applied only to buildings which served the colonized populations. But equally important were a series of political issues. Merlin had almost been killed by a bomb in Canton late in 1924; when the Vietnamese treated his would-be assassin as a national hero, the *colon* population grew even more hostile. Then, because of the electoral victory of the Cartel Des Gauches, a Socialist deputy from Puy de Dôme, Alexandre Varenne, was appointed governor-general in July 1925. It was the first time a member of the Socialist party had ever held such a position in the French Empire. Conservatives were highly suspicious, especially in the colony, even after the national congress of the Socialist party expelled Varenne from its ranks.

Varenne was caught between several different worlds, trusted by none of them. Perhaps this situation intensified his conviction that he could sidestep politics. He hoped to accomplish some well-intended reforms of a social nature, notably in the fields of labor, fiscal, and administrative reform, that would benefit the Vietnamese. Yet Varenne was unsuccessful in his naive efforts to placate every constituency and assert equitable, nonpartisan direction for the colony. Eloquent speeches and an austere public life—even forgoing the usual gold-braided uniform of his office—could not give him the authority he desired.

Varenne's priorities surely put in abeyance Hébrard's vision of a grandiose new governmental center. The situation worsened at the end of the year with the repercussions of a speech by Varenne. The governor-general dared suggest that Vietnam, with France's assistance, might one day regain its independence. The leftist minority felt betrayed by Varenne's ineffectiveness, while the majority of French colonial society, as well as their supporters in France, were infuriated. The anger further stymied all governmental undertakings. Varenne tried to make amends, even calling his statement about eventual independence an "error," but he was hounded from office after little more than two years in Indochina. Pierre Pasquier, a career administrator, now assumed the position.[115]

Hébrard remained oblivious to the political implications of his policies and his ideas—although this should not lead us to dismiss those aspects of his colonial career. His preferred project during his stay in Indochina, lasting through most of the 1920s, seemed to provide the autonomy and control he sought. Yet even here, we can see how Hébrard's urban plans illuminate the cultural complexities of French colonialism.

Dalat was to be a model city, in the sense of a controlled environment, an urbane retreat for the French elite (fig. 148). In location and in character, the town was far from the heat, the bickering, and the industrial pollution of Saigon, far from the violence, the rivalries, and the crowded streets of Hanoi. In their efforts to create a perfectly planned environment, Hébrard and the colonial government felt they could avoid the complexities of real cities. The plan downplayed industry and even large commercial districts, for Dalat was envisioned as a resort and summer capital. This city would supposedly inspire governmental efficiency, high-minded leisure, and health of body and mind through its site and design—at least for European residents. Strict racial and environmental controls characterized the town from its very origin. Although the emperor would later vacation here, other Vietnamese needed permission even to enter Dalat, and they lived only beyond the northern hills.

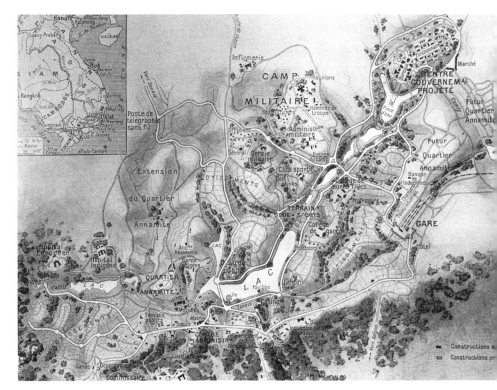

FIGURE 148. *Plan for Dalat by Ernest Hébrard, 1923, with a map of French Indochina. From* L'Illustration, *1923.*

Dr. Alexandre Yersin had first discovered this balmy plateau site during an 1897 excursion in the mountains of South Annam. Yersin, founder of the Institut Pasteur and the Medical School in Hanoi, specialized in research on malaria. He proposed using the area as a sanatorium for French families in the Orient, where they would be safe from tropical diseases like malaria and could regain the fortitude to face the difficult environments of the southeast Asian cities. Yersin had thereby hoped to still the government's insistence that the Institut Pasteur should work only in the region of Cochinchina's rubber plantations, where European enterprises might profit most directly from the scientists' efforts.[116]

Hearing that Dalat enjoyed a climate much like that of Nice, Doumer decided to proceed. He hired the military surveyor Champoudry to prepare a plan for a large luxury hotel, administrators' residences, and, to be sure, an imposing train station. The Palace Hotel was completed in the rococo style of hotels along the French Riviera, together with a few chalets reminiscent of the French Alps, but the continued lack of rail service meant that the fledgling town was abandoned at the time of World War I.

In 1921, when Long invited Hébrard to Indochina, the governor-general hoped to revive the idea of Dalat as a summer retreat for the colonial government, "providing not only the services of a military camp, but also a complete administrative capital."[117] Hébrard envisioned a perfect expression of his urbanistic principles: the separation of uses and races, made to seem organic by adaption to the natural terrain; and building guidelines to control height, materials, density, and basic proportions. Here he would create a visual harmony and a rational organization of spaces, similar to Prost's work in Rabat—or, indeed, to his own World Center.[118]

Despite Hébrard's insistent reprimands that colonial architects should take climate into account, he still treated environments in a rather abstract manner. The surveying he requested proved to be of poor quality, and since he never seems to have visited the site himself, Hébrard failed to take into account many of the splendid panoramic views.[119] Yet he did conceptualize an efficient modern city: an urban plan which facilitated orderly work, followed by relaxed pleasures in Dalat's parks, zoo, theater, and casino, then home along the lovely walks and curving drives to groups of picturesque private villas. The whole spared the Europeans any evidence of poverty or industry.

Once again, Hébrard conceived a plan and began work, only to have construction stop half-way through. The promenade around the lake and "a few mediocre villas crammed onto narrow lots" were the only aspects of his plan to be carried out during the 1920s.[120] What riled many *colons* about Hébrard's scheme was not so much its stylistic predilections as its insistence on zoning and design guidelines, curtailing the absolute freedom many Frenchmen believed to be their right, especially in the colonies. Only from Paris would he hear praise, and this precisely because of the progressive demands for such controls. In 1933 the Parisian journal *Urbanisme* lauded Hébrard's stand at Dalat. Zoning, the writer pointed out, "at first criticized in the name of liberty, would be accepted, several years later, as a safeguard against industrial intrusions, problems we suffer from so badly in the *métropole*."[121]

Regardless of the careful guidelines, most later building denied the actual setting and nostalgically evoked the distant French countryside. When construction of the villas recommenced in the 1930s, the designs expressed a nostalgia for the French countryside, with houses explicitly resembling cottages in Savoie, Provence, Alsace, and other provinces of France. Hébrard's concept of a complex cultural milieu had been reduced to a fairy-tale evocation of peaceful

French provincial life—much as Indochina's colonial cities of the nineteenth century had alluded to the urbane grandeur of France.

Hébrard sought to strike a balance between general principles of rational design and the particular texture of local cultures. Dalat was the proposal he emphasized most often in his articles for the French press, for this was truly the ideal environment to demonstrate his ideas, free from the bothersome intrusions of commercial interests. In this flawless planned environment he envisioned supremely healthy, reasonable, and uplifting life for all residents. In his utopian formulation Hébrard also hoped to create a new basis for the august tradition of French architecture, without sacrificing his awareness of the specific needs of the colonial government and the French residents—and even, to a lesser extent, those of the colonial subjects.

Hébrard's problem derived, in large part, from his very desire to fashion a perfectly harmonized system. His architecture supposedly embodied scientific reason and cultural tolerance, alluding to a perfect balance between past and future, aesthetics and industry, high art and vernacular. Such control, more than any formal paradigm, was for him the essence of modernism—or what he wanted modernism to be. Vietnam could, Hébrard hoped, provide a setting where he and others could experiment with this version of modernism, genially evoking history and cultural distinctions, while asserting the universal directives of scientific urban planning. As he told the Paris congress on colonial urbanism:

> French architects of our own day are capable, with the conditions imposed on them by the tropical climate and bearing in mind the situation they have been given, of creating a vital architecture that will not be inferior to the products of our glorious past I have just enumerated. In any case, instead of building in Indochina pastiches of what exists in Europe, why not direct the natives along a path that accords well with their traditions, their temperaments, and their aptitudes, making them evolve normally toward a modern art that will be particular to them?[122]

Hébrard's notion of French architects choosing to "direct the native" suggests the wide-ranging power he assumed, almost unconsciously, for the professional urbanist. In his view of culture, French aesthetic leadership and tutelage paralleled the political superiority of the colonial government over its "native charges."

5

MADAGASCAR: UNIVERSAL
ENGINEERING

ON THE LAST day of September, 1895, shortly before her fortieth birthday, Ranavalona III, Queen of Madagascar, stood with her courtiers in the well-tended garden of the royal palace, near a silver-gray cottage embellished with Gothic revival fretwork (fig. 149). As she watched French shells burst around her, the shrapnel killing many of the soldiers in attendance, Ranavalona decided to raise the white flag and surrender. For almost a year French colonial officials tried to maintain her on the throne, although they changed Ranavalona's title to a more local tribal sovereignty, Queen of the Merina, to emphasize their own dominance (fig. 150). But Ranavalona's tacit support of the ongoing insurrection throughout the island soon became too public for the French to tolerate. She was forced to abdicate, exiled in the middle of the night to the island of Réunion and from there to Algiers. This act ended the Imerina dynasty, a series of proud and popular monarchs who had ruled over most of Madagascar since 1787.[1]

A desire for autonomy and a firm commitment to the superiority of the Merina tribe had sustained the royal dynasty's aloofness from its subjects and from Westerners, a position given physical expression in the early choice of a capital city, Antananarivo (Tananarive to the French), high in the Antankara mountains at the center of Madagascar, with the royal palace perched on the Rova, the highest granite peak. Wheeled vehicles, even carts, were still unknown there when the French took control, for the Merina monarchs had accentuated their isolation by refusing to build roads across the island's rough and varied terrain.

The appeal of European ideas and products had nonetheless permeated many aspects of Malagasy life, especially in the distant capital. Ranavalona carried into her exile the costly sedan chair King Radama II had received from Emperor Napoleon III.[2] Ladies of the nobility followed the couture fashions of

FIGURE 149. *Palace of Manampisoa, built for Queen Rasoharina in Antananarivo, 1863–68. From* La Revue de Madagascar, *1933.*

Paris and London, only a year or two behind the latest modes, and gentlemen proudly displayed top hats or military dress uniforms. Tribunals and royal abodes emulated Western revival styles of the nineteenth century (fig. 151), while even ordinary dwellings and churches in Antananarivo often resembled Victorian cottages, their steeply pitched roofs ornamented with carved wooden tracery on the verge boards (fig. 152).

Europeans had long considered this city, like the Merina nobility (called the Imerina) who dominated it, a place of remarkable contrasts, at once orderly and cluttered in appearance, exotic to some and familiar to others, its inhabitants both sophisticated and suspicious about Western ways. Descriptions of Antananarivo tended, accordingly, to be widely divergent. Some visitors sharply criticized the place as a small town where "the houses are of thatch, in diverse styles and forms, built with no sense of the ensemble; the few more recent structures one notices from time to time blaspheme the ensemble without beautifying it."[3] Others described the first glimpse of a "far blue peak crowned with the towers and domes of palaces and churches; . . . well-built houses of red brick in a uniform style of architecture, generally surrounded with shrubberies, evoking reminiscences of the genteel but cheap suburbs of some of our large towns [in England]."[4] These varying responses related, in large part, to the author's attitudes about the appropriate appearance, whether highly structured or quaintly picturesque, for European cities.

FIGURE 150. *Queen Ranavalona III, who ruled Madagascar between 1883 and 1896. From Jean Devic,* Tananarive, 1952.

Marco Polo gave the name Madagascar to this, the fourth largest island in the world, less than 250 miles off the eastern coast of Africa, yet so isolated that

FIGURE 151. *High Court of the Queen, Antananarivo, built for Queen Ranavalona II by the English architect Parrett, 1883. From* La Revue de Madagascar, *1933.*

Eocene forms of life have been preserved. He did not visit the island but rather recounted the tales of Arab travelers.[5] Initial contact with the West came through Portuguese merchants who landed here in the sixteenth century but did not settle. European and American pirates in the mid- to late-seventeenth century proved to be a more lasting presence. They set up towns along the coast and intermarried with Malagasy women, establishing something of a democratic "pirates' republic" in their civil life, between attacks on the treasure-laden ships of the European powers.[6] Louis XIV tried to set up a French settlement at Fort Dauphin, far to the south, commissioning a grand commemorative obelisk from Claude Perrault to mark the site.[7] The settlement foundered thirty years later in 1665, when the king sent French girls to marry the settlers. Their common-law Antanoy wives, angered at being supplanted, easily incited their tribe to attack. Half the French were massacred and the rest fled, ending official European attempts to colonize for over a century.[8]

In 1820, during the reign of King Radama I, French and English missionaries were allowed to open schools and churches along the Malagasy coast. They soon introduced a printing press to produce educational and religious tracts, having transliterated the Malagasy language using the Latin alphabet. As the two foreign religions and two nationalities vied with one another at the court, receptivity to them both fluctuated wildly. In 1829, responding to a French gunboat attack on the recently established port city of Toamasina (Tamatave to the French), Queen Ranavalona I cut off contact with Europe, then banned Christianity a year later (largely because of its preachings about equality), and finally exiled all Europeans from the island between 1835 and 1857. She specified two individual exemptions to this dictum, but only one, a Frenchman, accepted her offer at the time. The legacy of these two individuals set the tenor for future development on Madagascar.

Jean Laborde, a French adventurer, had been shipwrecked in 1831 off the western coast of Madagascar, where he was searching for treasure aboard wrecked vessels. Laborde carried out a remarkable one-man industrial revolution after he

FIGURE 152.   *Protestant church near Antananarivo, c. 1870. Photograph by Don Rusillon, courtesy of the Musée de l'Homme, Paris.*

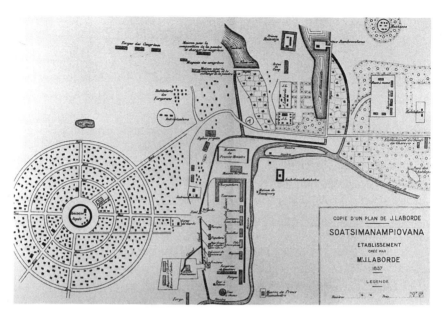

FIGURE 153. *Site plan of Jean Laborde's factory site at Mantasoa, 1837. From the* Bullétin de l'Académie Malgache, *1939.*

FIGURE 154. *Tomb (Fasan'ny) for Rainiharo at Isotry, north of Lake Anosy, by Jean Laborde, 1835. From Devic,* Tananarive.

gained the confidence of the queen. Soon this "universal engineer," as he depicted himself, began manufacturing a range of articles—including guns, cannons, textiles, porcelain, paper, sugar, and rum—from his factories, most notably at Mantasoa, close to an abundant supply of water, wood, and iron ore (fig. 153). More than 20,000 workers were eventually employed at Mantasoa, mostly slaves and conscript laborers provided by Ranavalona under the *fanompoana* system of obligatory labor to the crown.[9] Laborde showed some interest in health and welfare, providing housing for approximately 1,200 skilled employees.[10] Regardless, the Malagasy workers bitterly resented the unrelenting rigor of forced labor. In 1857, when Laborde was briefly required to quit the island, they rose up and demolished the machinery and buildings at Mantasoa. Only an abandoned furnace and an enormous hydraulic wheel remained as souvenirs of this early French experiment in industrial productivity.

Laborde's initial venture in monumental architecture had come in 1835, when he was invited to design a tomb for the recently deceased prime minister, Rainiharo, at Isotry on the outskirts of Antananarivo (fig. 154). A three-year stay in Bombay, shortly before his fateful shipwreck, gave a decided Hindu air to his design for the mausoleum, the first structure on Madagascar to use carved stone. By royal decree, only funerary architecture could employ stone, yet even royal and aristocratic tombs had never before explored the ornamental possibilities of the material.

Laborde recognized the basic design principles and the primal significance of funerary ceremony in Madagascar. Throughout the island, varying with the region, large family sepulchers are still adorned with carved wooden figures, enormous *zebu* (humpbacked cattle) horns, or massive stone monoliths. Well into the twentieth century, a majority of Merina in the central plateau region around the capital celebrated *famadihanas* (literally a turning over of the body) every three or four years, reclothing a corpse in a new shroud (the same *lamba* or shawl most people wear over their shoulders), dancing and feasting, and then returning the remains to the monumental tomb. Laborde's approach augmented the majesty and scale of a familiar vernacular building type without dramatically challenging tradition. Recognizing the Malagasy appreciation of funerary ritual, he celebrated Rainiharo in a new style.

Laborde was then given the opportunity to build a new palace for the queen in 1839. The hilltop site had originally been chosen by the first Merina monarch, Andrianampoinimerina, and his one-room wooden dwelling was left standing alongside the new residence. Laborde's design again specifically deferred to royal precedent and to the typical Malagasy buildings of the area (in this case, habitations for the living, always far less imposing than those for the

FIGURE 155. *Original Queen's Palace (Manjakamiadana), built for Queen Ranavalona I by Jean Laborde in Antananarivo, 1839, with typical Merina dwellings of the epoch. From the Reverend William Ellis*, Madagascar Revisited, *1867.*

deceased), while it introduced a new grandeur in size and complexity (fig. 155). After consultation with the queen, he adhered to the prevailing north-south orientation for houses, derived from mystical beliefs about healthy winds and the habits of ancestral spirits, which still pervade much of Madagascar. The basic module for construction continued to be the fathom, 5′3″, based on the height of the queen. Traditional wood construction was maintained but amplified, with an enormous ebony post at the center, some 130 feet high; three stories of massive high walls with surrounding verandas; and the steeply pitched two-sided roof. (Strict taboos forbade a roof with only one slope.) Now architecture, as well as location, could mark the royal family's special position, at once superior to and a part of the population they ruled.

The Manjakamiadana, as the palace is known locally ("Where It Is Meant To Reign"), respected established Malagasy traditions while it initiated a new trend in residential architecture. In fact, according to G. S. Chapus, a preeminent early historian of the city, the basic format of the palace became so popular and influential a structure among the upper classes that it came to seem "traditional." The modified Gothic revival forms—a multiple-story wood house with projecting balcony and steep, broken wood-shingle roof—soon became the characteristic vernacular in Antananarivo.[11]

FIGURE 156. *House for the Reverend J. Pearse, Antananarivo, by James Cameron,*
1840. From Joseph Mullins, Twelve Months in Madagascar, *1875.*

James Cameron, a Scottish carpenter turned missionary, preceded Laborde
by almost a decade, arriving in Madagascar in 1822 with the London Missionary
Society, by then a largely Nonconformist organization. As the church fathers
had hoped, Cameron used his artisanal skills to win the interest of the crown,
setting up factories and engineering a fresh-water reservoir. Once again, architecture served to mediate between European and Malagasy culture, innovating
even as it respected the precedents of both stylistic traditions.

Cameron's own house, a modest one-story dwelling, was the first structure
on the island to use sun-dried brick. This quickly became a popular building
material, since clay was abundant in many regions of the "Great Red Island." Its
deep-red color became especially characteristic of Antananarivo in the second
half of the nineteenth century, after Radama II lifted the ban on permanent
materials for ordinary citizens' dwellings in order to encourage more hygienic
habitations. Likewise, the house Cameron designed for a fellow missionary,
about the time Laborde built the Queen's Palace, provided another important
precedent. The balcony surmounting a broad front porch further developed the
creolized Gothic character of wooden and masonry architecture in the capital
city (fig. 156). [12] What seem long-standing vernacular traditions in building de-

FIGURE 157. *Typical Merina houses in Antananarivo, c. 1890, now using brick and balconies.* From C. Savaron, Mes Souvenirs á Madagascar. . . . (1885–1898), 1932.

rived, in part, from the example of these two Europeans replicating the style of dwellings they had known at home, adapting forms, meanings, and materials to their new surroundings (fig. 157).

Other amateur architects from the West followed this pattern as well. In the palace of the prime minister (the Andafiavaretra, today the president's residence), built between 1872 and 1874, the English missionary William Pool transformed European stylistic precedents even as he followed them, most notably with the brilliant choice of colors: bright pink walls set off in yellow. In a similar manner, paints of luminous red and white distinguished the Gothic detailing of the smaller Silver Palace (the Tramovola or Maison d'Argent) built by the French carpenter Louis Gros for Radama I in 1854.

When Cameron returned to Madagascar after Queen Rasoharina lifted the ban on Christianity in 1861, he agreed to transform Laborde's earlier design for the Queen's Palace. The Frenchman had been involved in an effort to overthrow the queen's now deceased husband, Radama II, and the new ruler wanted greater protection. Cameron enveloped the building in granite blocks, imposing a lordly, if rather lugubrious, more or less Renaissance-revival style to the new facade, completed in 1869 (fig. 158). For the first time, stone was used for a

Figure 158. *The Queen's Palace (Manjakamiadana) in Antananarivo with a new facade in stone by James Cameron, 1869. From Devic,* Tananarive.

dwelling rather than for a tomb. Cameron's ecclesiastical leanings show in four immense square towers at each corner, one of which contains a clock, much as a church belfry would do.

Indeed, while other houses did not follow this lead, stone now replaced wood as the most prevalent material for a spate of larger, European-designed

FIGURE 159. *Martyr Memorial Church at Ambohipotsy, south of the Queen's Palace, by James Sibree, 1863. From James Sibree,* Fifty Years in Madagascar, *1924. Courtesy of George Allen & Unwin, London.*

churches over the next two decades. This shift had first emerged with James Sibree's elegant Martyr Memorial Church at nearby Ambohipotsy (1863) (fig. 159); now it became quite widespread with such stately edifices as Father Alphonse Taïx's Catholic cathedral (1871), and William Pool's Anglican cathedral (1889), all fittingly Gothic in style. As Sibree declared in the *Antananarivo Annual* of 1887, "each of our churches became, so to speak, a professional school during its construction."[13] Western ecclesiastics sought to teach the Malagasy not only religious doctrine but also aesthetic appreciation and labor skills in the building crafts.

Cameron and Laborde paved the way for a renewal of contact with Europeans under a series of later Merina rulers. Their industrial accomplishments augmented the prestige and revenue of the crown. Their architecture—whether civic, residential, religious, or industrial—introduced Western aesthetic concepts, without abruptly challenging Malagasy principles of design and meaning. Mystical preferences for certain orientations or materials, and the symbolic allusions to the royal or tribal past could comfortably coexist with innovations in scale and style. The results had great appeal to the elite of the capital, stimulating extensive building and remodeling, and thus substantial overcrowding, throughout the second half of the century.[14]

As the Imerina nobles in Antananarivo experimented with Western fashions for their clothes, their houses, and their religion, the other inhabitants of the island grew increasingly fearful of offending ancestral spirits with such changes. Although most subjects were loyal to the throne, they resented what seemed the arrogance and disrespect of the Merina tribe and especially the Imerina oligarchy. These tensions undermined the authority of royal administrators to the point that, after Andrianampoinimerina, later monarchs of the nineteenth century never succeeded in imposing their rule over more than two-thirds of the island.

The various antagonisms overlapped, influencing both popular sentiment and official policy. In particular, the conscious decisions not to develop internal transportation greatly impaired the monarchy's control over outlying areas. Radama I had first refused to build a road from the coast to the capital, fearing it could facilitate a European invasion, and Prime Minister Rainilairarivony (also husband successively to the three queens he served between 1863 and 1895) continued this policy. He hoped to maintain Imerina power through the earliest and simplest techniques: a central but unassailable capital city, high in the mountainous plateau, together with a clear but absolute social hierarchy among the island's ethnic groups. Yet the isolation could not assure the Merina's dominance over all other tribes. Neither could it keep away European ideas and, eventually, European control.

What is striking, then, about Madagascar's precolonial history is the obvious and long-standing tensions between a reclusive stance, hostile to outside influence in economic or sociopolitical matters, and a fascination with Western aesthetic trends. If traditional modes of building, worship, or work could so easily be transformed, was culture only superficial? Or did the new forms change attitudes and help "civilize" these groups to accept the mores of modern industrial life? And how, in any event, did the styles disseminate through the various strata of Malagasy life when there seemed to be so much resistance to them?

In this quintessential colonial quandary one finds a key concern of the earliest Europeans who came to Madagascar, hoping to counter the initial antagonism of the local people with modern products, urban services, and architectural innovation. They hoped thereby to produce able workers and eager consumers. In particular, this colonial government enacted more ordinances regulating labor than any other French colony, to the point of establishing various forms of forced labor between 1897 and 1946.[15]

Their problems were by no means unique to this colony. The same antagonisms prevailed in many parts of France. French industrial groups like the Redressement Français also asked themselves how to modernize without losing their traditional authority as leaders and overseers. In the *métropole* or in the colonies, reformers had to decide which aspects of daily life were most susceptible to change, which were truly resistant, and which might introduce too precipitous a social revolution. Techniques that worked in the colonies might be able to transform French society, too, producing greater productivity and strong consumer interests, without destroying the charm or the social hierarchy of traditional society.

The Tache d'Huile

Only seven months after establishing a protectorate on the island, the French Parliament voted to annex the country as a full-fledged colony (fig. 160). In large part this simply showed expansionist pressure from businessmen, settlers, and missionaries who wanted a monopolistic position of strength. To a lesser extent, the decision resulted from liberal forces who wished to abolish slavery, relying on the 1848 law which freed any slave who set foot on French territory.[16] In any case, the rights and responsibilities of the French resident-general had never been spelled out clearly, for the primary goal in setting up a protectorate had been to foreclose British domination. The fact that neither of the men who

FIGURE 160. *Frontispiece, H. Galli [Henri Gallichet], La Guerre à Madagascar, 1896.*

first held office had been able to subdue the ever-present violence against Europeans seemed an obvious result of this vagueness.

The person chosen to head both the first official colonial government and the French colonial troops in Madagascar was Joseph-Simon Gallieni. He had already proven himself in the Sudan and Indochina. Now appointed to the rank of general, Gallieni arrived in Antananarivo on September 27, 1896, the day after Resident-General Larouche first read the emancipation proclamation to the populace. Gallieni was to serve as governor-general of Madagascar for the next nine years. He left his mark on virtually every aspect of the country's development in the twentieth century: education, health service, political structure, legal system, public works, and regional organization still show the impact of Gallieni's early policies.

From the start the new governor-general used the tactics he had evolved in Indochina, both the *tâche d'huile* approach to pacification, based on a gradual outreach of services through existing towns and new settlements, and the *politique des races*, whereby all ethnic groups were to be governed by their own leaders—selected by the French. Although Gallieni's strategies reflect a considered respect for local traditions and pride, the aims, if not the strategies, derived primarily from fervent nationalism. He wanted first to make Madagascar French (*"franciser Madagascar"*); secondarily, he believed it essential to humble the Merina elite and undermine the earlier strong influence of the British.[17] Despite certain manifestly good intentions, domination was the goal. The Malagasy recognized this, of course, and French troops continued to face armed resistance, causing the loss of many lives on both sides before "pacification" was declared a success in 1905.

Starting off with a calculated eye for tradition, Gallieni insisted on retaining Antananarivo as the capital of the new colony, as it had been under Ranavalona III and her predecessors. This decision came under attack from French military leaders, who considered the narrow footpath to Antananarivo laboriously cut by General Duchesne's conquering army from Mahajanja (Majunga), the nearest port city, entirely inadequate for protecting the inland capital. Public-works engineers in the army also contended that the city was simply too far from the coast, too hilly, and already too crowded for the kinds of improvements that were needed. Both groups wanted to maintain Toamasina as the temporary capital, until it was feasible to relocate the political center to a new site, the hill station of Antsirabé, south of the capital on a broad plateau—a former penal colony for political prisoners under the Imerina. Thirty years later, a major French urbanist based in Madagascar still concurred that Antsirabé seemed "more accommodating to a *ville nouvelle* based on the principles of modern urbanism."[18]

Figure 161. *The Avenue de France, Antananarivo, an 1899 street leading to the palace of the governor-general built by André Jully, 1889–92. Photographed in 1931. From* Le Monde colonial illustré, *1932.*

Gallieni argued that the health benefits of Antananarivo's mountainous site easily matched those of Antsirabé. More to the point, only in Antananarivo could the government fully establish its political authority. French dominance had to radiate out from the same center the Merina had used, where the colonial powers could likewise assert their superiority over the local elite and the distant tribes. Simultaneously, the French could "make Antananarivo a city in the European sense of the word," introducing improvements which would be highly visible here at the center of Malagasy urban life.[19] Gallieni prevailed, and the capital remained where it had been for more than a century.

Gallieni exercised the shift in authority with discretion but no lack of will, using historic preservation to suggest his respect for the Merina monarchy. After exiling the queen, he maintained her palace and the royal mausoleums as historic monuments, which they remain to this day. Nearby, the diminutive Manampisoa Palace ("Beauty's Increment") (see fig. 149) and part of the former palace of the prime minister were converted into museums with artifacts of the monarchy. (The rest served as a barracks for the 13th Infantry Regiment.)[20] The smaller Silver Palace (the Tramovola), by then abandoned, became the seat of the Académie Malgache in 1898 (see fig. 30). Here Gallieni encouraged scholarly research in Malagasy history, ethnography, and culture by European scholars. As would be the case several decades later in Indochina and Morocco, such

251

FIGURE 162.   Kabary *(public gathering) at the maison commune indigène of Fianarantsoa, built under Gallieni, c. 1900. National Archives.*

academies showed a certain respect for the civilization the French now dominated, although preservation actions focused entirely on the distant past, rather
than the evolving future, of the colonized culture and its leaders.

The new governor-general chose not to erect a headquarters for his own
regime, instead making do with the rather clumsy residential palace built for the
brief protectorate government in 1891–92. The architect, André Jully, had used
an overly self-conscious French Renaissance style to evoke the national grandeur
of the *grand siècle*. The spacious formal gardens, soon accentuated by the broad
Avenue de France on axis with the Residence, gave a feeling of elegance that
many observers indeed found not unlike that of the Trianon and its surroundings
(fig. 161). As Lyautey noted, the structure was near the "palace and the other
traditional installations of the former power."[21] Although the design scarcely
informs us about Gallieni's own preferences, the decision suggests that he was
reluctant to spend public funds simply on the glorification of France.

To encourage the semblance of local self-government, Gallieni revived the *fokon'olona* (village councils) of the central regions, through which tribal leaders had once settled disputes, collected taxes, and arranged for public works. The tactic sought to diminish the power of the Merina nobility and to fuel tribal antagonisms, rather than a sense of national unity. Gallieni considered the *fokon'olona* such a useful institution that he soon installed it throughout the island, including areas where the practice had never existed. Village squares became the setting for ceremonial gatherings (fig. 162), but the carefully staged events precluded any opportunities for significant local decision-making.

Despite such gestures of respect for Madagascar's earlier autonomy, the political and economic conditions of colonialism markedly altered life throughout the country. Private property, for example, had not existed in Madagascar, where all land belonged to the sovereign. Favorite nobles did receive sizeable holdings, but foreigners were never granted such exemptions. Through their councils the various tribes were allowed to farm and build houses and family tombs on royal land, in exchange for heavy taxes and services. Land not allocated to nobles or tribes constituted a kind of public domain which consisted primarily of forest or desert that would be difficult to cultivate. The French, in taking power from Ranavalona, became, like her, the ultimate owner and allocator of land. This might have allowed the opportunity to plan in a grand manner, with no concern for indemnities. But Gallieni believed it necessary to institute private property on the island. He thereby hoped to encourage European colonization, while promoting a strong desire for hard work and stability among the indigenous Malagasy—who could now aspire to become *propriétaires*.[22]

Whereas Gallieni did want to redistribute land in an equitable manner among the Malagasys themselves, his first commitment was to lure French farmers, merchants, and industrialists. A French national with a capital of only 5,000 francs could obtain 150 acres on the condition that he put them under cultivation. Even with such favorable terms, only 630 European farmers had been drawn to Madagascar by 1905, when Gallieni left. The vast majority of land grants during the first decade of French colonialism went to plantation owners or industrialists, especially mining companies, half of these grants (1.4 million acres) to only five large companies.[23]

Gallieni's land reforms proved unable to launch Madagascar as a truly successful French settlement for farmers or small-scale capitalists. Instead he soon established the preeminence of internationally based companies. Their leaders cared only about maximum exploitation of available resources, rather than the interests of either French or Malagasy people. Gallieni later regretted his naive trust in these powerful consortiums, but they would continue to pressure later colonial governments for improvements in their own self-interests, such as particular sites for roads and other public works.[24]

Perhaps the most dramatic aspect of change was the liberation of some 500,000 slaves on September 26, 1896.[25] The Imerina elite bitterly resented the loss of laborers and prestige, complaining about an inadequate and irresponsible work-force under the new system—complaints that would soon be echoed by French *colons*. Emancipation won gratitude from those who had been slaves, and very few of them would join the rebel groups which opposed the French. All the same, French law could not eradicate the fear of a return to slavery, a fear that would haunt French labor policies on the island for years to come. Nor could emancipation provide sources of income or housing for the former slaves, who already made up half the population of the capital city, soon joined by migrants from the countryside.[26] Vagabondage and thievery became major problems in Antananarivo, for the transition from feudal slavery to modern free labor occurred quite abruptly, with no anticipation of the changes this would entail.

In part to provide employment for this worrisome group, Gallieni felt compelled to revive forced labor. Every able-bodied Malagasy man between the ages of 16 and 60 was required to give a consecutive 50 (later 30) days of free labor, performing public works under the aegis of the French army. If he so desired, the individual could continue as a wage-earner after this time, and many did so, rather than return to their former owners. The workers were relatively well-housed in "liberty villages" near the major work sites, similar to those Gallieni had used in the Sudan in the 1880s.[27]

Still, as a good Republican, Gallieni could not help feeling uncomfortable about the system he had instituted. Officially the French system lasted only between 1896 and 1898 and it applied to fixed, limited periods of time devoted to a specific public purpose, rather than boundless individual gain. Anticipating the rationalizing discourse of future colonial administrations on the island, Gallieni could even contend that he was training the Malagasy people to be more productive workers, better adapted to French commercial interests.[28] In conjunction with the system of mandatory labor, he therefore established councils of French capitalists (Délégations Economiques et Financières) in every major city, calling on them to create jobs for the work force he was preparing. This became truly imperative in 1900, when the French legislature passed a law requiring that all colonies become economically self-sufficient within the next ten years.

The desire to modernize Madagascar's infrastructure certainly influenced Gallieni. New buildings, many of them entirely new kinds of buildings, repre-

FIGURE 163.   *Police station in the "indigenous village" of Toamasina, c. 1900.*
Postcard.

sented the associationist approach to colonization: clinics, nurseries, orphanages, post offices, town halls, and *maisons de tous*, as well as jails and police stations (figs. 163, 164). To take only one example of this mission, the colony had established 650 schools to train 50,000 future Malagasy workers by 1903, the curricula stressing practical and manual education.[29] Construction boomed, requiring a large corps of building workers.

More routine public works seemed, if anything, especially imperative if the colony were to flourish economically. The state of the capital's streets—simply foot paths—certainly required attention (fig. 165). Beginning with a project in the heart of Antananarivo, Gallieni called for the redesign of the city's major open space, the Andohalo. Under Merina rule, the Andohalo had consisted of a large irregular clearing where monarchs and prime ministers had assembled the entire population for speeches and celebrations known as *kabaries* (fig. 166). Like a Greek agora, this site served a diversity of uses, at once a place of political assembly and social gathering, a market and a religious center—for the immense blue basalt rock at the center was considered sacred. The French renamed the site the Square Jean Laborde, then beautified it with landscaping reminiscent of a nineteenth-century provincial capital: a lawn (divided into three terraces rising up the steep slope), flower beds, *allées* of trees, and a bandshell in the center

FIGURE 164. *First post office in Antananarivo, c. 1900. Postcard.*

where the military band played concerts on Sunday afternoons (fig. 167). A brick border around the square was eventually widened on all sides to become a street of standard width, reinforcing the sense of propriety, geometric order, and fast-paced movement the colonial government associated with its modernization efforts. French residents asserted that this setting would now "affirm the organizational spirit and genius of France."[30] Appropriately enough, the Square Jean Laborde was not only a stylish place for social gatherings but also the center for military parades and maneuvers.

With great fanfare the first wheeled vehicles entered the capital on November 10, 1897, passing by the Square Jean Laborde. Gallieni appointed a commission comprising engineers, military advisors, and commercial interests to study and oversee the city's internal street system. Following their recommendations, an initial edict ordered the removal of small stands and other encumbrances on the public way and forbade pigs to roam the streets. Within a year, two wider thoroughfares, the Rue Guillan and the Avenue de France, opened appropriate vistas to the Résidence de France, following the demolition of Malagasy houses which stood in the way. Substantial brick buildings soon lined the new thoroughfares, including the first post office (see fig. 164) and a department store, the Grands Magasins du Louvre, on the Avenue de France.[31] Gallieni demonstrated his confidence by shipping three automobiles from France, to-

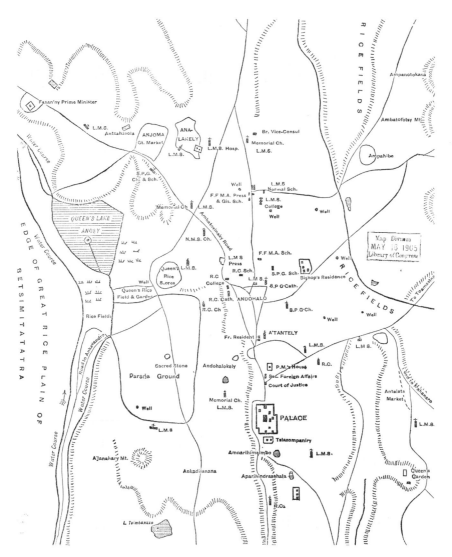

FIGURE 165. *Map of Antananarivo from the* London Times, 1895. *Library of Congress.*

gether with a dozen bicycles as gifts; every morning he took one of the vehicles out for a drive on the new roads.[32]

Connections to the rest of the island were, of course essential to Gallieni's *tâche d'huile* approach. In the interest of cultural and political decentralization, as well as widespread military presence, Antananarivo had to be more than the isolated symbol of power it had been under the Imerina. Beyond the city's bor-

FIGURE 166. *The Andohalo, Antananarivo, during a* kabary *under the reign of Ranavalona III. From* La Revue de Madagascar, *1933.*

ders, artillery troops undertook the widening of the trail to Mahajanja on the western coast, and then to Toamasina, the more distant port to the east. Until then, porters carried all merchandise on their heads, proceeding very slowly along narrow paths, and military officers used sedan chairs. When, in time, the improvements included blockhouses to protect travelers from bandits, traffic to the capital did begin to increase.

Railroad connections between the capital and both coasts took over a decade of laborious effort in this difficult and undeveloped terrain. A full ten years under construction, the railway station at Antananarivo was finally completed in 1910 by the architect Fouchard—a year after the first train on the island made its initial run.[33] The first *maire*, Paul Estebe, and the architect Delpeche platted the Avenue Fallières that year as a grand approach to the station; it opened to traffic in 1915.

Gallieni soon requested that Hubert Lyautey, his protégé in Indochina, join in the new colonial adventure. Thus it would be in rural Madagascar that Lyautey discovered the strategic and personal rewards of urban design. In 1898, as a young lieutenant-colonel in charge of the region just north of Antananarivo, Lyautey conceived his first urban design scheme, for the military camp of Ankazobé. Following the ancient Roman principle of converting military *cadastrae* into civilian *coloniae* (where the settlers would include former soldiers), he en-

FIGURE 167. *The Square Jean Laborde (formerly the Andohalo), relandscaped under Gallieni, c. 1905. From Piollet and Noufflard*, Madagascar, *n.d.*

visioned a simple core expanding with roads, parks, and a broad range of building types. The plan was based on a strong central axis running parallel to the surrounding waterways and ricefields, accented by large circular plazas from which radiated diagonal streets (fig. 168). Within this baroque site-plan for the little town, Lyautey stipulated a more picturesque architecture and setback scheme, derived not from indigenous precedents, but from "that stamp of the English colonial city to which I am so attracted: cottages and assymetry."[34] This, he contended, imprinted the feeling of colonial stability, of "home" (specifying the English word), and did so in a domestic rather than a militaristic sense (fig. 169).[35]

The principles of colonial urban design Lyautey would make so famous a decade later in Morocco emerged gradually during his early years with the French colonization effort in Madagascar. Between 1900 and 1902, now charged with pacifying the south of the island, he established his first true *ville nouvelle* adjacent to the Malagasy city of Fianarantsoa. With a population of only 5,000 people, this was already the second largest settlement on Madagascar, and Lyautey hoped to make the town thrive as "a little Tananarive."[36] Accord-

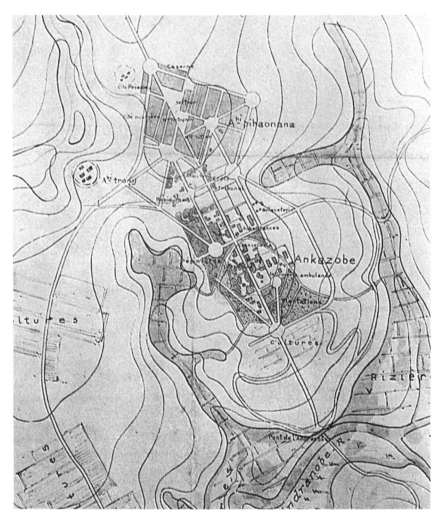

FIGURE 168. *Plan for Ankazobé by Hubert Lyautey, 1898. From J. S. Gallieni,* La Pacification de Madagascar, *1900.*

ingly the new red-brick houses and administrative buildings included a *maison de peuple*, school, post office, and military offices. The second-floor balconies supported by hefty brick pillars strongly resembled what the lieutenant-colonel had seen in the capital city. By now Lyautey had become adamant about creating a "pleasant, healthy setting" which "avoided as much as possible all uniformity, or any sense of the prison or barracks," even in the hospital district.[37] For this reason he decided to draw from the picturesque materials and proportions he had seen elsewhere in Madagascar, even though the plan again recalled a Ro-

FIGURE 169. *Design for a post office in Ankazobé by Hubert Lyautey, 1899. From* L'Urbanisme aux colonies.

man grid. Earlier European designers on the island had introduced Western styles while adapting to the basic construction and cultural pattern of Malagasy building types. Lyautey now self-consciously adhered to the architectural forms he saw around him—in order to soften the impact of dramatically new uses.

Public health, rather than aesthetics, preoccupied Gallieni, as well as every succeeding governor-general in Madagascar. The vast majority of French troops who died in the colony in the early years succumbed to disease rather than combat. A high incidence and great geographical range of malaria, tuberculosis, and leprosy took a heavy toll among the Malagasy people, as did alcoholism and venereal disease. Substantial rates of maternal and infant mortality affected most regions, urban and rural, augmented by deliberate abortions and infanticides.[38] Here were French health problems run wild.

Gallieni's response benefited the Malagasy people, at least more than comparable services in other French colonies. He created an auxilliary corps of doctors and nurses, the Assistance Médicale Indigène (AMI), working from a chain of new hospitals and smaller preventive health clinics (fig. 170). Beginning in 1897, all Malagasys were theoretically eligible to receive medical treatment free of charge. While chiefs-of-staff came from the French medical corps, many Malagasys received training in Western heath care at the medical school in Antananarivo, founded within months of Gallieni's arrival (fig. 171). The building

FIGURE 170. *Early French colonial hospital built under Gallieni in Fianarantsoa, c. 1900. National Archives.*

FIGURE 171. *Medical School, Antananarivo, 1897. National Archives.*

embodied the more glorious aspects of Beaux-Arts design. Its neoclassical facade alluded to universal principles of science and humanitarianism—a mainstay rationale for colonization. Gallieni then ordered the adjacent area south of Lake Anosy cleared of houses and small shops, establishing a well-defined district for the capital's medical complex. Here the staffs of Antananarivo's first "native hospital" (1898) and the Institut Pasteur (1902) undertook research as well as patient care (fig. 172).

The design of these other buildings suggests a more functional aesthetic (fig. 173). The army engineers who oversaw the work sought to maximize fresh air and sunshine with large windows opening onto spacious verandas. Whereas the earliest laboratory resembled the small missionary hospitals of mid-century, or even Cameron's Gothic revival dwellings, fitting comfortably into the hillside setting, the first hospital building was far and away the largest structure on the island. For this and all later additions to the complex, army engineers used prefabricated military barracks. Fortuitously the rows of plain, separate pavilions to isolate various groups from one another (men and women, contagious and noncontagious) broke the hospital up into units, even though the site plan showed no appreciation for a pleasant natural landscape as an element in the recuperation process.

Here and elsewhere Gallieni hoped that locating the primary health-care services for the Malagasys far from the center of the city would allay complaints from European *colons*, who were treated in their own facilities to the north, part of the French military hospital. While the basic layout of the medical district appealed to the Cartesian desire for order, and even served to buttress later arguments in favor of segregating races in everyday life, many French settlers considered that Gallieni allocated an excessive amount to medical care and education for the colonized population.[39] When insurrectionary violence again broke out in 1905, Gallieni's policies came under increased attack, and a new governor-general was appointed.

Unlike the majority of *colons* in Madagascar, most colonial health officials realized that illness depended on more than racial or social habits. It could not be dismissed as a local or "native" problem, for everyone could be affected in some way by the epidemic scale of certain diseases. Although Western medical care was indeed a positive aspect of colonization, the rationale behind it was largely self-serving. The desire for a healthier, more dependable work force and concern about the possible contagion of the European population motivated most public-health efforts in Madagascar, as they did elsewhere, even in France.

Health reform seemed urgent, in part because French cities suffered badly from two of the worst scourges in Madagascar, tuberculosis and venereal disease. These were not simply tropical ailments, and the colony could indeed function as a laboratory for evaluation of various strategies to contain them. Campaigns to combat the other two principal maladies, malaria and bubonic plague, centered around tactics of quarantine, segregation, and municipal upkeep—strate-

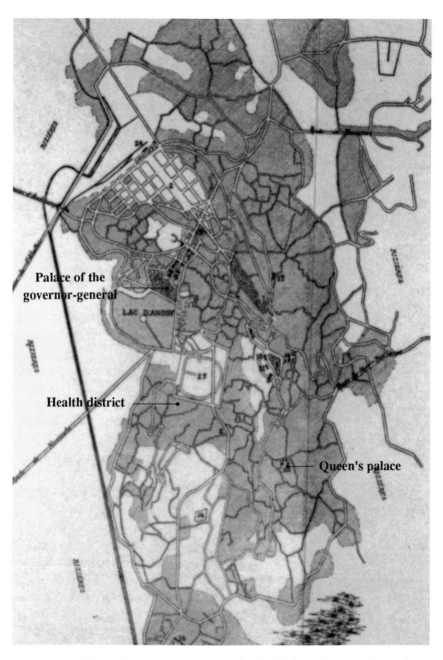

Palace of the
governor-general

LAC D'ANOSY

Health district

Queen's palace

FIGURE 172. *Map of Antananarivo in 1916. The "health district" was southeast of Lake Anosy; the palace of the governor-general north of the lake at the Place Colbert; the Queen's palace and other royal buildings stood atop the Rova. From* La Vie urbaine, *1919.*

FIGURE 173. *Hospital buildings in the "health district" of Antananarivo, c. 1910. From Devic,* Tananarive.

gies which had far-reaching health and political implications. As a French newspaper account in Antananarivo put the matter in 1924, segregation for sanitary purposes "is without doubt the best laboratory model for urbanism and ruralism."[40] Another article in the first issue of *Le Monde colonial illustré* stated unequivocally that epidemics lead directly to low birth rates and low worker productivity, two problems which obsessed the French public at home.[41]

When the Académie des Sciences d'Outre-Mer discussed psychiatric care in 1926, Dr. Gouzin stressed the importance of first defining general principles applicable everywhere, then elaborating different programs based on the conditions of a particular setting. For example, he explained, since research in the colonies could demonstrate that social problems are directly linked to a person's psychiatric state, all French health services should make better use of mental health assistants on the order of American social workers. At the same time, psychiatric facilities should carefully maintain the basic hierarchy and distinctions which prevail in a given society, thereby reinforcing the "normalcy" to which a patient should adapt.[42]

To understand both the local and the more far-reaching meaning of French public-health policies in Madagascar, to see how they affected urbanism in the colony and in France, we need to consider the state of knowledge about the most prevalent diseases in the tropics at the turn of the century. Only recently had advances in epidemiology revealed the true causes of malaria and yellow fever. In 1899 Dr. Ronald Ross, a British physician in Sierra Leone, established definitively that one breed of mosquito carries malaria, and that this insect can breed only in small pools of stagnant water.

In colonial nations throughout the tropics, two kinds of policies resulted from this discovery, both of them essentially environmentalist. The first approach, called "health segregation," predominated in the British colonies of Africa and Asia. More than ever before, white residential settlements were sited far from indigenous settlements. Not only would potential human carriers of the disease be kept at a distance but, in theory at least, the mosquitos that bred in the black and Asian villages where maintenance was negligible would not infest the white enclaves. Physicians explained with grave seriousness that, since mosquitos usually fed at night, segregation was only necessary for sleeping quarters. The minimum clearance between the two areas was ideally 1.25 miles—which they calculated to be the average distance an *anopheles* mosquito would fly.[43]

Public-health officials throughout the French empire discussed the British approach to malaria prevention, although never with exact statistics. They insisted that it was inappropriate in their milieu, arguing that official racial segregation did not characterize French colonial cities as much as it did those of Britain. As Paul Juillerat's course on colonial hygiene explained to students at the Ecole des Hautes Etudes Urbaines, tactics of separation and even segregation might be hygienic in theory, but cities are really too complex to adapt to such strategies.[44] Even advocates of racial segregation never contended that it should be absolute.

A second approach to the problem found more adherents in the French colonies—here, too, at least in theory. It involved the upkeep and extension outward of existing settlements, and especially improved techniques for the drainage of lowland swamps and marshes.[45] Most municipal campaigns stalled because of the high cost and centralized control necessary to clear all the ditches and other collecting places for stagnant water throughout a large area; in fact, in most instances, very little was done at all. French strategy seemed to exist more in the domain of principle than practice. Nonetheless, the basic tactic of municipal upkeep clearly had greater applicability in European cities than any forced segregation policy might have had, which accounted in part for its appeal to French colonial officials.

Antananarivo provides a case of such a strategy, with a slow and piecemeal policy of environmental improvement for health reasons. Beginning in 1898 resolutions called for the drainage of the marshes and rice fields on the periphery of the city. Cultural associations had made previous Malagasy governments dubious about such projects, for rice and its cultivation had mystical associations reaching back to the first Imerina king, who personally identified himself with the grain, saying "rice and I are one."[46] The French now made concerted efforts to clear the marshes, even with budgetary constraints. In 1900, for example, the first *maire* of the capital bought up the ricefields north of the city as the site for the future railroad station and Avenue Fallières, although the area would not be cleared for a decade. From 1898 up to the present day, successive reports on the city have criticized the same areas as major health hazards, suggesting that the government buy the land and convert it to other purposes.[47] In urban planning as in other realms, the identification of a problem has always been more readily forthcoming than the implementation of a solution.

In the case of tuberculosis, colonial officials closely watched the reforms being proposed in France. More astute than many of their French counterparts, they questioned the feasibility of trying to destroy all unsanitary housing in a city. Gallieni did order the demolition of some districts where large numbers of residents had contracted tuberculosis. More than simply ridding the city of contaminated dwellings, he hoped "to cut openings into the dense indigenous quarters"—the same kind of rhetoric as that used by French officials concerned about crowded working-class neighborhoods.[48] While Gallieni also encouraged new housing—between 1896 and 1903, over 9,000 building permits were issued in the capital—most of it was housing for Europeans.[49]

Recognizing that the *îlot insalubre* tactic of the Parisians had proven to be impractical and inadequate, administrators in Madagascar took another tack, based on preventive education and early detection. In every large city and at select regional centers in the countryside, beginning under Gallieni's successor, Dr. Victor Augagneur, tuberculosis dispensaries provided health services for patients and the general public (fig. 174). Dispensaries existed in France, too, of course, but they did not become numerous until the time of the First World War.[50] Madagascar's first tuberculosis dispensary had been founded a decade earlier; and by 1927 there were 125 medical outposts and special tuberculosis treatment centers concentrating on preventive health, as well as ten quarantined tuberculosis sanitoriums for victims recuperating from the disease.[51]

The attitude of the staffs differed fundamentally from that of French physicians. Employees in French dispensaries were strongly moralistic, seeking to "treat rationally" by changing their clients' habits—even sending away the children of affected patients to underscore the seriousness of the illness. Dispensary architecture usually reiterated this emphasis on purity and restraint, the mainstays of the *Neue Sachlichkeit* (New Objectivity) movement in architecture (fig. 10). Colonial counterparts tended to be far less severe. As one study explained, health workers "should not overload the intelligence of young natives with theoretical knowledge," only uncomplicated and specific directions to follow.[52] In

FIGURE 174. *Red Cross office and tuberculosis dispensary at Analakely, Antananarivo,*
1920. National Archives.

keeping with this attitude, the Malagasy dispensaries were simple, unintimidat-
ing places, even purposely pleasant, in a conscious effort to entice the indigenous population into a regime of better health.[53]

The results, while an improvement, can by no means be considered impressive. The antismallpox campaign seems to have been the only truly successful program; after several decades of extensive vaccinations, no cases were reported after 1918. If the population did begin to increase by 1912, the lowered
morbidity figures must still take account of the fact that malaria and tuberculosis
had worsened considerably since increased contact with Europeans in the late
nineteenth century, spreading inland off the coastal towns in Madagascar—an
indication of the disruptive changes Western influence would bring.[54]

Even today, tuberculosis continues to be a serious illness on Madagascar. At
issue here, as in France, are fundamental issues of causality. This disease does
indeed spread in close quarters, but it also tends to strike people who are over-
worked and undernourished, problems which worsened after the conquest. As
Alain Cottereau has argued with reference to Paris, health officials might well
have made more inroads in prevention by improving working environments,
wages, and living conditions, rather than by destroying any infected buildings.[55]

Bubonic plague, on the other hand, quickly takes epidemic form in a given locale, sparing no particular groups or areas, if especially prevalent in poorly maintained districts which harbor vermin. Outbreaks of plague had attacked the port cities of Madagascar, as other international ports, in the course of earlier centuries. When an epidemic reached the capital in 1917–18, the French decided to take strong action. Such action began with careful epidemiological studies of the city. Physicians discerned a topography of the epidemic, noting that it took the highest toll in the eastern regions, near the Malagasy hospital of Ankadinandriana. Overcrowding, the lack of paved streets, and the continued use of wood and thatch construction made it easier for the rats which carried the disease to hide. Analysis was based on environmental conditions per se, not suggestions about racial characteristics. Dr. Allain could say with authority, rather than with dismissive racism, that the "higher, healthier, more hygienic way of life" in the predominantly European areas helped protect both whites and Malagasys who lived there.[56]

Strategies to fight the epidemic fell into three categories, each one again centering around environmental action. The first step involved a full-fledged, multifaceted municipal cleaning campaign to eliminate rats. This included regular garbage collection, sewer cleaning, the destruction of all stables and animal shelters within the city, and the burning of contaminated dwellings, all paid for by municipal funds. Again, this was more a matter of principle than practice.

The second tactic created special camps for infected victims; six such establishments were quickly constructed near the Institut Pasteur, far from the densely populated center of Antananarivo. The Institut's medical staff established a veterinary service, a larger "native hospital," and a special Plague Research Pavilion. An enlarged Institut Pasteur was added to the site in 1928. Thus emerged a new specialized district for health.

The third and most dramatic move stemmed from the camps. When a second epidemic raged a few years later, the city issued a strict quarantine of infected individuals, either to their own houses or to treatment centers outside the city, adding ten more to the existing number. A wide greenbelt now surrounded the hospitals, treatment centers, and research facilities, first south and later adding new facilities to the southwest of the dense center of the capital city. Occupied in part by a military camp, this barrier isolated medical buildings and their occupants from the rest of the capital city. A *cordon sanitaire* now existed, based on disease, not race and racial implications of contamination.[57]

Even in such extreme circumstances, some colonial health officials in Madagascar showed an unusual sensibility to the human toll their reforms might take. In an article of 1925, Dr. Alfred Coury suggested that the municipality should never destroy or restrict entry to a house until all the inhabitants, both sick and well, had been assured of better housing. He went on to describe how the city could use vacant land it owned on the periphery to build new sanitary dwellings with controlled densities, available by priority to the dispossessed, most of whom would be Malagasys. Coury wisely noted that such a program would have to be implemented quickly and deliberately, so that speculation would not destroy the good intentions.[58] While his reform proposal was never carried out, it showed a perspicacity of vision far surpassing comparable debate in France. Moreover, aspects of Coury's approach certainly influenced his close friend, Georges Cassaigne, the urbanist who would carry out the first official plans for Antananarivo.[59]

Venereal disease in Madagascar had alarmed the French from the early nineteenth century, generating fear of contamination as well as a certain moral reprobation. Augagneur had been professor of "syphilography" at the University of Lyons during his term as mayor of that city, shortly before his appointment as governor-general. Both Gallieni and Augagneur considered the high incidence of syphilis to be the heart of the depopulation problem in Madagascar, and an indication of "a poorly developed sense of morality" among the indigenous people.[60] Once again, two themes that troubled social and physical scientists in France found their corollaries in the colonies.

Moral controls over sexual conduct were controversial, especially given the interest in the colonies as a laboratory for public-health procedures which could be implemented in French cities. Treatment of affected persons could, however, control the severity and spread of the disease. (In the days before penicillin, such treatment consisted of regular doses of mercury or, later, Salvarsan, a derivative of arsenic.) As early as 1900 Gallieni established a special hospital for venereal patients in Antananarivo, and the police began rounding up prostitutes for inspection. Medical staffs estimated that over half of the city's prostitutes had syphilis; when detection became definitive with the Wasserman test in 1906, the figure rose even higher. Since Augagneur's own investigations revealed that a quarter of all infants were born with the disease, he began construction of special maternity and children's hospitals to provide testing and early treatment (fig. 175). In 1920 an even broader-based system of detection, treatment, and tracing of contacts emerged. Specialized dispensaries for venereal disease were built, open free of charge to Europeans and Malagasys, first in the cities and then throughout the countryside. By 1927 the island had 135 maternity hospitals and 165 antivenereal dispensaries, indicating a real commitment to this health problem.[61]

FIGURE 175. *Children's Hospital, Antananarivo, 1928. Photograph by the Agence économique des colonies. From Pierre Launois,* Madagascar hier et aujourd'hui, *1947.*

A new aesthetic pertained only much later in the administrative office for the Institute for Social Hygiene in Antananarivo, built in 1932 (fig. 176). This building closely paralleled the contemporary European tendency to visualize scientific standards of purity and functional organization through architecture. Up until then, cost constraints eliminated supposedly hygienic materials such as ceramic tiles and electric lights for Malagasy dispensaries. Instead they used a picturesque wooden Gothic style, suggesting a cottage more than a hospital.

Each patient who visited a Malagasy dispensary had to be put on public police records, so that social workers could trace both past and future contacts. Health officials in France and in other French colonies seemed quite impressed with the Malagasy experiment in social hygiene, even if this "sanitary statism," in the words of the head of Indochina's health department, entailed a conflict between individual liberty and the health of the larger society that was difficult to reconcile.[62] The dispensaries and maternity hospitals represented a new phase in governmental health services: they functioned as local health centers and as branches of a centralized record-keeping system; the staffs dispensed free medication and information to individuals, while they gathered statistics on the city, its people, and their way of life.

It is perhaps in large part because of this surveillance, and the possible uses to which it might be put, that the majority of Malagasys shied away from the dispensaries.[63] Pleasant architecture and even free service could not necessarily

FIGURE 176. *Institute for Social Hygiene, Antananarivo, by J. H. Collet Cantelou,*
1932. From L'Illustration, *1936.*

FIGURE 177. *Administrative Place Colbert, Antananarivo, in 1902. From the* Revue
de Madagascar, *1933.*

win them over to "sanitary statism." Strategies for disease control had their own
internal logic, just as the facilities embodied aesthetic predilections which often
had little to do with health concerns, even if they could be rationalized in those
terms.

Rational Urbanism

By the time of World War I, the French administration felt the combined pressure of two recurrent urban problems: a relatively unproductive work force and grave public-health dangers, principally malaria outbreaks and a recent plague epidemic. These problems led to a step beyond gathering information, instituting sporadic cleanups, and building large hospital facilities. In addition, the colonial government needed to make a gesture to the local population, acknowledging that some 40,000 Malagasys had gone off to serve in European combat, one in ten dying in the trenches. More than protocol was at stake. Governor-General Abraham Schrameck had to counter the increasingly open criticism by educated Malagasys, especially given the discovery in 1915 of the VVS, a secret nationalist organization, and the example of the Russian Revolution—which indeed attracted Communist sympathizers.[64]

The response came in the form of an urban plan for the capital city. In 1918, Schrameck established a special commission to draw up an official plan, one based on the "principles of modern hygiene and urbanism." Quite self-consciously, Antananarivo "preceded Paris and most French cities" in its policies, following the example of Lyautey's Morocco rather than that of the *métropole*.[65]

The commission included health officers, governmental bureaucrats, and businessmen, but no Malagasys. Schrameck delegated sole responsibility for the urban design proposal to the man who had overseen the colony's Ministry of Hygiene and, before that, its Department of Streets. Georges Cassaigne was a Beaux-Arts-trained architect who had lived in Madagascar, serving the colonial administration, since 1900. He had not lost touch with Europe during this long period abroad. Cassaigne became a member of the SFU in 1912, and he ordered an impressive library of recent books on architecture, urbanism, and public health for the municipal library in the Place Colbert (today the Place de l'Indépendence), where any citizen could consult them (fig. 177).[66]

Such ties had led Cassaigne to explore on his own the problems of an urban plan for the capital; when he received the commission, he was able to deliver a carefully detailed proposal in only a week (fig. 178). The essential lines of analysis, as well as many of the specific design concepts, show him to be quite familiar with the recent urban problems and proposals of France, as well as the local circumstances of Madagascar. When Parisian journalist Léon Rosenthal, secretary of the School of Public Art, gave the plan high praise in *La Vie urbaine,* he went so far as to ask administrators in French cities, as well as other colonies, to follow Cassaigne's lead.[67]

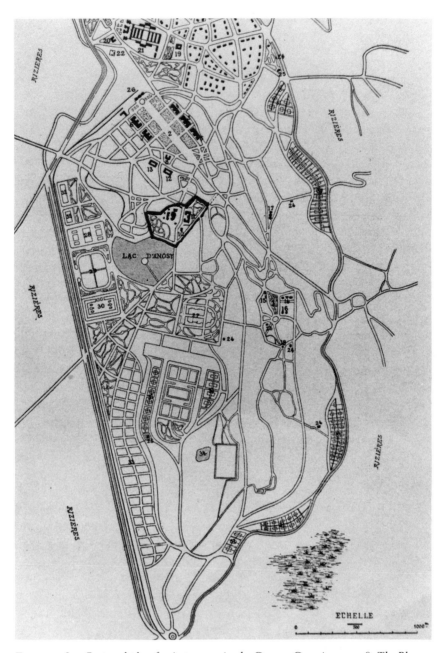

FIGURE 178.   *Proposed plan for Antananarivo by Georges Cassaigne, 1918. The Place Colbert is no. 9, linked by the stairs at Analakely to the Avenue Fallières at no. 2. The new medical district would be sited in former marshland to the north of the city. From* La Vie urbaine, *1919.*

274

Cassaigne fully appreciated the difficulty of his site, both its long and complex history for the Malagasy people, for whom place aroused strong spiritual and political associations, and also its extremely hilly, rocky terrain, which made new street and infrastructure services quite difficult to implement. In an effort to downplay the circulation problems of the city, he elected to stress the rational separation of activities. Through its geography, Cassaigne now divided the capital into an "upper city" on the original three hills, to be preserved as a historic district; a "middle city" to the north, reconceived for more elegant residential expansion, commercial and administrative districts, and a larger hospital zone at the outer edge; and finally a "lower city" to the south for transportation routes, industry, and workers' housing.[68] Often called "the city of a thousand districts," Antananarivo would now be grouped into a minimum of rationally organized quarters.

Cassaigne was aware of the contemporary obsession with transportation in Europe and the United States. Visionary theorists and workaday planners alike considered it the basis of all major urban design decisions. A dirigible landing field and an airplane hangar on a former ricefield to the west of Antananarivo took this predilection to a dramatic aerial scale. More practically, the proposal suggested that, in Antananarivo as in Paris, municipal "circulation is the key to modern urban planning."[69] While he necessarily downplayed cutting new streets in the center of town as exorbitantly expensive, Cassaigne insisted that he could remedy the congestion caused by over two thousand cars, as well as many animals and the continued use of sedan chairs. He would use the very techniques that had been introduced in certain parts of Paris: traffic circles (Hénard's *circulation à giration*), one-way streets, specified crosswalks, and off-street parking (fig. 179).[70] Antananarivo could demonstrate the effectiveness of these less disruptive adaptations to traffic. Cassaigne also utilized the older Malagasy pattern of steep stairways, cut into the rock, or occasionally modern traffic tunnels bored through the mountains, to link various parts of the city. The elliptical ring-road, initiated under Gallieni and finally completed following Cassaigne's plan of 1926, would join the various districts via the periphery.

The proposed new districts indicate Cassaigne's awareness of recent European and American prototypes, both formal and ideological, in urban design. He envisioned the Place Colbert as a monumental civic enter in the manner of the American City Beautiful.[71] The landscaped esplanade of the Avenue Fallières (today the Avenue de l'Indépendance) would be enlarged and a more impressive City Hall erected, flanked on one side by the Chamber of Commerce and a Museum of Commerce and Industry, on the other by a *maison de tous*. The urbanist hoped to promote both economic growth and social goodwill as

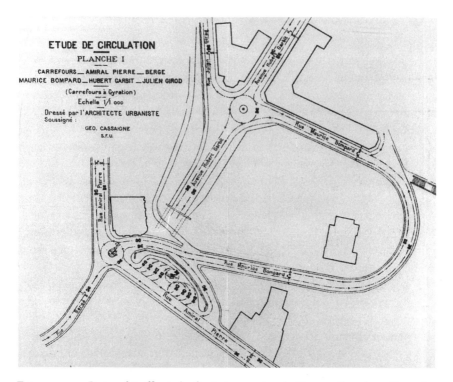

FIGURE 179. *Proposed traffic circles for Antananarivo, by Georges Cassaigne. From the* Bulletin économique de Madagascar et dépendances, 1927.

the capital flourished. Across the esplanade would rise a modern hotel to serve the train station at the terminus of the avenue, and a new central post office.

In an intriguing gesture of self-restraint, Cassaigne left one site along this grand axis undesignated, specifically allowing for new needs that would surely arise as the metropolis grew. If he cited the French urbanist Léon Jaussely, who proposed organizing cities according to the principles of "Taylorism: everything has a place," Cassaigne recognized that planners can never anticipate all the things that will have to be located strategically in a large, complex city. [72] And large it did become. Antananarivo's population had now reached some 60,000 people, only slightly more populous than in the early days of colonization, but it soon expanded precipitously, reaching 140,000 by 1940. [73] Each of Cassaigne's plans tried to anticipate a dramatic influx of people.

More than his counterparts in other colonies, Cassaigne considered new housing in his urban design proposals. This he grouped into three *cités-jardins* to the north, intended for French functionaries and commercial employees who worked near the Place Colbert, and five much simpler *villages-jardins* farther south. Malagasys would live there, creating a new edge to both east and west, some near proposed industrial sites and others in farming cooperatives. Ideally all of these garden cities, whether suburban or rural in character, would replace malarial swamps and ricefields. Cassaigne's concept of regional development anticipated a spontaneous process of drainage and "decongestion" as *colons* and colonial subjects moved out of the crowded central city of their own accord, seeking more pleasant surroundings.[74] Density remained a problem, nonetheless, for only the northern *cités-jardins*, all intended for French families, were constructed over the next several years.

The various garden-city developments in Cassaigne's proposal again raise the issue of separation between the races. In Antananarivo itself, intermixing was more or less taken for granted, in part because the rugged topography limited the scope of possible transformations. Class tensions, as much as racial attitudes, were voiced in critiques of the unhealthy, disorderly houses along many streets.

The European predilection for some form of racial segregation certainly found expression in the French newspapers of the capital, even if it did not determine land use. In 1923 the *Indépendant de Madagascar* proclaimed the "necessity of having an indigenous city and a European city," belittling the "sentimental tendency toward racial equality" espoused by some Frenchmen.[75] The author evoked the spirit of Lyautey's Morocco where considerably segregated cities had been achieved in terms of other goals, thereby distancing the majority of colonized people—especially the poor—from European residential districts, while sidestepping the specter of racism.[76] As Marcel Olivier, the next governor-general of Madagascar, was to put the matter:

> The segregation of indigenous districts, indispensable in colonial cities, in no way constitutes, at least for the present, a grievous racial discrimination for those to whom it applies. In other words, segregation can be based, not on race, but on a standard of living . . . and in Madagascar certain districts will be reserved for inhabitants with "a European standard of living."[77]

Following this lead, a 1928 law established such zones in which only "European construction" would be allowed. As in Morocco or Indochina, standards of size and sanitary equipment ruled out all but the wealthiest Malagasys.

French regulations unequivocally established the right of nonwhites to own land and reside in the predominantly European districts of all Malagasy cities.[78] Yet culture could again play a subtle role in dissuading them from doing so. The Malagasy rituals that governed the orientation of rooms and of the house itself found no place in the design of subdivisions intended for Europeans. A journalist defending the regulations seemed pleased that "by the simple technique of building inspections, Madagascar has achieved the principle of segregation, without recourse to dangerous legislation concerning racial discrimination." [79] Cassaigne himself, in an interview for the *Tribune de Madagascar* in 1924, had condoned segregated neighborhoods for "those who cannot or will not live by European standards," a group that included the white proletariat of the colony, although he again stressed the necessary interdependence of all zones or districts in a city or region. [80]

Outside the capital with its dense mix of people and activities, Cassaigne advocated a more open policy of segregation. In 1924 Governor-General Olivier asked him to redesign the hill station of Antsirabé as a spa and resort town. The plan evolved over the next three years, done with the assistance of the landscape architect Gustave François and research by Cassaigne's brother Albert (fig. 180). Both Cassaignes acknowledged that class and racial segregation had to be explicit in "the Vichy of the Indian Ocean," especially if English colonists from South Africa were one potential group of tourists. [81] Accordingly, the plan anticipated inexpensive Malagasy housing to the southwest, near the market, the industrial district, and the military barracks. Picturesque residential settlements for Europeans proceeded from a resort hotel near the spacious villa districts through small cottages, farther to the east (figs. 181, 182). This sequence formed another edge of the city, separated by parkland from the center of Antsirabé.

Various sizes of detached dwellings seemed, in Cassaigne's mind, a necessary formula for housing in Europe or the colonies, since he associated apartment living with France's low natality rate. Single-family houses were available to all residents of Antsirabé, whatever their class or race. Cassaigne viewed the scheme as a progressive urban model for the entire island, and indeed for France. [82] The European parallels become especially vivid in the suggestion that a "linear city" would eventually link Antsirabé to "satellite cities" such as Vinavinkarena, an industrial town to the south, forming a connected sequence of settlements from Antananarivo to Antsirabé and then to Fianarantsoa. [83] The regional scheme complemented Cassaigne's vision for the capital city. Rapid transit would directly link the commercial, administrative, and industrial districts with various residential suburbs. Both the discourse and the scale of the regional vision alluded to European urbanistic debate.

In many ways, of course, Cassaigne's plans for Madagascar drew from Lyautey and Prost's work in Morocco, as well as contemporary European ideas about urbanism. Cassaigne and Schrameck readily acknowledged their debt to the Moroccan precedent, though Cassaigne cheerily reminded audiences that Lyautey's first efforts in urban design had taken place on Madagascar. [84] After World War I, Cassaigne often joined with his Moroccan colleagues at conferences and pub-

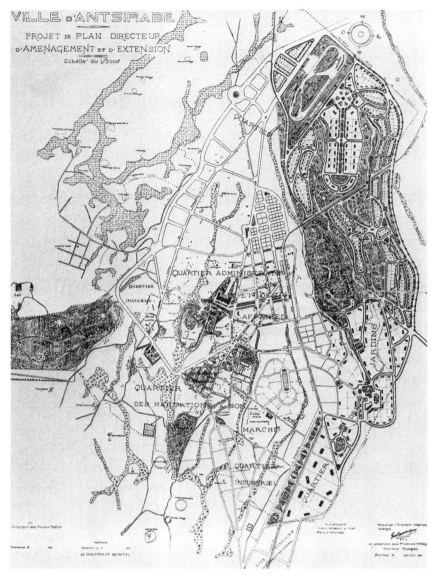

FIGURE 180. *Plan for Antsirabé by Georges Cassaigne, 1924. From* La Vie urbaine, 1934.

lic lectures in France: at the Musée Social, the Académie des Sciences d'Outre-Mer, the Société Française des Urbanistes, and the Strasbourg Congress on Urbanism of 1923.[85] In each of these forums Lyautey, Prost, and Cassaigne presented a common theoretical and formal approach to urban design, stressing a

279

FIGURE 181. *The Hotel Terminus in Antsirabé, 1929. National Archives.*

balance between traditional architectural forms and modern social science in the evolution of guidelines. The fundamental difference involved the sciences each colonial administration sought to apply: ethnography and geography in Morocco, biology and sociology in Madagascar.

The distinctions become clear in two examples of Cassaigne's work. Sounding much like Lyautey, he insisted that the "tropical sanitorium" of Antsirabé had to look different from Vichy or Paris, using local materials and vernacular adaptations to the climate, such as verandas and balconies, even for the major resort buildings.[86] Since Cassaigne believed the Gothic-revival wooden buildings of the nineteenth-century capital to be authentic indigenous structures, he unknowingly relied on European architectural precedents. As yet, few expert historians could instruct him about the actual evolution of Malagasy housing forms. All the same, the creolized Gothic had become a local style over the years, meaningful to this population, handled in particular ways by Malagasy craftsmen, even if it originally derived from European fashions. More important, the gist of Cassaigne's approach had little to do with the glorification of a distant historic past in contrast to a supposedly decadent present. Cassaigne indeed recognized the need to modulate between traditional and innovative forms, considering first how each aesthetic would correlate with public-health considerations. He, too, understood the dynamic nature of cities.

The debate over Antananarivo's major marketplace clarifies the strengths and limits of Cassaigne's stance. In 1898 Gallieni had first decided to transfer the Zoma, or Friday marketplace, from the Andohalo to Analakely, the monumental stairway at the base of the new Avenue Fallières, leading up to the Place Colbert. This setting was proportionately smaller, given that the original Zoma had consisted largely of a slave market, but the form and placement of market stalls were left to the Malagasy merchants (fig. 183). Twenty-five years later the city council again decided to rebuild the Zoma, this time without moving it, in anticipation of a major trade exhibition later that year. Cassaigne proposed retaining the picturesque local character of the earlier Zoma, to the point of using umbrellas in the open plaza, despite counterproposals for a large metallic structure from the self-styled "modernists" of the colony. He did, all the same, specify more hygienic materials for permanent structures around the periphery, notably glazed brick, tile, and cement, rather than straw thatch and wood.

Cassaigne's proposal seemed too timid to the Chamber of Commerce, which preferred a more dramatic gesture. The immense metallic exposition facility was erected, but since the weight proved totally unsuitable for the marshy site, it had to be dismantled within a year.[87] Cassaigne's scheme finally prevailed in 1926, with the beginning of yet another refurbished market place. His "Zoma

FIGURE 182. *Small cottages in Antsirabé, c. 1930. Postcard.*

FIGURE 183. *The second Zoma or Friday Market in Antananarivo, which the French moved to the Analakely district in 1897. From Piollet and Noufflard,* Madagascar.

des pavilions" was paved with cement and the market stalls rebuilt in brick with hygienic white tiles (fig. 184). They retained the traditional steeply pitched roofs and the basic proportions of earlier huts, while subtly introducing modern improvements that would help with disease control.

Public health remained a central concern with the new governor-general, Marcel Olivier, appointed in 1924. With twenty years of experience in the colonial service, mostly in French West Africa, he knew how to assert his views in a manner that would impress the French at home. Like his close friend Lyautey, Olivier saw urban design as a key tool and propaganda device in his political strategy. For Olivier, urbanism was based on health, and health in turn should produce a more reliable labor force.[88]

Within two years of taking office, Olivier issued a "Charter for Urbanism." He appointed an Urbanism Council to generate plans for every city on the island—the first of which was a new plan by Cassaigne for Antananarivo (fig. 185). Cassaigne again responded within weeks of the commission's request. This time he dealt less with local motifs and historical traditions, gearing his revised plan to the predilections of the new government. Parks and sports fields dot the map, replacing marshlands, to provide healthful recreation for the entire popu-

FIGURE 184. *Masonry pavilions at the renovated Zoma, by Georges Cassaigne, 1926. Postcard.*

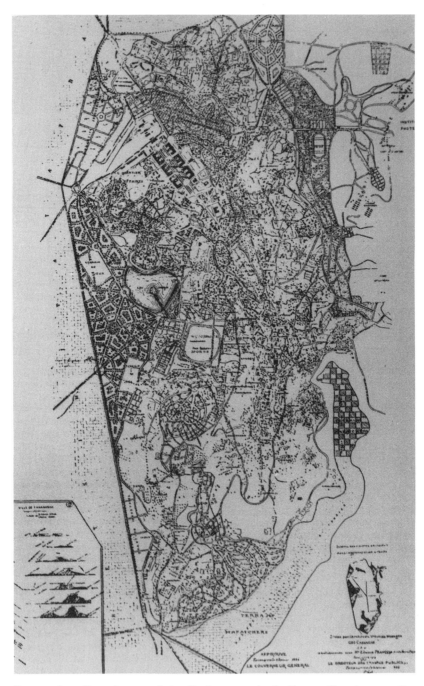

FIGURE 185. *Second proposed plan for Antananarivo by Georges Cassaigne, 1926.*
From L'Urbanisme aux colonies.

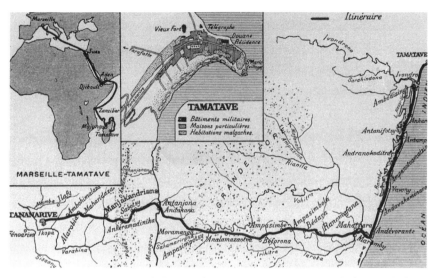

FIGURE 186.   *Toamasina and the French route to Antananarivo in 1896. From J. S. Gallieni,* Neuf ans à Madagascar, *1908. Courtesy of Librairie Hachette.*

lation—following contemporary European interest in encouraging workers to exercise during their leisure hours. Larger industrial zones and more abundant housing for all classes frame the southern and eastern extensions of the city. Now working in collaboration with Dr. Coury, Cassaigne distributed public services, especially public baths and social hygiene dispensaries, throughout Antananarivo, in an effort to reach every group of residents.[89]

The major differences are purely formal rather than conceptual. Cassaigne's plan of 1926 features bold geometric patterns in overlapping circles, checkerboard grids, or baroque radial tridents. By contrast, the 1918 plan seems almost naive, its gently curving streets aligned to the topography, suggesting something of a talented engineer's approach to site planning. The patterns of the new plan self-consciously emulated recent prototypes in Europe. The most obvious case is the garden cities and agricultural cooperatives. Several of them used a modernist grid; others duplicated almost literally the schematic drawing Ebenezer Howard had published in *Garden Cities of Tomorrow* (1901)—a copy of which Cassaigne had donated to the colony's public library.[90]

The principal impetus for the changes Olivier wanted to see came precipitously in 1927, when a cyclone destroyed most of the coastal city of Toamasina (Tamatave to the French). Founded in 1800, this had been the first colonial capital and was still an important port, although its population did not surpass 20,000 (fig. 186).[91] Since the city required a plan that could be implemented quickly, Jean-Henri Collet de Cantelou, architect-in-chief of the rebuilding ef-

FIGURE 187.   *Post-cyclone map of Toamasina, c. 1930, based on the 1927 plan by
Cassaigne and Collet de Cantelou. Library of Congress.*

fort, saw an opportunity. He would demonstrate the benefits of modernist principles of design, notably efficiency and standardization in construction.[92] The
governor-general endorsed de Cantelou's vision wholeheartedly, recognizing the
parallel between this architectural stance and the industrial productivity he
wanted to encourage. Within a few years journalist Maurius-Ary Leblond could
praise a new setting at Toamasina that fulfilled Olivier's expectations. The colonial administration, he wrote, "profited from this 'blank slate' to act with resolution and firmly root a powerful, spacious city, worthy of the imperial glory of
France."[93]

Cassaigne collaborated on Collet de Cantelou's site plan for Toamasina, five
times larger than the city had been only a year earlier. They maintained the
gridiron established in the early years of colonization, but aggrandized and rationalized the street system (fig. 187). Major boulevards trumpeted the names of
illustrious Frenchmen—Gallieni, Poincaré, Foch—as they speeded the movement of goods and people from one district to another. The placement of principal and subsidiary routes established precise zones.

The ensemble reinforced the spirit of "standardization for buildings and,
even more so, for their constituent elements" that de Cantelou hoped to achieve
throughout Madagascar.[94] In contrast to Cassaigne, de Cantelou had arrived in
the colony at age 30, already imbued with the avant-garde thinking of the 1910s
and 1920s which favored austere, standardized housing as the epitome of modern architecture. For this reason, Toamasina's new buildings in no way resembled the simple wooden boxes with Gothic ornament that had once lined
the streets—even though the early use of prefabricated parts, most notably along
the Rue de Commerce, must surely have appealed to de Cantelou. He carried
Toamasina's initial, rather simple, Western technology to a new level of sophistication. In terms of economic policy, de Cantelou wanted to modernize the
production of building materials on the island while he standardized both prices
and components. In terms of aesthetics, he envisioned uniform prototypes,
modified somewhat according to region and use.[95]

Strict guidelines pertained to all new buildings, public or private, throughout the city. De Cantelou did not point out, as he well might have done, that
the former Imerina monarchs had imposed numerous building regulations, especially concerning materials, which had also produced a certain uniformity.[96]
While public competitions for a variety of services—housing, administrative
offices, clinics, a court house, police station, publications center, and so forth—
engaged architects from France and other colonies, de Cantelou's controls governed their overall production and appearance in every instance. Reinforced
concrete became the mandatory building material, for he believed it to be the

most durable material for a modern city, especially in the tropics.[97] The new offices along the Boulevard Gallieni therefore resemble one another quite noticeably: sited on axis, their unrelieved white walls based on the same proportional system and the same materials, the Moderne geometry of their entrances providing the only ornamentation (fig. 188). Uniformity in the port area came under even stricter controls. Here the commercial well-being of the entire colony depended on real efficiency, and the image of progress would have to impress newcomers at first glance.[98]

Having drawn up the urban design guidelines for Toamasina, de Cantelou began to oversee new construction throughout the island. In 1927 Olivier named him the first director of the Bureau of Architecture and Urbanism, a governmental post comparable to that held by Prost and Hébrard. Two years later the administration decided that standardized prices and goods would indeed promote economic growth, so it seemed appropriate to reward the individual who had promoted the concept. A Bureau of Economical Housing was established, again with de Cantelou as director, to produce inexpensive prototypes (*modèle-types*) for new housing. Here, too, de Cantelou promoted uniform building materials and techniques, in an effort to keep down costs and elevate the visual quality of new construction.

FIGURE 188. *Tribunal, Toamasina, by Collet Cantelou's Bureau of Architecture and Urbanism*, 1928. *From* La Revue de Madagascar, 1933.

Figure 189. *Military housing, Camp des Manguiers, Toamasina, by Collet de Cantelou's Bureau of Economic Housing, 1929. From* L'Urbanisme aux colonies.

The prevalence of flat roofs and smooth white walls in the new housing estates shows an undeniable affinity with contemporary European modernism (fig. 189). Yet we should not dismiss this architecture as a mere imitation of German *siedlung*. The prototypes vary somewhat, as indeed they did in Weimar. While white, cubic massing prevailed in Toamasina, Antananarivo, or Mahajanja, the details and scale differ from one city to the next. Large single-family villas predominated in certain garden-cities, while others were composed primarily of two-family houses or small apartment buildings. The modifications were as intentional as the uniformity. "There is not 'one,' but an infinity of types," explained de Cantelou, "which we had to conceptualize in order to respond to the most diverse conditions."[99]

Such conditions also included regional differences. De Cantelou expressed a certain appreciation for the vernacular architecture of the country, describing Madagascar as "a primitive civilization, but nonetheless sufficiently evolved to suggest some guidelines for housing."[100] One sees such guidelines in the bands of deep-red brick in Antananarivo (fig. 190) and the perforated concrete screens of Toamasina, evoking the local masonry and the wooden fretwork of nineteenth-century dwellings in each town. The garden-cities of the capital even have slightly hipped roofs, alluding to the steep pitches of earlier Malagasy

289

FIGURE 190. *Garden City on the outskirts of Antananarivo, by Collet de Cantelou's Bureau of Economic Housing, 1928. From* La Revue de Madagascar, *1933.*

dwellings there. Nevertheless, the continuities were quite abstract, something to be savored by a professional audience rather than passersby.

The majority of new housing estates in Madagascar provided for the growing number of French military personnel and administrative functionaries, since here, too, the government employed almost half of the Europeans in the colony in the 1930s. [101] A minor portion of the new housing was intended for Malagasy governmental employees. The incoming governor-general, Léon Cayla, speaking to the colony's business leaders in 1932, justified the expense in familiar terms: "The regrouping of the natives on well-placed reservations assures colonialism in all its forms [i.e., both the private and the public sectors] of its needs for a labor force and clientele, while facilitating the policing and administration of the colony." [102]

In its overall scope and aesthetic, de Cantelou's program signaled a shift away from Cassaigne's conspicuous interest in local forms and traditional building practices toward more universalistic conceptions of architecture favored by the European avant-garde. Like Olivier, de Cantelou was intrigued with the notion of urbanism as "a principal means of action in social politics, . . . as a means for propaganda and the penetration of European standards of living." [103] In particular, he wanted to prove the capacity of a construction system to mediate between past traditions and future aspirations. Standardized construction seemed a way to upgrade Madagascar's public image, proving that the colony was on the leading edge of modern architecture and industrial productivity.

De Cantelou's accomplishments sought to transform Antananarivo "from a primitive village into a modern city," putting Madagascar in the class of Morocco and Indochina as an exemplar of "French urbanism and moral works."[104] The full scale of the transformation required the assistance of an immense loan from France, initiated by Olivier and implemented by his successor, Cayla. They proposed a vast program, borrowing almost 200 million FF in 1931. While the loan pertained specifically to public works, administrative architecture claimed a major portion of the allocations.[105] Cayla affirmed de Cantelou's role as head of a new Department of Architecture, Parks and Gardens (later the Department of Architecture and Urbanism). As one of his next projects he in fact delved into landscaping, erecting a number of pergola-bridges, all of a uniform module and planting, to traverse some of the ravines in Antananarivo. But the real significance of the office lay in the autonomy given its design staff and the authority vested in de Cantelou himself. The service removed designers from the more utilitarian concerns and aesthetics which prevailed in the Department of Public Works, under whose auspices he had been. Now was the chance to demonstrate what modern architecture could do.

De Cantelou's functionalist aesthetic metamorphized Madagascar, especially the capital and the major provincial cities, during the early 1930s. Construction boomed with the loan funds, despite the worldwide economic depression. The range of work is quite impressive. New post offices and dispensaries proliferated, simple structures in smaller towns, massive variations of these same forms in the larger cities (fig. 191). New and rebuilt marketplaces served both the Malagasy and the European populations. Those of Toamasina, Tulear, and other small towns all used the same large open structure made of prefabricated metal struts (fig. 192). But in Antananarivo de Cantelou chose a different tack (fig. 193). On axis at the center of the Zoma he placed a large building with a clock, built of concrete with metal components, yet designed to the same proportions and style as Cassaigne's recent market stalls (fig. 194). The Tranompokonolona ("Maison de Peuple") provided space for larger commercial displays and after-hours festivities. In the opinion of the editors of La Revue de Madagascar, the new Zoma was able to "reconcile the necessities of hygiene with respect for a setting that many tourists praise for its picturesque local color."[106]

With the upper city from the Andohalo to Ambohipotsy finally declared a historic district, as Cassaigne had recommended more than a decade ago, de Cantelou could rebuild much of the center of the capital as he wished.[107] He centralized services and imposed rigorous design guidelines, concentrating on two areas. The busy Avenue Fallières, running between his new train station

FIGURE 191. *New Central Post Office, Antananarivo, by Collet de Cantelou's Bureau of Architecture and Urbanism, 1930. From* L'Illustration, *1936.*

(1936) and the Zoma market, furnished grandeur to the commercial core of the new development. A new city hall by de Cantelou (1936) (fig. 195) dominated the end of the long axis. Its blocky, three-story massing provided the template, strictly enforced, for new buildings all along the avenue, whether public or private (fig. 196). Rooftop pergolas were specified at regular intervals; uniform double windows alternated with angular bow-windows at the second floor, both set within a continuous band of dark brick. Owners were required to install small boutiques in the continuous ground-floor arcade level, in an effort to maintain the commercial animation of the earlier streets.[108]

FIGURE 192. *Marketplace, Toamasina, by Collet de Cantelou's Bureau of Architecture and Urbanism, 1930. From* La Revue de Madagascar, 1933.

A few blocks away, another monumental complex at the Place Colbert (today the Place de la Libération) provided over one hundred new governmental offices (fig. 197). Here, too, the site already served as the center of the colonial bureaucracy, but now all services were brought together, their collective purpose reaffirmed in the unified architecture. Once again, the necessity of low-rise buildings with a marshy subsoil generated the forcefully horizontal aesthetic. All of the five-story structures had flat roofs, flat concrete facades, and bands of dark brick. The new administrative district created an imposing presence, in keeping with the more directive governmental policies under Olivier and Cayla. As de Cantelou told his audience at the Parisian Congress on Colonial Urbanism, "We have quit the technical terrain to enter into the realm of social politics, of which urbanism is evidently one of the principal means of action." [109] His functionalist concerns had taken on an increasingly ideological tone, suggesting how architecture could present a modern image of the colony, evoking health and efficiency to both European visitors and Malagasy laborers.

At a more practical level, the new building policies also illuminate certain problems that can emerge because of an avid determination to use modernist forms and materials, with little regard for local circumstances. The flat roofs, prohibited as *fady* (taboo) in traditional Malagasy architecture, quickly developed leaks in the heavy rainfall, especially in the center of the island. [110] Reinforced concrete proved to be exceedingly expensive, since limestone deposits were only minimal on the island and cement had to be imported from Mozam-

293

FIGURE 193.   *Aerial view of the new Zoma, Antananarivo, seen from the stairs leading to the Place Colbert, 1930. Photo by Albert Robillard, courtesy of the Musée de l'Homme, Paris.*

FIGURE 194.   *Tranompokonolona ("Maison de Peuple") of the new Zoma in Antananarivo, by Collet de Cantelou, 1930. From* L'Architecture d'aujourd'hui, *1945.*

FIGURE 195.   *New Hôtel de Ville, Antananarivo, by Collet de Cantelou, 1933–36. From* La Revue de Madagascar, *1933.*

FIGURE 196.   *Renovation of the Avenue Fallierès, Antananarivo, following design guidelines set by Collet de Cantelou, completed in 1936. From* L'Illustration, *1936.*

FIGURE 197.   *First segment of the new colonial administrative offices at the Place Colbert, Antananarivo, by Collet de Cantelou's Bureau of Architecture and Urbanism, 1933. From* La Revue de Madagascar, *1933.*

bique. Nonetheless, modernist imagery continued to dominate official construction throughout the colonial period, and even after national liberation in 1960, for it reinforced the up-to-date self-image which leaders wanted to project.

Not everyone approved of de Cantelou's resolutely modernist approach to architecture and urban design. The Ministry of Colonies even issued a strongly worded report on Madagascar's Bureau of Architecture and Urbanism, criticizing the lack of adaptation to local materials and styles, especially the use of reinforced concrete, as overly expensive and intrusive. The author cited a French architect on the island, speaking before the Délégations Economiques et Financières, who deplored the "importation here of completely preconceived ideas, notably a construction formula applied indiscriminately to all regions, with no thought for local contingencies."[111]

The aesthetic was not a matter of whim or purely formal preferences. The colonial government wanted to project a unified image of modernity while it laid the groundwork for an economy based on standardized goods and mass production. All the same, the private building trades could not supply a large enough number of skilled workers to carry out this agenda. With this dilemma emerged another critical problem in many modernization schemes, again made especially vivid in the colonial context. Recognizing the predicament as early as 1925, Governor-General Olivier announced that henceforth all public works would be carried out by a new agency, the Service de la Main d'Oeuvre des Travaux d'Intérêt Général. Widely known as SMOTIG (one could translate the name as the Labor Force in the Public Interest), this service used Malagasy military recruits. Since the government also passed a law requiring all ablebodied Malagasy men to serve three (later two) years in the military service, SMOTIG can only be called compulsory labor.

Olivier's "Charter of Labor," published that same year, established the terms and goals of SMOTIG. Responding to the recurring complaints from *colons* that Malagasy manual laborers were unreliable and slow, Olivier promised this service would reform "the thousands and thousands of men who do absolutely nothing and are determined to do nothing, unless they are forced."[112] SMOTIG would solve the "crisis of manpower" on the island, providing itinerant workers with "the maximum of moral health in the maximum of material comfort."[113] Olivier reassured colonial employers that he was not taking potential laborers away from the plantations and factories, for such employees would be exempt.[114] Instead, he asserted, like "Schools of Work," SMOTIG camps would train future laborers through the discipline and rigor of their new environments.[115]

Some eight to ten thousand young men were enlisted each year, and twenty-three "pioneer camps" were built around the country, close to major public-

FIGURE 198. *SMOTIG camp in Madagascar in 1928. From* L'Afrique française, *1929.*

works sites in the cities and countryside. Every settlement housed three to four hundred men, half of them with their families (though some camps had up to a thousand recruits).[116] Houses for the "pioneers" (as Olivier preferred to call the workers) ranged from one-room family cottages to small dormitories for single men, all well-ventilated and neatly arranged in rows (fig. 198). The materials were inexpensive local products like bamboo, rather than reinforced concrete, for the government intended these to be temporary settlements, not permanent proletariat housing projects. In sum, the architecture and layout of the "pioneer village" resembled that of "a native village . . . except for the benefits of order and hygiene."[117] The aesthetic synthesis would, he hoped, win favor.

Realizing that a forced-labor system would elicit criticism, Olivier tried to justify it in various ways. Medical care ranked high, with health specialists overseeing diet, vaccinations, and individual records to keep the work force thriving. Looking to the past, he emphasized that the *fanompoana* had been routine under the earlier Imerina monarchy, Gallieni's first colonial government, and even the eighteenth-century ancien régime in France. A "traditional" form of labor organization, Olivier contended, SMOTIG mitigated the potentially disruptive aspects of modernization for the colonized people. Yet the *fanompoana* had been exclusively tribal obligation to the monarchy—versions of it continue even today in the upkeep of royal lands and mausoleums—and the Malagasys refused to transfer this ceremonial relationship to the French colonial government. [118]

For the most part, however, Olivier tried to defend his system by pointing to SMOTIG's positive impact on modernization: it would build up the colony's industrial base and reorganize its cities. In fact, he argued, "the conception of the camps could serve as a model for urban centers." [119] And indeed, this labor force proved essential in the vast urban expansion programs of the late 1920s and in the 1930s. SMOTIG camps were put at the disposal of de Cantelou's various agencies, first in the rebuilding of Toamasina, then in the construction of model garden-cities, finally in the 1930s campaign for public works and new administrative buildings in the major cities. Once again, urban settlements served as both means and ends for political and economic policy in a French colony.

Industrialists' organizations in France, most notably the Redressement Français, heartily endorsed Olivier's accomplishments, for they too worried about how to increase worker productivity through urban planning, better health conditions, and tighter discipline—even if they would never have ventured to suggest such a system at home. [120] Unconvinced, the International Labor Organization attacked SMOTIG in the French Parliament. The government reached an accord with the critics in 1931, agreeing to phase out the SMOTIG camps, in the meanwhile using them only for works of direct benefit to the Malagasys—housing, for example, rather than ports or railroads. Still defending the system, Cayla pointed out that many "pioneers" chose to stay with the camps after their work contracts expired, since their wages were three times higher than what most private employers on the island were willing to pay. [121]

It was the protests of these employers, convinced that the colonial government was depleting their supply of cheap labor, together with the criticism from French labor and liberal organizations, that brought about the demise of SMO-TIG. In 1936, when the Popular Front gained control of the government in Paris, SMOTIG was finally and definitively abolished. Simultaneously, for the first time, independent trade unions were authorized in Madagascar. Over the remaining years of the decade, less than 10 percent of the potential working population was employed, and the vast majority of Malagasys lived a quiet, rural existence which the French demeaned as lazy and unproductive. [122]

In Madagascar then, as in Europe, political leaders considered modern construction technology an integral part of their program for urban improvement and economic growth. The call for rationalization did not, in fact, generate a close analysis of truly economical local materials and production techniques. Nor did the system grant much dignity to the laborers themselves, only to the advanced technology they were trained to employ. The image of modernity seemed necessarily universal, rather than inherently specific to a place and a culture. Only from the perspective of those in power did modernization promise a better life in underdeveloped regions and backward cities, initiating their populations into the world market and guaranteeing profits for European investors.

Officials here also pondered the usefulness of historic preservation. Government and the private sector hoped to retain not just the quaint charm of French provinces and exotic colonial terrains, but also the hierarchy of authority associated with the island's premodern culture. Traditional architectural forms were integrated into modern Western building types in an effort to downplay resistance and disguise the autocratic control.

Traditionalism and modernism formed a unified urban policy for the powerful interest-groups which supported industrial and commercial expansion during the first half of the twentieth century. This was true to some extent throughout Europe and the United States, but it was especially evident in the French colonies. A 1936 article in the *Revue de Madagascar* documents the two-part agenda. Echoing Vaillat's analysis of Morocco, Maurius-Ary Leblond contended that most of the colony's inhabitants, French and Malagasy alike, "do not fully realize that this little Continent is simultaneously one of the most extraordinary laboratories and museums that the universe has offered cilivized man." [123] Official urban policy thus sought to experiment while it preserved, to innovate without disrupting traditions. Despite the humanitarian arguments, this cultural strategy was of use primarily to French interests, to "civilized man" at home and abroad.

Conclusion

"WE HAVE THEREFORE a political facet to art in Morocco," declared Alfred de Tarde in 1915, "and it is by no means the least aspect of our native policy (fig. 199).[1] De Tarde nonetheless granted too much to the abstract powers of representation. He assumed that Morocco's architecture would ensure the stability of the colonial regime because it represented the supposed strength and the benevolence of that domination. From our perspective, the situation appears far more complex. There are further ramifications, both formal and political, at home as in the colonies, of so self-consciously politicized an urban milieu. They now merit closer attention.

The first instance is most purely political. In each of the three countries I have described, a powerful nationalist movement emerged during the 1930s, based in the very settings the French believed would reinforce their colonial power. Whereas earlier resistance had been concentrated in rural areas, opposition to colonial domination now took on new force in cities. Nationalism thrived in the *hadara* cities of Rabat, Fez, Salé, and Tetuan, once renowned for their civilized urban culture; in the bustling Vietnamese cities of Saigon, Haiphong, and especially Hanoi; and in the Malagasy capital of Antananarivo. Here, as at home, the French had created a concentrated public domain—represented in institutions like the state schools, hospitals, governmental offices, public parks, even post offices and train stations. Now those settings came to be seen in a radically different light. The new generation of young nationalists demanded equal access to the benefits of modern technology and economic development; they believed in Western concepts of democracy and liberty, insisting that France live up to those ideals. Vietnamese nationalists such as Phan Chu Trinh and Phan Boi Chau had argued that it was crucial to assimilate Western ideas and techniques. Now the "Jeunes Annamites," like the "Jeunes

FIGURE 199.   *Mural of a skyscraper rising out of the tropical oceans, by Duclos de la
Haille, from the Colonial Museum at the 1931 Colonial Exposition, Paris. Courtesy of
the Musée des Arts Africains et Océaniens, Paris.*

Marocains," both graduates of French universities in colonial cities, amplified
those demands. Their efforts to "transform their country into a modern state"
presupposed political independence—but not a rejection of their own cultural
traditions.[2]

In Morocco or Vietnam the urban "free schools" had emphasized an amalgam of traditional national culture with modern Western sciences, in the interest
of preparing the country for independence.[3] Each nationality retained a vivid
sense of its own autonomy, its own potent history and cultural integrity which

302

deserved respect—even as it underwent necessary change. Continuity would retain and even expand its pivotal role in the demands for political independence. In the 1950s Jacques Rabemananjara eloquently articulated "the cultural foundations of Malagasy nationalism."[4] Demonstrations had erupted in 1938 in the streets of Antananarivo when the remains of Queen Ranavalona were returned to the royal tombs in Antananarivo.[5] Ho Chi Minh skillfully employed Confucian terms such as "loyalty," "humaneness," and "virtue," recalling Vietnam's long history of independence (fig. 200). Moroccan nationalism drew much of its strength from Islam and the continued prestige of the sultan, two institutions protected by the French through their preservation of mosques, medersas, and royal palaces.

Social scientists of the period, drawing from Max Weber and Louis Wirth, regarded all cities as harbingers of modernism.[6] In part for this reason, French specialists in the colonies ignored the full significance of powerful links with national pasts. Colonial cities were considered " 'de-tribalized' communities par excellence"—with the exception of touristic monuments preserved by the French.[7] Yet cultural identity, embodied in the particularity of a city, soon became a self-conscious force which fueled nationalism.

The bustling colonial cities of the 1920s and 1930s provided important settings where the colonized intelligentsia could form a new vision of the future. That vision, too, showed the possibility of combining modernism and tradition. Western and indigenous culture could coexist under autonomous governments, far better than they had under imperialism. New technology, health care, education, productivity, and other improvements did not require colonial auspices. Benefits had accrued primarily to Europeans and a small segment of the colonial bourgeoisie, but they could be allocated more equitably. Paradoxically, the French had created a demand for the modern amenities they had brought, a desire that fueled demands for independence.

We also learn a great deal about the European response to imperialism by this focus on French colonial cities. The acceptance, even the widespread endorsement of colonialism cannot by explained solely in terms of economic advantage or political strength. Culture, too, had its role. Imagery helped make colonial ambitions seem tangible and exciting to the public. The cultural message of their colonial cities enticed the French imagination. These cities seemed exotic and even mysterious settings, "primitive" in comparison to Europe; simultaneously, they represented the epitome of rational Western organization. As such they were always inferior, yet always worthy of investment and pride. The polarity allowed both sides of the vision to coexist, each extreme buttressing the

徵王殺漢將

FIGURE 200. *Engraving of Trung Trac, the legendary "Killer of Chinese Generals" in the first century* A.D., *who became a celebrated national heroine during the 1930s. Courtesy of the Ecole Française d'Extrême-Orient, Paris.*

304

FIGURE 201. *Lyautey and Sultan Moulay Youssef with their principal advisors in the Résidence de France at Rabat, 1920. From* L'Illustration, *1934.*

other. The myths of colonialism could remain potent, even when the enterprise might have seemed a dubious undertaking (fig. 201).

Yet colonialism was an artificial construction. It could no more endure forever in the French consciousness than for the colonized populations themselves. By the 1930s it was clear that associationism could not curtail resistance to the French. The recurrence of strikes and urban violence made opposition evident. It was also difficult to argue the economic benefits of colonialism for most French businessmen, farmers, and workers—or for an unchanging "native" economy. International economic interests determined policy in the colonies. The colonies really only benefited two major French banks and a handful of large industrial concerns—notably producers of phosphates in Morocco and rubber in Indochina. These enterprises had no use for the myths of association. At the same time, architectural fashions had changed, shifting toward a severe classicism or a *Sachlichkeit* "objectivity." By 1930 the romantic narrative of association sounded very naive indeed.

The shift can readily be seen in the Colonial Exposition of 1931, a swan song of the associationist approach to colonial urbanism which had held sway for two decades. Even the peripheral site, outside Paris at the Bois de Vincennes, emphasized that the colonies no longer seemed so central a comparison with French cities. Most of the buildings were only temporary structures, including the exotic pavilions for each colony (see figs. 126, 202) and the monumental structures which centralized information (fig. 203). Only the Museum of the Colonies, a collaboration between Jausseley and Laprade, would remain after six months (fig. 204). Its stripped classicism and reinforced concrete, wrote Marcel Olivier, "illustrates the art of our time."[8] The key images of colonialism had been reduced to fleeting impressions and a mere collection of objects, both indigenous arts and raw materials for production. Lyautey, in his preface to the official report on the exposition, regretted the distant site and the "ephemeral nature of this enterprise." These circumstances, he realized, curtailed his dream of instructing the French public about urbanism and political strength through colonial policies.[9]

All the same, there was a real legacy in the colonial cities and the strategies which had been implemented there. These experiments had demonstrated the potential value of urban design and strong urban policies, whatever the setting. Historic preservation by entire districts could romantically capture the past in certain neighborhoods, making them alluring to tourists, while leaving other parts of the city to modernize quite dramatically. This and other de facto policies of residential segregation, carried out in part by restricting modern improvements to certain districts, could be applied anywhere. Rationalized street systems and zoning plans could encourage economic growth in certain districts. Centralized governmental complexes accentuated the authority of the state. Public institutions and public spaces could serve as a stage for new kinds of interaction, instilling particular attitudes and skills. Maintaining or recreating certain traditional public settings could also help sustain a hierarchical order.

Colonial urban designers and social scientists believed they had formulated general principles of design and social order. They chose not to recognize the particular circumstances under which they worked. The colonies provided more than the ideal laboratory setting so often invoked, and more than the "mirror" we might refer to today. They functioned like a magnifying glass, revealing with startling clarity the ambitions and fears, the techniques and policies that pertained at home, here carried out almost without restraints.

As Michel Foucault has so adroitly shown, there is no privileged domain outside of power, but rather a web of interrelations in which everyone, even the dominant, is intertwined. Culture, far from being extraneous, often binds the seams. Analyzing it closely, one can discern its force.

FIGURE 202. *The Malagasy Pavilion at the 1931 Colonial Exposition, Paris, by Collet de Cantelou and Vessière. From* L'Illustration, *1931.*

The most obvious group to be enmeshed in this web were the colonized populations, exploited economically and denied the right to determine the course of their own culture. This control did not prevent the rise of nationalism, the rejection of European domination, and later the resurgence of traditional–even fundamentalist–values.

Colonial architects were also entangled. Eager to assert new approaches to style, urban design, and historic preservation, they touted the benefits of granting exceptional authority to experts like themselves. One can understand how these professionals could see themselves above politics, in the sense of partisanship, since the leaders of every political party had more or less the same agenda in the colonies. Yet the circumstances of the colonies made the architects all too dependent on authoritarian regimes that would support their policies.[10] That chance for control remains a principal appeal for today's designers.

Colonial administrators recognized more fully the political implications of buildings, urban plans, even styles and policies. Yet they, too, were caught,

FIGURE 203. *The Metropolitan Building at the 1931 Colonial Exposition, Paris, by Roger-Henri Expert. From Marcel Olivier,* Rapport générale de l'Exposition Coloniale, *1931.*

unable to wield power arbitrarily because of the need to influence others: to win support among the colonized population, to regulate the actions of the *colons* and the market itself, to interest settlers and investors, and finally to capture the imagination of the French public. Thus no one group was fully able to assert control over the urban domain, even those actors who considered themselves most autonomous.

Because of their rich complexity and the extreme milieu of power in which policy was carried out, colonial cities help orient us to the possible uses and inequities of urban design. We realize irrefutably that these reside not so much in particular styles or even policies, but in their *implementation*. Political ambitions are not inherent in architectural forms, whether the forms are modern or historicist, whether the politics of the patrons are conservative or radical. Politics inevitably come into play as goals, stylistic choices, and techniques are interwoven. This is true even in the initial planning stage, but all the more so once a policy is carried out, as professionals' decisions affect the day-to-day life of actual cities and residents—sometimes, of course, in a very different way than what the designers and their clients had intended.

This colonial model, by the authoritarian ways in which it was implemented, actually brings into focus some of the underlying problems which cloud the major formal polemics of the West. Consider first the modernist vision. In the early twentieth century the cities of these three colonies, especially their European districts, exemplified many of the principles espoused by avant-garde modernists in Europe: more standardized construction, more rationalized organization of public services and industry, efficient circulation routes, and greater attention to the hygienic aspects of design, such as the need for fresh air and sunlight. We also see many of the inequities and abuses that might be incurred by such improvements. Unequal access to the benefits of modern urbanism, while more visible in colonial cities—where the broad boulevards, spacious parks, new housing, and up-to-date services were provided, for the most part, only in the European districts—affects Western metropolises and postcolonial cities as well. So, too, with the loss of autonomy and even livelihood for many handicraft workers in construction trades and other aspects of a local market economy; an uneconomical commitment to inappropriate materials and techniques; a sense of alienation from the past; and over-reliance on expertise.

At the same time, by studying this somewhat exaggerated case, we can discern some of the inherent problems in what we now call post-modernism, in many ways a legacy of the historically minded architecture of the colonies. In both France and her colonies, modernization engendered a nostalgic call for

FIGURE 204.   *The Colonial Museum at the 1931 Colonial Exposition, Paris, by Léon Jausseley and Albert Laprade. Painting by Bazin from* L'Illustration, *1931.*

historic preservation and contextual design. The result, in fact, represents a sharp break with history. As specialists chose certain monuments to isolate and venerate, promoting particular stylistic idioms as prototypical forms, dismissing others as minor variations or impure combinations of styles, architectural design could no longer be considered the complex product of a diverse, vital culture. The variety of forms and uses within any society, the ongoing adaptations of styles, seemed inchoate to educated professionals. Despite the interest in so-called "vernacular arts," the gulf between privileged conceptions of "architecture" and the domain of ordinary building, supposedly unchanging and unselfconscious, grew wider. The historic fabric of cities was commercialized into a tourist commodity, an expression of quaint charm. And the efforts to replace certain groups' actual involvement in political life with a purely visual expression of their cultural autonomy demonstrate how historicist design, intentionally or not, can reinforce political authority.

These stylistic issues are by no means minor considerations today. Throughout the world, questions of "appropriate style" have recently come to the fore. The heyday of Third World modernism during the 1950s and 1960s was in part a reaction to the quaint historicism of earlier colonial urban design, a sign that newly independent countries could be part of modernized international development. That phase is, by and large, over now, just at the time when the Western elite is also looking to vernacular traditions to reinvigorate their own cities. Ironically, the "authentic" buildings now popular in many non-Western countries often recall French colonial architecture from the 1920s. It is all too easy, in either setting, to assume that one can maintain a sense of place, preserving a national or regional heritage simply by choosing historicist architecture. But is it possible for architectural styles to offer more than nostalgia, unless the architect carefully considers the economy of production and the social life of the space?

Invoking history and tradition can be a significant endorsement of continuity, but contemporary architects also need to acknowledge change. No one can evade historical change simply by the use of a supposedly untainted, traditional typology. Continuity is immensely important, yet one must be cautious about invoking the term "traditional," especially if it carries connotations of an unchanging, ahistorical, stable past. The challenge is to take fuller account of the process of history, its innovations and conflicts, and its multiplicity of forms and meanings. The past cannot simply mean a retreat to a golden age before the Europeans, before modern industrialization, for these factors have changed us all irrevocably. Respect for the past in the so-called Third World must include a coming to terms with the stage of colonialism.

Architects everywhere still debate the merits of historical or more resolutely modernist styles. They do so with moral fervor, touting one style for its positive effects on society and lambasting the other. According to the critic's aesthetic predilections, historical styles make manifest either local pride or consumeristic artifice; modernism brings either equality and widespread improvements, or a disintegration of the public sphere. The history of the French colonies suggests that no stylistic stance can ever guarantee certain results. The discussion must go beyond style.

The question to pose, once again, is whether we learn anything truly new from this juxtaposition of culture and politics. The answer is not simply empirical, though the comparative narrative does highlight many particular aspects about architecture, imperialism, national identity, and urban policy that might otherwise be overlooked. It is mostly an epistemological reorientation which emerges. We learn to look at urbanistic policy in a new way. On the one hand, this means accepting the validity of different aesthetic preferences. Neither modernism nor historical continuity has a moral mandate. This does not mean that design has no political implications. We should never dismiss style as a superficial epiphenomenon. Nor can design be reduced to simplistic ambitions, for architectural choices always involve more than the political intentions of the clients.

In this complexity lies the core of urban life. The city is at once something shared and particular: it draws together diverse groups, creating a common ground. At the same time, every space or building is inevitably seen and experienced in distinctive ways by different people; the city nurtures the particularity and autonomy of different groups. There is no single reading of a city, a place, or a style of architecture that should dominate all other meanings. Architecture is a public arena, a world of contention and consensus. It must always be read in multiple ways, in terms of the specific artistic goals of designers, the social or economic goals of powerful figures, and the associations or uses of diverse groups. Each perspective is valid; they cannot even be ranked, although certain groups have considerably more power to assert the hegemony of their views and their values.

Colonialism, too, is a complex enterprise, never reducible to any one motive or goal, never viewed uniformly by all citizens—not even in the lands being colonized. Cities, through their spaces and the policies which created them, help us unravel this imbroglio. In doing so we learn something about the nature of colonialism, and about the nature of architecture as well.

The colonial cities of the early twentieth century are not settings that can be isolated from other Western metropolises. They shared many of the same problems, and the administrators used variations of urban policies familiar in Europe. In the extremity of their political authority and the visual impact of diverse streets and quarters, they point up the complexities of modern urban design throughout the world. One can still find the imprint of these earlier experiments in both Western cities and postcolonial cities of our own day.

Perhaps it is now possible to acknowledge the positive lessons of this earlier effort: the recognition of cultural differences; the attempts to preserve historical traditions and streetscapes through urban design; and the sensibilities of architects trying to engage the complex layers of urban life. There in part lies the compelling visual appeal of these colonial cities. All the same, such good intentions and even real successes cannot overshadow the fundamental inequalities that urban design—even good urban design—can engender.

The truly essential lesson we can learn from these examples is the need *always* to raise issues about what any urbanistic project will do to the economy of a region, the social life of residents, their understanding of the past, and the political engagement of all groups in their collective future. We cannnot help but recognize the intensely political implications of certain design decisions in a colonial context. In doing so, we learn to ask relevant questions about the diverse meanings and potential implications of any architectural style or urban policy, whatever the setting.

Notes

ABBREVIATIONS

AF	*L'Afrique française*
AG	*Annales de géographie*
AA	*L'Architecture d'aujourd'hui*
AMPC	*Annales de médecine et de pharmacie coloniales*
AOM	Archives Nationales, Section d'Outre-Mer, Aix-en-Provence
BAM	*Bulletin de l'Académie Malgache*
BASO	*Bulletin de l'Académie des Sciences d'Outre-Mer*
BEFEO	*Bulletin de l'Ecole Française d'Extrême-Orient*
BEMD	*Bulletin économique de Madagascar et dépendences*
BESM	*Bulletin économique et sociale du Maroc*
BRF	*Bulletin du Redressement Français*
BSEI	*Bulletin de la Société des Etudes Indochinoises*
CM	*La Construction moderne*
CNA	*Chantiers nord-africains*
CRA	*Les Cahiers de la recherche architecturale*
FL	Fonds Lyautey, Archives Nationales, Paris
IM	*L'Indépendant de Madagascar*
MCI	*Le Monde colonial illustré*
MS	*Le Musée Social*
PP	Prost Papers, Académie d'Architecture, Paris
RFHOM	*Revue française d'histoire d'outre-mer*
RM	*Revue de Madagascar*
TM	*La Tribune de Madagascar*

INTRODUCTION

1. Joseph Marrast, "Dans quelle mesure faut-il faire appel aux arts indigènes dans la construction des édifices?" *L'Urbanisme aux colonies et dans les pays tropicaux*, ed. Jean Royer, 2 vols. (La-Charité-sur-Loire: Delayance, 1932–35), 2:24. (All translations from the French are mine.) Prost had outlined the basic parameters of the design in 1915 with their site plan for the Grand'Place; the building was completed in 1925.

2. Among the most important recent critiques of "colonial" representation, see James Clifford, *The Predicament of Culture: Twentieth-Century Ethnography, Literature, and Art* (Cambridge: Harvard University Press, 1988); Terry Eagleton, Fredric Jameson, and Edward Said, *Nationalism, Colonialism, and Literature* (Minneapolis: University of Minnesota Press, 1990); Timothy Mitchell, *Colonising Egypt* (Cambridge and New York: Cambridge University Press, 1988); and *Anthropology and the Colonial Encounter*, ed. Talal Asad (London: Ithaca Press, 1973).

3. Maurius-Ary Leblond, "Passé et avenir de l'art colonial," *L'Art vivant* no. 219–20 (February 1938): 71.

4. Léandre Vaillat, *Le Visage français du Maroc* (Paris: Horizons de France, 1931), p. 40.

5. Robert Delavignette, *Soudan—Paris—Bourgogne* (Paris: Editions Bernard Grasset, 1935), p. 253, cited in Raoul Girardet, *L'Idée coloniale en France, 1871–1965* (Paris: Pluriel, 1978), p. 187.

6. Louis Hubert Gonzalve Lyautey, speech at the distribution of lycée prizes, Oran, Algeria, July 12, 1907, *Paroles d'action: Madagascar—Sud Oranais—Oran—Maroc (1900–1926)* (Paris: Armand Colin, 1927), p. 52.

7. A typical example of this sentiment is Eugène Brieux of the Académie Française, writing in *Le Matin*, who envisioned the 1922 Colonial Exposition at Marseilles as a cure for "our national 'depression,' discouragement or scepticism . . . for national disparagement, the incomprehensible crisis of humility from which the French are suffering" (cited in Adrien Artaud, *Rapport général de l'exposition coloniale de Marseille, 1922* [Marseille: Commissarist Général, 1923], p. 522). On this theme, see Barnard Semmel, *Imperialism and Social Reform: English Social-Imperial Thought, 1895–1914* (1960; Garden City, N.Y.: Anchor Books/Doubleday, 1968); and Henri Brunschwig, *Mythes et réalités de l'imperialisme coloniale française, 1871–1914* (Paris: Armand Colin, 1960). My earlier article, "Tradition in the Service of Modernity: Architecture and Urbanism in French Colonial Policy, 1900–1930," *Journal of Modern History* 59 (June 1987): 291–316, treats many of the issues I will consider in this book, but in a far more condensed manner.

8. There is now an abundant literature on European colonization during this period, most of which focuses, with considerable internal controversy, on political and

economic motivations. Among the most useful for this study were Ronald Robinson and John Gallagher, with Alice Denny, *Africa and the Victorians: The Official Mind of Imperialism* (London: Macmillan, 1961); *Robinson and Gallagher and Their Critics*, ed. William Roger Louis (New York: Frederick Watts, 1975): Eric J. Hobsbawm, *Industry and Empire* (Baltimore: Penguin, 1968); idem, *The Age of Empire, 1875-1914* (New York: Pantheon, 1988); Samir Amin, *L'Economie du Maghreb*, 2 vols. (Paris: Editions de Minuit, 1966); idem, *Imperialism and Unequal Development* (New York: Monthly Review Press, 1979); *Colonialism in Africa, 1870-1960*, ed. Peter Duignan and L. H. Gann, 4 vols. (Cambridge: Cambridge University Press, 1975); Immanuel Wallerstein, *The Capitalist World Economy: Essays* (Cambridge: Cambridge University Press, 1979); *The Colonial Situation*, ed. Immanuel Wallerstein (New York: John Wiley, 1966); and Jean-Louis Miège, *Expansion européene et décolonisation de 1870* (Paris: Presses Universitaires de France, 1973).

There have, of course, been several notable attempts to consider a more cultural analysis of colonialism, and in particular to highlight the role of urban design. Among the best such work is Janet L. Abu-Lughod, *Rabat: Urban Apartheid in Morocco* (Princeton: Princeton University Press, 1980); François Béguin, *Arabisances: Décor architectural et tracé urbain en Afrique du Nord, 1830-1950* (Paris: Dunod, 1983); Brian Brace Taylor, "Planned Discontinuities: Modern Colonial Cities in Morocco," *Lotus International* 36 (1979): 52-66; Jacques Marseille, *L'Age d'or de la France coloniale* (Paris: Albin Michel, 1986); Raymond Betts, *Tricoleur: The French Overseas Empire* (London: Gordon and Cremonissi, 1978); and *Colonial Cities: Essays on Urbanism in a Colonial Context*, ed. Robert J. Ross and Gerald J. Telkamp (Dordrecht, Netherlands: Kluwer Academic, 1985). Material on colonial India is especially rich. See Anthony King, *Colonial Urban Development: Culture, Social Power and Development* (London: Routledge-Kegan Paul, 1976); Robert Grant Irving, *Indian Summer: Lutyens, Baker, and Imperial Delhi* (New Haven: Yale University Press, 1981); Norma Evenson, *The Indian Metropolis: A View towards the West* (New Haven: Yale University Press, 1989); and Thomas R. Metcalf, *An Imperial Vision: Indian Architecture and Britain's Raj* (Berkeley: University of California Press, 1989). Also see my joint article with Paul Rabinow, "Savoir et pouvoir dans l'urbanisme moderne colonial d'Ernest Hébrard," *CRA* no. 9 (1982): 26-43.

9. Project for a "Bibliothèque des Beaux-Arts et du Tourisme au Maroc," p. III, carton 19, dossier 88, FL.

10. Jean-Louis Cohen, "L'Union sacrée: technocrates et architectes modernes à l'assaut de la banlieue parisienne," *CRA*, no. 9 (1982): 6-25; and Anatol Kopp, Frédérique Boucher, and Danièle Pauly, *L'Architecture de la reconstruction en France, 1945-1954* (Paris: Editions du Moniteur, 1982).

11. Norma Evenson, *Chandigarh* (Berkeley and Los Angeles: University of California Press, 1966); "Venturi, Rauch & Scott Brown," *Progressive Architecture* 65 (October 1984): 88-89. Among the numerous recent discussions of these terms, perhaps the

most cogent is Alan Colquhoun, "Three Kinds of Historicism," *Oppositions* 26 (1984): 29–39, and, more generally, his *Essays in Architectural Criticism; Modern Architecture and Historical Change* (Cambridge: MIT Press, 1981). An excellent source of images and ideas in postcolonial architecture and urban design, especially projects dealing with the interrelation of local traditions and international modernism, is *Mimar: Architecture in Development* (Singapore). See in particular Bernard Huet, "The Modernity in a Tradition: The Arab-Muslim Culture of North Africa," *Mimar* 10 (October–December 1983): 49–57, and Dogan Kuban, "Modern versus Traditional: A False Conflict," *Mimar* 9 (July–September 1983): 54–58.

12. The most notable and best-known example of this endeavor is Carl E. Schorske's provocative *Fin-de-Siècle Vienna: Politics and Culture* (New York: Alfred A. Knopf, 1980). Other important examples include Thomas Bender, *New York Intellect: A History of Intellectual Life in New York City, from 1750 to the Beginnings of Our Own Time* (New York: Alfred A. Knopf, 1987); Richard A. Goldthwaite, *The Building of Renaissance Florence: An Economic and Social History* (Baltimore: Johns Hopkins University Press, 1980); Barbara Miller Lane, *Architecture and Politics in Germany, 1918–1945* (1968; Cambridge, Mass.: Harvard University Press, 1985); Serge Guilbaut, *How New York Stole the Idea of Modern Art* (Chicago: University of Chicago Press, 1983); Lynn Hunt, *Politics, Culture and Class in the French Revolution* (Berkeley: University of California Press, 1984); T. J. Clark, *The Painting of Modern Life: Paris in the Age of Manet and His Followers* (Princeton: Princeton University Press, 1984); and Debora L. Silverman, *Art Nouveau in Fin-de-Siècle France: Politics, Psychology, and Style* (Berkeley: University of California Press, 1989).

13. *The Invention of Tradition*, ed. Eric J. Hobsbawm and Terence Ranger (Cambridge and New York: Cambridge University Press, 1983).

14. A notable exception is Marshall Berman, *All That Is Solid Melts into Air: The Experience of Modernity* (New York: Simon and Schuster, 1982).

15. See Thomas Bender, "The Culture of the Metropolis," *Journal of Urban History* 14 (Fall 1988): 492–502.

16. Rhoads Murphy, "Traditionalism and Colonialism: Changing Urban Roles in Asia," *Journal of Asian Studies* 29 (1969): 68. Murphy of course acknowledges the effect of historical chronology and national cultures in this broadly limned portrait.

17. Representative books which emphasize this theme of the laboratory include Joseph Chailley-Bert, *La France et la plus grande France* (Paris: *Revue politique et parlementaire*, 1902); J. B. Piollet, *La France hors de France* (Paris: Felix Alcan, 1910); Alfred de Tarde, *Le Maroc, école d'énergie* (Paris: Plon, 1915); Albert Sarraut, *La Mise en valeur des colonies françaises* (Paris: Payot, 1923). On this general tendency in European intellectual life, see Edward W. Said, *Orientalism* (New York: Pantheon, 1978).

CHAPTER ONE

1. François Caron, *An Economic History of Modern France*, trans. Barbara Bray (New York: Columbia University Press, 1974), pp. 27–43, 133–34, 142–65; and Leonard R. Berlanstein, *The Working People of Paris, 1871–1914* (Baltimore: Johns Hopkins University Press, 1984); pp. 4, 9.

2. J. N. Birabeu, "Quelques aspects de la mortalité en milieu urbaine," *Population* 30 (May–June 1975): 514; and Michel Huber, *La Population de la France* (Paris: Presses Universitaires de France, 1943), pp. 187, 221.

3. Louis Greenberg, *Sisters of Liberty: Marseille, Lyon, Paris, and the Reaction to a Centralized State, 1868–1871* (Cambridge: Harvard University Press, 1971); Jeanne Gaillard, *Communes de province, Commune de Paris* (Paris: Flammarion, 1971); and J. Rougerie, "Espace populaire et espace révolutionaire, Paris, 1870–1871," *Recherches et travaux de l'Institut d'histoire économique et sociale à Paris*, vol. 1 (Paris, 1977).

4. Berlanstein, *The Working People of Paris*, p. 169; Edward Shorter and Charles Tilly, *Strikes in France, 1830–1968* (Cambridge: Harvard University Press, 1974); Michelle Perrot, *Les Ouvriers en grève, 1781–1890*, 2 vols. (Paris: La Haye-Mouton, 1974); *Le Socialisme français et le pouvoir*, ed. Michelle Perrot and Annie Kriegel (Paris: Etudes et documentation Internationales, 1966); Tony Judt, *Socialism in Provence, 1871–1914* (Cambridge and New York: Cambridge University Press, 1979); John M. Merriman, *The Red City: Limoges and the French Nineteenth Century* (New York: Oxford University Press, 1985); and *Consciousness and Class Experience in Nineteenth-Century Europe*, ed. John M. Merriman (New York: Holmes and Meier, 1979).

5. See, in particular, the excellent work by Nicholas Bullock and James Read, *The Movement for Housing Reform in Germany and France, 1840–1914* (Cambridge and New York: Cambridge University Press, 1985), pp. 305–8.

6. Jean Izoulet, *La Cité moderne et la métaphysique de la sociologie* (Paris: Felix Alcan, 2d ed., 1895), p. ix.

7. Emile Durkheim, *Suicide: A Study in Sociology*, trans. John H. Spaulding and George Simpson (1897; New York: The Free Press, 1951), p. 368.

8. Prof. Barthelemy, "Exposé des mésures en vigueur en France, et d'un projet de réorganisation de la surveillance de la prostitution," cited in Alain Corbin, *Les Filles de noce: misère sexuelle et prostitution au XIXe et XXe siècles* (Paris: Aubier, 1978), p. 364. Also see Robert A. Nye, *Crime, Madness and Politics in Modern France: The Medical Concept of National Decline* (Princeton: Princeton University Press, 1984); idem, "Degeneration and the Medical Model of Cultural Crisis in the French *Belle Epoque*," in *Political Symbolism in Modern Europe: Essays in Honor of George L. Mosse*, ed. Seymour Drescher, David Sabean, and Allan Sharlin (New Brunswick: Transaction Books, 1982), pp. 19–42; and Koenraad Swart, *The Sense of Decadence in Nineteenth-Century France* (The Hague: M. Nijhoff, 1964).

9. Raymond Escholier, *Le Nouveau Paris: la vie artistique de la Cité Moderne* (Paris: Editions Nilsson, 1923), p. 44; Georges Benoit-Lévy, *Paris s'entendu* (Nice: Société générale de l'imprimerie, 1927), p. 10. Similar statements appear in Gustave Kahn, *L'Esthétique de la rue* (Paris: Bibliothéque Charpentier, 1901); Max Doumic, *L'Architecture d'aujourd'hui* (Paris: Schmid, 1903); A.-Augustin Rey, *Le Cri de la France: Des Logements!* (Paris: M. Rivière, 1912); Emile Magne, *L'Esthétique des villes* (Paris: Société du Mercure de France, 1908); Robert de Souza, *Nice, capital d'hiver. L'avenir de nos villes. Etudes pratiques d'esthétique urbaine* (Paris: Berger-Levrault, 1913); and Charles Lortsch, *La Beauté de Paris et la loi* (Paris: Recueil Sirey, 1913).

10. This point is very well made in Kenneth Eric Silver, *"Esprit de Corps": The Art of the Parisian Avant-Garde and the First World War, 1914–1925* (Princeton: Princeton University, 1990).

See, among many such general pleas, Lucien Lévy-Bruhl, *La Morale et la science des moeurs* (Paris: Felix Alcan, 1903); Emile Durkheim, *L'Education morale* (his 1902–3 course at the Sorbonne) (Paris: Felix Alcan, 1925); Max Leclerc, *Le Rôle social des universités* (Paris: Armand Colin, 1895) (Leclerc was later the author of *Au Maroc avec Lyautey* [Paris: Armand Colin, 1927]); Paul Desjardins, *Le Devoir présent* (Paris: Armand Colin, 1896); and the most important statement of this attitude, Léon Bourgeois, *Solidarité* (Paris: Armand Colin, 1896; 11 editions to 1926).

On architecture, see, in particular, François Loyer, *Paris Nineteenth Century: Architecture and Urbanism*, trans. Charles Lynn Clark (New York: Abbeville, 1988); idem, *Architecture of the Industrial Age, 1789–1914*, trans. R. F. M. Dexter (Geneva: Skira, 1983); Marc Gaillard, *Paris au XIXe siècle* (Paris: Fernand Nathan, 1981); Peter M. Wolf, *Eugène Hénard and the Beginning of Urbanism in Paris, 1900–1914* (New York and Paris: International Federation for Housing and Planning/Centre de Recherce d'Urbanisme, 1968); and Norma Evenson, *Paris: A Century of Change, 1878–1978* (New Haven: Yale University Press, 1979).

11. Unidentified speech, PP. Also see Prost's *L'Urbanisme au point de vue technique*, no. 16 of *Les Cahiers du Redressement français* (Paris: Editions de la S.A.P.E., 1927), pp. 1–2.

12. Léon Bourgeois's *Solidarité* (1896) spurred the publication of many related works, such as the Ecole des Hautes Etudes Sociales study, *Les Applications sociales de la solidarité* (Paris: Felix Alcan, 1904). Solidarity was called "the charter of the French Republic" in Maurice Baumont, *L'Essor industriel et l'impérialisme colonial (1878–1914)* (Paris: Presses Universitaires de France, 1949), p. 458. On the movement in general, see Celestin Bouglé, "L'Evolution du solidarisme," *Revue politique et parlementaire* 35 (1903): 480–505; and J. E. S. Harward, "Solidarity: The Social History of an Idea in Nineteenth-Century France," *International Review of Social History* 4 (1959): 261–81, and idem, "The Official Social Philosophy of the French Third Republic: Léon Bourgeois and Solidarism," 6 (1961): 19–48.

13. An indication of the extent of Le Play's influence is the fact that Lyautey, around the age of twenty and under the tutelage of Albert de Mun, learned by heart passages from all three volumes of *Le Réforme sociale* (see Lyautey, *Lettres du Sud de Madagascar* [1900–1912] [Paris: Armand Colin, 1935], p. 187).

On Le Bon, see Susanna Barrows, *Distorting Mirrors: Visions of the Crowd in Late Nineteenth-Century France* (New Haven: Yale University Press, 1981); Robert A. Nye, *The Origins of Crowd Psychology: Gustave Le Bon and the Crisis of Mass Democracy* (Beverly Hills: Sage, 1975); and Roger L. Geiger, "Democracy and the Crowd: The Social History of an Idea in France and Italy, 1890–1914," *Societas* 7 (Winter 1977): 47–71. On Durkheim, see Steven Lukes, *Emile Durkheim, His Life and Work, a Historical and Critical Study* (New York: Harper and Row, 1982); and Ernest Wallwork, *Durkheim: Morality and Milieu* (Cambridge: Harvard University Press, 1972). On Le Play, see Michael Z. Brooke, *Le Play: Engineer and Social Scientist* (London: Longman, 1970); and *Frédéric Le Play on Family, Work, and Social Change*, ed. Catherine Bodard Silver (Chicago: University of Chicago Press, 1982).

For general discussion of the social sciences in France during this period, see Henri Hauser, *L'Enseignement des sciences sociales* (Paris: Chevalier-Masescq, 1903); Dick May [Jeanne Weill], *L'Enseignement social à Paris* (Paris: Arthur Rousseau, 1896); and Terry Nichols Clark, *Prophets and Patrons: The French University and the Emergence of the Social Sciences* (Cambridge: Harvard University Press, 1973).

14. De Souza, *Nice*, pp. ix–x, 377–78.

15. Ibid., pp. 389–423. An important addition to this list took place shortly after de Souza's book was published, in 1917, when Ernest Hébrard was named head of the French army's Archaeological Service in Thessalonika, Greece. Here he supervised reconstruction projects for the center of the city. An earthquake and fire in 1919 gave him the chance to realize many aspects of these proposals. The Greek government then invited Hébrard to Athens, where he succeeded in preventing the destruction of the area around the Parthenon, before political dissension and the fall of the government foreclosed other work there. See Y. Yerolympos, *The Replanning of Thessalonika after the Fire of 1919* (Thessalonika, 1975); Jacques Cohen, "Evolution de Salonique," thesis, Institut d'Urbanisme de la Ville de Paris, 1935); Pierre Lavedan, "L'Oeuvre de Ernest Hébrard en Grèce," *Urbanisme* 2 (May 1933): 148–68; and Gwendolyn Wright and Paul Rabinow, "Savoir et pouvoir dans l'urbanisme moderne colonial d'Ernest Hébrard," *CRA* no. 9 (January 1982): 32.

16. Speech in Casablanca, July 14, 1914, in *Paroles d'action: Madagascar—Sud Oranais—Oran—Maroc (1900–1926)* (Paris: Armand Colin, 1927), pp. 116–17.

17. Charles Lortsch cites such a statement by M. Chastenet at the Chamber of Deputies session of June 24, 1909, in *La Beauté de Paris et la loi*, pp. 15–16.

18. On this general history, see Bullock and Reed, *The Movement for Housing Reform*, esp. pp. 465–504; Roger H. Guerrand, *Les Origines du logement social en France*

(Paris: Les Editions Ouvrières, 1967); Anne-Marie Shapiro, *Housing the Poor of Paris, 1850–1902* (Madison: University of Wisconsin Press, 1985); and Anthony Sutcliffe, *The Autumn of Central Paris: The Defeat of Town Planning* (London: Edward Arnold, 1970).

19. For detailed coverage of French urban reform proposals, see, in particular, Anthony Sutcliffe, *Toward the Planned City: Germany, Britain, the United States, and France, 1780–1914* (Oxford: Basil Blackwell, 1981); *Histoire de la France urbaine,* vol. 4, *La Ville de l'âge industriel: le cycle haussmannien,* ed. Maurice Agulhon (Paris: Le Seuil, 1983); *Metropolis 1890–1940,* ed. Anthony Sutcliffe (Chicago: University of Chicago Press, 1984); Bernard Marrex, *Louis Bonnier* (Brussels: Mardaga, 1988); *L'Haleine des faubourgs: ville, habitat et santé au XIXe siècle,* ed. Lion Murard and Patrick Zylberman (Paris: Recherches, 1978); Evenson, *Paris;* Gaillard, *Paris;* and Loyer, *Architecture.*

20. The best analysis in English is Sanford Elwitt, "Social Reform and Social Order in Late-Nineteenth Century France: The Musée Social and Its Friends," *French Historical Studies* 11 (1980); 431–51. Also see Emile Cheysson, *Le Musée Social* (Paris: Imprimerie Nationale, 1894); Alain Cottereau, "Les Débuts de planification urbaine dans l'agglomération parisienne," *Revue de sociologie du travail* 12 (October–December 1970): 362–92; Henri Deroy, "Du Musée Social au CEDIAS," *CEDIAS* (Paris: Musée Social-OCOB, 1964); Roger Merlin, *Jules Siegfried, sa vie, son oeuvre* (Paris: Musée Social, 1922); and André Siegfried, "Discours: Cinquantenaire du Musée Social," *Les Cahiers du Musée Social* n.s. 3 (1945): 157–74.

Jules Siegfried, president of the Musée from 1894 to 1922, had grown up in Mulhouse, a center of early nineteenth-century housing reform, then served as mayor of Le Havre, before coming to Paris, first as a deputy and then as a senator, where he was engaged in housing reform and colonial politics. As early as 1896, soon to be president of the Groupe Colonial du Sénat, Siegfried had been responsible for appraising the colonial budget, whereupon he insisted on a new policy of decentralization and social reform—what would soon come to be called "association." Prost maintained professional ties with the Musée through the 1920s, even occasionally returning to Paris as a consultant to the group.

21. Commission d'Extension de Paris, Préfecture du Départment de la Seine, *Considérations techniques,* vol. 2 (Paris: Chaux, 1913), p. 49, cited in Evenson, *Paris,* p. 37.

22. See Lortsch, *La Beauté de Paris et la loi;* Kahn, *l'Esthétique de la rue;* Magne, *L'Esthétique des villes;* and Paul Léon, *Histoire de la rue* (Paris: La Taille-Donce, 1947), pp. 200–220. An excellent discussion of these issues appears in Evenson, *Paris,* pp. 21–51, 150–59. Rapid transit merited some consideration, too, of course, in part because of its relationship to the problem of unplanned and unregulated growth around the periphery. When suburban rail lines and urban tramways came under their control in the 1890s, the Parisian council openly encouraged suburban development—for the most

part a working-class exodus to more affordable housing, often quite ramshackle, on the outskirts of Paris. Certainly the most dramatic new service was the Métropolitan, the Parisian subway system, inaugurated in 1900, after years of contentious debate, to serve the crowds of tourists visiting the International Exposition that year.

23. Robert de Souza, "L'Urbanisme en Dix Commandements," *Le Musée Social* 36 (April 1929): 138–39; Léandre Vaillat, *La Cité renaissante* (Paris: Librairie Larousse, 1918); Vaillat et al., *L'Urbanisme dans la région parisienne* (Paris: Musée des Arts Décoratifs, 1935); and Vaillat's weekly articles on "Le Décor de la Vie" in *Le Temps*. We should note, however, that Le Corbusier attended meetings both of La Renaissance des Cités and the 1923 Congrès International d'Urbanisme et d'Hygiène Municipale at Strasboug, also organized by the SFU. See his presentation, "Le Centre des grandes villes," published in *Où en est l'urbanisme en France et à l'étranger? Edité par la SFU à l'occasion du Congrès International d'Urbanisme et d'Hygiène Municipale* (Strasbourg: SFU, 1923), pp. 247–57.

24. Paul Lafollye, "Exposition des documents concernant l'aménagement et l'embellissement des cités, organisée par la Renaissance des Cités au Musée des Arts décoratifs," *L'Architecture* 22 (December 1, 1919): 727. Also see A. Antoine, *Les Routes américaines* (Paris: Dunod, 1926); Henry Crosat, *La Cité idéale ou l'urbanisme social rationnel* (Paris: Besson, 1920); and *La Cité moderne. Catalogue de l'Exposition de l'Habitation* (Paris: Science et Industrie, 1929).

25. Eugène Hénard, *Etudes sur les transformations de Paris. Fascicule 7: Les voitures et les passants. Carrefours libres et carrefours à giration* (Paris: Librairies-Imprimeries Réunies, 1906), p. 282. On Hénard's work and influence, see Wolf, *Eugène Hénard*; and Jean-Louis Cohen's edited reissue of the *Etudes* (Paris: L'Equerre, 1982).

26. Jean-Claude-Nicolas Forestier, *Grandes villes et systèmes de parcs* (Paris: Hachette, 1908), p. 22. Also see idem, *Jardins. Carnet de plans et de dessins* (Paris: Emile-Paul Frères, 1920); idem, "Les Parcs urbains et ruraux en France et à l'étranger," *Annales du Musée Social* (1910): 162–66; and Henri Prost, "Hommage à Forestier," *Urbanisme* 21 (1952): 74–75.

27. Forestier, *Grandes villes*, p. 49. For a vivid and thoughtful discussion of Forestier, see Jean-Louis Cohen's unpublished paper, "Americanism and the Paris Planning Discussion in the Work of Forestier and Jaussely."

28. These two terms appear, for example, in the *Annales du Musée Social* (January 1909): 58, and (November 1909): 34. Also see *Où en est l'urbanisme en France et à l'étranger?*; Léon Jaussely, "Chronique dc l'urbanisme," *La Vie urbaine* 1 (1919): 181–225; Jean Marcel Aubertin and Henri Blanchard, *La Cité de demain dans les régions devastées* (Paris: Armand Colin, 1917); Léon Rosenthal, *Villes et villages françaises après la Guerre. Aménagement. Restauration. Embellissement. Extension* (Paris: Payot, 1918); Eugène Beaudouin, "La Société Française des Urbanistes," *Urbanisme* 31 (1962): 16–19 (part of a special issue on "Cinquante ans d'urbanisme"); Jacques Lucan,

"Chronique d'années de guerre," *Architecture, mouvement, continuité* 44 (February 1978): 70–73; Jean-Christophe Tougeron, "Donat-Alfred Agache: un Architect Urbaniste, un Artiste, un Scientifique, un Philosophe," *CRA* 8 (April 1981): 30–49; and Mary McLeod, "'Architecture or Revolution': Taylorism, Technocracy, and Social Change," *Art Journal* 43 (Summer 1983): 132–47.

The founders of the SFU included eight architects—Ernest Hébrard, Henri Prost, Léon Jaussely, D.-Alfred Agache, Marcel Aubertin, André Bérard, Eugène Hénard, and Albert Parrenty—as well as J. C. N. Forestier and Edouard Redont, both landscape architects, and Edouard Herriot, mayor of Lyons. Georges Risler of the Musée Social was honorary president.

29. *Comment reconstruire nos cités détruites. Notions d'urbanisme s'appliquant aux villes, bourgs, et villages*, ed. D.-Alfred Agache, Marcel Aubertin and Edouart Redont (Paris: Armand Colin, 1915), p. 5.

30. Georges Risler, "Les Plans d'aménagement et d'extension des villes," *MS* (1912): 301–51, republished that year by Arthur Rousseau; idem, "L'Expropriation pour cause d'insalubrité," *La Réforme sociale* (December 1, 1910); and idem, preface to *Comment reconstruire*, p. 2.

31. Georges Risler, preface to *Comment reconstruire*, pp. 2–13.

32. For example, Léon Jaussely's classes in urban art considered master plans, open-space allocations, and cohesive architectural groupings, including garden cities and civic centers. See George B. Ford, *Out of the Ruins* (New York: Century, 1919), p. 230; *Ecole des Hautes Etudes Urbaines* (Paris: Institut d'Histoire, de Géographie, et d'Economie Urbaines, 1920); "Chronique de l'Institut d'Histoire, de Géographie, et d'Economie Urbaines de la Ville de Paris," *La Vie urbaine* 1 (March–June 1919): 203–25; and Jaussely, "Chronique de l'urbanisme." In a similar vein, see Adolphe Dervaux, *L'Edifice et le milieu* (Paris: Ernest Leroux, 1919); Léon Anscher and Georges Rozet, *Urbanisme et tourisme* (Paris: Leroux, 1920); and André Vera, *L'Urbanisme ou la vie heureuse* (Paris: R.-A. Correà, 1936). It is interesting to note that the Institut d'Urbanisme theses on foreign and colonial cities made greater and more imaginative use of historical research than the theses on French cities.

33. Marcel Poëte, *Introduction à l'urbanisme. L'évolution des villes. La leçon de l'antiquité* (Paris: Boivin, 1929); idem, *Une Vie de cité. Paris de sa naissance à nos jours*, 4 vols. (Paris: Picard, 1924–31); and idem, "L'Esprit de l'urbanisme français," *AA* n.s. 10 (March 1939): 4–5.

34. Léon Jaussely, "Avertissement" to the French edition of Raymond Unwin's *Town Planning in Practice*, translated as *L'Etude pratique des plans de villes* (1922; reprint ed., Paris: L'Equerre, 1980), p. iii. The scheme was a joint project by Jaussely, Expert, and Sollier.

35. Bullock and Reed, *The Movement for Housing Reform*, p. 370; Jean-Louis Cohen, "L'Union sacrée: Technocrates et architectes modernes à l'assaut de la banlieue

parisienne," *CRA* no. 9 (January 1982): 6–25; and "Vingt ans d'urbanisme appliqué," special issue of *AA* n.s. 10 (March 1939).

36. Georges Benoit-Lévy, *La Cité-Jardin* (Paris: Henri Fouve, 1904), p. 7; also in the second revised edition, 2 vols. (Paris: Editions des Cités-Jardins de France, 1911), 1:31.

37. See Charles S. Maier, *Recasting Bourgeois Europe: Stabilization in France, Germany, and Italy in the Decade after World War I* (Princeton: Princeton University Press, 1975), pp. 70–83; idem, "Between Taylorism and Technocracy: European Ideologies and the Vision of Industrial Productivity in the 1920s," *Journal of Contemporary History* 5 (1970): 27–61; Jean-Marie Mayeur and Madeleine Rebérioux, *The Third Republic from Its Origins to the Great War, 1871–1914* (Cambridge and Paris: Cambridge University Press, 1984), pp. 269–71; Richard F. Kuisel, *Capitalism and the State in Modern France* (Cambridge and New York: Cambridge University Press, 1981); Henry W. Ehrmann, *Organized Business in France* (Princeton: Princeton University Press, 1957), pp. 19–26; Henri Fayol, *Administration industrielle et générale* (Paris: Dunod, 1916; reprinted as *General and Industrial Management*, trans. Constance Storrs, New York: Pitman, 1949); and McLeod, "'Architecture or Revolution.'"

38. See Richard F. Kuisel, *Ernest Mercier, French Technocrat* (Berkeley and Los Angeles: University of California Press, 1967); Marc Bourbonnais, *Le Néo-Saint-Simonisme et la vie sociale d'aujourd'hui* (Paris: Presses Universitaires de France, 1923); and Klaus-Jurgen Muller, "French Fascism and Modernization," *Journal of Contemporary History* 11 (1976): 92–93.

39. "Pour l'urbanisme. Un code, une méthode d'application," supplement to the *BRF* 2 (May 15, 1928): 1. Also see Jean Levêque and J. H. Richard, *Une Politique du logement*, no. 15 of the *Cahiers du Redressement Français*, n.d.

40. M. Malkiel-Jirmounsky, "Reflexions sur l'architecture contemporaine," supplement to the *BRF* 2 (September 1, 1928): 3–4.

41. Le Corbusier, *Vers le Paris de l'époque machiniste*, supplement to the *BRF* 2 (February 15, 1928) and *Pour bâtir: Standardiser et tayloriser*, supplement to the *BRF* 2 (May 1, 1928). One pamphlet elaborated on his ideas for the Plan Voisin for Paris (through purportedly functionalist arguments, and therefore without illustrations), while the second advocated Taylorized standardization, putting forth his housing at Stuttgart and Pessac as examples. The thirty-five separately published volumes of these supplements and the *Cahiers*, collectively called a "citizens' library" by the organization, reached some 20,000 people within the first year of their publication (Kuisel, *Ernest Mercier*, p. 50).

In 1927 the Redressement Français organized its first congress, under the patronage of Maréchals Foch and Lyautey, which included a Commission de l'Habitation et de l'Urbanisme. Prost, de la Casinière, and Le Corbusier all took part, which resulted in the two publications by Le Corbusier, as well as Prost's *L'Urbanisme au point de vue technique*, and de la Casinière's *Le Rôle des pouvoirs publics dans l'urbanisme*, both supplements to the *BRF* 2 (March 1, 1928). In addition, other especially pertinent articles include "Urbanisme," *BRF* 1 (September 1, 1927): 9–11; "Le Gouvernement et l'urbanisme," *BRF* 2 (April 1, 1928): 3; and Paul Duléry, "La Tâche municipale," *BRF* 3 (May 1, 1929): 5–12.

42. Kuisel, *Ernest Mercier*, pp. 47, 57, 66; Guillaume de Tarde, *Lyautey, le chef en action* (Paris: Gallimard, 4th ed., 1959), p. 154. Mercier's youngest brother, Louis, was also an aide to Lyautey in Morocco and a member of his circle.

43. Even as late as 1914 France's colonies accounted for only 11 percent of the nation's exports, 9 percent of imports, and 9 percent of foreign investment. See Madeleine Réberioux, *La République radicale (1898–1914)* (Paris: Editions du Seuil, 1975), p. 125; Henri Brunschwig, *Mythes et réalités de l'impérialisme coloniale française, 1871–1914* (Paris: Armand Colin, 1960), pp. 80–89; and Jacques Marseille, *Empire colonial et capitalisme français: Histoire d'un divorce* (Paris: Albin Michel, 1984).

44. Joseph Chailley-Bert, *Le Rôle social de la colonisation* (Paris: Comité de Défense et de Progrès Social, 1898), pp. 10–19. (This piece also appeared in the Le Playist journal *La Réforme social*.)

45. Albert Sarraut, *La Mise en valeur des colonies françaises* (Paris: Payot, 1923), pp. 88–90. Note that the growth of the automobile industry—one of the "new industries" favored by the Redressement Français—gave new financial impetus to colonial investment, notably in Southeast Asia, as the Michelin Tire Company and other enterprises set up large, well-organized, and highly exploitative rubber plantations, turning Indochina's balance of trade from a liability to a marked success during the 1920s. (See Martin J. Murray, *The Development of Capitalism in Colonial Indochina, 1870–1940)* [Berkeley and Los Angeles: University of California Press, 1980], pp. 119–29).

46. Sarraut, *La Mise en valeur*, p. 90. Also see idem, "Nationaliser l'idée coloniale," *L'Europe nouvelle* 428 (May 1, 1926): 581, cited in Thomas G. August, *The Selling of the Empire: British and French Imperialist Propaganda, 1890–1940* (Westport: Greenwood, 1985), p. 53.

47. See Lion Murard and Patrick Zylberman, "L'Ordre et la règle: l'hygiènisme en France dans l'entre-deux-guerres," *CRA* no. 15–17 (1985): 42–53; idem, "La Cité eugénique," in *L'Haleine des faubourgs*, pp. 423–53; Georges Canguilhem, *On the Normal and the Pathological*, trans. Carolyn Fawcett (1943; Boston: D. Reidel, 1978); and Nöel Bernard, *La Vie et l'oeuvre d'Albert Calmette, 1863–1933* (Paris: Albin Michel, 1961). Dr. Robert-Henri Hazemann called the dispensary "un piège à prophylaxie" in *Le Service social municipal* (Paris: Le Mouvement sanitaire, 1929), p. 98. Note, by way of contrast, that Calmette's earlier "hygiene monitors" had offered public-health advice in the home to any working-class family who requested it.

48. Sicard de Plauzolles, *Revue de prophylaxie sanitaire et morale* (1920), cited in Jacques Donzelot, *La Police des familles* (Paris: Minuit, 1977), p. 169.

49. There was only a slight decrease during the ensuing decade. See Cecile Tardieu-Gotchac, "Les Fleaux sociaux," in *Histoire économique de la France entre les deux guerres*, ed. Alfred Sauvy, 4 vols. (Paris: Fayard, 1965–75), 3: 405–6; Michel Huber, *La Population de la France pendant la guerre* (Paris: Presses Universitaires de France, 1931), p. 51; Dr. Bouchet, "Le Péril tuberculeux," *BRF* 5 (September 1930): 6–16.

50. Municipal Council report of 1906, cited in Anthony Sutcliffe, *The Autumn of Central Paris* (London: Edward Arnold, 1970), p. 110. Also see Paul Juillerat, *La Tuberculose et l'habitation* (Paris: Masson et Cie., 1905), and idem, *L'Hygiène et l'habitation* (Paris: Ecole des Hautes Etudes Urbaines, 1920).

51. Alain Cottereau, "La Tuberculose: maladie urbaine ou maladie de l'usure au travail?—Critique d'une epidémiologie officielle: Le cas de Paris," *La Revue de sociologie du travail* 20 (1978): 192–224.

52. Evenson, *Paris*, p. 216.

53. Not even hospital design showed much attention to current research in public health, despite recurrent criticisms that these settings were outmoded by Pasteur's theories of contagion. Edouard Herriot and Tony Garnier did collaborate on the Hôpital de la Grange-Blanche in Lyons, beginning as early as 1909, but the complex was not completed until 1932. Their primary concern, moreover, stressed the functional organization of services, more than patient comfort, public access to services, or hygienic settings per se. See Rosenthal, *Villes et villages*, pp. 191–94; Abraham Flexner, *Medical Education, A Comparative Study* (New York: Macmillan, 1925), pp. 15–27, 118, 166–70; Charles Danielson, *La Santé publique* (Paris: Eugène Figuière, 1936); Theodore Zeldin, *France, 1848–1945*, 2 vols. (Oxford: Oxford University Press, 1977), 2: 327; John D. Thompson and Grace Goldin, *The Hospital: A Social and Architectural History* (New Haven: Yale University Press, 1975), pp. 189–97.

54. Thompson and Goldin, *The Hospital*, p. 208; Anita Hirsch, "Le Logement," in Sauvy, *Histoire économique*, 3: 99; Berlanstein, *The Working People of Paris*, p. 59.

55. André Armengaud, *La Population française au XIXe siècle* (Paris: Presses Universitaires de France, 1971), pp. 47–108.

56. The houses could not be too near a church, school, or public building; they had to be shuttered and further sequestered with curtains or glazed windows; all of the prostitutes within had to be registered with the police and undergo weekly examinations for signs of venereal disease; known prostitutes were forbidden even to appear on the main streets or in public gardens. See Corbin, *Les Filles de noce*; and Marcel Lods, "L'Urbanisme," in Sauvy, *Histoire économique*, 3: 411–14.

57. Jill Harsin, *Policing Prostitution in Nineteenth-Century Paris* (Princeton: Princeton University Press, 1985), pp. 39–43.

58. Eugène Couturaud, *Guide pratique pour la reconstruction, l'extension, l'aménagement et l'embellissement des villes et des communes rurales* (Paris: Librairie de la

Construction Moderne, 1915), p. 28. Also see Jacques Bertillon, *La Dépopulation de la France* (Paris: Felix Alcan, 1911); Paul Leroy-Beaulieu, *La Question de la population* (Paris: Felix Alcan, 1911); and E. Maurel, *Causes de notre dépopulation* (Paris: Doin, 1902). For more recent analyses, see Karen Offen, "Depopulation, Nationalism, and Feminism in Fin-de-Siècle France," *American Historical Review* 89 (June 1984): 648–76; and Francis Ronsin, *La Grève de ventres: Propagande néo-malthusienne et baisse de la natalité française, XIXe–XXe siècles* (Paris: Aubier-Montaigne, 1980).

59. See, among many such sources, Henri Sellier, *La Lutte contre la tuberculose dans la région parisienne, 1896–1927*, 2 vols. (Paris: Editions de l'Office d'Hygiène Sociale, 1928), 1: 3, 157; and Juillerat, *L'Hygiène et l'habitation*, p. 15.

60. William MacDonald, *Reconstruction in France* (New York: Macmillan, 1922), pp. 24–28, citing the official statistics of the French Ministry of the Liberated Regions.

61. Henri Sellier and A. Bruggeman, *Le Problème du logement* (Paris: Presses Universitaires de France, 1927), p. 26.

62. Cited in Hirsch, "Le Logement," p. 81.

63. Sellier and Bruggeman, *Le Problème du logement*, pp. 1–2. In 1926 some two-fifths of the Parisian population was estimated to be inadequately housed, with 25 percent living in apartments averaging two residents per room. See Louis Loucheur, *Le Carnet secret, 1908–1932* (Brussels: Brepol, 1962), p. 145. On the Parisian housing problems, see Ginette Batty-Tornikian, *Un Projet urbain idéal typique: l'agglomération parisienne, 1919–1939* (Paris: CORDA, 1979); and Henri Sellier's numerous publications, especially *La Crise du logement et l'intervention publique*, 4 vols. (Paris: Editions de l'Office Public des Habitations à Bon Marché du Département de la Seine, 1921).

64. Jean Bastié, *La Croissance de la banlieue parisienne* (Paris: Presses Universitaires de France, 1964); and Henri Sellier, *Les Banlieues urbaines et la réorganisation administrative du Département de la Seine* (Paris: Marcel Rivière, 1920).

65. M. Bonnefond, "Les Colonies de bicoques de la région parisienne," *La Vie urbaine* 6 (April 15, 1925): 525–26.

66. Ibid.

67. See Sellier, *Les Banieues urbaines*; idem, "L'Effort français pour l'habitation populaire," *L'Illustration* 87 (March 30, 1929); Raphael Alibert, "L'Aménagement de la région parisienne," *BRF* 5 (January 1, 1930): 7–11, (April 1, 1930): 12–23; Camille Dépaule, "Les Sociétés d'Habitations à Bon Marché et l'urbanisme," thesis, Institut d'Urbanisme of the University of Paris, 1923; Berthe Leymarie, "Organisation sociale des cités-jardins du grand Paris," thesis, Institut d'Urbanisme, 1926; Jean Taricat and Martine Villars, *Le Logement à Bon Marché. Conronique, Paris, 1850/1930* (Paris: Editions Apogée, 1982); and Evenson, *Paris*, pp. 208–32.

68. M. Peirotes, "Le Problème du logement et l'intervention de la ville de Strasbourg," *Où en est l'urbanisme*, pp. 435–44.

69. Prost, writing in 1927, after his return from Morocco, straightforwardly declared that such zoning would prevent declines in property values (Prost, *L'Urbanisme au point de vue technique*, p. 3). Also see Georges Risler, "De la Reconstruction des villes détruites," *La Question de la réconstruction des villes* (Paris: Société Française des Habitations à Bon Marché, 1916), pp. 7–18.

70. "L'Urbanisme dans nos colonies: une exposition d'urbanisme colonial," MCI 88 (Decembber 1930): 130.

71. See *Henri Sauvage, 1873–1932* (Brussels: Archives d'Architecture Moderne, 1976).

72. Edith Elmer Wood, "The Cités-Jardins of Lyons and Rheims," *The American City* 28 (March 1923): 229–30; Tony Garnier, *Les Grands travaux de la ville de Lyon* (Paris: Charles Massin, n.d.).

73. Société Française des Habitations à Bon Marché, *La Question de la reconstruction des villes et villages détruites par la Guerre* (Paris: Société Française des HBM, 1916), p. 25.

74. In *Villes et villages*, Rosenthal declared that "the crisis of nineteenth-century architecture was the disappearance of regional styles [and] archaeological mania . . . a contradictory evidence of chaos and monotony" (p. 42).

75. Wood, "The Cités-Jardins of Lyons and Rheims," p. 230.

76. Raymond Escholier could thus celebrate "department stores [which] welcome modern art" (Escholier, *Le Nouveau Paris*, pp. 248–49). Also see Achille Duchêne, *Pour la reconstruction des cités industrielles* (Paris: Bibliothéque de la Renaissance des Cités, 1919), pp. 28–29; and Tourgeron, "Donat-Alfred Agache," p. 34. As early as 1908 Emile Magne praised the store as "the ardent soul of the street" (*L'Esthétique des villes*, p. 89).

77. The books were published in 1923, 1924, and 1926, with an enthusiastic introduction by Vaillat. See Jean-Claude Vigato, "L'Architecture du régionalisme: les origines du débat (1900–1950)" (unpub. paper, Ecole d'Architecture de Nancy, n.d.). I would like to thank Robin Middleton for this useful source.

78. Vaillat would take up this term in his book on Morocco, *Le Visage français du Maroc* (Paris: Horizons de France, 1931).

79. Léon Jaussely, "Avertissement," p. xiv.

80. Juarès in the *Revue de l'enseignement primaire et primaire supérieures*, June 11, 1909, cited in Mayeur and Rebérioux, *The Third Republic*, p. 188.

81. Claude-Roger Marx, *L'Art social* (Paris: Eugène Fasquelle, 1913).

82. France had 157 Bourses de Travail by 1908, only twenty years after the first one had been erected in Paris. See R. D. Anderson, *France, 1870–1914: Politics and Society* (London: Routledge and Kegan Paul, 1977), p. 138. John M. Merriman describes in detail the program of the Bourse de Travail in Limoges, established in 1895

by the CGT and the municipal government (*The Red City*, p. 182).

83. Emile Dubuisson, *Construction d'un nouvel hôtel de ville: rapport de l'architect* (Lille: Imprimerie Centrale du Nord, 1922); *Le Nouvel Hôtel de Ville de Lille* (Paris: *Le Génie civil*, 1928); François Loyer, "Ornement et caractère," in *Le Siècle de l'éclecticisme, Lille 1830–1930*, ed. Maurice Culot, Lise Grenier, and Hans Wieser-Benedetti (Paris and Brussels: Archives d'Architecture Moderne, 1975), p. 101; and Pierre Pierrard, *Lille et les Lillois* (Paris: Bloud et Gay, 1983), p. 289.

84. Duchêne, *Pour la reconstruction*, pp. 60–61, 9. Also see Pierre Dourdeix, "La Maison de Tous," *CM* 30 (November 7, 1920): 18–20; Rosenthal, *Villes et villages*, p. 187; Escholier, *Le Nouveau Paris*, pp. 23–85.

85. Maurice Agulhon, "Le Mairie: Liberté. Egalité. Fraternité," in *Les Lieux de mémoire*, ed. Pierra Nora, vol. 1, *La République* (Paris: Gallimard, 1984), pp. 167–93; and idem, *Marianne into Battle: Republican Imagery and Symbolism in France, 1789–1880*, trans. Janet Lloyd (1979; Cambridge and New York: Cambridge University Press, 1981); "Imagerie civique et décor urbain," *Ethnologie française* 5 (1975): 33–46; "La Statuomanie et l'histoire," *Ethnologie française* 8 (1978): 3–4; and Françoise Choay, "Pensées sur la ville, arts de la ville," in *La Ville de l'âge industriel*, pp. 197–230. For a general overview of such architectural representation, see Eric J. Hobsbawm, "Mass-Producing Traditions: Europe, 1870–1914," in *The Invention of Tradition*, ed. Eric J. Hobsbawm and Terence Ranger (Cambridge and New York: Cambridge University Press, 1983), pp. 263–307.

86. Rosenthal, *Villes et villages*, p. 277.

87. Escholier, *Le Nouveau Paris*, pp. 236–37.

88. Kahn, *L'Esthétique de la rue*, pp. 205–6. Also see Louis Bonnier, *Les Règlements de voirie* (Paris: Schmid, 1903); and Charles Magny, *Des Moyens juridiques de sauvegarder les aspects ethétiques de la ville de Paris* (Paris: Bernard Tignol, 1911). On other French cities and their urbanistic dilemmas, see Jules Scribe-Loyer, *Les Conditions anthropogéographiques du développement de l'agglomeration lilloise* (Lille: Imprimerie de L. Danel, 1922); Catherine Bruant, *Une Métropole social-democrate: Lille, 1896—1919—1939* (Paris: CORDA, 1979); Jacques Gréber, *Ville de Marseille. Plan d'aménagement et d'extension* (Paris: Fréal, 1933); Association Française pour l'Avancement des Sciences, *Lyon, 1906–1926* (Lyon: A. Rey, 1926); and Claude Collet and R. M. Dion. *L'Urbanisation de Nancy entre 1871 et 1914* (Nancy: Université II, 1980).

89. Lortsch, *La Beauté de Paris et la loi*, pp. xii, 202.

90. Albert Guérard, *L'Avenir de Paris: Urbanisme français et urbanisme américain* (Paris: Payot, 1929), p. 28.

91. Lortsch, *La Beauté de Paris et la loi*, p. 99.

92. Guérard, *L'Avenir de Paris*, p. 28; Lucien Magne, *L'Architecture française du siècle* (Paris: Imprimerie Nationale, 1890), p. 39.

93. Robert de Souza, *L'Art Public* (Paris, 1900), p, 19; Emile Magne, *L'Esthétique des villes*, p. 9.

94. George B. Ford, *Out of the Ruins*, p. 220.

95. Paul Léon, *La Vie des monuments français, déstruction, restauration* (Paris: A. et J. Picard, 1951); idem, *La Renaissance des ruines, maisons, monuments* (Paris: H. Laurens, 1918); idem, *Les Monuments historiques: conservation, restauration* (Paris: H. Laurens, 1917); and Charles Magne, *La Beauté de Paris: conservation des aspects artistiques* (Paris: Pignol, 1911).

96. Paul Léon, introduction to Léon Anscher and Georges Rozet, *Urbanisme et tourisme* (Paris: Leroux, 1920); and Maxime Leroy, *La Ville française: institutions et libertés* (Paris: Marcel Rivière, 1927), p. 105.

97. D.-A. Agache, "Cités-Jardins et villes futures," *Exposition de la Cité Moderne* (Nancy, 1913), pp. 189–200. Also see Risler's early statement on "Les Plans d'aménagement et d'extension des villes," pp. 111–28.

98. Donat-Alfred Agache, *Nos Agglomérations rurales. Comment les aménager: étude monographique, analytique, comparée d'un concours de plans de bourgs et villages* (Paris: Librairie de La Construction Moderne, 1917), cited in Lucan, "Chronique d'années de guerre," p. 71. Also see Léon Jaussely, "Les Cité devastées par la guerre. Etudes de reconstitution," *La Vie urbaine* 1 (March–June 1919): 109–44.

99. Léandre Vaillat, preface to *L'Architecture régionale dans les provinces envahies* (Paris: SADG, 1917), p. 9. We should note that George Ford, a leading proponent of the "scientific" approach to urban design, had first organized this exhibit for the YMCA in the years before the war; the original material was then lost, found, then reformulated into a more "culturalist" display of 150 documents.

100. Le Corbusier, *Vers une architecture* (Paris: Editions Cres, 1923; reprint ed., Paris: Moniteur, 1977), p. 189; translated into English by Frederick Etchells as *Towards a New Architecture* (1927; New York: Praeger, 1960)—although this passage is omitted. Also see Le Corbusier's *Urbanisme*, p. iii.

101. Vaillat, preface to *L'Architecture régionale*, p. 13.

102. See Eugen Weber, *Peasants into Frenchmen: The Modernization of Rural France* (Stanford: Stanford University Press, 1976); idem, *The Nationalist Revival in France, 1905–1914* (Berkeley and Los Angeles: University of California Press, 1959); Edward W. Fox, *History in Geographical Perspective: The Other France* (New York: W. W. Norton, 1971); Jack E. Reece, *The Bretons against France; Ethnic Minority Nationalism in Twentieth-Century Brittany* (Chapel Hill: University of North Carolina Press, 1977); *French Cities in the Nineteenth Century*, ed. John M. Merriman (New York: Holmes and Meier, 1981); and Alain Demangeon and Bruno Fortier, *Les Vaisseaux et les villes: l'arsenal de Cherbourg* (Brussels: Pierre Mardaga, 1978). On the general concept of internal colonialism, see Antonio Gramsci, "The Southern Question" in *The Modern Prince and Other Writings* (New York: International Publishers, 1959);

and Pablo Gonzales-Casanova, "Internal Colonialism and National Development," *Studies in Comparative International Development* 1 (1965): 27–35.

103. See Jean Charles-Brun, *Le Régionalisme* (Paris: Blond, 1911); idem, *Le Problème du régionalisme* (Paris: Presses Universitaires de France, 1924); Henri Hauser, *Les Régions économiques* (Paris: Librairie Bernard Grasset, 1918); Jules Milhau, "Le Mouvement régionaliste," in Sauvy, *Histoire économique*, 3: 128–51; and Gérard Bélorgey, *La France décentralisée* (Paris: Berger-Levrault, 1984).

104. Charles-Brun, *Le Régionalisme*, p. 67, cited in Vigato, "L'Architecture de régionalisme."

105. François Pinardel, *La France et ses colonies, classe de primeur* (Paris: Gabriel Beau Chesne, 1930), p. 82.

106. Cited in Daniel Bellet and Will Darvillé, *Ce que doit être la cité moderne* (Paris: H. Nolo, 1914), p. 22.

107. George B. Ford, "Town Planning in the Devastated Regions of France," *The American City* 22 (March 1920): 219.

108. Alfred Potier, *L'Application par la ville de Lille des lois du 14 mars 1919 et du 19 juillet 1924, rélatives au plans d'aménagement, d'extension, et d'embellissement* (Lille: Imprimerie G. Santai, 1929), p. 184.

109. George B. Ford, *Aide-mémoire de l'urbaniste* (Paris: Renaissance des Cités, 1916); idem, *L'Urbanisme en pratique* (Paris: E. Leroux, 1920); and *Out of the Ruins*, p. 196. Also see M. N. Forestier, *La Reconstruction de Reims* (Paris: La Construction Moderne, n.d.); Raoul Dautry, "La Rationalisation de la cité," *L'Illustration* 87 (March 30, 1929); n.p.; Georges Hewrsent, *Une Politique de la construction après la guerre* (Paris: Payot, 1919); and Leroy, *La Ville française*.

110. Duchêne, *Pour la reconstruction*, pp. 7, 15. See, in particular, Alfred Agache, et al., *Comment reconstruire nos cités détruites (1915)*; Aubertin and Blanchard, *La Cité de demain (1917)*; Ed. Joyant, *Traité d'urbanisme*, 2 vols. (Paris: Librairie Technique, 1923); Le Corbusier, *L'Urbanisme (1924)*; Jean Raymond, *L'Urbanisme à la portée de tous* (Paris: Dunot, 1925); Pierre Lavedan, *Qu'est-ce que l'urbanisme?* (Paris: Henri Laurens, 1926); and A. A. Rey, Justin Pidoux, and Charles Barde, *La Science des plans de villes. Les applications à la construction, à l'extension, à l'hygiène et à la beauté des villes* (Paris: Dunod, 1928).

CHAPTER TWO

1. *Recueil des délibérations du Congrès Colonial National, Paris, 1889–90* (Paris, 1890), vol. 1, pp. 90–91, cited in Martin Deming Lewis, "One Hundred Million Frenchmen: The 'Assimilation' Theory in French Colonial Policy," *Comparative Studies in Society and History* 4 (January 1962): 140. Lewis also notes that other participants

claimed, "Experience demonstrates that the black who has received too developed an education acquires a distaste for labor" (ibid., p. 24, cited in *Recueil*, pp. 140–41).

2. M. Bonnefond, "Les Colonies de bicoques de la région parisienne," *La Vie urbaine* (1925): 554 (emphasis added). A similar example is in Adolphe Dervaux, "Le Beau, le Vrai, l'Utile et la réorganisation de la cité," *La Grande revue* 90 (April 1916): 330.

3. R. Thomas, "Le Politique socialiste et le problème colonial de 1905 à 1920," *RFHOM* 46 (1959): 213–45; Georges Oved, *La Gauche française et la nationalisme marocain, 1905–1955*, vol. 1 (Paris: Editions L'Harmattan, 1984); Tony Judt, *La Reconstruction du parti socialiste, 1921–1926* (Paris: Presses de la Fondation Nationale des Sciences Politiques, 1976). Juarès later refuted these early views. An important opposition voice from the left was that of Henri Cartier, *Comment la France "civilise" ses colonies* (Paris: Bureau d'Editions, 1932).

4. Charles Lemire, *Les Colonies et la question sociale en France* (Paris: Challamel Ainé, n.d.), p. 21.

5. Raymond Postal, "Visions et prévisions de Lyautey. Lumières pour la France nouvelle," *Construire: études et croquis* (Paris: J. Demoulin, 2d ed., 1941), p. 15. Postal was referring specifically to Lyautey's "Du Role social de l'officier," *La Revue des deux mondes* 150 (March 15, 1891): 443–59 (reprinted, Paris: Plon for the Association National Maréchal Lyautey, 1935; Paris: Editions Albert, 1984).

6. See Jean-Louis Miège and Eugène Hughes, *Les Européens à Casablance au XIXe siècle (1856–1906)*, vol. 14 of the Institut des Hautes Etudes Marocaines Notes et Documents series (Paris: Librairie Larose, 1954); Miège, *Le Maroc et l'Europe, 1830–1894*, 4 vols. (Paris: Presses Universitaires de France, 1961–64); Edmund Burke, III, *Prelude to Protectorate in Morocco: Precolonial Protest and Resistance, 1860–1912* (Chicago: University of Chicago Press, 1976); and Martin J. Murray, *The Development of Capitalism in Colonial Indochina, 1870–1940* (Berkeley: University of California Press, 1980).

7. Jean-Marie Mayeur and Madeleine Rebérioux, *The Third Republic from Its Origins to the Great War, 1871–1914* (Paris and Cambridge: Cambridge University Press, 1984), p. 273. Also see note 43, chap. 1.

8. Gaston Rambert, "L'Urbanisme à l'Exposition Coloniale de Marseille," *La Vie urbaine* 4 (December 15, 1922): 425.

9. *Revue générale de l'architecture et des travaux publics* 22 (1864), cited in Richard Chafee, "The Teaching of Architecture at the Ecole des Beaux-Arts," in *The Architecture of the Ecole des Beaux-Arts*, ed. Arthur Drexler (New York: Museum of Modern Art, 1977), p. 101. The first section of this chapter draws upon my joint article with Paul Rabinow, "Savoir et pouvoir dans l'urbanisme moderne colonial d'Ernest Hébrard," *CRA* no. 9 (January 1982): 26–43. Also see *The Beaux-Arts and Nineteenth-Century French Architecture*, ed. Robin Middleton (London: Thames and Hudson,

1982); and Donald Drew Egbert, *The Beaux-Arts Tradition in French Architecture*, ed. David Van Zanten (Princeton: Princeton University Press, 1980).

10. See "Tony Garnier from Rome to Lyons," special issue of *Rassagna* 17 (1984); Dora Wiebenson, *Tony Garnier: The Cité Industrielle* (New York: Braziller, 1969); Christophe Pawlowski, *Tony Garnier et les débuts de l'urbanisme fonctional en France* (Paris: Bibliothèque de C.R.U., 1967); *L'Oeuvre de Henri Prost: architecture et urbanisme* (Paris: Académie d'Architecture, 1960); "Henri Prost, l'urbanisation," special issue of *Urbanisme* 88 (1965); and Wright and Rabinow, "Savoir et pouvoir," pp. 28-29.

11. See Chafee, "The Teaching of Architecture"; Neil Levine, "The Romantic Idea of Architectural Legibility: Henri Labrouste and the Neo-Grec," in Drexler, *The Architecture of the École*, pp. 325-416; Egbert, *The Beaux-Arts Tradition*, pp. 62-86; and Mary McLeod, "Urbanism and Utopia: Le Corbusier from Regional Syndicalism to Vichy," PhD. diss., Princeton University, 1985.

12. "Paris—1900," manuscript in PP, p. 9.

13. Ibid., p. 13.

14. Procès-Verbaux de l'Académie des Beaux-Arts, June 29, 1901, Institut de France, n.p. We must base our appraisal of Garnier's 1900 *envoi* upon the version he published almost two decades later. It seems, from verbal descriptions, that the early version did have smooth, unornamented white walls, though the roofs were not yet flat.

15. Ibid.

16. Th. Leveau, "Istanbul," in *L'Oeuvre de Henri Prost*, pp. 183-205; Albert Gabrielle, "Henri Prost et son oeuvre à Stamboul," *Revue archéologique* (April–June 1960): 211-17; and Marida-Ida Talamona, "Henri Prost, architecte et urbaniste, 1874–1954," mémoire de DEA, Ecole des Hautes Etudes en Sciences Sociales, Paris, 1983.

17. Jean Hulot, *Selinote: la ville, l'acropolie, et les temples* (Paris: Librairie Générale de l'Architecture et des Art Décoratifs, 1910); Paul Bigot, *Rome antique au IVe siècle* (Paris: Editions Vincent Fréal, 1955).

18. Lyautey, too, honored the example of *imperium*, stating that one must "always look to the history of Rome for eternal examples of organization and sang-froid" (speech at the opening of the Paris-Maroc department store in Casablanca, November 17, 1914, from *Paroles d'action: Madagascar—Sud Oranais—Oran—Maroc (1900–1926)* [Paris: Armand Colin, 1927], p. 166).

19. On Jaussely's Barcelona plan, see Robert de Souza, *Nice, capital d'hiver. L'avenir de nos villes. Etudes practiques d'esthétique urbaine* (Paris: Berger-Levrault, 1913), pp. 410-23; and George R. Collins, *The Designs and Drawings of Antonio Gaudi* (Princeton: Princeton University Press, 1983), pp. 52, 69.

20. See Temma Kaplan's unpublished paper, "Civic Rituals and Patterns of Resistance in Barcelona, 1890–1930."

21. Examples of his drawings appear in *Pompei: travaux et envois des architectes*

français au XIXe siècle (Paris: Ecole National Supérieure des Beaux-Arts, 1981), pp. 130–43, 347–64.

22. Ernest M. Hébrard and Jacques Zeiler, *Spaleto: le palais de Dioclétien* (Paris: Librairie Général de l'Architecture et des Arts Décoratifs, 1912), p. 174.

23. Ernest M. Hébrard and Hendrik Christian Andersen, *Creation of a World Center of Communication*, 2 vols. (Paris, 1913), 2:14–15. Also see Wright and Rabinow, "Savoir et Pouvoir," pp. 29–32; and Juliano Gresleri and Dario Matteoni, *La Città mondiale: Hébrard, Otlet, e Le Corbusier* (Venice: Marsilio, 1982).

24. Hébrard and Anderson, *World Center*, 1:79.

25. Ibid., 1:77.

26. Ibid., 1:71.

27. Ibid., 1:pp. 78, 77.

28. Ibid., 1:79.

29. *World Conscience: An International Society for the Creation of a World Center* (Rome, 1913), pp. 53–139. The novelist Henry James, however, proved quite negative about such a grandiose project, even though he had fallen in love with the young sculptor Andersen, bemoaning that "when you write me that you are now lavishing time and money on a colossal ready-made City, I simply cover my head with my mantle and turn my face to the wall, and there, dearest Hendrik, just bitterly *weep* for you. . . . As if, beloved boy, any use on all the mad earth can be found for a ready-made city, made-while-one-waits, as they say. . . . Cities are living organisms that grow from within and by experience and piece by piece; they are not bought all hanging together, in *any* inspired studio anywhere whatsoever" (Letter of April 14, 1912, in *The Selected Letters of Henry James*, ed. Leon Edel [New York: Farrar, Straus and Cudahy, 1955], pp. 199–200).

30. Illustrations for these possible sites appeared in *World Conscience*.

31. A. Trystan Edwards, "A World Centre of Communication," *Town Planning Review* 5 (April 1914): 19, 29.

32. See M. Brincourt, "Création d'un centre mondial: La Cité Future," *L'Architecture* 27 (January 17, 1914): 17–18 and (January 24, 1914): 30; Paul Otlet, "Un Projet grandiose de Cité Internationale," *Premier Congrès International. Union de Villes et Communes Belges* (Brussels: Union International des Villes, 1913), pp. 79–85; idem, "The Foundations of World Society and Need for an Intellectual and Civic Center of International Reconstruction," *Survey: Journal of Social Work* 41 (February 1, 1919): 598–601; and Major H. Barnes, "Messrs. Andersen and Hébrard's Scheme," *Architectural Review* 46 (December 1919): 137–42.

33. *World Conscience* (Rome, 2d ed., 1938), pp. 2,10; Antonio Nezi, "Una città come nessun'altra: anima, cuore e cervello del mondo," *Emporium* 64 (July 1926): 32–50.

34. Terry Nichols Clark, *Prophets and Patrons: The French University and the Emergence of the Social Sciences* (Cambridge: Harvard University Press, 1973), pp. 122–247; George Weisz, "The French Universities and Education for the New Professions, 1885–1914: An Episode in French University Reform," *Minerva* 17 (Spring 1979): 98–128; and Lucien Lévy-Bruhl, "L'Institut d'Ethnologie de l'Université de Paris," *MCI* 3 (March 1926): 51–52. This institution should not be confused with the Ecole Pratique des Hautes Etudes, one of the most productive innovations of the Second Empire. The Ecole d'Alger might also be mentioned as an important site for social-science research.

35. Alfred de Chatelier, named to the first chair in Muslim Sociology and Sociography [sic] in 1903, was director of the Mission Scientifique du Maroc. A disciple of Durkheim, he even questioned the pieties of colonialism during these early years. Especially important is the journal he edited between 1906 and 1926, *Revue du Monde musulman*, describing the variations within the Islamic world, as well as the changes it was undergoing—an implicit pan-Islamic stance. This was the only such journal of the period that sought a Muslim as well as French readership, opening its pages to a variety of opinions. See Edmund Burke, III, "The Sociology of Islam: The French Tradition," in *Islamic Studies: A Tradition and Its Problems*, ed. Malcolm H. Kerr (Malibu: Undena Publications, 1980), p. 86.

36. Henri Rimbault, "L'Institut Musulman et la grande mosquée de Paris," *Le Monde colonial illustré* 3 (August 1926): 170–71; and Max Tournon, *Notre Protectorat marocain* (Paris: Afrique française, 1923).

37. "Paris," *American Architect and Building News* 59 (February 26, 1898): 98; Xavier Trevy, "L'Ecole coloniale," *La Revue politique et parlementaire* 17 (1898): 577–91; and William B. Cohen, *Rulers of Empire: The French Colonial Service in Africa* (Stanford: Hoover Institution Press, 1971).

38. On the Lyon school, see John F. Laffey, "Municipal Imperialism in Decline: The Lyon Chamber of Commerce, 1925–1938," *French Historical Studies* 9 (Fall 1975): 340; *Lyon, 1906–1926: Cinquantième Congrès de l'Association Française des Sciences* (Lyons: Société Anonyme de l'Imprimerie A. Rey, 1926), pp. 548–56; Catherine Coqnery-Vidrovitch, "French Colonization in Africa to 1920: Administration and Economic Development," in *Colonialism in Africa, 1870–1960*, ed. L. H. Gann and Peter Duignan, vol. 1, *The History and Politics of Colonialism, 1870–1914* (Cambridge and New York: Cambridge University Press, 1969), pp. 165–98. Coqnery-Vidrovitch notes that England, with no such centralized schooling for colonial officers, emphasized distinctions of culture and geography much more emphatically.

39. "Fondation de l'Académie des Sciences Coloniales," *Comptes-Rendus des Séances et Communications de l'Académie des Sciences Coloniales* 1 (Paris: Société d'Editions Géographiques, Maritimes et Coloniales, 1922): 27. The academy still exists today, publishing a journal entitled *Mondes et cultures* which bears the association's motto: "Savoir. Comprendre. Respecter. Aimer."

40. "Fondation," p. 20.

41. Burke, "Sociology," p. 76.

42. Jacques Berque, "Quatre-vingt-cinq ans de sociologie maghrebine," *Annales ESC* (1956): 320, cited in Burke, "Sociology," pp. 87–88.

43. Paul Vidal de la Blache, "Les Caractères de la géographie," AG 22 (July 15, 1913): 299. Also see Anne Buttimer, *Society and Milieu in the French Geographic Tradition* (Chicago: Rand McNally for the Association of American Geographers, 1971), p. 44. For intriguing comparisons, see Lewis Pyenson, *Cultural Imperialism and Exact Sciences: German Expansion Overseas, 1900–1930* (New York: Peter Lang, 1985).

44. Paul Vidal de la Blache, "Les Genres de vie dans la géographie humaine," AG 20 (May 15, 1911): 193–212; (July 15, 1911): 289–304; idem, "Les Grandes agglomérations humaines," AG 26 (November 15, 1917): 401–22 and 27 (January 10, 1918): 91–101; idem, *Principles of Human Geography*, trans. Millicent Todd Bingham (1922; New York: Henry Holt, 1926).

Genre de vie was one of Vidal's key terms. Also see *La Renaissance de la géographie française* (Paris: Ligue Maritime et Coloniale Française, 1926). The concept is strikingly similar to what French urbanists of the time called the *cadre de vie*, referring to their Anglo-American colleagues' concern for the entire living environment, not just housing units. On parallels with the concept of *cadre de vie*, see Annelise Gérard, *Quartier et unité de voisinage dans la pratique urbanistique française, 1919–1973* (Strasbourg: Unité Pedagogique d'Architecture de Strasbourg, 1980).

45. Paul Vidal de la Blache, "Le Chemin de fer transsaharien," *Annales coloniales* 4 (1904): 19–20; idem, review of A. Bernard's *Les Confins algero-marocains* in AG 20 (September 15, 1911): 450. The engineer Auguste Choisy, who advocated architectural theory based on the inherent rationality of modern construction, had promoted this same railroad in the late nineteenth century. As early as 1877 the minister of public works had advocated a "ribbon of steel" to link Algeria with Senegal. See Donald McKay, "Colonialism and the French Geographical Movement, 1871–1881," *Geographical Review* 33 (April 1943): 230–31.

46. Augustin Bernard, "La Capitale du Maroc," AG 22 (January 15, 1913): 460–63.

47. Pierre Lavedan, *Géographie des villes* (Paris: Gallimard, 1936); Buttimer, *Society and Milieu*, p. 318.

48. Georges Hardy, *Géographie et colonisation* (Paris: Gallimard, 1933), p. 203.

49. Buttimer, *Society and Milieu*, pp. 113–14; Alfred Demangeon, *Problèmes de géographie humaine* (Paris: Armand Colin, 1942).

50. Address to the Union Colonial Française, published in the *Quinzaine coloniale*, March 25, 1910, p. 226, cited in Jean Brunhes, *Human Geography: An Attempt at a Positive Classification. Principles and Examples*, trans. I. C. LeCompte (from the third rev. ed., 1925) (Chicago and New York, 1925), p. 532.

51. Ibid., p. 543.

52. Ibid., p. 567. Also see his "Caractères des faits de géographie humaine," *AG* 22 (January 15, 1913): 1–40, for an explanation of the French role in preserving the artistic motifs of various Islamic countries.

53. Agathon [Henry Massis and Alfred de Tarde], *Les Jeunes gens d'aujourd'hui* (Paris: Plon-Nourrit, 1911). The original articles appeared in *L'Opinion* in 1910. The book is skillfully analyzed in Robert Wohl, *The Generation of 1914* (Cambridge: Harvard University Press, 1979), pp. 5–18. "Only outside France, and preferably in the colonies," concludes Wohl, "could a young bourgeois intellectual . . . discover 'reality'" (p. 40). (Careful readers will note that Alfred restored the *de* to the family name of his father, Gabriel Tarde.) Also see Gabriel Hanotaux, "L'Apport intellectuel des colonies à la France," *La Revue des deux mondes* 37 (January 1, 1927): 129–40.

54. Joseph Chailley-Bert, *La France et la plus grande France*, extract from the *Revue politique et parlementaire* (August 1902): 31–32.

55. Joseph Chailley-Bert, *La Vie intime: les discours du Président Roosevelt* (Bourdeaux, 1903), p. 32, cited in Raymond Betts, "The French Colonial Frontier," in *From the Ancien Régime to the Popular Front*, ed. Charles K. Warner (New York: Columbia University Press, 1969), p. 131.

56. Speech in Oran, Algeria, July 12, 1907, in *Paroles d'action*, p. 53. By 1926, the industrialist Octave Homberg suggested, "It has become a banality to say that France will reawaken herself through her colonies" (*Les Conferences Coloniales du "Panorama"* [Paris: Ecole des Hautes Etudes Sociales, 1926]).

57. Edouard Herriot, "L'Ordre dans la création: l'oeuvre du Général Lyautey au Maroc," *France-Maroc* 1 (January 15, 1918):1.

58. See Clifford Geertz, "'From the Native's Point of View': On the Nature of Anthropological Understanding," in his *Local Knowledge: Further Essays in Interpretive Anthropology* (New York: Basic Books, 1983), p. 69; and John D. Legge, *Southeast Asian History and Historiography: Essays Presented to D. G. E. Hall*, ed. C. D. Cowan and O. W. Wolters (Ithaca: Cornell University Press, 1976), p. 402.

59. See Raymond F. Betts, *Assimilation and Association in French Colonial Theory, 1890–1914* (New York: Columbia University Press, 1961); Lewis, "One Hundred Million Frenchmen," pp. 129–51; M. M. Knight, "French Colonial Policy—The Decline of 'Association,'" *Journal of Modern History* 5 (June 1933): 208–24; and Gerald Joseph Doiron, "The Policy of Association in Morocco under Marshal Lyautey, 1912–1925," Ph.D. diss., Boston University, 1971.

60. [Anonymous but attributed to Durkheim], "L'Effort colonial," *La Revue de Paris* (September 15, 1902), cited in Raoul Girardet, *L'Idée coloniale en France, 1871–1962* (Paris: La Table Ronde, 1972), p. 158.

61. René Maunier, *The Sociology of Colonies: An Introduction to the Study of*

Race Contact, 3 vols., ed. and trans. E. O. Lornmer (1932; London: Routledge and Kegan Paul, 1949), 2:454.

62. Prost, *L'Urbanisme au point de vue technique*, p. 16.

63. Lyautey, who was pivotal in implementing the new policies, maintained close contacts with the Musée, and even found Henri Prost through his contacts in the organization. Paul Doumer, a former governor-general of Indochina, also frequented meetings, and Emile Cheysson, a statistician and vice-president of the Musée, published a book entitled *L'Homme social et la colonisation* (Paris, 1905), calling for the increased use of social and physical sciences in the colonies.

On procolonial French politics, see Georges Hardy, *Histoire sociale de la colonisation française* (Paris: Larose, 1953), pp. 147-48, 311; Charles-Robert Ageron, *France coloniale ou parti colonial?* (Paris: Presses Universities de France, 1978); Peter Grupp, *Deutschland, Fankreich und die Kolonien: des französische "Parti Colonial" und Deutschland von 1890 bis 1914* (Tubingen: J. C. B. Mohr, 1980); Stuart Michael Persell, *The French Colonial Lobby, 1889–1938* (Stanford: Hoover Institution Press, 1983); and L. Abrams and D. J. Miller, "Who Were the French Colonialists? A Reassessment of the *Parti Colonial, 1890–1914*," *The Historical Journal* 19 (1976): 685–725.

64. Cited in Louis Vignon, *Un Programme de politique coloniale: les questions indigénes* (Paris: Plon Nourrit, 1919), p. 160.

65. Joseph Chailley-Bert, *Dix anées de politique coloniale* (Paris: Armand Colin, 1902), p. 45. This passage is also cited in Lyautey, *Dans le Sud de Madagascar* (Paris: Lavauzelle, 1903), p. 381.

66. Jules Harmond, *Domination et colonisation* (Paris: Flammarion, 1910), p. 160.

67. See Jean-Marie de Lanessan, *Principes de colonisation* (Paris: Félix Alcan, 1897); and Lallier de Coudray, "Gallieni et Lyautey," *Bulletin de la Société de geographie et d'études coloniales de Marseille* 45 (1925): 5–21.

68. "Instructions du Gouvernement-Général, le 22 mai 1898," in *Gallieni, la pacification de Madagascar*, ed. F. Hellot (Paris: Librairie Militaire R. Chapelet, 1900), pp. 332–44. Also see Gallieni, *Neuf ans à Madagascar* (Paris: Hachette, 1908), pp. 325–27; Lyautey, "Du Rôle colonial de l'armée," *La Revue des deux mondes* 162 (January 15, 1900): 443–59; reprinted in his *Lettres du Tonkin et de Madagascar (1894–1899)* (Paris: Armand Colin, 1921), pp. 629–53. On Gallieni, see *Gallieni pacificateur: écrits coloniaux de Gallieni*, ed. Hubert Deschamps and Paul Chauvet (Paris: Presses Universitaires de France, 1949); Gallieni, *Trois colonnes au Tonkin (1894–1895)* (Paris: Librairie Militaire R. Chapelot, 1899); idem, *Gallieni au Tonkin (1892–1896)* (Paris: Berger-Levrault, 1941); *Lettres de Madagascar, 1896–1905* (Paris: Société d'Editions Géographiques, 1928); and Roger-François Didelot, *Gallieni, soldat de France* (Paris: P. Dupont, 1947).

69. Lyautey, letter to Eugène-Melchoir de Vogüe, June 25, 1901, *Lettres du Sud*

de Madagascar (1900–1912) (Paris: Armand Colin, 1935), p. 119. Also see Daniel Rivet, "Lyautey l'Africain," *L'Histoire* 24 (December 1980): 16–24.

70. See, for example, Albert Laprade, *Lyautey urbaniste, souvenirs d'un témoin* (Paris: Horizons de France, 1934), p. 5; Tournon, *Notre protectorat*, p. 246; Henri Deschamps, "Maroc," *CM* (November 26, 1930): 54; and Charles Brisson, *Lyautey l'Africain* (Paris: Paul Duval, n.d.), p. 16. Lyautey sometimes substituted the word "hôpital" for "chantier," or varied "m'évite" for "vaut."

71. Lyautey, "Du Rôle social de l'officier"; also see David B. Ralston, *The Army of the Republic: The Place of the Military in the Political Evolution of France, 1871–1914* (Cambridge: MIT Press, 1967), pp. 286–87; and Raoul Girardet, *La Société militaire dans la France contemporaine (1815–1935)* (Paris: Plon, 1953), pp. 279–311.

72. Address to the Congrès des Hautes Etudes Marocaines, May 26, 1921, in *Paroles d'action*, p. 341. For an overview of these metaphors, see, in particular, *Lyautey l'écrivain, 1854–1932*, ed. André Le Révérend (Paris: Ophrys, 1976).

73. Georges Hardy, *Les Colonies françaises: Le Maroc* (Paris: Henri Laurens, 1930), p. 63.

74. Lyautey, *Rapport générale sur la situation du protectorat du Maroc au 31 juillet 1914* (Rabat: Résidence Générale de la République Française, 1916), p. xiv.

75. For excellent studies of similar events in British India, see Bernard S. Cohen, "Representing Authority in Victorian India," in *The Invention of Tradition*, ed. Eric J. Hobsbawm and Terence Ranger (Cambridge and New York: Cambridge University Press, 1983), pp. 165–209; Thomas R. Metcalf, "Architecture and the Representation of Empire: India, 1860–1910," *Representations* 6 (Spring 1984): 37–65; and, for more formalist accounts, Robert Grant Irving, *Indian Summer: Lutyens, Baker and Imperial Delhi* (New Haven: Yale University Press, 1981); and *Architecture of the British Empire*, ed. Robert Fermor-Hesketh (New York: The Vendome Press, 1986).

76. Lyautey, "Politique du protectorat," statement of November 18, 1920, in *Lyautey l'Africain—textes et lettres du Maréchal Lyautey*, 4 vols., ed. Pierre Lyautey (Paris: Calmann-Levy, 1962), 4:28.

77. Service Historique des Armées, Série H 225, *Etat d'Alger à la fin de 1832*, cited in François Béguin, *Arabiscances: décor architectural et tracé urbain en Afrique du Nord, 1830–1950* (Paris: Dunod, 1983), p. 11.

78. Cited in Stephen A. Roberts, *The History of French Colonial Policy, 1870–1925* (1929; reprint ed., Hamden: Archon Press, 1963), p. 456.

79. Gallieni, "Instructions," pp. 339–43; idem, *Neuf ans*, pp. 47, 325–27.

80. Quote from the "Instructions" in Lyautey's *Lettres du Tonkin et de Madagascar*, p. 638.

81. Lyautey, Speech to the Université des Annales, Paris, December 10, 1926, in *Paroles d'action*, pp. 452–53.

82. Lyautey, speech to the Université des Annales, p. 454. On Lyautey's life, his own writings evoke the many dimensions and passionate emotions of this unusual yet representative individual. See, in particular, *Lettres de jeunesse: Italie (1883), Danube, Grèce, Italie (1893)* (Paris: B. Grasset, 1931); *Lettres du Tonkin et de Madagascar (1894–1899)*, 2 vols. (Paris: Armand Colin, 1921); *Lettres du Sud de Madagascar (1900–1902)* (Paris: A. Colin, 1935); *Vers le Maroc. Lettres du Sud-Oranais (1903–1906)* (Paris: A. Colin, 1937); *Lyautey l'Africain—textes et lettres du Maréchal Lyautey*, 4 vols., ed. Pierre Lyautey (Paris: Calmann-Levy, 1962); *Les Plus belles lettres de Lyautey*, ed. Pierre Lyautey (Paris: Calmann-Levy, 1962); *Un Lyautey inconnu: correspondance et journal inédits, 1874–1934*, ed. André Le Révérend (Paris: Perrin, 1980); and *Lyautey l'écrivain, 1854–1932*, ed. André Le Révérend (Paris: Ophrys, 1976).

Principal works on Lyautey include Sonia E. Howe, *Lyautey of Morocco* (London: Hodder and Stoughton, 1931); André Maurois, *Lyautey* (Paris: Plon, 1930; trans. Harmish Miles, New York: D. Appleton, 1931); André Lichtenberger, *Sous le signe du Lyautey: la leçon marocaine* (Paris: Editions Musée Social, 1939); Albert Laprade, *Lyautey urbaniste: souvenirs d'un témoin* (Paris: La Renaissance du Livre, 1947); Berthe Georges Gaulis, *La France au Maroc: l'oeuvre de Général Lyautey* (Paris: A. Colin, 1919); Guillaume de Tarde, *Lyautey, le chef en action* (Paris: Gallimard, 1959); Georges Hardy, *Portrait de Lyautey* (Paris: Blond et Gay, 1949); Jacques Benoist-Méchin, *Lyautey l'Africain ou le rêve immolé* (Lausanne: Clairefontaine, 1966); Patrick Heidsieck, *Rayonnement de Lyautey* (Paris: Gallimard, 1947); General Maurice Durosoy, *Avec Lyautey: homme de guerre, homme de paix* (Paris: Nouvelles Editions Latines, 1976); and Alan Scham, *Lyautey of Morocco: Protectorate Administration, 1912–1925* (Berkeley and Los Angeles: University of California Press, 1970).

83. Letter to Eugène-Melchoir de Vögué, November 20, 1897, in *Lettres du Tonkin et de Madagascar*, 1:550.

84. Letter to Max Leclerc, May 27, 1904, in *Vers le Maroc*, p. 68.

85. Address to the Congrès des Hautes-Etudes Marocaines, May 26, 1921, in *Paroles d'action*, p. 341.

86. Journal entry, November 16, 1894, *Lettres du Tonkin et de Madagascar*, 1:71.

87. "Ce que pensait Lyautey de l'oeuvre de Henri Prost," in *L'Oeuvre de Henri Prost*, p. 119.

88. Cited in Georges-Gaulin, *La France au Maroc*, p. 79 (repeated p. 210).

CHAPTER THREE

1. Léandre Vaillat, *Le Périple marocain* (Paris: Flammarion, 1934), p. 55. Also see J. Célérier, *Le Maroc* (Paris: Armand Colin, 1931), who discusses the problem of two architectural aesthetics on p. 118.

2. Maurice Long, *Bulletin de l'Afrique française* (1916), cited in Max Tournon, *Notre protectorat marocain* (Poitiers: Texier, 1927), p. 248. A similar eulogy appears in *Memorial Lyautey, l'oeuvre de la France au Maroc* (Casablanca: Résidence Générale de la France, 1953).

3. Kenneth L. Brown, *People of Salé: Tradition and Change in a Moroccan City, 1830–1930* (Cambridge: Harvard University Press, 1976), pp. 119–211; Augustin Bernard, *L'Afrique du Nord pendant la guerre* (Paris: Presses Universitaires de France, 1926), p. 85; Robin Bidwell, *Morocco under Colonial Rule: French Administration of Tribal Areas, 1912–1956* (London: Frank Cass, 1973), p. 20; and David Cohen, "Lyautey et le sionisme, 1915–1925," *RFHOM* 67 (1980): 269–300.

4. Lyautey, "Note, Rabat, le 18.6.13," carton 19, dossier 88, FL.

5. Léandre Vaillat, "Un Paysage industriel au Maroc," *Urbanisme* 22 (January 1934): 70–74. Train stations, too, reflected this formal austerity, so different from their nineteenth-century European counterparts. The expanded new *gares* of Casablanca and Rabat, built in the late 1920s, offered a significant public benefit, in that the tracks were relocated in underground tunnels.

6. Alfred de Tarde, *Le Maroc, école d'énergie* (1915; Paris: Plon-Nourrit, 1923), p. 21.

7. Speech to the Université des Annales, Paris, December 10, 1926, in Lyautey, *Paroles d'action: Madagascar—Sud Oranais—Oran—Maroc (1900–1926)* (Paris: A. Colin, 1927), pp. 452–53.

8. Lyautey, "Architecture," *AA* 1 (June–July 1931): 14.

9. Lyautey, "Allocation du 9 octobre 1916 aux chefs indigènes," *Paroles d'action*, p. 195.

10. Lyautey, *Rapport générale sur la situation du protectorat du Maroc au 31 juillet 1914* (Rabat: Résidence Générale de France, 1916), pp. 311–12, as cited in Janet Abu-Lughod, *Rabat: Urban Apartheid in Morocco* (Princeton: Princeton University Press, 1980), pp. 174–76, 192–93. Also see Edmund Burke, III, "The Sociology of Islam: The French Tradition," in *Islamic Studies: A Tradition and Its Problems*, ed. Malcolm H. Kerr (Malibu: Undena Publications, 1980), pp. 73–88. The multivolume *Villes et tribus du Maroc*, a compendium assembled by the Direction des Affaires Indigènes, dutifully described the ongoing roles of the *pasha*, the *mohtaseb*, the *amin el-moustafad*, and the *nâdir*. (See Direction des Affaires Indigènes, *Villes et tribus du Maroc: documents et renseignements*, 7 vols. [Paris: Leroux, 1915–20], esp. vol. 4, *Rabat et sa région: les villes après la conquête* [1919], pp. 83–88.)

11. The most thorough history of the city is Jacques Caillé, *La Ville de Rabat jusqu'au protectorat français*, 3 vols., Publications de l'Institut des Hautes Etudes Marocaines (Paris: Vanoest Editions d'Art et d'Histoire, 1949). Janet Abu-Lughod gives an excellent and highly critical account of the French intervention there, juxtaposing the colonial account with other, quite eloquent portraits of Rabat before and after coloniza-

tion in *Rabat: Urban Apartheid in Morocco.*

12. Henri Post, "L'Urbanisme au Maroc," p. 4, unidentified lecture notes, PP. In an earlier text on Morocco, the geographer Augustin Bernard declared, equally oblivious to the intervening changes, that Moroccan industry "has remained stationary; the worker of today employs tools in use a thousand years ago and labors according to the same methods as his predecessors of antiquity, without change or improvement" (*Le Maroc* [Paris: Felix Alcan, 1913], p. 183).

13. Lucien Deslinières, *La France nord-africaine* (Paris: Editions du Progrès Civique, 1928), p. 646. Deslinierès was an Algerian *colon* and union organizer among the European population in Morocco. Earlier, in *Le Maroc socialiste* (1912), he had suggested that the protectorate offered the perfect opportunity to experiment with socialism—at least for the European population residing there—while still maintaining colonial power.

14. Edmund Burke, III, *Prelude to Protectorate in Morocco: Precolonial Protest and Resistance, 1860–1912* (Chicago: University of Chicago Press, 1976), pp. 26–40.

15. "L'Oeuvre social de la France au Maroc," lecture by Lt.-Col. Huot and Maréchal Lyautey, Paris, February 27, 1922, *Le Musée Social* 4 (April 1922): 127. The point is reiterated in Bernard, *L'Afrique du Nord pendant la guerre*, p. 85.

16. Charles André Julien, *Le Maroc face aux impérialismes, 1415–1956* (Paris: Editions Jeune Afrique, 1978), p. 8; Jacques Berque, *French North Africa: The Maghreb between Two World Wars*, trans. Jean Steward (New York: Praeger, 1962), pp. 71–72. As Berque says elsewhere, "What the men of the Arab Bureaux sought was finally not sociological understanding of these societies, but the key to their operation, the secret of secrets that, once known, would permit their domination" ("Cent-vingt-cinq ans de sociologie maghrebine," *Annales ESC* [1956], p. 320, cited in Burke, "Sociology," pp. 87–88).

17. Lt. Charles Juntz, *Souvenirs de campagne au Maroc* (Paris: Lavauzell, 1913), p. 87, cited in Robin Bidwell, *Morocco under Colonial Rule* (London: F. Cass, 1973), p. 15. Also see Burke, *Prelude*, and Jean-Louis Miège, *Le Maroc et l'Europe, 1830–1894*, 4 vols. (Paris: Presses Universitaires de France, 1961–64). Written records first refer to the town of Anfa, a small but active commercial center of the thirteenth century. The Portuguese occupied the town briefly, naming it Casa-Branca (white house), but destroyed and abandoned the settlement around 1468. In 1770 the sultan of Morocco established a village on the site, naming it Dar-el-Beïda (Arabic for "white house"), which the Spanish later translated into Casablanca.

18. Speech to the Université des Annales, p. 456; also see Léandre Vaillat, *Le Visage français du Maroc* (Paris: Horizons de France, 1931), p. 8; and Lyautey's letter of June 17, 1913, in *Lyautey l'africain*, ed. Pierre Lyautey (Paris: Plon, 1953), 1:162.

19. Speech to the Université des Annales, p. 453.

20. Ibid.

21. Vaillat, *Visage*, p. 7.

22. *Questions diplomatiques et coloniales* (October 1, 1901), pp. 390–91, and a statement by the art historian Georges Marçais, both cited in Marewan A. Buheiry, "Colonial Scholarship and Muslim Revivalism in 1900," *Arab Studies Quarterly* 4 (September 1982): 11, 13.

23. Caillé, *La Ville de Rabat*, 1:569; Lyautey's letter of June 17, 1913, in *Lyautey l'africain*, 1:145–58; and Vaillat, *Visage*, p. 27.

24. Vaillat, *Periple*, pp. 74–75.

25. "Rabat," *Encyclopedia of Islam*, 1st ed., ca. 1936, cited in Abu-Lughod, *Rabat*, p. 150.

26. *Lyautey l'africain*, 1:148, 157; Pierre Pelletier, "Valeurs financières et urbanisme au Maroc," *BESM* 19 (June 1955): 10.

27. In fact, as Julien charges, Lyautey and his officers often celebrated the Berber as noble and independent because he resisted Islam and the Arab sultan. See *Le Maroc*, p. 99; Bernard, *Le Maroc*, p. 411; Berque, *French North Africa*, p. 229; Abu-Lughod, *Rabat*, p. 137; M. E. Michaux-Bellaire, "Sociologie Marocaine," *Archives marocaines*, vol. 27 (preparatory classes for the Service des Affaires Indigènes) (Paris: Librairie Ancienne Honoré Champion, 1927), pp. 293–311; and Charles-Robert Ageron, *Politiques coloniales au Maghreb* (Paris: Presses Universitaires de France, 1973), pp. 109–50.

28. Walter Harris, *The Morocco That Was* (London: W. Blackwood, 1921), cited in Clifford Geertz, "Centers, Kings, and Charisma: Reflections on the Symbolics of Power," in *Culture and Its Creators: Essays in Honor of Edward Shils*, ed. Joseph Ben-David and Terry Nichols Clark (Chicago: University of Chicago Press, 1977), pp. 162–67.

29. By 1921 Europeans constituted less than 1 percent of the population in Marrakesh, 3 percent in Fez, and 11 percent in Meknes (most of these converted the adjacent plains into farmland). See Henri de la Casinière, *Les Municipalités marocains, leur développement, leur legislation* (Casablanca: Imprimerie de la Vigie Marocaine, 1924), appendix, n. p. Also see *Les Guides bleus. Maroc* (Paris: Hachette, 1925), p. 13. Fifty years after Lyautey's decision, half of Morocco's urban dwellers lived in Casablanca, Rabat, and Kenitra—a coastal axis whose land area represented less than 1 percent of the total country ("Rabat," *Mimar* 22 [October–December 1986]: n.p.).

30. Prost, "Les Plans d'extension," in *Où en est*, pp. 202–3.

31. J. C. N. Forestier, *Espaces libres et jardins publics du Maroc* (Rabat: Résidence Générale de la République de France, 1913), n. p.

32. De la Casinière, *Municipalités*, p. 90.

33. Ibid.; and Abu-Lughod, *Rabat*, p. 166. Five bases for land tenure existed in Morocco before the coming of the French, though only three concerned urban areas. Under the direction of Henri de la Casinière, French legal consultants drew up propos-

als for "modernizing" the supposedly archaic Islamic system, proposals which effectively alienated the Moroccans from their land. In the first case, that of domainal lands held by the state, the sultan was allowed to keep most of his palaces and gardens, but other property fell to the French as representatives of the protectorate government.

In the second instance, concerning lands held by religious foundations called habous (*hubus*), municipalities often bought land outright for low prices or else expropriated it for a "public purpose," which could be either the construction of a European *ville nouvelle* or, at a later date, a "new medina" for Moroccans.

In terms of the third category, that of privately owned freehold, the interpretation of property law again showed a definite bias toward French settlement and the Napoleonic legal code. In 1913 the Moroccan government, speaking through the sultan but acting on behalf of the French, instituted a new landed-property regime, *immatriculation*, which called for the reregistration and arbitration of private landownership; each parcel had to be distinctly delimited under a name, a number, and a proper topographic specification. All registration took place through French *livres fonciers*, with protests against illegalities only allowed for a short period after such registration, and litigated through the French legal system. (See Abu-Loghod, *Rabat*, pp. 163–67; and Charles F. Stewart, *The Economy of Morocco, 1912–1962* [Cambridge: Harvard Middle Eastern Monograph Series, 1964], pp. 17–26.).

34. L. Glorieux-Monfred, "L'Urbanisme en Afrique de Nord," AA (March 1939): 67; Henri Prost, *Lyautey et les méthodes françaises de colonisation* (Bucharest: Editura Contemporana, 1944), 15; Jean Marrast, "Maroc," in *L'Oeuvre de Henri Prost: Architecture et urbanisme* (Paris: Académie d'Architecture, 1960), p. 51.

35. Edith Wharton, "Madame Lyautey's Charities in Morocco," *France-Maroc* 10–11 (1918): viii, cited in Abu-Lughod, *Rabat*, p. 146. Also see Wharton's *In Morocco* (New York: Macmillan, 1920), dedicated to Lyautey.

36. Marrast, "Maroc," p. 52.

37. Prost, "Le Développement de l'urbanisme," in *L'Urbanisme aux colonies et dans les pays tropicaux*, ed. Jean Royer, 2 vols. (La Charité-sur-Loire, 1932), 1:71, 59.

38. Cited in Jean Royer, "Henri Prost urbaniste," *Urbanisme* 88 (1965): 12–13, a special issue devoted to Prost's work.

39. De Tarde, *Le Maroc*, p. 17; André Adam, *Casablanca, essai sur la transformation de la société marocaine au contact de l'occident*, 2 vols. (Paris: C. N. R. S., 1968), 2: 50. Among the most profitable ventures of this early period which imposed virtually no constraints on land development were Colonel Baudin's plats at the Quartier de la Liberté—bought through an associate to circumvent restrictions on military officers engaging in real-estate development—and Léonard Julien's development of Anfa-Supérieur in the suburbs of the city.

40. Laprade, "Lyautey urbaniste," p. 53; Prost, "Casablanca"; idem, "Le Port de Casablanca," *France-Maroc* 1 (August 15, 1917): 4; Bernard Champignuelle, *Perret*

(Paris: Arts et Metiers Graphiques, 1959), pp. 36, 143.

41. See Lyautey's speech in Casablanca, July 14, 1914, in *Paroles d'action*, p. 116, for a typical criticism.

42. Prost, "Casablanca," and Adam, *Casablanca*, 2: 57-60. The typhus epidemic was precipitated by the unregulated expansion of the city's European population. See Célérier, *Le Maroc*, p. 83.

43. Prost, "Le Plan de Casablanca," *France-Maroc* 1 (February 15, 1917): 4; idem, "L'Urbanisme au Maroc," CNA, p. 119.

44. Marrast, "Maroc," p. 55.

45. Adam, *Cassablanca*, 1: 149; Katherine Marshall Johnson, *Urban Government for the Prefecture of Casablanca* (New York: Praeger, 1970), p. 16. Johnson also notes that conservative estimates indicate the city will have over four million inhabitants in the year 2000.

46. The most readily accessible discussions of this legislation appear in Alan Scham, *Lyautey in Morocco: Protectorate Administration, 1912-1925* (Berkeley and Los Angeles: University of California Press, 1970); Henri Prost, "Le Développement de l'urbanisme dans le protectorat du Maroc, de 1914 à 1923," in *L'Urbanisme aux colonies*, 1: 59-80; Henri de la Casinière, "La Législation de l'urbanisme au Maroc," in *L'Urbanisme aux colonies*, 2: 103-8; idem, "Les Plans d'extension des villes et l'urbanisme au Maroc," in *Où en est l'urbanisme en France et à l'étranger?* (Paris: Librairie de l'Enseignement Technique, 1923), pp. 202-12, 296-321; and Louis Sablayrolles, *L'Urbanisme au Maroc: les moyens d'action—les résultats* (Albi: Imprimerie Coopératif du Sud-Ouest, 1925). Prost's article follows closely the unsigned chapter entitled "L'Urbanisme au Maroc" in *La Renaissance du Maroc: dix ans de protectorate, 1912-1922* (Poitiers: Résidence Générale de la République Française au Maroc, 1923), pp. 361-93, and "Urbanisme au Maroc," CNA (February 1932): 117-20.

47. Prost, "Développement," p. 62; idem, "L'Urbanisme," in *Où en est*, p. 17; Sablayrolles, *L'Urbanisme*, p. 46; Myriam Boccara, "Casablanca—histoires d'architecture," thesis, Ecole des Beaux-Arts, U.P. 8, Paris, 1985.

48. Prost letter to M. Buan of the Bureau Immobilier du Maroc, September 4, 1922, PP; Prost, "Le Plan de Casablanca," *France-Maroc*, 12.

49. Albert Laprade, "Lyautey urbaniste et constructeur," AA (March 1936): 57.

50. Vaillat, *Visage*, p. 54.

51. André-Marie-Henri Rigollet, speech to the Ecole des Beaux-Arts, Paris, December 19, 1955, cited in Marrast, "Maroc," p. 57.

52. *La Renaissance du Maroc* included an article by Prost. For a similar argument, see Albert Laprade, "Les Influences possibles du Maroc sur l'art français," *France-Maroc* 1 (May 15, 1917): 37-39.

53. Loggias were more common to the Jewish *mellahs*, but virtually unknown in

Islamic Moroccan architecture before the first European houses in the late-nineteenth century.

54. Speech to the Université des Annales, p. 450. On Jonnart's term in Algeria, see François Béguin, *Arabisances: décor architectural et tracé urbain en Afrique du Nord, 1830–1950* (Paris: Dunod, 1983), pp. 20–34; and Berque, *French North Africa*, pp. 204–12.

55. See the excellent article by Janet L. Abu-Lughod, which outlines the persistence, evolution, and manipulation of this aesthetic, "The Islamic City—Historic Myth, Islamic Essence, and Contemporary Relevance," *International Journal of Middle East Studies* 19 (1987): 155–76.

56. Jean Gallotti, "La Beauté des villes marocaines," *L'Art vivant* 5 (October 15, 1930): 804. Also see Georges Marçais, *Manuel d'art musulman* (Paris: A. Picard, 1926–27), since reissued as *L'Architecture musulmane d'occident: Tunisie, Algérie, Maroc, Espagne* (Paris: Arts et Métiers Graphiques, 1954), still the most important book on the subject, as well as Joseph de la Nézière, *Les Monuments mauresques du Maroc* (Paris: Albert Lévy, 1921); Henri Terrasse, *L'Art hispano-mauresque des origines au XIIIᵉ siècle* (Paris: Publications de l'IHEM, 1932); Victor Piquet, *Monuments historiques du Maghreb*, vol. 3, *Le Maroc* (Paris: Librarie Orientale et américaine, 1949); R. Guy, *L'Architecture moderne de style arabe* (Paris: Librairie de la Construction moderne, n.d.); Prosper Ricard, *Le Maroc* (Paris: Hachette, 1930); and idem, *Pour comprendre l'art musulman dans l'Afrique du Nord et en Espagne* (Paris: Hachette, 1924).

57. Jean Gallotti, *Le Jardin et la maison arabes au Maroc*, with drawings by Albert Laprade and photographs by Lucien Vogel, 2 vols. (Paris: Albert Levy, 1924). A fascinating analysis of the underlying architectural principles of this book can be found in Mohammed El Malti, "The Architecture of Colonialism, Morocco, 1912–1932: An Inquiry into the Determinants of French Colonial Architecture," Ph.D. diss., University of Pennsylvania, 1983, p. 36. Much later, Laprade's own sketchbooks, *Croquis: Portugal, Espagne, Maroc* (Ivry: Editions Serg, n.d.) reproduced many of the illustrations featured in the joint publication.

58. Laprade, *Croquis*, n.p.

59. Thus when the French added a new *makahma* to the palace and new medina of Casablanca, Albert Cadet, the building's architect, declared that the pasha's earlier residence was inappropriate for meetings with foreign dignitaries, since it lacked "the decor of a rich mansion of Fez with sculpted plaster, rich *zelligs*, and ceilings in painted wood" (Albert Cadet, *Le Mahakma de Casablanca* [Paris: Paul Hartman, 1953], n.p.). This building was designed "in the Moorish style" in 1937, but not completed until 1952.

60. Ibid. This was just what Prost had warned against at the Congrès International de l'Urbanisme aux Colonies in 1931.

61. Ibid.

62. *Le Jardin et la maison*, p. vii.

63. Prost, "L'Urbanisme au Maroc," *La Renaissance du Maroc*, p. 391.

64. Bernard Huet, "The Modernity in a Tradition: The Arab-Muslim Culture of North Africa," *Mimar* 10 (October–December 1983): 50; Besim Selim Hakim, *Arabic-Islamic Cities: Building and Planning Principles* (London and New York: K.P.I., 1986), pp. 102–14.

65. Prost, "L'Urbanisme au Maroc," p. 42, PP.

66. Prost, "Rapport général," in *L'Urbanisme aux colonies*, 1:22.

67. Brian Brace Taylor, "Planned Discontinuity: Modern Colonial Cities in Morocco," *Lotus International* 36 (1979): 58.

68. Huet, "The Modernity in a Tradition," p. 54.

69. Lyautey, speech to the Université des Annales, p. 457.

70. Prost, "L'Urbanisme au Maroc," pp. 36–37; also see Taylor, "Planned Discontinuity," p. 60.

71. Prost, "Développement," p. 70.

72. Prost, "L'Urbanisme au Maroc," in *La Renaissance du Maroc*, p. 374; Henri Basset and Evariste Lévi-Provençal, *Chella: une nécropole mérinide* (Paris: Emile Larose, 1923).

73. Direction Générale de l'Instruction Publique, des Beaux-Arts, et des Antiquités, *Historique (1912–1930)* (Rabat: Résidence Générale, 1931), pp. 98–107.

74. Emile Pauty, "Rapport sur la défense des villes et la restauration des monuments historiques," *Hesperis* 2 (1922): 449. Also see Prost, "L'Urbanisme au Maroc," *La Renaissance du Maroc*, p. 367; and Lyautey's letter of December 11, 1913, in *Lyautey l'africain*, 1:166–69.

75. Cited in Prost, "Développement," p. 66.

76. André Colliez, *Notre protectorat marocain, la première étape, 1912–1930* (Paris: Librarie des Sciences Politiques et Sociales, 1930), p. 204.

77. Henri Descamps, "L'Architecture française, IV. Rabat," *CM* 46 (February 8, 1931): 300. More recently, Jean-Louis Miège, the preeminent historian of Moroccan-French relations, still calls this area "the most beautiful urban success of North Africa" (Jean-Louis Miège, *Le Maroc* [1952; Paris: Presses Universitaires de France, 1971], p. 71).

78. Vaillat, *Visage*, p. 33.

79. Ibid., p. 35.

80. Maurice Tranchant de Lunel, "Du Collège d'Isphahan aux medersas de Fez," *France-Maroc* 1 (December 15, 1917): 10. By 1929 there was one preparatory school exclusively for the Moroccan elite in each of the six major cities. The student body numbered only 802 students in 1926. See Colliez, *Notre protectorat*, p. 274; Direction

Générale de l'Instruction Publique, *Historique*, pp. 37–89, 117–33; Charles Terrasse, *Medersas du Maroc* (Paris: Editions Albert Morancé, 1928).

81. Georges Hardy, "L'Education au Maroc," *Revue de Paris* (April 15, 1921), cited in Daniel Rivet, "Ecole et colonisation de Maroc: la politique de Lyautey au début des années vingt," *Cahiers historiques de Lyon* 21 (1976): 174.

82. Lyautey, "Note sur l'enseignement mixte franco-arabe, secondaire et supérieure," Fez, June 2, 1922, p. 3, and "Examen de conscience au sujet de l'enseignement musulman," Casablanca, June 11, 1922, both cited in Rivet, "Ecole et colonisation," p. 175.

83. Brown, *People of Salé*, p. 194. "Free schools" meant nontuition schools.

84. "Le Maroc en 1932."

85. The Boulevard de la Gare renovation cost the protectorate only 100 FF at the time. See Adam, *Casablanca*, 1:60; de la Casinière, *Municipalités*, p. 99; Taylor, "Planned Discontinuity," 57. Taylor provides an excellent short overview of Prost's and Lyautey's urbanistic policies.

86. Direction Générale de l'Instruction Publique, *Historique*, p. 139.

87. Laprade, "Les Influences possibles," pp. 37–38; Henri Descamps, "L'Architecture française, II. L'Oeuvre de M. Prost," *CM* 46 (October 26, 1930): 74.

88. Ibid. p. 54.

89. Vaillat, *Visage*, p. 40.

90. Gaston Bardet, *Le Nouvel urbanisme* (Paris: Vincent, Fréal, 1948), p. 28.

91. Maurice Tranchant de Lunel, "L'Art et les monuments du Maroc," *Conferences Franco-Marocaines*, vol. 1, *L'Oeuvre du protectorat* (Paris: Plon-Nourrit, 1916), pp. 269–70. (This text comprises the speeches given at the 1916 Exposition Franco-Marocain at Casablanca.) Also see Tranchant de Lunel's rather florid autobiography, *Au Pays de paradoxe* (Paris: Bibliothèque Charpentier, 1924).

92. Prost letter to Lyautey, dated 1916, FL, carton 19, dossier 88.

93. Lyautey's letter of April 23, 1913, in *Lyautey l'africain*, 1:264; also see Descamps, "L'Architecture . . . II," p. 173; Sablayrolles, *L'Urbanisme*, p. 48; and Jacques Ladreit de La Charrière, *La Création marocaine* (Paris: Peyronnet, 1930), p. 141.

94. Tranchant de Lunel to Lyautey, "Note, Paris, 24 janvier 1916" FL, carton 19, dossier 88.

95. Maurice Tranchant de Lunel, "Une Exposition des arts marocains," *France-Maroc* 1 (May 15, 1917): 7; "Rapport de M. Tranchant de Lunel relatif à la vente des objets d'art marocains, septembre 1917," FL, carton 19, dossier 88; Emile Bayard, *L'Art de reconnaître les styles coloniaux de la France* (Paris: Garnier Frères, 1931), pp. 316–17. On this theme also, see *Ethnic and Tourist Arts*, ed. Nelson Graburn (Berkeley and Los Angeles: University of California Press, 1976).

96. Bayard, *L'Art*, p. 304.

97. Alfred Bel, "Les Industries d'art indigène en Afrique du Nord (Algérie, Tunisie, Maroc)," AF (supplement, October 1931): 591.

98. "Note," April 2, 1922, in Lyautey l'africain, v. 4, pp. 194–95.

99. Georges Hardy, Portrait de Lyautey (Paris: Bloud et Gay, 1949), p. 289; Lyautey speech to the Université des Annales, Paroles d'action, p. 455; Jules Borély, Mon Plaisir au Maroc (Paris: André Delpenche, 1927); and idem, Le Maroc au pinceau (Paris: Editions Dunoël, 1950).

100. Sablayrolles, L'Urbanisme, p. 50; and Borély, "L'Architecture nouvelle et l'urbanisme au Maroc," L'Art vivant 5 (October 15, 1930): 834–39.

101. Direction de l'Instruction Publique, Historique, pp. 147, 152.

102. Sablayrolles, L'Urbanisme, p. 52; Prost, "Les Plans d'extension," in Où en est.

103. Lyautey, speech to the Université des Annales, p. 451. Also see Alfred de Tarde, "Note: Projet d'une Bibliothéque des Beaux-Arts et du Tourisme du Maroc," FL, carton 19, dossier 88.

104. Ed. Joyant, Traité d'urbanisme, 2 vols. (Paris: Librairie de l'Enseignement Technique, 1923), 2: 79–91; Jean Raymond, Précis d'urbanisme moderne (Paris: Dunod, 1934), p. 3. Both men had been adjuncts of Prost's service in Morocco.

105. Lyautey, "Architecture," p. 14.

106. Georges Hardy, Historie sociale de la colonisation française (Paris: Larose, 1953), p. 209.

107. Albert Laprade, "L'Architecture moderne au Maroc," L'Art vivant 13 (February 1938): 22–23.

108. Le Corbusier, Urbanisme (Paris: G. Crès, 1925), pp. 272, 158; Le Corbusier Sketchbooks, 1914–1964 (Cambridge: MIT Press, 1981), vol. 1, ms pp. 440–45. Le Corbusier would of course go on to do an unexecuted Obus Plan for Algiers, begun in 1931, encompassing a monumental curving building along the coast surmounted by a multilane highway. He did, all the same, allow for some intermixing of "Moorish" dwellings with his Citrohan houses.

109. Borély, "L'Architecture nouvelle et l'urbanisme," p. 834.

110. R. d'Arcos, "L'Urbanisme au Maroc," CNA 2 (October 1929): 583–84; Henri Ponsich, "Urbanisme," CNA 2 (September 1929): 309; Jacques Felze, "L'Architecture, art éminement social," CNA 6 (July 1933): 715–17; "Casablanca, cité moderne," CNA 2 (April 1929): 271–74.

111. Th. de Chabot, "Faudra-t-il un jour démolir Casablanca?" CNA 3 (October 1930): 907, 910. Representative examples of articles on Le Corbusier include Paul Romain, "Le Corbusier à Alger: 'une revolution architecturale,'" CNA 4 (April 1930): 360–78; and, the following month, "La Ville radieuse: Le Corbusier à Alger," 473–82.

112. De Chabot, "Faudra-t-il un jour démolir Casablanca?" p. 908; "Le Palais de

Justice de Rabat," *CNA* 3 (February 1930): 90; Victor de Stahl, "La Construction de nouvelles voies ferrées au Maroc," *CNA* 4 (April 1931): 412–19; "L'Institut d'Hygiène à Rabat," *CNA* 4 (April 1931): 407–8; Vaillat, *Visage*, pp. 5–7, 20.

113. See, in particular, Prost, "L'Urbanisme en Afrique du Nord," pp. 2, 5; idem, "L'Urbanisme au Maroc," esp. pp. 4, 10, 42.

114. One can compare the Moroccans' ability to modernize without losing their sense of national and religious heritage with the Algerians' more fanatical swings between state-socialist industrialism and religious fundamentalism. I would certainly not say that the cultural policies employed during the colonial periods of these two countries' histories explain the disparities. Nonetheless, the policies did create two very different cultural attitudes toward modernism and tradition—to say nothing of two very different settings. In one, monuments of the past were protected while modern cities were constructed; in the other, there was no sound basis for preservation and an evangelical belief in the universal applicability of architectural modernism.

115. Abu-Lughod, *Rabat*, p. 147. This legal system drew extensively from recent urban legislation in Germany, Italy, Switzerland, and Egypt, countries Prost had visited on his Musée Social commission studying contemporary urbanism elsewhere in Europe, shortly before his move to Morocco.

116. Lyautey, *Rapport générale sur la situation*, p. xiv.

117. Sablayrolles, *L'Urbanisme*, p. 46. For an extensive discussion of this legislation, see Abu-Lughod, pp. 150–95.

118. In contrast, speculation in the undeveloped areas such as the elite western districts of Casablanca resulted in virtually no benefits to the state.

119. De la Casinière, *Municipalités*, p. 98; Abu-Lughod, *Rabat*, p. 169.

120. Lyautey, speech to the Université des Annales, pp. 445–46.

121. Letter cited in Bidwell, *Morocco*, p. 202.

122. Prost, "L'Urbanisme au Maroc," p. 19, PP.

123. Sablayrolles, *L'Urbanisme au Maroc*, p. 9. He even cited Henry George as part of the critique.

124. Letters to André and Max Lazard (to whom Lyautey considered himself "le grand frère") appear in *Un Lyautey inconnu, correspondance et journal inédits, 1874–1934*, ed. André Le Révérend (Paris: Librairie Académique Perrin, 1980); and *Choix de lettres, 1882–1912*, ed. André Le Révérend (Paris: A. Colin, 1947). On the financial scandals, see Julien, *Le Maroc*, p. 107; and Pierre George, *La Ville: le fait urbain à travers le monde* (Paris: Presses Universitaires de France, 1952), p. 286. Further evidence of this affinity is Lyautey's creation of an advisory group he called the Board of Directors of the Morocco Company. Beginning in 1919, this body, which consisted of the officers of the chambers of commerce from each major *ville nouvelle*, met bimonthly in Rabat to discuss the allocation of funds from the budget and to suggest priorities for public works. See Abdullah Larouri, *The History of the Maghrib: An In-*

terpretive Essay, trans. Ralph Mannheim (Princeton: Princeton University Press, 1977), p. 339.

125. Vaillat, *Visage*, p. 39. Vaillat, to his credit, regretted the lack of participation available to the French public in Morocco, though he did not sense any problem in restricting the rights of Moroccans themselves.

126. "Consultation juridique sur l'expropriation pour cause d'utilité publique: Si Larci Naciri," FL, carton 19, dossier 88.

127. Abu-Lughod, *Rabat*, pp. 169–73; de la Casinière, *Municipalitiés*, pp. 99–100.

128. Sablayrolles, *L'Urbanisme*, p. 58.

129. Abu-Lughod, *Rabat*, pp. 161–73; Melvin Knight, *Morocco as a French Economic Venture* (New York, D. Appleton-Century, 1937), pp. 57–67. Pierre Pelletier shows the French with almost twice as much average value in landholdings as the Moroccans in 1937, and twice as much in surface, with urban landholdings slightly higher than this average, especially in Rabat and Casablanca ("Valeurs financières et urbanisme au Maroc," *BESM* 19 [June 1955], pp. 13–14).

130. Henri Prost and Gaston Monsarrat, *L'Urbanisme au point de vue technique* (Paris: S.A.P.E., 1927), p. 3.

131. Pelletier, "Valeurs," p. 39. Also see Abu-Lughod, *Rabat*, p. 147.

132. Richard Parker, *A Practical Guide to Islamic Monuments in Morocco* (Charlottesville: Baraka Press, 1981), p. 85; Francis Ambrière, *Le Maroc* (Monaco: Les Documents d'Art, 1952), p. 109.

133. Philip Khoury, "Syrian Urban Politics in Transition: The Quarters of Damascus during the French Mandate," *International Journal of Middle Eastern Studies* 16 (1984): 507; T. H. Greenshields, " 'Quarters' and Ethnicity," in *The Changing Middle Eastern City*, ed. G. H. Blake and R. I. Lawless (London: Croom, Helm, 1980), p. 124; and Brown, *People of Salé*, pp. 34–39; Sablayrolles, *L'Urbanisme*, p. 21; Lyautey, "Note, fin novembre, sur Marrakech," FL, carton 55; Georges Hardy, *Le Maroc* (Paris: H. Laurens, 1930), pp. 32–34; and Berque, *French North Africa*, p. 159.

134. Bernard, *L'Afrique du Nord*, p. 86; Hardy, *Colonies*, pp. 82–84; "L'Urbanisme aux Colonies et dans les Pays Tropicaux," *La Vie urbaine* (November 15, 1933): 385.

135. Prost, "Notes," n.p. PP.

136. Robert Montagne, *Naissance du prolétariat marocain* (Paris: Peyronnet, 1952), p. 140. *Chantiers nord-africains* took special notice of the "*very* modern bathroom" and facade, in one such house for a vizier of the sultan, designed by the modernist architect Marius Boyer ("Boyer & Balois, Palais de S. E. El-Mokri, grand vizier de S. M. le Sultan du Maroc," *CNA* [July–August 1929]: 467–70).

137. "Note, fin novembre, 1913, sur Marrakech," FL, carton 55. I would like to thank Daniel Rivet for this citation.

138. Here I take issue with the title of Abu-Lughod's *Rabat: Urban Apartheid in Morocco*, though I find it an extraordinary book. The author herself notes that few Moroccans agree with her label (pp. xvii, 216).

139. Prost, "Le Plan de Casablanca," pp. 4–12.

140. Prost, "L'Urbanisme en Afrique du Nord," p. 5.

141. Adam, *Casablanca*, 1:19. On speculation, also see René Hoffherr, *L'Economie marocaine* (Paris: Sirey, 1932); Emmanuel Durand, "L'Evolution de l'urbanisme dans le protectorat du Maroc, de 1923 à 1931," in *L'Urbanisme dans les colonies*, 1:81–93; Jean-Claude Delorme, "De Henri Prost à Michel Ecochard," *Architecture, Mouvement, Continuité* 42 (June 1977): 5–12; Abu-Lughod, *Rabat*, pp. 167–68; and Taylor, "Planned Discontinuity," pp. 53–66. Michael Ecochard, Morocco's French colonial urbanist just after WWII, emphasized that this rampant speculation was responsible for many of Casablanca's later problems (*Casablanca: le roman d'une ville* [Paris: Editions de Paris, 1955], p. 31).

142. Taylor, "Planned Discontinuity," p. 65.

143. Durand, "L'Evolution de l'urbanisme," p. 83.

144. Whereas 75 kilometers of sewers existed before 1913 in Fez, Rabat, and Casablanca, 193 kilometers were in use a decade later. This service did help control the problem of typhus, which had been rampant in 1913, although another epidemic struck in 1938, due to inadequate facilities and overcrowding in the medinas. See Sablayrolles, *L'Urbanisme*, pp. 104–5; and René Janon, "L'Oeuvre d'une municipalité marocaine: Casablanca," *CNA* 6 (July 1932): 563–67.

145. Abu-Lughod, *Rabat*, p. 190, cites Xavier Durrieu, *The Present State of Morocco: A Chapter of Mussulman Civilisation* (London: Longman, Brown, Green and Longmans, 1854), pp. 59–60, and Hugh Stutfield, *El-Maghreb: 1200 Miles' Ride through Morocco* (London: Sampson Low, Marstan, Searle, and Rivington, 1886). Also see M. Delure, "Les Travaux publics au Maroc," *Conferences Franco-marocaines*, 2:145; and *Rabat et sa région*, vol. 2 (1919), p. 27.

146. Adam, *Casablanca*, 1:149.

147. Montagne, *Naissance*, p. 135. The number of Moroccan Jews in these figures remained constant at about one-third of the indigenous population, mostly residing in the crowded *mellahs*, until three years after 1940 when tensions in the countryside with the rise of Zionism drove many more Jews into the larger coastal cities.

148. Augustin Bernard, "Afrique du Nord," in *L'Habitation indigène dans les possessions françaises*, ed. Augustin Bernard, Henri Labouret, Georges Julien, Charles Robequain, and Maurice Leenhardt (Paris: Société d'Editions Géographiques, Maritimes et Coloniales, 1931), p. 20.

149. Prost, "Rapport général," in *L'Urbanisme aux colonies*, 1: 24.

150. Adam, *Casablanca*, 1: 85–100; Montagne, *Naissance*, pp. 133–78; and Brown, *People of Salé*, p. 175.

151. Jacques Berque, "Médinas, villeneuves et bidonvilles," *Cahiers de Tunesie* 6 (1958): 5–42; Yvonne Mahé, "L'Extension des villes indigènes au Maroc," thesis, University of Bordeaux, 1928; Pierre Mas, "Les Phenomènes d'urbanisation et les bidonvilles au Maroc," thesis, Institut d'Urbanisme, Paris, 1950; idem, "L'Urbanisation actuelle du Maroc: les 'bidonvilles,'" *La Vie urbaine* 61 (1951): 185–221; Henri Morestin, "Les Faubourgs indigènes de Rabat," *Les Cahiers d'outre-mer* 3 (1960): 66–76; Adam, *Casablanca*, 1: 84–86; Pelletier, "Valeurs," p. 16, and Abu-Lughod, *Rabat*, pp. 161, 200.

152. Stephane Delisle, "Le Prolétariat marocain de Port-Lyautey," *Cahiers de l'Afrique et l'Asie*, vol. 1, *L'Evolution social du Maroc* (Paris: Peyronnet, 1949), pp. 120–21; Adam, *Casablanca*, 1:85–86; and Montagne, *Naissance*, pp. 161–62.

153. Abu-Lughod, *Rabat*, p. 200; and Montagne, *Naissance*, pp. 141, 158–60.

154. Adam, *Casablanca*, 1:50.

155. Prost, "Rapport général," p. 24.

156. Prost, "Casablanca," n.p.

157. Lecture notebook, entry under "Cités-Jardins," PP.

158. Albert Laprade, "Une Ville créée spécialement pour les indigènes à Casablanca," in *L'Urbanisme aux colonies*, 1: 98.

159. Ibid., p. 97. Also see Adam, *Casablanca*, 1:69–84; Vaillat, *Visage*, pp. 13–16; and idem, "La Nouvelle médina de Casablanca," *L'Illustration* (October 18, 1930): 30.

160. Laprade, "Une Ville créée," p. 97.

161. Edward W. Said, *Orientalism* (New York: Pantheon, 1978). Also see Abdallah Larouri, *The Crisis of the Arab Intellectual*, trans. Diarmid Cammel (1974; Berkeley and Los Angeles: University of California Press, 1976).

162. Vaillat, *Visage*, p. 16. The Moroccan bourgeoisie, I should note, also became attached to the *Derb el-Habous*. When additional administrative offices for the pasha were established nearby, adjacent to the palace, just before the Second World War, Casablanca's habous became the new center of Muslim life in the city.

163. Sablayrolles, *L'Urbanisme*, p. 7.

164. Ibid., p. 172.

CHAPTER FOUR

1. Gaston Bonnefont, *Aventures de six Français aux colonies* (Paris: Garnier Frères, n.d.), p. 680.

2. Mat Gioi [a pseudonym meaning "The Sun" in Vietnamese, adopted by Alfred de Pouvourville], *Le Tonkin actuel, 1887–1890* (Paris: Albert Sarine, 1891), p. 18.

3. In *La Vie quotidienne des Français en Indochine, 1860–1910*, Charles Meyer describes this aversion to extravagance as "Quaker" ([Paris: Hachette, 1985], p. 83).

4. De Pouvourville, *Le Tonkin actuel*, p. 25.

5. Letter of November 10, 1894, in *Lyautey, Choix de lettres, 1882–1919*, ed. André Le Révérend (Paris: A. Colin, 1947), p. 35.

6. Eugène Brieux, *Voyages aux Indes et Indochine* (Paris: Delagrave, 1910), p. 38.

7. See, for example, Brieux, *Voyages*; Claude Bourrin, *Le Vieux Tonkin . . . 1884 à 1889* (Saigon: J. Aspar, 1935); and Virginia Thompson, *French Indochina* (New York: Macmillan, 1937), p. 219.

8. The term "Vietnam," as used in this book, applies to the present-day unified country made up of three parts of French Indochina—Tonkin, Annam, and Cochinchina (divided, in part, to obliterate their historical unity)—which once formed the unified Empire of Vietnam. After a long period of domination by China, the empire had been refounded by the Nguyen emperor Gia Long in 1802, with its capital at Hué. The Nguyens briefly annexed Laos (1832) and Cambodia (1834), though these cultures, more oriented toward Indian civilization than Chinese, remained quite hostile. The term "Vietnam" was deliberately dropped from Western usage with the French conquest; they insisted upon the Chinese appellation "Annam," which alluded to the nation's former dependent status upon another great power. The term was again taken up in 1905 by the nationalist leader Phan Boi Chau, who founded the Viet Nam Duy Tan Hoi (Association for the Modernization of Vietnam). Ho Chi Minh (then Nguyen Ai Quoc) used it, too, when he founded the Viet Nam Cach Menh Than Nien Dong Chi Hoi (Vietnam Revolutionary Youth League) in Canton in 1925. Two years later the Viet Nam Quoc Dan Dang (Vietnam Nationalist Party) spread the term throughout the colonized population as a symbol of national liberation.

9. Thomas E. Ennis, *French Policy and Developments in Indochina* (New York: Russell and Russell, 1936), pp. 36–52; and Lê Thành Khoi, *Le Viêt-Nam: histoire et civilisation* (Paris: Les Editions de Minuit, 1955), pp. 365–79, provide excellent summaries of this approach.

10. Thompson, *French Indochina*, p. 425. Thompson provides an excellent background on colonial Vietnam, as does Milton Osborne, *The French Presence in Cochinchina and Cambodia: Rule and Response (1859–1905)* (Ithaca: Cornell University Press, 1969); Joseph Buttinger, *Vietnam: A Dragon Embattled*, 2 vols. (New York: Praeger, 1967), vol. 1, *From Colonialism to the Vietminh* (pp. 19–23 deal specifically with the tensions of Cochinchina); and Rudolf von Albertini, *European Colonial Rule, 1880–1940: The Impact of the West on India, Southeast Asia, and Africa*, trans. John G. Williamson (Westport, Conn.: Greenwood Press, 1982), pp. 193–224. For firsthand accounts, see Paulin Vial, *Les Premières années de la Cochinchine française*, 2 vols. (Paris: Challamel, 1874); and *Documents pour servir à l'histoire de Saigon, 1859 à 1865*, ed. Jean Bouchet (Saigon: Editions Albert Portail, 1927).

11. Eugène Jung, *La Vie européene au Tonkin* (Paris: Flammarion, 1901), p. 125.

12. Ernest Hébrard, "L'Urbanisme en Indochine," in *L'Urbanisme aux colonies et dans les pays tropicaux*, ed. Jean Royer, 2 vols. (La-Charité-sur-Loire: Delayance, 1932), 1:288; idem, "L'Urbanisme en Indochine," *L'Architecture* 36 (1923): 3.

13. Vu Quoc Thuc, "Les Villes vietnamiennes," in *Pour le comprehension de l'Indochine et de l'Extrême-Orient*, ed. H. Bernard (Hanoi: Taupin, 1939), p. 210.

14. Xavier Guillaume, "Saigon, or the Failure of an Ambition (1858–1945)," in *Colonial Cities*, ed. Robert J. Ross and Gerard J. Telkamp (Dordrecht and Boston: Martinus Nijhoff, 1985), p. 182.

15. P. Cultru, *Histoire de la Cochinchine française des origines à 1883* (Paris: A. Challamel, 1910), p. 274. The heights of the city were occupied in prehistoric times. The word "Saigon" first came into use in the letters of eighteenth-century French missionaries, probably a transliteration of the ancient Khmer name "Prei-kor" (forest of the capital). The government of Gia Long called the upper governmental and military city "Gia-dinh" and the commercial riverbank "Ben-nghé." "Saigon" is still much more widely used than "Ho Chi Minh City."

16. Ibid., pp. 274–78; "Saigon hier et aujourd'hui," in *Perspectives d'outre-mer*, a special issue in vol. 14 of *Notre Maroc* (March 1955): 25; Thompson, *French Indochina*, pp. 228–30; Jean Bouchet, "La Naissance et les premières années de Saigon, ville française," *BSEI*, n.s. 2 (1927): 42, 49–51. The population before the French conquest had reached at least 100,000 in the various villages constituting Saigon; early in the nineteenth century, John White estimated it to be as high as 180,000 (*A Voyage to Cochin China* [London: Longman, Hurst and Green, 1824], p. 232).

17. David G. Marr, *Vietnamese Anticolonialism, 1885–1925* (Berkeley: University of California Press, 1971), p. 81.

18. Cultru, *Histoire*, pp. 278–79.

19. "Promenades historiques dans les rues de Saigon," in *Perspectives d'outre-mer*, p. 32; Hilda Arnold, *Promenade dans Saigon* (Saigon: SILI, 1948), p. 9; Antoine Brébion, "Monographie des rues et monuments de Saigon," *Revue indochinoise* 16 (October 1911): 363.

20. Vial, *Les Premières années*, 2:227; Le Thi Ngoc Anh, "Etude de quelques monuments répresentatifs de l'art française à Saigon dans les années 1877–1908," resume of a *mémoire*, Faculté des Lettres, University of Saigon, 1973, p. 508, AOM; Bouchet, "Naissance,"p. 38.

21. "La Cathédrale de Saigon," *CM* 10 (June 15–August 10, 1895): 441–43, 454–56, 489–90, 509, 537–38: R. P. Parret, "La Cathédrale de Saigon," *Indochine* 4 (July 8, 1943): 13–16.

22. Le Thi Ngoc Anh, "Etude": 582–84. The building was erected on the same site Codry had tried to use twenty-seven years before—two other sites had been contemplated in the meantime.

23. Ibid., 583.

24. Ibid.

25. Buttinger, *Vietnam*, p. 53. In 1925 André Malraux acerbically commented that "Cochinchina is the only French territory where it is forbidden . . . to profess republicanism" (cited in Philippe Devillers, *Histoire du Viet-Nam de 1940 à 1952* [Paris: Editions du Seuil, 1952], p. 44). Also see Georges Hardy's policies as director of public education in Morocco, set forth in his article "L'Education au Maroc," *Revue de Paris* (May 15, 1921), where he wrote, "The time has passed when one can believe that all science is good and that teaching for its own sake is a formula without danger" (p. 774).

26. Bouchot, "Naissance," p. 42; Tran Van Tat, "Mémoire sur l'évolution et l'aménagement de la ville de Saigon-Cholon," *mémoire*, Institut d'Urbanisme, University of Paris, 1928. Pierre Simon, who notes that almost all the Vietnamese *métis* lived in the cities of Saigon or Hanoi, has pointed out that in popular imagery, the term *métis* acquires only the negative qualities of both races. ("Aspects de la colonisation de la décolonisation de l'Indochine orientale," thesis, Université de Paris V, 1973), pp. 108, 114.

27. Jean-Marie de Lanessan, *Principes de colonisation* (Paris: Félix Alcan, 1897) and idem, *La Colonisation française en Indo-Chine* (Paris: Félix Alcan, 1895); Hébrard, "L'Urbanisme en Indochine," *L'Architecture*, p. 5; Alain Forest, *Le Cambodge et la colonisation française: histoire d'une colonisation sans heurts (1897–1920)* (Paris: Librairie-Editions L'Harmattan, 1980), p. 234.

28. Letter to his sister from Lang-Son, February 2, 1895, in *Choix de lettres*, p. 62.

29. Paul Doumer, *L'Indochine française: souvenirs* (Paris: Buibert et Nony, 1903), pp. 335, 343; Buttinger, *Vietnam*, pp. 28–35; Charles Robequain, *The Economic Development of French Indochina*, trans. Isabel A. Ward (London and New York: Oxford University Press, 1944), pp. 89–116; Henry Marc and Pierre Couy, *Indochine française* (Paris: Editions France-Empire, 1946), pp. 126–38; and Lê Thành Khoi, *Le Viêt-Nam*, pp. 413–18.

30. Buttinger, *Vietnam*, p. 30. Also see Le Van Kim, *Les Travaux publics en Indochine* (Paris: Imprimerie "Labor," 1926); and Tren Van Trai, *Les Chemins de fer en Indochine* (Paris: L. Rodstein, 1941).

31. Thompson, *French Indochina*, p. 206.

32. Paul Bernard, *Nouveaux aspects du problème économique indochinois* (Paris: F. Sorlot, 1937), p. 23; also see Pierre Lanvin, *La France en Indochine* (London: Publications de la France Combattante, 1943), p. 17.

33. Brieux, *Voyages*, p. 37. Nonetheless the bridge withstood years of American bombing, remaining the main conduit for supplies between Hanoi and Haiphong.

34. Thompson, *French Indochina*, p. 219; Stephen A. Roberts, *The History of French Colonial Policy, 1870–1925* (1929; Hamden: Archon Press, 1963), p. 456.

35. Alcide Bléton, *Journal officiel de la Cochinchine*, October 22, 1885, cited in Paulin Vial, *Nos Premières années au Tonkin* (Voiron: Imprimerie Baratier et Mollaret, 1889), p. 419.

36. Ibid., p. 359.

37. This very disparity is criticized in "Situation ensemble, Mission du 30 mars 1920 au Tonkin, Inspection Générale des Colonies," carton 169, dossier 14, Direction des Travaux Publics de l'Indochine, AOM. Also see Léon Fayet, *Les Egouts de Hanoi* (Hanoi: Imprimerie d'Extrême-Orient, 1939).

38. De Pouvourville, *Le Tonkin actuel*, p. 14; "Hanoi: From Prehistory to the Nineteenth Century," *Vietnamese Studies* 13 (1977): 9–57; and Georges Azambre, "Hanoi," *BSEI* 30 (1955): 355–63. The word "Hanoi" first came into use in 1831 with the political grouping of districts under the aegis of Gia Long's vast citadel of Trang Long, another Vauban-inspired fortress, almost a kilometer long on each side, which functioned as the royal city until the French conquest. In the previous two centuries the settlement had been known as "Ké-Chô."

39. Thompson, *French Indochina*, p. 219.

40. Meyer, *La Vie quotidienne*, pp. 73–74. Saigon rickshaw drivers in time organized, going out on strike in 1921 to protest bad working conditions.

41. Marc and Couy, *L'Indochine française*, p. 127.

42. Roberts, *History*, p. 471; Thompson, *French Indochina*, p. 73; Paul Isoart, *Le Phénomène national vietnamien* (Paris: Librairie Générale de Droit et de Jurisprudence, 1961), p. 200; and Buttinger, *Vietnam*, pp. 17–19.

43. See Buttinger, *Vietnam*, p. 37; and Ennis, *French Policy*, p. 71.

44. Isoart, *Le Phénomène national*, p. 207; Buttinger, *Vietnam*, pp. 59–60; and Jean Chesneaux, *Contribution à l'histoire de la nation vietnamienne* (Paris: Editions Sociales, 1955), p. 156. Doumer accomplished his purposes largely through the Superior Council, which established expensive state monopolies on opium, alcohol, and salt, creating in the process an overbearing burden on the Indochinese population. This was especially the case with salt, used to preserve fish and to make the highly seasoned fish sauce, *nouc mam*. When the price of salt rose fourfold, then sixfold, many fishermen could no longer afford to conserve and sell their catch, which created a spiral of poverty and malnutrition throughout the country. In the interest of revenue, moreover, the French encouraged the consumption of alcohol and the use of opium.

45. Doumer, *L'Indochine*, p. 322.

46. *L'Indochine française*, vol. 1, *L'Annam* (Paris: Société d'Editions Géographiques, Maritimes et Coloniales, 1919), n.p.

47. In 1903 the French government sent Ajalbert, trained as a lawyer, to Indochina. He remained there for five years and then left, returning recurrently and becoming increasingly vehement in his criticism. See in particular his *L'Indochine en péril*

(Paris: P. V. Stock, 1906); and *Les Nuages sur l'Indochine* (Paris: Louis Michaud, 1912).

48. Numerous examples appear in Eugène Teston and Maurice Percheron, *L'Indochine moderne: encyclopédie administrative, touristique, artistique et économique* (Paris: Librairie de France, 1932). By 1912, some 85 percent of funds collected from direct taxation of the Vietnamese people went to officials' salaries (Roberts, *History*, p. 481).

49. Albert Sarraut, *La Mise en valeur des colonies françaises* (Paris: Payot, 1923), p. 122.

50. For an overview, see John S. Furnivall, *Educational Progress in Southeast Asia* (New York: International Secretariat, Institute of Pacific Relations, 1942), pp. 38–41, 81–88; Vu Tam Ich, "A Historical Survey of Educational Developments in Vietnam," *Bulletin of the Bureau of School Service of the University of Kentucky* 32 (December 1959): 1–135; and Drep Van Ky, "L'Enseignement des indigènes en Indochine," *Comptes-rendus de l'Académie des Sciences Coloniales* 4 (1924–25): 377–87.

51. Ennis, *French Policy*, p. 170.

52. *Un Empire colonial français: l'Indochine*, ed. Georges Maspero, 2 vols. (Paris: Van Oest, 1929), 2: 91; *Le Lycée Albert Sarraut à Hanoi* (Hanoi: Imprimerie d'Extrême-Orient, 1925).

53. David G. Marr, *Vietnamese Tradition on Trial, 1920–1945* (Berkeley and Los Angeles: University of California Press, 1981), p. 34. Buttinger offers a far more ambitious estimate of 80 percent literacy (*Vietnam*, p. 46). An important expression of the pro-education sentiment among the urban Vietnamese is the Dông Kinh Nghia Thuc, or Tonkin Free (i.e. Non-Tuition) School, founded in 1907 in Hanoi and espousing the ideals of the popular nationalist leader Phan Chau Trinh. His goal was that of a democratic republic in which the Vietnamese people, again unified and independent, would share the rewards of industrial science and indigenous culture. Some one thousand students and numerous nationalist supporters considered this school a "pagoda of modernizaiton." The French resented their autonomy and closed the school after only eight months, arresting the leaders and sending Phan Chau Trinh into exile. (See Vu Duc Bang, "The Dông Kinh Free School Movement," in *Aspects of Vietnamese History*, ed. Walter F. Vella [Honolulu: University Press of Hawaii, 1973], pp. 30–95; and Marr, *Vietnamese Tradition*, pp. 200–201.)

54. Gail P. Kelly, "Franco-Vietnamese Schools, 1918–1938," Ph.D. diss., University of Wisconsin, 1974, tables 1 and 4; Marr, *Vietnamese Tradition*, pp. 35, 414; and Thompson, *French Indochina*, pp. 384–87. By 1950 Carol Quigley estimated that the French had allowed illiteracy to reach 90–95 percent ("Education in Overseas France," *Current History* 35 [1958]: 102).

55. "L'Action de l'Ecole Française d'Extrême-Orient au point de vue social," pp. 1–2 (report of the Geurnut Commission, Hanoi, 1937), Direction du Tourisme de l'Indochine, carton 22, AOM.

56. Ibid.

57. Ibid., p. 5; Walter G. Langlois, *André Malraux: The Indochina Adventure* (New York: Praeger, 1966), pp. 3–50; Ernest Hébrard, "La Conservation des monuments anciens et des veilles villes indigènes de l'Indochine," in *L'Urbanisme aux colonies,* 2: 25. Malraux, who was caught stealing sculpture from Angkor, became critical of the colonial government in Indochina and helped organize leftist opposition newspapers among the Vietnamese population.

58. Interview with Nguyén-Ba Long, March 25, 1981, Paris. Also see *La Cinquantenaire de l'Ecole Française d'Extrême-Orient,* ed. Louis Malleret (Paris: Editions de Boccard, 1953), pp. 161–70; and Bernard Philippe Groslier, *Indochine* (Geneva: Nagel, 1966).

59. Speech of Pierre Pasquier at the inauguration of the Musée Louis Finot, Hanoi, November 30, 1932, reprinted in the *BEFEO* 33 (1933): 481.

60. Ibid.

61. Speech of Governor-General Martial Merlin, *Conseil de Gouvernement de l'Indochine, Session Ordinaire de 1923* (Hanoi: Imprimerie de l'Extrême-Orient, 1923), p. 13.

62. Ennis, *French Policy,* p. 103.

63. Thompson, *French Indochina,* p. 90.

64. Long had been a delegate from the French legislature during the establishment of the protectorate in Morocco and the issuing of its first state loan. See Lyautey's preface to Benard, *Au Service de l'Indochine,* and Benard's comment that Long considered Lyautey "a master" (p. 14).

65. "Instructions du Ministère de l'Intérieur aux Préfets des Départements relatives à l'etablissement des plans d'aménagement et d'extension des villes," March 20, 1920, sent to Governor-General Long by the ministry of colonies, and Long's telegram of May 3, 1920, requesting the brochures (Direction des Travaux Publics de l'Indochine, carton 82, dossier 4, AOM).

66. Cited in Hébrard, "L'Urbanisme en Indochine," in *L'Urbanisme aux colonies,* 1: 282.

67. Ibid.

68. Telegram from the minister of colonies to the governor-general of Indochina, June 24, 1921, and "Rapport sur le fonctionnement du Services, Années 1922–23," p. 6, Direction des Travaux Publics de l'Indochine, carton 82, dossier 4, AOM; letter from Prost to Hébrard, February 18, 1921, PP. For an overview of Hébrard's carrer, see Gwendolyn Wright and Paul Rabinow," "Savoir et pouvoir dans l'urbanisme moderne colonial d'Ernest Hébrard," *CRA* no. 9 (1982): 26–43.

69. See note 14, chapter 2. Hébrard did return to Greece regularly during the 1920s at the invitation of the junta, to confer about urbanism and historic preservation.

70. Buttinger, *Vietnam*, p. 102.

71. Ernest Hébrard, "Rapport général sur l'urbanisme en Extrême-Orient," "L'Urbanisme en Indochine," "L'urbanisme aux Iles Phillipines," "L'Urbanisme aux Indes Anglaises, en Birmanie et dans les États Malais," "L'Urbanisme en Chine.—Les villes des concessions," in *L'Urbanisme aux colonies*, 1: 261–62, 278–89, 294–310; idem, "L'Architecture locale et les questions d'esthétique en Indochine," "La Conservation des monuments," "L'Habitation en Indochine," and "L'Habitation aux Indes" in *L'Urbanisme aux colonies*, 2: 25–34, 58–64.

72. Hébrard, "L'Architecture locale," p. 32.

73. Ibid.

74. Ibid., p. 32.

75. Hébrard, "L'Urbanisme en Indochine," in *L'Architecture*, p. 2; and Azambre, "Hanoi," 355–60.

76. Hébrard, "L'Architecture locale," p. 34.

77. Hébrard, "L'Urbanisme en Indochine," In *L'Architecture*, p. 2; and idem, "L'Urbanisme en Indo-Chine," in *Urbanisme* 1 (1932): 72. A brief overview, translated during the American intervention, may be found in Nguyen Quang Nhar and Nguyen Nang Dac, *Vietnamese Architecture* (Washington, D.C.: Embassy of Vietnam, 1970).

78. Hébrard, "L'Urbanisme en Indochine," in *L'Architecture*, p. 16.

79. "Chronique: Indochine Française: École Française d'Extrême-Orient," *BE-FEO* 26 (1926): 445. Quite similar is the Musée Blanchard de la Brosse (1929) at the entrance to the Botanical Garden in Saigon, designed by Hébrard's friend Delaval in the "style vietnamienne." See Bernard Philippe Groslier, "Le Musée de Saigon" in *Perspectives d'outre-mer*: 33–38, and *Indochine: Documents Officiels* (Paris: Société des Études Géographiques, Maritimes, et Coloniales, 1931), pp. 190–95.

80. Ibid; Louis;-Georges Pineau, "L'Aménagement et l'extension des villes en Indochine," *La Vie urbaine* n.s. 6 (November 15, 1930): 353–59; idem, "L'Urbanisme en Indochine," *Indochine* (October 26, 1943); 1–33.

81. Marr, *Vietnamese Tradition*, p. 6; Martin J. Murray, *The Development of Capitalism in Colonial Indochina (1870–1940)* (Berkeley: University of California Press, 1980), pp. 124–27; Ennis, *French Policy*, p. 92.

82. On page 463 of *La Mise en valeur des colonies françaises*, Sarraut declares that Indochina has become "the most important, the most developed, and the most prosperous of our colonies."

83. Pierre Brocheux, "Les Grands Dien Chen de la Cochinchine occidentale pendant la période coloniale," in *Tradition et révolution au Vietnam*, ed. Jean Chesneaux, Georges Boudarel, and Daniel Hémery (Paris: Éditions Anthropos, 1971), p. 158.

84. Marr, *Vietnamese Tradition*, pp. 5–6.

85. Charles A. Michaud, "French Indochina," in *The New World of Southeast Asia*, ed. Lennox A. Mills et al. (Minneapolis: University of Minnesota Press, 1949), pp. 221-22.

86. From the mid-1930s onward, some companies provided workers with cleaner and more sanitary individual dwellings, constructed by the residents themselves in traditional thatch and mud, thereby providing an enormous saving (Murray, *Development of Capitalism*, pp. 276-77). Also see Tran Tu Binh, *The Red Earth: A Vietnamese Memoir of Life on a Colonial Rubber Plantation*, trans. John Spragens, Jr., and ed. David G. Marr, South East Asia series no. 66 (Athens, Ohio: University of Ohio Press, 1985).

87. Michaud, "French Indochina," p. 225; Charles Robequain, *L'Evolution economique de l'Indochine française* (Paris: Hartmann, 1938), p. 54.

88. Murray, *The Development of Capitalism*, pp. 185-86.

89. Jean Chesneaux, "L'Implantation géographique des interêts coloniaux aux Vietnam et ses rapports avec l'économie traditionnelle," in *Tradition et révolution*, p. 77.

90. T. G. McGee, *The Southeast Asian City: A Social Geography of the Cities of Southeast Asia* (New York: Praeger, 1967), p. 57; Robequain, *L'evolution économique*, pp. 117-20; Rhoads Murphy, "Traditionalism and Colonialism: Changing Urban Roles in Asia," *Journal of Asian Studies* 29 (1969): 67-84.

91. Hébrard, "L'Urbanisme en Indo-Chine," *Urbanisme* 1: (1932) 74; Tran Van Tat, "Memoire," p. 69; J. M. Kermadec, *Cho-Lon, Ville chinoise* (Saigon: Société Asiatique d'Éditions, 1955); Le Van Lam, "Les Problème d'urbanisme dans la région de Saigon-Cholon," *mémoire*, Institut d'Urbanisme, University of Paris, 1957.

92. Hébrard, "L'Urbanisme en Indochine," in *L'Architecture*, p. 1.

93. Hébrard, "L'Architecture locale," p. 32.

94. Murray, *The Development of Capitalism*, p. 189.

95. A. A. Pouyanne, "Les Travaux publics de l'Indochine," *Bulletin economique de l'Indochine* n.s. 4 (1925): 513-42; (1926): 265-320, 357-506; summarized in *Les Travaux publics de l'Indochine* (Hanoi: Imprimerie de l'Extreme-Orient, 1926).

96. Hébrard, "L'Urbanisme en Indochine," in *L'Architecture*, p. 5; idem, "L'Urbanisme en Indochine," in *L'urbanisme aux colonies* 1, 289. His plan for Saigon-Cholon called for additional tramway lines (including covered shelters for waiting passengers) to serve the Vietnamese and a network of broad arcaded streets geared to pedestrian and automobile traffic to serve the French and wealthy Vietnamese. Hébrard, "L'Urbanisme en Indochine," in *L'Urbanisme aux colonies*, p. 282.

97. Hébrard, "L'Urbanisme en Indochine," in *L'Architecture*, p. 5.

98. Hébrard, "L'Urbanisme en Indochine," in *L'Urbanisme aux colonies*,1: 288.

99. Hébrard, "L'Urbanisme en Indochine," *L'Architecture*, p. 1; Hébrard comments in M. Cohen-Stuart, Hébrard, and Durand, "A propos de la séparation des villes

au Maroc et aux Indes néerlandaises," in *L'Urbanisme aux colonies*, 1: 276–77.

100. Remarks of M. Cohen-Stuart, delegate from the Dutch East Indies, in "A propos de la séparation," p. 276.

101. Hébrard, "L'Urbanisme en Indochine," in *L'Urbanisme aux colonies*, 1: 279, 285.

102. Tran Nguyen Chan and the city of Saigon, *Recueil des textes concernant l'hygiène et la santé publique* (Saigon: Union Nguyen-Van-Cha, 1929), p. 338, carton 169, Direction des Travaux Publics de l'Indochina, AOM.

103. Ibid.

104. Tran Van Tat, "Mémoire," p. 64.

105. See, in particular, John Rex, *Race, Colonialism and the City* (London and Boston: Routledge and Kegan Paul, 1973); and Philip Mason, *Patterns of Dominance* (London and New York: Oxford University Press, 1970).

106. Philip D. Curtin, "Medical Knowledge and Urban Planning in Tropical Africa," *American Historical Review* 90 (June 1985): 594–613.

107. "Saigon," *Perspectives d'outre-mer*, has several examples of such structures. Also see Nguyen Khac Kham, *An Introduction to Vietnamese Culture* (Tokyo: Center for East Asian Cultural Studies, 1967), which mostly explores the history of Western influence; and Pierre-Richard Féray, *Le Viêt-Nam au XXe siècle* (Paris: Presses Universitaires de France, 1979).

108. Dr. P. Noël Bernard, "Les Instituts Pasteur d'Indochine," Session of March 3, 1927, *Comptes-Rendus de l'Académie des Sciences Coloniales* 8 (1928): 415–24.

109. Pierre Lavedan, "Le Lycée de Saigon," *L'Architecture*.

110. Alfred de Pouvourville, *Histoire populaire des colonies françaises: L'Indochine* (Paris: Éditions du Velin d'Or, 1932), p. 238.

111. Jean Baptiste Alberti, *L'Indochine d'autrefois et d'aujourd'hui* (Paris: Société d'Éditions Géographiques, Maritimes, et Coloniales, 1934), p. 470.

112. Hébrard, "L'Architecture locale," p. 34.

113. Ibid. This was the autonomy Hébrard had requested when he took the post. Although the governor-general's office sent letters to the heads of every relevant bureau in the administration, asking for their collaboration and Hébrard's "complete independence," this was scarcely the welcome he found (letters of July 18, August 13, and September 7, 1921, Direction des Travaux Publics de l'Indochine, carton 169, dossier 10, AOM).

114. Hébrard, "L'Urbanisme en Indochine," in *L'Urbanisme aux colonies*, 1: 282–83; idem, "L'Urbanisme en Indo-Chine," *Urbanisme*: 73–74; Henri Cucherousset, "Nouvelles constructions à Hanoi: la Direction des Finances," *Eveil économique de l'Indochine* (September 18, 1927): 137; and A. Piglowski, "La Ville de Hanoi, 1884–1928," *Indépendance Tonkinoise* (February 3–14, 1929).

115. William H. Frederick, "Alexandre Varenne and Politics in Indochina, 1925–1926," in *Aspects of Vietnamese History*, pp. 96–159; Langlois, *Malraux*, pp. 163–80; Camille Devilar, *Comment on perd une colonie* (Paris: Presses Modernes, 1927); R. Thomas, "La politique socialiste et le problème colonial, de 1905 à 1920," *RFHOM* 46 (1959): 213–45; and Alexandre Varenne, "La situation de l'Indochine," *Revue du Pacifique* 5 (February 1926): 71–108; (December 19, 1926): 197–246.

116. Dr. Laurent-Joseph Gaïde, *Les Stations climatiques de l'Indochine* (Hanoi: Imprimerie d'Extrême-Orient, 1930): 18.

117. Louis-Georges Pineau, "Le Plan d'aménagement et d'extension de Dalat," *La Vie urbaine* 49 (1939): 34.

118. Ibid., p. 46, where Pineau cites Léandre Vaillat's description or Rabat's formal unity from *Le Visage français*, p. 36. Also see Pineau, "Dalat, capital adminstratif de l'Indochine," *Revue indochinoise juridique et économique* 2 (1937): 45–81, and all of Hébrard's writings on Indochina.

119. Pineau, "Le Plan d'aménagement," pp. 37, 40. Pineau was commissioned to adapt Hébrard's ambitious plan to a more modest scale in 1932. During WW II Dalat functioned as the colony's capital. Today, partially restored and boasting a population of 100,000, it is becoming an important socialist resort (*New York Times*, August 22, 1987, p. A4).

120. Ibid., p. 37. Also see François de Tessan, "Une Station d'altitude en Indochine," *L'Illustration* 161 (February 17, 1923): 156–59.

121. "Ernest Hébrard en Indochine," *Urbanisme* 2 (January 1933): 170.

122. Hébrard, "L'Architecture locale," p. 34.

CHAPTER FIVE

1. I use the appellation "Madagascar" since the term first used after independence, the "Malagasy Republic," has now been changed to the "Democratic Republic of Madagascar." On the early history of the island, see, in particular, Raymond K. Kent, *From Madagascar to the Malagasy Republic* (London: Thames and Hudson, 1962); Edouard Ralaimihoatra, *Histoire de Magadascar* (Antananarivo: E. Ralaimihoatra, 1966); Mervyn Brown, *Madagascar Rediscovered: A History from Early times to Independence* (London: Damien Tunnacliffe, 1978); Hubert Deschamps, *Histoire de Madagascar* (Paris: Editions Berger-Levrault, 1961); Sonia E. Howe, *The Drama of Madagascar* (London: Methuen, 1938); Phares M. Mutibwa, *The Malagasy and the Europeans: Madagascar's Foreign Relations, 1861–1895* (Atlantic Highlands, N.J.: Humanities Press, 1974); and G. S. Chapus, "Quatre-vingts années d'influences européenes en Imerina," *BAM* n.s. 8 (1925): 1–352.

2. Howe, *Drama*, p. 315.

3. "Tananarive et ses environs," *Journal officiel de Madagascar et dépendences* (December 9, 1903), cited in A. Bruggeman, "L'Urbanisme aux colonies: Tananarive, son passé, son évolution, son avenir, I," *La Vie urbaine* 16 (1933): 9.

4. E. F. Knight, *Madagascar in War Time* (London: 1896), p. 128, cited in Brown, *Madagascar Rediscovered*, p. 236.

5. Marco Polo describes tales he heard in 1294 in *The Travels of Marco Polo* (London: Penguin, 1958), pp. 274–75.

6. Daniel Defoe, *A General History of the Robberies and Murders of the most notorious Pyrates*, 2 vols. (London: C. Rivington, 1724–26); Hubert Deschamps, *Les Pirates à Madagascar* (Paris: Berger-Levrault, 1949); and Robert Drury, *Madagascar; or Robert Drury's Journal* (1890; reprint ed., Westport, Conn.: Negro Universities Press, 1969).

7. Joseph Jacquiot, "Médailles et projets de monument et de jetons pour la colonie de Madagascar au 1665 et la fondation de la Compagnie Française des Indes au 1664," *Actes du 91e congrès national des sociétés savantes* (Paris, 1968), pp. 407–26.

8. Brown, *Madagascar Rediscovered*, pp. 49–54.

9. J. Chauvin, *Jean Laborde, 1805–1878* (Antananarivo: Pitot de la Beaujardière, 1939), p. 27.

10. Ibid., pp. 25–30. The site plan of the installation faces page 16. Laborde even made occasional efforts to develop profit-sharing.

11. Chapus, "Quatre-vingts années": 194–210; J. Devic, *Tananarive, essai sur ses origines, son développement, son état actuel* (Antananarivo: Imprimerie Officielle, 1952), pp. 70, 107; Jacques Dez, "L'Habitat traditionnel (essai d'interprétation)," *Bulletin de Madagascar* 19 (August 1969): 701–13.

12. James Cameron, *Recollections of Mission Life in Madagascar during the Early Days* (1868; Antananarivo: Imprimerie Imerina, 1967); Devic, *Tananarive*, p. 107; Joseph-Simon Gallieni, *Neuf ans à Madagascar* (Paris: Hachette, 1908), p. 209; Léon Rosenthal, "Le Plan d'aménagement et d'extension de Tananarive," *La Vie urbaine* 1 (1919): 304; André Jully, "L'Habitation à Madagascar," *BAM* 1 (1898): 288; Henri Mager, *La Vie à Madagascar* (Paris: Librarie de Paris, 1899), pp. 162–63; and Michel Thiout, *Madagascar* (Paris: Horizons de France, 1961), p. 146.

13. Cited in Chapus, "Quatre-vingts années," p. 215. Also see James Sibree, *Fifty Years in Madagascar: Personal Experiences of Mission Life and Work* (London: Allen and Unwin, 1924), pp. 20–30, on his designs for some fifty churches and hospitals in Madagascar; M. C., "Tananarive et ses environs," *BEMD* 23 (1926): 31–39; Jean Poirier, "Aspects de l'urbanisation à Madagascar: les villes malgaches et la population urbaine," *Civilisations* 18 (January 1968): 89; and Devic, *Tananarive*, p. 107.

14. Christian Mantaux, "Tananarive d'autrefois," *RM*, n.s. 47–48 (1964): 10; Devic, *Tananarive*, p. 107.

15. Maureen Covell, *Madagascar: Policies, Economics and Society* (London and New York: Francis Pinter, 1987), p. 20.

16. Howe, *Drama*, pp. 292–93; Gallieni, *Neuf ans*, pp. 34–35.

17. The *"franciser"* statement is from a letter to Alfred Grandidier, Antananarivo, November 25, 1896, in Joseph-Simon Gallieni, *Lettres de Madagascar, 1896–1905* (Paris: Sociéte d'Editions Géographiques, Maritimes, et Coloniales, 1920), p. 15. Also see Gallieni, *Neuf ans*, pp. 44–63.

18. Georges Cassaigne, "Le Plan de Tananarive: travaux des sections," session of May 23, 1924, Section d'Hygiène Urbaine et Rurale et de Prévoyance Sociale of the Musée Social, *Le Musée social* 29 (September 1924): 274.

19. "Tananarive et ses environs" (1903), cited in Albert Bruggeman, "Tananarive: son passé, son évolution, son avenir, II," *La Vie urbaine* 16 (March 15, 1933): 81. Also see M. Gontard, "La Politique relative de Gallieni à Madagascar pendant les premières années de l'occupation française (1896–1900)," *RFHOM* 58 (1971): 183–214; and Gallieni, *Neuf ans*, pp. 25–32. The city was founded about 1610, and first given the name Analamanga ("Blue Forest"). The name Antananarivo ("the City of a Thousand") was adopted during the next century when a tribal king reputedly brought in some 1,000 guards.

20. Robert Boudry, "Les Villes malgaches: Tananarive," *RM* 1 (July 1933): 69, 85; Poirier, "Aspects," p. 89; and Razafy Andriamihaingo, "L'Urbanisme à Tananarive," *BAM* 32 (1954): 783–802.

21. Lyauty's introduction to "Séjour à Ankazobé: organisation du territoire, octobre 1897–mars 1989," in *Lettres de Tonkin et de Madagascar*, 2 vols. (Paris: A. Colin, 1935), 2: 215. Also see Devic, *Tananarive*, p. 109; Bruggeman, "Tananarive . . . II," p. 73; and Pierre Camo, "Tananarive," *La Revue de Paris* 25 (April 15, 1928): 796. The same building and its park remain today as the Maison de France in postcolonial Antananarivo.

22. Gallieni, *Neuf ans*, p. 66.

23. Stephen H. Roberts, *History of French Colonial Policy (1870–1925)* (1929; Hamden: Archon Press, 1963), p. 408; and Thompson and Adloff, *Malagasy Republic*, p. 330.

24. Thompson and Adloff, *Malagasy Republic*, p. 19.

25. Joseph-Simon Gallieni, *Madagascar de 1896 à 1905*, 2 vols. (Antananarivo: Imprimerie Officielle, 1905), 1:10; and Ed. C. André, *De la condition de l'esclave dans la société malgache avant l'occupation française et l'abolition de l'esclavage* (Paris: A. Rousseau, 1899).

26. Devic, *Tananarive*, p. 48.

27. Joseph-Simon Gallieni, *Deux Campagnes au Soudan française, 1886–1888* (Paris: Hachette, 1891), pp. 142–47.

28. Gallieni, *Neuf ans*, pp. 63–64.

29. Roberts, *History*, pp. 403, 410; Gallieni, *Madagascar*, 1: 281; and Michel

Massiot, *L'Administration publique à Madagascar* (Paris: Librairie Générale de Droit et de Jurisprudence, 1977), p. 127. Edouard Ralaimihoatra of the Académie Malgache comments that the construction of the country's first prisons supplanted the tribal punishments of torture and death (*Histoire de Madagascar*, p. 230).

30. Devic, *Tananarive*, p. 50; Gallieni, *Neuf ans*, pp. 90–91; Charles Robequain, *Madagascar et les bases dispersées de l'union française* (Paris: Presses Universitaires de France, 1958), p. 321; and Bruggeman, "Tananarive . . . I," p. 10.

31. Bruggeman, "Tananarive . . . I," p. 14; Devid, *Tananarive*, p. 52; E. Baudin and J. J. Rabearivelo, *Tananrive: ses rues et ses quartiers* (Antananarivo: Imprimerie de l'Imerina, 1937), p. 96.

32. Gallieni, *Neuf ans*, pp. 90–91, 98, 116–18, 245; Ralaimihoatra, *Histoire*, p. 237; Charles Robequain, *Une Capitale montagnarde au pays tropical:Tananarive* (Grenoble: Allier, 1949), p. 300.

33. Devic, *Tananarive*, p. 110.

34. Hubert Lyautey, letter to his sister, January 10, 1898, in *Lettres de Tonkin et de Madagascar*, 2: 21. Also see General Vacher, "Lyautey urbaniste," in *L'Urbanisme aux colonies et dans les pays tropicaux*, 2 vols., ed. Jean Royer (La Charité-sur-Loire: Delayance, 1932), 1: 115–25; and Lyautey, speech to the *colons* of Fianarantsoa, October 5, 1900, in his *Paroles d'action: Madagaqscar—Sud Oranais—Oran—Maroc (1900–1926)* (Paris: A. Colin, 1927), p. 14.

35. Letter to his sister, January 10, 1898, in *Lettres du Tonkin et de Madagascar*, 2: 221.

36. Cited in Férnand Labatut, "Le Site et les paysages de Fianarantsoa," *Cahiers d'outre-mer* 68 (October–December 1964): 347.

37. Lyautey, *Dans de Sud de Madagascar* . . . , 1900–1902 (Paris: H. Charles Lavauzelle, 1903), p. 354. Also see Vacher, "Lyautey urbaniste," pp. 124–25; and Maurius-Ary Leblond, "Fianaratsoa et sa région: l'âme du Betsileo," *RM* 3 (January 1935): 91–122.

38. Gallieni, *Madagascar*, 1: 277–332; Marcel Olivier, *Six ans de politique sociale à Madagascar* (Paris: Bernard Grasset, 1931), p. 147; Charles Richard, "Le Gouvernement de Victor Augagneur à Madagascar (1905–1910)," thèse de 3ème cycle, University of Paris, 1969,p. 87; Guillaume Grandidier, *Le Myre de Vilers, Duchesne, Gallieni: quarante années d'histoire de Madagascar, 1880–1920* (Paris: Sociéte d'Editions Géographiques, Maritimes et Coloniales, 1923), pp. 162–63; and Louis Chevalier, *Madagascar: Populations et ressources* (Paris: Presses Univcrsitaires de France, 1952), pp. 16–62.

39. Dr. G. Girard, *L'Institut Pasteur de Tananarive* (Antananarivo: Imprimerie Moderne de l'Emyre, 1930), p. 92; idem, "La Santé publique et ses problèmes à Madagascar entre les deux guerres mondiales (1917–1940)," *BAM* 42 (1964): 13; Direction du

Service de Santé de Madagascar, "Notice sur l'organisation de l'assistance médicale indigène" s.d., carton 919, dossier 10, Direction des Travaux Publics de Madagascar, AOM; André You, *Madagascar, colonie française (1896–1930)* (Paris: Sociéte d'Editions Géographiques, Maritimes, et Coloniales, 1931), pp. 248–72; and Dr. Chippaux, "De l'hôpital colonial à l'hôpital 'Girard et Robie': 70 ans de politique hospitalière," *BASO* n.s. 8 (1966): 362.

40. [Urbs Nus], "La Maison du colon," *IM* (February 2, 1924): 2. This phrase was repeated again and again, for example in Dr. Abbatucci's "La Téchnique sanitaire aux colonies," *AMPC* 25 (January–March 1927): 109.

41. Dr. Neveu-Lemaire, "L'Assistance médicale et l'avenir de nos colonies," *MCI* 1 (January 1924): 80. Also see Dr. Bouchet, "Le Péril tuberculeux," *BRF* 5 (September 1930): 6–16, which discusses this same point with specific reference to France.

42. Dr. Gouzin, "L'Assistance psychiatrique et l'hygiène mentale aux colonies," speech to the Académie des Sciences Coloniales, 1926, *AMPC* 25 (July–September 1927): 291, 295, 301.

43. Leo Spitzer, "The Mosquito and Segregation in Sierra Leone," *Canadian Journal of African Studies* 2 (1968): 49–61; H. Harold Scott, *A History of Tropical Medicine*, 2 v. (London: Edwin Arnold, 1939), v. 1, pp. 168–74; Raymond E. Dummett, "The Campaign against Malaria and the Expansion of Scientific Medicine and Sanitary Services in British West Africa, 1898–1918," *African Historical Studies* 1 (1968): 153–97.

44. Paul Juillerat, "L'Hygiène et l'habitation," lecture notes for a course at the Ecole des Hautes Etudes Urbaines, 1919–20, Institut d'Urbanisme, University of Paris; Dr. Alfred Coury, "Le Fonctionnement du Service de Défense contre le Paludisme à Madagascar (1923–1924)," *AMPC* 23 (May–July 1925): 238–64; Scott, *History of Tropical Medicine*, v. 1, pp. 163–74; and George Rosen, *A History of Public Health* (New York: MD Publications, 1958), pp. 278–90.

45. "Pour le développement, l'hygiène et l'esthétique de nos villes," *IM* (February 18, 1922): 2; "L'Hygiène urbaine," *TM* (September 18, 1926): 2; "L'Assainissement intégrale de Tananarive," *TM* (October 2, 1926): 3; Dr. Félix Putzeys and Dr. F. Schoofs, "Extension des villes, création de nouveaux quartiers," in *Extension des villes: hygiène dans la construction*, vol. 2 of the *Traité de technique sanitaire*, 6 vols., ed. Félix Putzeys, F. Schoofs, et al. (Paris: Librairie Polytechnique Ch. Bernager, 1927), p. 9; Juillerat, "L'Hygiène," pp. 26–29; and Dr. W. Dufougère, "La Médecine et l'assistance médicale aux colonies," in *Le Domaine colonial français*, 4 vols. (Paris: Editions du Cygne, 1930), 4: 337–65.

46. Brown, *Madagascar Rediscovered*, p. 129.

47. Georges Bechmann, *Salubrité urbaine, distribution d'eau et assainissement*, 2 vols. (Paris: Baudry, 1898), 2: 150–280; Dr. Georges-Félix Treille, *Principes d'hygiène coloniale* (Paris: G. Carre et C. Naud, 1899), pp. 210–40; Dr. Charles Joyeux, *Hygiène*

de l'européen aux colonies (Paris: A. Colin, 1928), pp. 110–32; Robequain, *Une Capitale*, p. 301; Christian Mantaux, "Tananarive d'autrefois," *RM* 36 (1969): 59; H. Razafindralambo, "Extension de la ville de Tananarive dans la zone ouest et ses problèmes," thèse de 3ème cycle, Institut d'Urbanisme, University of Paris, 1971.

48. Gallieni, *Neuf ans*, p. 223.

49. Alfred and Guillaume Grandidier, *Histoire physique, naturelle, et politique de Madagascar*, 9 vols. (Paris: Société d'Editions Géographiques, Maritimes et Coloniales, 1907), 1: 565.

50. Dr. R. H. Hazeman, "L'Hygiène social des villes. I. L'Urbanisme et le travail social," *La Vie urbaine* 14 (July–August 1937): 221–42; *Le Rôle des associations d'hygiène social (Congrès des Associations d'Hygiène Sociale tenu au Musée Social le 7 novembre 1925)* (Paris: Masson, 1926), pp. 4, 15–16; Prof. Paul Courmont, *Les Dispensaires d'hygiène sociale de l'Institut Bacteriologique de Lyon, 1905–1933* (Lyons: Société Anonyme de l'Imprimerie A. Rey, 1933), pp. 7–17; Noël Bernard, *La Vie et l'oeuvre d'Albert Calmette, 1863–1933* (Paris: Albin Michel, 1961); Emile Guillot and Marius Bousquet, *Edifices publics pour villes et villages* (Paris: Dunod, 1927), p. 382.

51. Dr. Maurice Rousseau, "Les Services sanitaires dans les différentes colonies en 1927," *AMPC* 27 (October–December 1929): 518–19.

52. A. Chantemesse and E. Mosny, *Hygiène coloniale*, vol. 11 of the *Traité d'hygiène*, ed. G. Bourardel and E. Mosny (Paris: Librairie J.-B. Baillière et Fils, 1907), p. 203.

53. You, *Madagascar*, p. 512.

54. Dr. G. Girard, "Le Succès le plus marquant de l'oeuvre sanitaire de la France à Madagascar: la disparition de la variole depuis 45 ans," *Revue médicale d'hygiène d'outre-mer* no. 270 (August–September 1958): 102–8.

55. Alain Cottereau, "La Tuberculose: maladie urbaine ou maladie de l'usure au travail?" *Sociologie du travail: politique urbaine* 19 (1978): 192–224; also see idem, "Les Débuts de planification urbaine dans l'agglomération parisienne," *Sociologie du travail* 12 (1970): 362–92.

56. Dr. Allain, "La Second épidemie de peste de Tananarive (novembre 1921–février 1922)," *AMPC* 20 (September–December 1922): 320.

57. Dr. Cachin, "La Peste dans la province de Tananarive en 1922 et 1923," *AMPC* 21 (May–July 1923): 186–204; Dr. Alfred Coury, "Organisation de la lutte contre la peste dans la commune de Tananarive," *AMPC* 23 (January–April 1925): 33–49; "Histoire de l'Institut Pasteur de Madagascar," p. 152; L. Fabian Hirst, *The Conquest of Plague: A Study of the Evolution of Epidemiology* (Oxford: Clarendon Press, 1953), pp. 358–60; Faranirina Esoavelomandroso, "Résistance à la médecine en situation coloniale: la peste à Madagascar," *Annales ESC* 36 (March–April 1981): 168–90.

58. Coury, "Organisation de la lutte," p. 38.

59. Georges Cassaigne, "Il faut décongestionner Tananarive, III," *TM* (November 28, 1924): 1.

60. Gallieni, *Madagascar*, 1: 277; Charles Richard, "Le Gouvernement de Victor Augagneur à Madagascar (1905–1910)," thèse de 3ème cycle, University of Paris, 1969, p. 84; and Louis Chevalier, *Madagascar: populations et ressources* (Paris: Presses Universitaires de France, 1952), p. 54.

61. "Notice sur l'organisation de l'assistance médicale indigène," p. 44; Rousseau, "Services," p. 519; Richard, "Augagneur," p. 84. Victor Augagneur, *Erreurs et brutalités coloniales* (Paris: Editions Montaigne, 1927), p. 202; Y. G. Paillard, "Victor Augagneur: socialisme et colonisation," *BAM* 52 (1974): 66–79; Dr. Allen and Dr. Augagneur, "Organisation de la lutte antivénerienne à Madagascar," *AMPC* 20 (May–July 1922): 130. Augagneur (in fact a Republican-Socialist) published numerous articles on this subject in the *Annales de médecine et de pharmacie coloniales* between 1909 and 1920.

62. Dr. Laurent-Joseph Gaïde, *Le Péril vénerien en Indochine* (Hanoi: Imprimerie d'Extrême-Orient, 1930), p. 35.

63. Chevalier, *Madagascar*, pp. 62–70.

64. Brown, *Madagascar*, pp. 258–60; Thompson and Adloff, *Malagasy Republic*, pp. 21–23; A. Dandouau and G. S. Chapus, *Histoire des populations des Madagascar* (Paris: Presses Universitaires de France, 1952), p. 279. The VVS, founded in 1913, stood for VY Vato Sakelika ("Iron, Stone, and 'Network'"). Its principles were quite similar to those of Phan Chau Trinh in Vietnam. Many of the members were medical-school or university students, priests or Protestant pastors. They wanted to preserve their own cultural heritage and, at the same time, to have access to Western science and technology, all in the course of obtaining once again their independence.

65. Georges Cassaigne, "Les Plans d'aménagement des villes de Madagascar," *L'Urbanisme aux colonies*, 1: 130.

66. Georges Cassaigne, "La Ville moderne: documentation," *BEMD* 24 (1927): 179–82, lists representative volumes, including Joyant's *Traité d'urbanisme* (1923), de la Casinière's *Les Municipalités marocaines* (1924), A. Antoine's *Les Routes américaines* (1926), Henri Sellier's *Hygiène urbaine, habitations à bon marché, cités-jardins* (1921), Sellier's *Cités-jardins et maisons-ouvrières* (1922), numerous works by Georges Benoît-Lévy, Jacques Gréber's *L'Architecture aux Etats-Unis* (1920), and George B. Ford's *L'Urbanisme en pratique* (1920).

67. Léon Rosenthal, "Le Plan d'aménagement et d'extension de Tananarive," *La Vie urbaine* 1 (1919): 310.

68. Razafindralambo, "Extension," p. 20; "Madagascar en plein évolution," *MCI* 106 (June 1932): 118.

69. Georges Cassaigne, "La Ville moderne: la circulation," *BEMD* 24 (1927): 174.

70. Ibid., p. 177.

71. Casaigne, "Il faut décongestionner Tananarive, III," *TM* (November 28, 1924): 1.

72. "Il faut décongestionner . . . , I," *TM* (November 21, 1924): 1; Rosenthal, "Le Plan d'aménagement," p. 307.

73. Poirier, "Aspects," p. 85; Ed. Joyant, "Villes de Madagascar," in *Traité d'urbanisme*, 2 vols. (Paris: Librairie de l'Enseignement Technique, 1928–29), 1: 159–61.

74. "Il faut décongestionner . . . , III," p. 1.

75. [Urbanus], "L'Urbanisme à Madagascar, II," *IM* (June 23, 1923): 1. Also see Paul Le Bourdiec, "Croissance et organisation de l'espace urbaine et suburbaine: la morphologie des villes malgaches," *La Croissance urbaine en Afrique noir et à Madagascar*, 2 vols. (Paris: CNRS, 1972), 1: 168.

76. [Urbanus], "L'Urbanisme à Madagascar, I," *IM* (June 20, 1923) 1.

77. Olivier, *Six ans*, p. 191.

78. Report of the head of the Mission d'Inspection à Madagascar to the Minister of Colonies, April 22, 1923, carton 333, dossier 6, Division des Affaires Politiques de Madagascar, AOM.

79. Léon Geisman, "L'Urbanisme à Madagascar," in *L'Urbanisme aux colonies*, 1: 127.

80. Cassaigne, "Il faut décongestionner . . . IV," *TM* (December 2, 1924): 1.

81. Georges and Albert Cassaigne, "Antsirabé: Vichy de l'Océan Indien," *La Vie urbaine* 17 (May 15, 1934): 179; Also see Dr. Guerrini, *Antsirabé thermale et touristique* (Antananarivo: Imprimerie Officielle, n.d.), p. 26; and Robequain, *Madagascar*, pp. 317–22.

82. Cassaigne, "Il faut décongestionner . . . I," p. 2.

83. Cassaigne, "Antsirabé," p. 180.

84. Cassaigne, "Les Plans d'aménagement," p. 131. Also see Gérard Donque, "Les Problèmes fondamentaux de l'urbanisme tananarivien," *Madagascar: revue de géographie* 13 (1968): 43–51; and "L'Urbanisme à Madagascar," decree of December 24, 1926, in the report of Léon Perrier, Minister of Colonies, *Journal Officiel de la République Française* (December 24, 1926): 18.

85. Cassaigne, "Le Plan de Tananarive," *MS*, pp. 273–377; idem, "Les Plans d'aménagement," in *L'Urbanisme aux colonies*, 1: 128; *Où en est l'urbanisme en France et à l'étranger?* (Strasbourg: SFU, 1923).

86. Bruggeman, "Tananarive . . . II," p. 112.

87. Devic, *Tananarive*, p. 110; and C. Savaron and M. Fleurial, "L'Hôtel de Ville et son quartier," *RM* 3 (October 1936): 130.

88. Gérard Donque, "Le Zoma de Tananarive, étude géographique d'un marché urbain," *Madagascar: revue de géographie* 3 (July–December 1965): 93–227, and 4 (Jan-

uary–June 1966): 93–273.

89. Geismar, "L'Urbanisme à Madagascar," pp. 126–27; Cassaigne, "Les Plans d'a-ménagement," pp. 128–31; Bruggeman, "Tananarive. . . . II," pp. 109–12, and Joyant, *Traité d'urbanisme*, vol. 1, pp. 159–61. Edouard Ralaimihoatra calls the colony a "po-litical laboratory" under Governor-General Marcel Olivier (*Histoire de Madagascar*, p. 242).

90. The book was not translated into French until 1923, though a French Société des Cités-Jardins was founded in 1903. Georges Benoît-Lévy publicized Howard's con-cept, as well as examples of garden cities from many diverse countries, throughout the early twentieth century.

91. "Le Problème de la rue," *TM* (December 14, 1926): 2; "Plans d'aménagement et d'extension des villes à Madagascar," report of the Ministry of Colonies, December 24, 1926, carton 330, dossier 12, Direction des Travaux Publics de Madagascar, AOM; and Olivier, *Six ans*, pp. 190–200.

92. J.-H. Collet de Cantelou, "L'Architecture et l'urbanisme à Madagascar," *L'Ur-banisme aux colonies*, 1: 132–40; and idem, "Madagascar," in *AA* 16 (Marc 1945): 91–96.

93. Maurius-Ary Leblond, "Les Villes malgaches: Tamatave," *RM* 1 (October 1933): 12. Also see "Activité du Service des Travaux Publics en 1928–1929," carton 330, dossier 11, Direction des Travaux Publics de Madagascar, AOM; "L'Ere des grands travaux," *MCI* 103 (1929): 176–77; and Pierre Raxaly-Andriamihaingo, "L'Urbanisme de Tamatave," *Bulletin de Madagascar* 5 (1954): 105–62.

94. De Cantelou, "L'Architecture," p. 133.

95. Ibid., pp. 132–40.

96. Bruggeman, "Tananarive, I," p. 27.

97. De Cantelou, "L'Architecture," p. 134.

98. Leblond, "Les Villes malgaches: Tamatave," p. 123.

99. De Cantelou, "L'Architecture," p. 138. Also see Charles Lebel, "Le Standardi-sation à Madagascar," thèse de doctorat, Faculty of Law, University of Paris, 1937, pp. 2–21.

100. De Cantelou, "L'Architecture," p. 133.

101. F. Labatut and R. Raharinarivonirina, *Madagascar, étude historique* (Paris: Nathen Madagascar, 1969), p. 170; and Massiot, *L'Administration publique*, p. 324.

102. Léon Cayla, "Madagascar pendant la crise," *RM* 1 (January 1933): 26.

103. De Cantelou, "L'Architecture," p. 133.

104. Gaston Pelletier and Louis Roubaud, *Images et réalités coloniales* (Paris: André Tournon, 1931), p. 288.

105. *Madagascar: le pays, la production, la vie sociale* (Paris: Agence Economique

du Gouvernement Général de Madagascar, 1932), p. 180.

106. "Renovation du Zoma," *RM* 1 (January 1933): 131–32;"Urbanisme," *RM* 2 (October 1934): 131.

107. "Une Grande métropole coloniale: Tananarive," *L'Illustration* 94 (December 26, 1936): 529; and M. Pegourier, "Rapport de l'Inspection Générale des Colonies, Missions 1927–1928," July 7, 1928, p. 7, carton 333, dossier 9, Affaires Politiques de Madagascar, AOM.

108. Devic, *Tananarive*, p. 110; de Cantelou, "L'Architecture," pp. 132–40; Boudry, "Les Villes malgaches: Tananarive," pp. 110–12; Charles Dumont, "Paysages et villes malgaches," *L'Art vivant* 13 (February 1938): 46–47, 92.

109. De Cantelou, "L'Architecture," p. 132; "Note," *RM* 1 (January 1933): 131–32. Michel Massiot considered Madagascar the colony that best exemplified the long-standing French tension between local liberties and centralism (*L'Administration publique à Madagascar* [Paris: Librairie Générale de Droit et de Jurisprudence, 1971], pp. 3–30).

110. Devic, *Tananarive*, p. 110; Jacques Dez, "L'Habitat traditionel (essai d'inter-prétation)," *Bulletin de Madagascar* 20 (August 1969): 103–4.

111. R. Lebègue, "Rapport sur le Service d'Architecture, des Parcs, et Jardins," n.d., p. 22, carton 330, dossier 8, Direction des Travaux Publics de Madagascar, AOM.

112. Olivier, *Six ans*, p. 105.

113. Ibid., pp. 69, 271.

114. Ibid., pp. 69–98.

115. *Les Travaux publics*, 1927–28 (Antananarivo: Direction des Travaux Publics de Madagascar, 1928), n.p.; "SMOTIG: Rapport de l'Inspection Général des Travaux Publics sur l'emprunt authorisé par la loi du 22 fevrier 1931," p. 9, carton 334, dossier 12, Direction des Travaux Publics de Madagascar, AOM; "Nôte sur le régime de la main d'ouevre à Madagascar," carton 331, dossier 6, Affaires Politiques de Madagascar, AOM; François Valdo, "Le SMOTIG malgache," *AF* 38 (1929): 510–16; and Thompson and Adloff, *Malagasy Republic*, pp. 444–46.

116. Ministry of Colonies, Cabinet of Ministers, "De l'Empoi du 2ème contingent" (February 10, 1927), p. 3, carton 2942, Affaires Politiques de Madagascar, AOM.

117. Olivier, *Six ans*, p. 116.

118. Ibid., pp. 73–76, 100–101; R. Cherrier, "La Legislation concernant le travail indigène à Madagascar," thèse de doctorat, Faculty of Law, University of Paris, 1932, p. 7; and Dr. Trautman, "Service de la Main d'Oeuvre des Travaux d'Intérêt Général," *AMPC* 27 (July–September 1929): 344–68. On *fanampoana* labor today, see M. Feeley-Harnik, "Ritual and Work in Madagascar," in *Madagascar: Society and History*, ed. Conrad Phillip Kottak, Jean-Aimé Rakotoarisoa, Aidan Southall, and Pierre Verin

(Durham: Carolina Academic Press, 1986), p. 163.

119. Ministry of Colonies, "De la 2ème contingent," p. 6.

120. "Six ans de politique sociale à Madagscar," *BRF* 6 (August–September 1931): 11.

121. Thompson and Adloff, *Malagasy Republic*, p. 446; and R. Koerner "Le Front Popularie et la question coloniale à Madagascar, l'année 1936," *RFHOM* 61 (1974): 436–54.

122. Thompson and Adloff, *Malagasy Republic*, p. 446.

123. Maurius-Ary Leblond, "Madagascar et les sciences," *RM* 4 (1936): 18.

CONCLUSION

1. Alfred de Tarde, *Le Maroc, école d'énergie* (1915; Paris: Plon-Nourrit, 1923), p. 5.

2. Henri Grimal, *La Décolonisation, 1919–1963* (Paris: A. Colin, 1965), p. 75; Kenneth L. Brown, *People of Salé: Tradition and Change in a Moroccan City, 1830–1931* (Cambridge: Harvard University Press, 1976), pp. 217–20; Charles-André Julien, *L'Afrique du Nord en marche; nationalismes musulmans et souveraineté français* (Paris: Julliard, 1942; 4th rev. ed., 1972); and Jacques Berque, *Le Maghreb entre deux guerres* (Paris: Seuil, 1962), pp. 115–20. David G. Marr's masterful study of this issue, *Vietnamese Tradition on Trial, 1920–1945* (Berkeley: University of California Press, 1981), recounts in particular the evocation of Einstein's theory of relativity, with the intellectual "jumping out of one's shadow to find some elements of the truth" in a radically different context. (His reference is to an article by Truong Truc Kinh and Nguyen Dong Ha in 1923, cited on p. 331 of his work.)

3. The debate continues to the present day. Kenneth Brown specifically refutes the Weberian argument that the Islamic city never developed the associational character of Western cities, existing only as a conglomeration of separate units. (*People of Salé*, p. 211).

4. Paul Bairoch, *The Economic Development of the Third World since 1900*, trans. Cynthia Postan (Berkeley: University of California Press, 1975), p. 153.

5. See Abdallah Laroui, *Les Origines sociales et culturelles du nationalisme marocaine (1830–1912)* (Paris: Maspero, 1977); Julien, *L'Afrique du Nord en marche*; idem, *Une Pensée anti-coloniale: positions, 1914–1979* (Paris: Sindbad, 1979); Brown, *People of Salé*, pp. 210–20; Alexander Woodside, *Community and Revolution in Modern Vietnam* (Boston: Houghton Mifflin, 1976); idem, "Problems of Education in the Chinese and Vietnamese Revolutions," *Pacific Affairs*: 648–66; and David G. Marr, *Vietnamese Anticolonialism, 1885–1925* (Berkeley: University of California Press, 1971).

6. Jacques Rabemananjara, *Nationalism et problèmes malgaches* (Paris: Présence Africaine, 1958), pp. 121–50; also see idem, *Témoinage malgache et colonialisme* (Paris: Présence Africaine, 1956), p. 14.

7. The Queen had died in exile in Algiers in 1917.

8. Governor-General Marcel Olivier, *Rapport général. Exposition coloniale internationale et des pays d'outre-mer*, 2 vols. (Paris: Imprimerie Nationale, 1931), 2:66. Allusions to the colonies appear in the immense sculpted facade by Janniot, representing the economic history of French colonialism, as well as the interior murals. Olivier reasoned as well that the "simple geometric lines recall primitive civilizations" (ibid.).

On the Colonial Exposition, see in particular "L'Exposition Colonial," *L'Architecture* 49 (1931): 317–40, 365–86; *Revue des deux mondes* (1931): 45–55 265–87, 329–45; André Demaison, *Guide officiel de l'Exposition Coloniale Internationale* (Paris: Editions Mayeux, 1931); and Charles-Robert Ageron, "L'Exposition Coloniale de 1931: mythe républicain or mythe impérial?" in *Les Lieux de mémoire*, vol. 1, *La République*, ed. Pierre Nora (Paris: Gallimard, 1984), pp. 561–91.

9. Preface to *Rapport général*, vol. 1, p. vi.

10. This argument suggests an important source for Le Corbusier's authoritarian approach to urbanism during the 1930s. Conversely his Algiers plans, especially the interplay of the carefully preserved Casbah and the Cité des Affaires, or business district, can be seen as the culmination of the associationist approach he so deprecated.

Index

Note: A page number in italic indicates that an illustration of the indexed item appears on that page.